S0-ADC-179

A History of the British Secret Service

By the same author:

THE PRIVATE LIFE OF MR GLADSTONE
MADOC AND THE DISCOVERY OF AMERICA
JOHN DEE

Richard Deacon

A HISTORY OF THE BRITISH SECRET SERVICE

TAPLINGER PUBLISHING COMPANY
NEW YORK

First Published in the United States in 1970 by
TAPLINGER PUBLISHING CO., INC.
29 East Tenth Street
New York, New York 10003

Library of Congress Catalog Card Number 72-107017
Standard Book Number 8008-3865-3

Printed in the United States of America

Contents

Illustrations

A History of the British Secret Service

1

Introduction

To WRITE a history of any Secret Service is to tilt against a great many windmills.

Not the least of these windmills is the orthodox historian's distrust of the very subject of espionage in the context of history. Such distrust is relevant to the extent that it is neither wise nor logical to relate the activities of Secret Services to the actual course and development of the history of a nation. Yet it is undeniable that espionage has provided some splendid, often unsung victories, as in the case of the notorious Zimmermann Telegram in World War I.

Another problem that confronts the would-be historian of a Secret Service is that his task becomes progressively more difficult as he approaches the present day. Whereas the distant past is reasonably adequately documented, the closer one gets to the present the more cunningly are facts hidden, and, inevitably, the more hazardous the shoals of the law and Official Secrets Acts, not to mention the laws of libel. To be too close to the subject, to have participated oneself in Intelligence work, to draw on documents covered by the Official Secrets Act, is not merely a disadvantage but on occasions a veritable barrier to tackling such a work.

To exemplify some of these hazards I cannot do better than quote from the *S.O.E. in France: An Account of the Work of the British Special Operations Executive in France 1940-44,* by M. R. D. Foot. Mr. Foot wrote in his preface: "Naturally I have tried to produce as complete, as accurate, and as fairly balanced an account as time permitted. No one will be less surprised than myself if inaccuracies remain; for the whole published literature on the subject is pitted with them, and the unpublished archives are often contradictory as well as confusing and confused."

Another windmill that, consciously or unconsciously, one tilts against is the windmill of prejudice—of one's own in the first place and of one's sources as well. The aim of this book is at least to avoid the prejudice that can be inflicted by the official mind. In short, this particular history is one that declines to be circumvented, circumscribed or inhibited, as far as is humanly possible, by officialdom. It is, in fact, in no sense an official history. Nor has it been submitted to any form of censorship.

But by adopting the aim mentioned in the preceding paragraph the author's prejudices are left isolated and unchallenged. There is no restraining influence except the facts themselves, and sometimes one set of facts cancels out another. In such cases the author is forced to do his own detective work by way of interpretation.

I think that documentation and facts show that the British Secret Service in all its branches has fluctuated more in both its strength and efficiency than that of any other comparable national espionage organisation. In some epochs there were brilliant successes, in others a long run of dismal failures. In some decades too little money was spent to obtain worthwhile results, whereas in others an increase in funds allotted to the Secret Service brought about revolutionary and desirable changes in organisation and methods.

Generally speaking, the success or failure of the Secret Service will be shown to be in direct relation to the amount of money spent on it; the ability of its titular heads; and the attitude of the government of the day towards it.

A great power that lacks an efficient Intelligence force is automatically doomed: that has been the lesson from the hey-day of Troy to the present time. But the maintenance of an efficient intelligence force, however cheaply it is run, is as important for small and neutral powers as for the larger ones. Switzerland's neutrality has been achieved and maintained as much through its modest but extremely efficient counter-espionage service as anything else, while Israel is the supreme example of a small power not only holding its own but winning a six-day war almost entirely on the strength of the reports of its espionage organisation.

One point needs to be made absolutely clear at the outset. By the somewhat loose phrase "British Secret Service" I do not refer to any one branch of national Intelligence. The phrase, and indeed this study of it, is intended to cover all branches of British Intelligence—the S.I.S., M.I.5 and M.I.6, the Naval and Military Intelligence departments and other lesser known organisations. To have concentrated on any one single section of Intelligence would have been to give a distorted picture. Sometimes one section, sometimes another has predominated in the history of the Service, while from time to time such temporary organisations as the S.O.E. and the intelligence section of the Ministry of Economic Warfare have played vital rôles at crucial moments.

"To begin at the beginning", as the narrator of *Under Milk Wood* eagerly starts his story, but to pinpoint the actual beginning of British national Intelligence is historically, or factually, almost impossible. All history, and for that matter legend, too, shows that Intelligence in some form or other is as old as man himself. One could point to Noah, when he sent out the dove to see whether the waters had abated, as attempting the first known form of aerial reconnaissance. Sir Basil Thomson, the creator of the Special Branch at Scotland Yard, once remarked that "if the Pharoah Memptah had been given an efficient Intelligence service, there would have been no exodus".

In Europe national espionage developed slowly by the employment of ambassadors and envoys as spies. Diplomacy and theft were almost synonymous. But in the Middle Ages this form of espionage was used mainly against the English and hardly practised at all by English ambassadors overseas. Indeed during the Anglo-French war of 1293–98 an English knight, Sir Thomas Turberville, was a spy in the service of the French King, Philip IV. Turberville was sent back to Britain to incite the Scots and the Welsh against Edward I. It was only after many years of this kind of one-sided espionage that the English gradually overcame their insularity and realised the importance of having envoys who could supply them with information about foreign countries' policies and imbroglios. Modern diplomacy was born in Venice and as far back as 1268 the Venetian ambassadors had to deliver in writing full reports of their missions and answers to questions submitted by their government within fifteen days of their arrival home.

The activities of the Venetian ambassadors stimulated the

embryo of counter-espionage in England for the first time under the Tudors. Henry VII found it was essential for him to be kept well informed of the moves of his opponents. Both at home and abroad he employed agents to obtain Intelligence of the conspiracies of Warbeck and Suffolk, but these men could in no sense be described as an organised security force. Henry VII's reign marked an inauspicious beginning to national Intelligence in its untidiest and least effective form.

But in the following reign there was a slight improvement and even one or two conspicuous successes in counter-espionage. Giustiniani, the Venetian Ambassador in London, discovered in 1515 that his letters were being opened by agents of the English Government. He lodged a strong complaint with Cardinal Wolsey and reported back to the Doge in Venice: "The letters received by me from your Sublimity had been taken out of the hands of the courier at Canterbury by the royal officials and opened and read: the like being done by private letters from the most noble, the ambassador Badoer of France and others."[1]

The interception of diplomatic communications was common practice all over Europe and this forced many countries to introduce codes and ciphers. Here again the Venetians proved themselves supreme and it was not until 1868 that two scholars finally found the key to the cipher used by Michel, the Venetian Ambassador to England in the reign of Mary I.

But it is to the Tudors in general that Britain owes the development of national espionage. Henry VII, when harried from one place to another by Richard III in the years before he came to the throne, had learned at first hand the importance of a personal espionage system. It was only through the vigilance of his own agents that he foiled a plot by Richard III to have him kidnapped in Brittany. In this instance the man to whom he particularly owed his life was Christopher Urswick, who became Recorder of London. But Henry VII's espionage organisation was more in the nature of a personal than a national service. His son, Henry VIII, was less wary about his own safety and left all questions of Intelligence to his Ministers of State, first to Wolsey and later to Thomas Cromwell. But while Wolsey served his royal master comparatively loyally, he failed in one of the subsidiary aims of his espionage service—that of getting himself elected Pope.

Thomas Cromwell, no less ambitious, was made of sterner stuff. With ruthless efficiency he took charge of the patchwork espionage service that was bequeathed to him and made some attempt to co-ordinate it. He increased the number of agents and created a systematic machine of terror inside England. Again, as was typical of the early Tudors, there was more counter-espionage than active spying abroad, for Henry VIII had determined on a policy of splendid isolation for England and regarded foreign Intelligence with at best mild interest and at worst complete indifference. The machine Cromwell created was designed to trap all discontented Englishmen of any consequence and remove them by trial or murder, whichever was the more convenient. Cromwell was faced by the machinations of Chapuys, the Spanish Ambassador, who was just as ruthlessly seeking to disrupt the English government in the north, the west and Wales and, but for Cromwell, could undoubtedly have had some success in London, too. The perjury of Rich at the trial of Sir Thomas More showed how easily Cromwell was able to influence the course of justice by means of his agents.

Yet England still lacked an Intelligence service devoted solely to the purpose of espionage and counter-espionage. Cromwell's Intelligence was often merely incidental to his main purpose. The visitation of the monasteries, which he organised and which lasted for nine months, produced confidential reports exceeding the required amount of information for containing and disciplining and dissolving the monasteries. Dr. Richard Layton, Archdeacon of Buckingham, and one of his more assiduous agents, wrote to Cromwell in October 1535, that "there is neither monastery, cell, prior, nor any other religious house in the north, but Dr. Legh and I have familiar acquaintance within ten or twelve miles of it, so that no knavery can be hid from us in the country."[2]

Certainly Cromwell's visitation of the monasteries was closer to a witch-hunt than to a respectable commission of inquiry. It was not until 1533 that Cromwell attempted any serious espionage on foreign soil and even then it was a barely concealed effort at obtaining Intelligence. His intention was to by-pass his royal master's indifference and to seek allies for England on the Continent, and he decided to investigate the prospects in Germany.

He dispatched two agents to make a tour of Germany and to report on the political and religious situations there. One of these agents was his friend, Stephen Vaughan. But little came of the venture; the Lutheran princes showed scant interest in allying themselves with Henry VIII.

Cromwell had many of the attributes of the ideal Intelligence administrator. Not only was he tidy-minded and efficient, but he believed in avoiding possible future dangers by prompt action, by leaving nothing to chance and in making long-term plans. At home this policy paid off, but in the field of foreign affairs it only brought about the downfall of Cromwell himself: here his very virtues became fatal flaws. "Masterly inactivity often rewarded England", wrote Professor Dickens in his *Thomas Cromwell & The English Reformation*, "however dark the reports, for the complexion of Europe changed swiftly enough to make short-term and opportunist policy the wisest. So often we may observe this antithesis between opportunism and doctrinarism in the chequered story of Tudor diplomacy. Always the opportunists like Henry VIII and Elizabeth emerge unscathed, while the doctrinaires, the would-be builders of systems like Wolsey and Mary Tudor, end in confusion. Henry VIII and Cromwell both stood somewhere between the extremes, but the latter leaned somewhat towards the doctrinaires."

In this clash between opportunism and doctrinairism the organisation of an Intelligence service was bound to suffer, especially as, generally speaking, the opportunists and isolationists won. Henry VII, in somewhat unorganised fashion, had first sought to protect his throne by developing a system of secret service, and Christopher Urswick, Recorder of London, was his chief agent, but the latter's rôle was much more that of a personal spy for his royal master than a director of espionage. But, as will be seen in the next chapter, one man by his pertinacity, patriotism, commonsense and generosity forged an organisation which justly won for him the title of the creator of the British Secret Service.

This service has through the ages generally served the country well in all serious crises and times of war, but there have been occasions, both in the lesser wars and in times of peace, when it has failed abysmally. Its most consistent record of success lay in

Ireland where for nearly four centuries it was supremely efficient. The Irish section of the Secret Service was kept on its toes, not merely by Irish rebels but because several foreign countries, France, Spain and the United States, used the Irish to intrigue and stir up trouble. Yet in the last three years of these four centuries the Secret Service in Ireland was disorganised, infiltrated and literally destroyed.

There have also been times when the Secret Service was hindered and obstructed by the Foreign Office, or when its warnings have been unheeded by the governments of the day. The most recent example of this was during Neville Chamberlain's premiership.

Obviously there can be no such thing as a complete history of any Secret Service. Even if every document or record on the whole subject was available for inspection, one would still have to contend with inaccuracies, with exaggerated reports and the problem of interpreting conflicting and contradictory material. What does emerge from a detailed study of the Service over four hundred and fifty years is a picture of the development of espionage and counter-espionage, of changing methods and unchanging qualities and trends peculiar to the British, and, not least, of the diligence, courage and effectiveness of individual agents and Intelligence chiefs.

It is noteworthy that individualism has played a much greater rôle in British espionage than in that of any other Intelligence service. Despite the growing trend towards team-work, the individual even in the twentieth century not only remained supreme but has frequently achieved more than a whole team of Intelligence experts.

2

Throgmorton and Walsingham

In the middle of the sixteenth century some of the precepts of Machiavelli began to be adopted in ruling English circles. Thomas Cromwell himself moulded much of his policy on the Machiavellian concept of *virtu*, that by bold endeavour a great man can control at least that part of his future which is not dependent on fate. As for that staunch protestant, Sir Nicholas Throgmorton, he was frequently described as a Machiavellist.

In May 1559, Sir Nicholas was appointed English Ambassador to France and in this post he became the first serious organiser of Intelligence, albeit on a very small scale, of our ambassadors overseas. His Intelligence was extensive and useful and Sir Nicholas was the chief informer for Cecil, the Secretary of State, on the French policy *vis-à-vis* both England and Scotland. Cecil used one of Throgmorton's dispatch men, Sandy Whitelaw, as a confidential go-between with the Scots rebels.

One of the problems of handling secret agents has always been that of anticipating their reactions in certain circumstances and in allowing for their prejudices. Throgmorton gave Cecil a most comprehensive report on Sandy Whitelaw, saying that he was "a sober, honest, godly man . . . very religious and therefore you must let him see as little sin in England as you may".[1]

But Throgmorton was a little too zealous in his quest for information. Catherine de Medici was quick to realise he was a potential trouble-maker as well as a spy and she put such restrictions on him that he was almost a prisoner for a while. This forced Cecil to write a memorandum on French affairs which in effect recommended that if Throgmorton was not given greater liberty he must be replaced by someone else. Cecil was not so much concerned with Throgmorton's personal freedom as he was that his ambassador, however able an informer, might be siding with Robert Dudley, and the "war party" at Court. Cecil was more interested in negotiations and an accommodation with France than in any direct confrontation. However, Elizabeth, who at this time thought highly of Throgmorton, decided to hand over all negotiations with the French to her ambassador.

In the end Throgmorton's ambition, his aggressive Protestantism and meddling in politics proved his undoing. Thus he repeated the errors of all the early Tudor organisers of Intelligence in that, not content with the power which their information gave them, they threw away their advantages by pursuing independent policies against the wishes of their rulers.

The result to date of all this amateurism in the field of Intelligence was that any semblance of organisation in obtaining information faded away the moment the organiser fell out of favour, or was executed. Throgmorton's organisation disappeared with him; Cecil was too closely occupied with the day-to-day business of politics to have time to devote to creating any substantial Intelligence machine and the slow business of deciphering messages often took up time which might more usefully have been devoted to improved organisation.

The situation changed with the advent of Sir Francis Walsingham, whose ancestors came from the Norfolk village of that name. It was through the chance illness of Sir Nicholas Throgmorton that Walsingham first came to the notice of Queen Elizabeth. Being too ill to write himself, Throgmorton asked Walsingham, then a young man in his thirties, to compose a letter to Cecil. It was a letter of a highly confidential nature concerning a Mr. Robert Stewart who had been sent from France by the Huguenot leaders to seek the Queen's help.

The letter did not reveal the exact position Walsingham then held, but it seems obvious that he was already working for either Throgmorton or Cecil, or was at least in the close confidence of both men.

Both Elizabeth and Cecil were impressed by the competence and intelligence of the letter writer and from then on Walsingham seems to have found favour at Court. Walsingham on his part was not slow to take advantage of this. Of his own accord he began to send Intelligence reports to Cecil. He sent one such report which, he declared, was "from Franchiotto, the Italian". It urged that the Queen should pay attention to her food, her bedding and examine her furniture in case poison be given to her secretly. For good measure Walsingham sent a list of persons suspected of being actively hostile to the Queen who had recently entered the country.

Walsingham had a special talent—invaluable in an age of religious upheaval—for smelling out Protestants and Protestant sympathisers in the most unlikely places on the Continent. Thus the Franchiotto he referred to was a Captain Thomas Franchiotto, of Lucca, an Italian Protestant who had been in the pay of France. Where Wolsey, Cromwell and Throgmorton had paid the penalty by being too ambitious and too involved in active politics, Walsingham increasingly devoted his attention solely to obtaining intelligence. He would not let himself be lured away from this objective either by offers of advancement, or even by personal preferences. Politically he was probably closer to the "war party" and to Robert Dudley (Earl of Leicester) than to Cecil, but he never overplayed his hand or sought to intrigue against Cecil. His mind was subtle, but not devious, he was ambitious to serve his country in the best way he knew, but not ambitious enough to wish to be politically dominant. If he feared that sooner or later England would have to fight Spain, he did not openly advocate a war policy, but saw to it that the reports he presented to Cecil and Elizabeth supported his unspoken contentions. When he did express a view he did so with diffidence but with quiet assurance that was much more effective than the arguments of the more flamboyant Leicester. To Cecil on 20 December 1568, he wrote: "I beseech your honour that I may without offense conclude that in this division that reigneth among us, there is less danger in fearing too much than too little, and that there is nothing more dangerous than security."[2]

This was far calmer and less prejudiced advice than Elizabeth was receiving from some of her advisers. Some feared that France and Spain would together link up against England; others supported the plea of the Huguenot envoys that England should make common cause with them and declare war on France; a few openly wanted war with Spain. Walsingham's sole concern was to ascertain the facts.

In the early stages of his career Walsingham was more concerned with counter-espionage in England than with intelligence from abroad. Indeed at this time he relied on the latter as a by-product of the former. He was always searching for potential enemies on English soil. He arranged with the Lord Mayor of London to have weekly reports on all foreigners who stayed in the city. As these reports were all passed on to Cecil it is fairly clear that Walsingham was then assisting Cecil in Secret Service work.

While Thomas Cromwell had used his spies to increase his personal authority and to stamp his own political ideas on the realm, Walsingham was mainly concerned with the safety of the nation from foreign attack and the exposing of plots against the Queen. Loyalty paid off. By helping to unmask the Babington, Ridolfi and Throgmorton plots he staved off a series of attempts against the Crown.

In 1570 Walsingham was appointed Ambassador to France and it was during this period that he began to build up an Intelligence service overseas as well as at home. He lost no time in making this the most influential ambassadorial post in Europe during a critical epoch, but it was obvious that he was none too happy in France. One letter, which he wrote to an unnamed woman, possibly his wife, reveals as much:

"My hope is . . . that her Majesty will find so small taste in this my present service that she will forbear to employ me any further by making choice of some other of more sufficiency. . . . If I might be my own carver I had rather be our neighbour in Sothery (which you wish and I most desire) with a piece of bread and cheese than to have in the country to which I am going their best delicates and entertainments, but seeing I am born a subject and not a prince, I am tied to the condition of obedience and commandment."[3]

The most probable reason for Walsingham's reluctance to accept the ambassadorship in Paris was that it loomed before him as a financial hazard. Elizabeth, in common with that other Tudor, Henry VII, could be parsimonious on public expenditure, especially overseas, unless there was a certainty of a worthwhile return on the outgoings. From his correspondence back to Whitehall it was clear that Walsingham protested about the lack of funds to run the Embassy properly. His courteous but firm arguments on this subject seem to have borne some fruit, for apart from a grant for living expenses the Queen also conferred on Walsingham certain special privileges for the export of wool.

From such privileges he may, in part at least, have financed some of his Secret Service work. Soon he had engaged a number of agents in France. There was a certain Captain Thomas, an Irishman who pretended to be a Catholic refugee who had escaped to France; he was instructed by Walsingham to report on the activities of Archbishop of Cashel in Ireland, who was suspected of anti-English intrigues in France. Yet another of his agents was that strange, erudite Elizabethan mystic, John Dee, the Queen's astrologer. Dee's relations with Walsingham were close throughout the latter's life, but many of the missions Dee undertook for Walsingham are still matters of conjecture rather than of fact.

While Walsingham was ambassador in Paris he was involved in the protracted negotiations for the proposed marriage of Elizabeth to the Duc d'Anjou. In coping with the French side of these negotiations Walsingham had to walk a tight-rope path of diplomacy. For at the English court there were three distinct views on the subject of Elizabeth's marriage to a Frenchman: Leicester and the "war party" were frankly hostile to the plan, lining up with the Puritans in opposing it on religious grounds; Cecil was cautiously, but certainly not enthusiastically, in favour of exploring all possibilities, hoping it would detach France from Spain and make her an ally of England; Elizabeth was the unknown quantity, playing it along by ear and never allowing either of the factions to guess at her real feelings in the matter.

The Secret Service was brought fully into play in all these negotiations. Walsingham saw the whole question of Elizabeth's proposed marriage as a matter of national security. From the beginning he almost certainly opposed the proposition, but he did not wish to appear to side with Leicester against Cecil, so he avoided stressing the religious difficulties and scruples during his negotiations. At the same time, by employing John Dee he made use of an agent who had the fullest confidence of the Earl of Leicester. Elizabeth wanted fuller information about what was happening in Paris and how the marriage talks were progressing and, during 1571, at Walsingham's behest, she asked Dee to go to France.

Exactly what Dee achieved on that mission is not clear, but it involved a journey to the Duchy of Lorraine and almost certainly concerned the question of Elizabeth marrying not only the Duc d'Anjou but his brother. Dee, who had drawn the Queen's horoscope, was asked to cast horoscopes of both prospective suitors. This latter action may not have been so innocuous as it seemed. Elizabeth had been deeply impressed by Dee's horoscope-casting since she was a princess in imprisonment at Woodstock, and when she came to the throne one of her first requests was that he should calculate the most propitious date for her Coronation. It may well have been that the wily Walsingham was anxious that Dee should produce horoscopes of the two suitors which might be a warning to the Queen to steer clear of marriage with a French prince. And Dee himself reported that the political possibilities of an alliance were more attractive than "anythinge so unpropitious as matrimonie for which the starres give no brief and the factes as seene in France the more soe". This was certainly what Walsingham believed and wanted to hear. As for the Queen, she must have been hugely delighted when, without matrimonial entanglements, she concluded the Treaty of Blois a year later.

In 1573 Walsingham returned to England and became Principal Secretary and a member of the Privy Council. Shortly after this he was writing to Lord Burghley on Secret Service matters: "If your Lordship have any suspicion of any unsound meaning in the Low Countries towards her Majesty, I think he [Captain Sassetti] would be a very good instrument to decipher the same, having as he hath, great familiarity with Chiapin Vitelli. Your Lordship wrote unto me to find out one to be employed in Spain. If you think any such employment presently necessary I think I could find the means to place my old servant Jacomo in the French King's ambassador's resident's house in Spain."[4]

The duties of Secretary, which Walsingham carried out, were set out in some detail and included this important dictum: "to have care to the intelligence abroad". But though he had tracked down rebellious Catholics, unmasked plots against the Queen's life and organised a powerful counter-espionage network at home, Walsingham was still far from satisfied with the Intelligence obtained from overseas. He still needed a steady stream of information from France to keep him posted on all the vagaries and movements of the various political groups in that country. Elizabeth was anxious to keep her lines open to her other suitor, Alençon, "the little frog" as she dubbed him, for he was now placed under close surveillance in the chateau of Bois de Vincennes, along with the King of Navarre. But Walsingham was unhappy about the inadequacy of these communications so he established his own contacts with Alençon and the King of Navarre, using for this purpose Jacomo Manucci, already mentioned, and Thomas Wilkes. Both men were sent to France with secret instructions from Walsingham in 1573. What those instructions were is not clear, but their messages back to London provide some clues. Wilkes writes to Walsingham that he had met "a gentlewoman" who had promised to carry messages to the two prisoners. Shortly afterwards Wilkes reported that he had spoken to the King of Navarre himself.

It was in the hard school of sifting the plots and ploys behind the various plans for marrying Elizabeth to Alençon or Anjou that Walsingham learned the lessons of espionage. To build up the Intelligence service which his royal mistress so ardently desired he had to experiment and to improvise, to check and double-check: it was an admirable opportunity to learn how best an espionage service could be organised. On the political side Walsingham's keen analytical mind enabled him to take an essentially realistic view of what was and what was not practical. It was this training, plus his own acute sense of anticipation, which enabled him to retain the position of Principal Secretary until his death. While some at court wanted an alliance with France at all costs, others, foolishly, were so suspicious of French motives that they wanted England to ally herself with Spain against France. Walsingham shared neither view. He had no doubts whatsoever that sooner or later the real enemy of England would prove to be Spain, whether on the high seas, in the new colonies or at home. Equally he mistrusted French motives, especially Catherine of Medici's, and his information told him that England's best policy lay in allying herself with the French

Huguenots while raising troops in Germany and assisting Alençon and Navarre to gain their freedom.

This was advice which Elizabeth may have secretly respected but outwardly, at least, resisted. Walsingham, however, bore all the frustrations of his royal mistress's obduracy with patience; perhaps he knew that, given time to be proved right, some, if not all, of his advice would be followed. He always had the air of a man who, though on the surface humble and modest, inwardly had great confidence in his own intuition and judgement. The Queen would sometimes tease him; she called him "my Moor"—a laughing tribute to his dark, good looks. But more often she would exasperate Walsingham by refusing him the necessary funds to carry on his Secret Service work.

At this time probably none of the Great Powers of Europe spent less on Secret Service work than England. That England eventually had a properly organised Secret Service in Elizabethan days was due first to Walsingham's intense patriotism and, secondly, to the fact that he frequently footed the bill for it himself. What Elizabeth allowed for funds for espionage was never enough. Eventually Walsingham bankrupted himself by the personal monies which he expended on his Secret Service. Camden testified that Walsingham weakened his estate by his considerable expenditure for Secret Service and died "surcharged with debt". Only a year before his death when Walsingham made his will he declared in that testament that "I will that my body in hope of a joyful resurrection be buried without any such extraodinary ceremonies as usually appertain to a man serving in my place, in respect of the greatness of my debts and the mean state I shall leave my wife and heirs in".[5]

There have been many criticisms by historians, including Walsingham's own biographer, Dr. Conyers Read, that the extent and organisation of his Secret Service have been exaggerated and that it was in fact a very modest concern. But such criticisms are grossly unfair. He alone first provided a semblance of a truly national and permanent Secret Service and if it was small and far from universal it was extraordinarily effective when one considers that he financed it largely himself, frequently borrowing money on the security of his own modest estates to keep it going.

It must be remembered that in the earliest days of his attempts to build up a Secret Service Walsingham's prime task was to protect the Queen and unmask plots which either threatened her life or were intended to force her from the throne. Most of his work concentrated on counter-espionage in England and no sooner had he unmasked one plot than another was discovered; the multiplication of plots forced him to spend more money and, like other espionage chiefs after him, he was sometimes compelled to exaggerate, or even invent threats, in an attempt to conjure more funds from the royal coffers.

Walsingham had to contend with opponents skilled in the arts of subterfuge. At the time when plans were afoot for a marriage between Mary Queen of Scots and the Duke of Norfolk the latter set up a network of agents who passed messages between him, various Catholic rebels, the Duke of Alva and Mary Queen of Scots herself. Walsingham, through the aid of John Dee, found that the messages were passed in bottles of wine.

It was one of Walsingham's rules that even an English ambassador overseas must be regarded with suspicion and mistrust until he had proved his integrity. He was well aware of the temptations and webs of intrigue with which our envoys were beset. The case of Sir Edward Stafford, the first concrete example of a double-agent in British history, revealed something of these temptations. Stafford, a relative of the Queen, was appointed Ambassador to Paris in 1583. He was inexperienced in diplomacy and suffered from the further handicap of not having been properly briefed by Sir Henry Cobham when he took up his post. Apart from having doubts as to his ability, Walsingham appears to have disliked and mistrusted him in the beginning, though in the end he gave him every benefit of the doubt.

The Spaniards were quick to notice that Stafford was short of money and they put him on their pay-roll. That he provided them with intelligence is clearly proved, but he may in the long run have been able to convince Walsingham that what he obtained from the Spaniards was far more important to England's cause than what he gave to Spain.

Cobham seems to have been not merely unhelpful but positively obstructive when he handed over to Stafford. He refused to give the new Ambassador any information whatsoever about secret agents, or of those well disposed towards England. Nevertheless Stafford was determined to impress the authorities at home and he sent in frequent dispatches. For these he was not thanked, but was informed rather frigidly by Walsingham that the Queen "is many times offended with the charges of often posting as I dare not make her privy of all the despatches I receive from you".

Stafford suspected that Walsingham was concealing his dispatches from the Queen. It was probably true that to suit his own purposes Walsingham was anxious that too much attention to Stafford's reports should not be paid by Elizabeth. For Walsingham was not merely suspicious of Stafford's devotion to Elizabeth but frankly disbelieved his assertions of loyalty. He sent one Rogers to Paris to keep a watch on Stafford and it was quickly learned that Stafford had contacts with two agents of Mary Queen of Scots, Charles Paget and the Archbishop of Glasgow.

But worse reports were to come from Rogers. He said that Stafford was a go-between between French Catholics and English papists and that he had been bribed by the Duke of Guise to show him the English despatches. This information should have been enough to have forced Stafford's recall from Paris and immediate imprisonment, but curiously Walsingham took no action. He was a cautious man and may have doubted Rogers' reports; on the other hand he may have felt that Stafford could be used as an unwitting tool in the diplomatic game Walsingham sought to play. If Stafford possessed the confidence of the enemy, then they would believe any information which Stafford passed on to them. What could suit Walsingham's purpose better than to feed Stafford with false reports to bewilder the French and the Spaniards, with whom he was also in touch?

For there is little doubt that Rogers' disturbing reports were accurate. In 1585 Bernardino de Mendoza, Spain's ablest ambassador, at that time Minister in Paris, informed his government that he believed Stafford could be bribed to give information to Spain. In a letter to Philip of Spain the Spanish ambassador wrote that "now was the time for Your Majesty to make use of him [Stafford] if you wished any service done. . . . you should see by his acts how willing he was to do so. . . . This ambassador is much pressed for money." The reply from Philip was that Stafford should be given "2,000 crowns, or the jewel you suggest".

Stafford kept the Spanish King informed of many movements of English ships. Yet he was never brought to trial and returned to England without any visible stain on his character. But one cannot say for certain that he was an absolute traitor any more than one can say Walsingham was seriously at fault in not having him impeached. That Stafford was being secretly urged by the Spanish ambassador in Paris to prevent an alliance between France and England cannot be doubted. Possibly by reporting to London that the Queen might persuade the King of Navarre to change his religion, he was misrepresenting the facts in order to ruin negotiations. Or he may have been playing off Burghley, who shared Stafford's views to some extent, against Walsingham. But one cannot be sure as there is no record available of discussion in the English Privy Council on the French question at this time. It may also have been that Walsingham did not feel himself to be in a strong enough position to bring down Stafford, or that, had he tried to do this, he might have weakened his own position. Another, though less likely possibility, is that Stafford, despite his chicaneries, was more use to Walsingham in Paris than any other ambassador. Walsingham may have felt content to take a chance and to obtain what genuine intelligence Stafford could bring him.

If Walsingham was really playing so subtle a game, it certainly paid off later, for Stafford, while telling the Spaniards of England's preparations against the Armada, also reported to Walsingham about the Spanish fleet. "The Spanish party here [in Paris] brag that within three months Her Majesty will be assailed in her own realm, and that a great army is preparing for it", he wrote in July 1586.

This single item of information may have outweighed any harm Stafford had caused through his dealings with the Spaniards. For he alone of any Englishman in Paris would be likely to gain such confidential intelligence from the Spaniards, who were taking great pains to mask their preparations against England. Within six months Walsingham had further news which confirmed what Stafford had reported. An agent reported that "King Philip manifestly has some great design against us, having made the agreement with the Focchers for money payable here in a special place".

No doubt it was partly because Walsingham was not sure of the reliability of his own ambassador in Paris that he started to build up an independent Secret Service which was not dependent on official sources and by means of which he could double-check his ambassadors' despatches. Not having the funds to embark on any expensive espionage, he relied mainly on patriotic young students, mostly men of good family, who were resident abroad. Most of these young men were living in Italy, a country which Walsingham regarded as ideal as an espionage base because reports of Spanish affairs were more easily obtained there than in France or in Spain where spying was difficult.

It is clear, however, that it took many years before Walsingham was able to build up an effective network overseas. The system never really got under way until about 1587, by which time Walsingham had sufficient reports coming in to convince him that Spain was amassing a vast Armada of ships for an attack on England. It is not possible to trace the whole system of Walsingham's espionage service, because it was conducted entirely by the man himself and details were rarely committed to paper. But in the spring of 1587 he was able to draw up his *Plot for Intelligence out of Spain*, which is still preserved in the State Paper Office. It is almost the sole documentary evidence of the organisation of his Secret Service.[6]

This plan sets out the organisation of his system as follows:

1. The need to obtain some correspondence from the French Ambassador in Spain. [Here, obviously, was a cross-check on what Stafford was supplying from the Spanish Ambassador in Paris.]

2. "To take orders with some at Rouen to have frequent advertisements from such as arrive out of Spain at Nantes, Havre and Dieppe."

3. Sir Edward Stafford (English Ambassador in France) to obtain information from the Venetian Ambassador.

4. To set up an Intelligence post in Cracow for receiving reports on Spanish matters coming from the Vatican. [Undoubtedly one of his chief informants in Cracow was John Dee, who

at that time was offering his services as an astrologer to Count Laski; he was in close touch with Francesco Pucci who was known to have attempted to steal correspondence between the Vatican and Philip of Spain.]

5. To nominate persons (French, Flemish, or Italians) to travel along the Spanish coasts and report what preparations are being made at ports, furnishing them with letters of credit as a cover.

6. To obtain Intelligence from the Court of Spain and from Genoa.

7. To arrange Intelligence at Brussels, Leyden and in Denmark.

8. To employ Lord Dunsany [presumably as an agent].

This was a comprehensive and detailed plan. It was possible to put it into operation because during this year Walsingham managed to obtain £3,300 from the Queen for espionage. It was the largest single sum he had ever obtained from Elizabeth for this kind of work, but even so it was insufficient and had to be augmented from his private means.

Gradually *The Plot for Intelligence out of Spain* produced results. Early in 1587 Richard Gibbes, an Englishman who had been to Spain, reported to Walsingham that he had himself seen about one hundred and fifty warships in various ports and had heard "talk of 300 gallies [galleons]". In Lisbon, Gibbes had posed as a Scotsman and was therefore received sympathetically by the Spaniards who regarded Mary Stuart's countrymen as their allies.

When the Spaniards questioned Gibbes on British ports and rivers he pleaded ignorance as often as he dared, but questioned about whether the Thames was a suitable river on which to bring in a navy he replied that it was "a very ill river, full of sands within and without sight of land and not possible to bring in a navy".

Walsingham's other agents all performed effectively. In Venice, Stephen Paule picked up the gossip on the Rialto and noted every scrap of information about Spain. It was one of Walsingham's maxims that, as he put it, "if there were no knaves, honest men should hardly come by the truth of any enterprise against them". Acting on this assumption, Walsingham was daring enough and imaginative enough to use rogues and even improbable allies in his task of gleaning information on Spanish intentions. Two of his most active agents were two young English Catholics—the Standen brothers—who were notorious for their reckless behaviour and indulgent living. Superficially they would seem to have been a serious security risk; in fact—and again this is tribute to Walsingham's judgement—they were brilliantly successful. Their Catholicism was not of a fanatical kind and in no sense checked them from spying on Spain.

Antony Standen struck up a friendship with Giovanni Figliazzi, the Tuscan Ambassador to Spain, who had been asked by the King of Spain to go to Florence to try to arrange a marriage between Ferdinand, the new Grand Duke of Tuscany, and a Spanish princess. Standen adopted the name of Pompeo Pellegrini, and, using this *nom de plume* in a letter to Walsingham in February 1587, he wrote enthusiastically about the Tuscan ambassador. "This gentleman", wrote Standen, "is very discreet and passing courteous . . . he hath divers times dealt with the King of Spain about our matters so commanded by him, in which reasonings he hath often debated with the King of Spain and alleged just reasons why her Majesty was to be offended with that manner of dealing, and especially about the affront used to her Majesty's messenger when he was there, whose counsel, if Mr. Waad had followed, things had no doubt fallen out better. . . . If you will write him a letter of thanks, inferring that you have understood his goodwill to her Majesty and to that crown, as to yourself also, I think it to very good purpose, he having good means out of Spain, and, writing this letter, make me the deliverer."[7]

The utmost importance was attached by Walsingham to the rôle played by the Tuscan ambassador. He encouraged Standen to make fullest use of this source of information. Shortly afterwards Standen, still signing himself Pompeo Pellegrini, wrote to Walsingham saying that four galleys of the Genoese fleet had gone to Spain and that he had learned of others which were to be dispatched there from Naples. Referring to Walsingham's last letter, Standen added, ". . . you desire diligence in intelligence of Spanish matters. I have borrowed one hundred crowns and dispatched to Lisbon a Fleming who hath there a brother in service with the Marquis of Santa Cruz—I have given him address for his letters to me at the ambassador's house in Madrid who straight will send them to me."

Some hint of Standen's importance as an agent may be gauged from the fact that about this time Queen Elizabeth granted him a pension of £100 a year. It was a wise investment in an agent who during the summer and autumn of 1587 sent Walsingham regular reports which were invaluable in their revelations of Spanish naval and military preparations. The Fleming he mentioned proved to be a most assiduous informant in his capacity as a servant to the Marquis of Santa Cruz who was Grand Admiral of the Spanish Navy. Communications must have been hazardous, slow and hampered by the necessity for deciphering most of the messages, but Walsingham must have felt the risks and delays were more than outweighed by the fact that eventually he was able to pass to his Queen copies of Santa Cruz's reports to Philip of Spain which gave the most detailed accounts of the Armada, the number of ships involved, stores, armaments and personnel.[8]

Walsingham followed up this new avenue of intelligence by corresponding regularly with Figliazzi, when the Tuscan envoy returned to Florence from Madrid. At the same time he expressed the greatest anxiety that Standen's cover should not be revealed, or that this agent should in any way be put in danger. In a postscript to Burghley Walsingham wrote: "I humbly pray your Lordship that Pompey's letter may be reserved to yourself. I would be loathe the gentleman should have any harm through my defeault."[9]

Walsingham went far beyond being simply a receiver and co-ordinator of intelligence. On the strength of what he learned he set out deliberately to play for time—a ploy which has throughout history been a vital factor in British Intelligence—and to scheme so that the Armada preparations were delayed. Through his influence bankers in Genoa were persuaded to withhold, or at least to delay loans to Philip so that the source of revenue to the Spanish war effort came to be controlled by the English Secret Service. Dr. James A. Welwood, in his *Memoirs*, described how Walsingham found a way to retard the Spanish invasion by a whole year by arranging for the Spanish bills to be protested at Genoa. Thomas Sutton, a wealthy merchant, was said to be largely responsible for having the Spanish bills of exchange protested. As a result of all this Standen was able to report in June 1587, that the Spaniards could not mount sufficient naval strength to launch an offensive against England that year. Thus triumphantly Walsingham informed Burghley that "Your Lordship by the enclosed from Florence may perceive how some stay is made of the foreign preparations".

The "Grand Tour" of Europe did not become an automatic phase of the education of scions of the British aristocracy and middle classes for another hundred and fifty years, but to a limited extent it was practised in Tudor times. As Italy was the centre of Renaissance culture it became the magnet for the young English tourists completing their education and it was through these people that the English Secret Service was developed. Walsingham himself had spent five years as a young man completing his education in Europe and much of this time had been spent in Italy. Here he had not only learned the technique of counter-espionage as practised by the Venetians, but had come to realise that Italy was the most useful listening post for events in Spain.

The truth was that intelligence direct from Spain was hard to come by. Very few Englishmen went to Spain except to trade and since trade had been virtually cut off, an Englishman in Spain was always an object of suspicion. But Spain had the closest contacts with all parts of Italy, not merely at the Vatican but in Milan, through which city Spanish reinforcements for the Low Countries were dispatched, in Genoa, where loans were negotiated, and in Rome, Tuscany and Savoy. Then again Philip of Spain owed a considerable proportion of his naval resources to his Neapolitan possessions.

Garrett Matingly in his *Defeat of the Spanish Armada* has written that Walsingham's Secret Service was dependent upon "a few under-paid agents of varying ability . . . a system hardly larger or more efficient, except for the intelligence of its direction and the zeal of its volunteer aids, than that which every first-rate ambassador was expected to maintain from his own information, one which the governments of Florence or Venice would have smiled at as inadequate for the police of a single city".

This is a somewhat unfair comparison. Certainly the provision of funds for espionage was woefully inadequate, but probably no other Secret Service in Europe had such a brilliant director, nor one so generous in providing his own money for operations. The truth is that never in history, except perhaps during the First World War of 1914-18 did England owe so much to Intelligence than in the years which immediately preceded the Spanish Armada's onslaught against our coasts.

3

Tudor Cryptography and Psychological Warfare

In Tudor times the effectiveness of espionage from overseas depended in the last resort on the efficiency of the ciphers used for messages. It was in this period that code-breakers came into their own and there began a private war between rival espionage services to break each other's ciphers.

But while Latin Europe was still pursuing Latin ciphers both for speed and precision, in the north attempts were being made to develop a coded jargon. Walsingham had studied secret communications and the methods used on the Continent both in Venice and Florence. He brought back to England with him a copy of a manual on cryptography by one Alberti and soon put this into use. Thereafter both Burghley and Walsingham paid particular attention to new cryptographical developments and relied heavily on the advice of John Dee, who had made a great study of the subject. It was Dee who became closely acquainted with Jerome Cardan and introduced the Cardan grille system. This was basically a very simple cipher and is sometimes referred to as the "Trellis Cipher", consisting of a block of letters which are read downwards vertically and then upwards again. Dee appreciated the simplicity of this system, but maintained that it was "a childish cryptogram such as eny man of knowledge shud be able to resolve".

Walsingham set up an elaborate cipher department in his house in London and here was undertaken not merely the deciphering of intelligence reports coming into London, but those intercepted from enemy sources, as well as setting up a section to specialise in forgeries for the planting of false documents. That this branch of Walsingham's work was effective may be judged from a letter from the Spanish King's Governor of the Netherlands, complaining that the news he sent home, even in secret cipher, was known in London before it reached Madrid.

One of the most skilled men employed by Walsingham in his cipher department was a young man named Gilbert Gifford, who belonged to a Catholic family and had at one time been trained as a Jesuit. However, he was not apparently cut out for the Church, or maybe he became disillusioned with it, for he landed himself in prison through some discreditable transaction and, while there, wrote to Walsingham, boldly offering his services to spy on the Jesuits.

Walsingham, who was cautious and boldly experimental in turn, personally interviewed Gifford and decided to give him a chance. The young man was told to return to his home, which was situated close to where Mary Queen of Scots was living. Very soon Gifford was, with Walsingham's connivance, offering his services to Mary. Soon the Scottish Queen was using Gifford as a messenger and he copied out the correspondence as soon as he got hold of it, replacing the seals so professionally that no one could tell they had been broken.

Soon Gifford succeeded in obtaining from Mary's entourage the methods of the Papal cipher department with a complete key to all correspondence. It was through this discovery that Walsingham was able to unmask the Babington plot for the assassination of Queen Elizabeth, but in the message which revealed this project the identity of the six men who were in the plot was concealed by code-numbers for which there was no clue in the context.

Numbers were frequently used in codes and ciphers to denote names in this period. In Sir Henry Wotton's code for example England was signified by 39, the Queen of Spain by 55, Genoa by 43 and Holland and Germany as 96 and 70 respectively. Sometimes alphabetical codes had to be substituted for numbers to obtain the key and other numerical codes, used by Walsingham, included 3 for Mary Queen of Scots, 30 for her son James and 6 for the intriguing Countess of Shrewsbury. It was the habit of the Elizabethan statesmen to use numerical codes for leading figures. Randolph used such numerical codes in his letters to Walsingham.[1]

When Walsingham uncovered the plot to assassinate Elizabeth he was particularly disturbed to learn that the six men, whose identities were hidden, were all supposed to be in Queen Elizabeth's own household. All he could do was to bide his time and hope that further correspondence when intercepted would provide some hint of their identities. Then Anthony Babington, the ardent supporter of the Scottish Queen and originator of the plot, walked into Walsingham's house one day to ask for his passport to be endorsed for a visit to the Low Countries. While Babington was waiting a message was brought in to the assistant who was dealing with him: it was from Walsingham himself and urged that an agent should be told to shadow Babington. While the assistant was studying the message Babington cunningly managed to catch a glimpse of its contents. The moment the assistant left the room—presumably to give instructions for Babington to be watched from the moment he left the house—Babington vanished. Shortly afterwards so, too, did six young men in the Queen's household. Then, relentlessly, Walsingham went into action. Within a month the six young men were arrested and Mary Queen of Scots was facing trial.

The history of English ciphering has been characterised by its oddities and eccentricities more than any logical development of the art. In this has lain both its strength and its weakness. Walsingham without question had the best cryptographic organisation in Europe, built up largely on the strength of his experts' knowledge of existing systems on the Continent, which he adapted for his own use as well as using to decipher the messages of his opponents. But he also owed much to the eccentricities and oddities of John Dee who re-discovered the long-lost cryptographical secrets of Trithemius. When on a visit to the Continent in 1562 Dee came across a book entitled *Stenographia*, written by Trithemius, Abbot of Spanheim (1462–1516), and he was sufficiently excited by this discovery to mention it in a letter to Sir William Cecil. The book he had purchased, he told Cecil, had been sought by others who had offered "a Thousand Crownes and yet could not be obteyned . . . a boke for which many a lerned man has long sought and dayly doth seeke; whose use is greater than the fame thereof is spread".[2]

For in Trithemius's book were cunningly contrived studies of the art of cipher writing, perhaps the most significant work on this theme yet written. That Dee's discovery was fully appreciated by Cecil is evident from a certificate of the Elizabethan statesman, dated 28 May 1563, in which Cecil testified that Dee's time beyond the seas had been of inestimable value and "well bestowed".

Dee adapted the cryptographical ideas of Trithemius and made them available to Walsingham. He also produced a book on the subject, *The Monad, Hieroglyphically, Mathematically, Magically, Cabbalistically and Analogically Explained.* But though the book became famous in Europe, it was not popular in the universities, for it was never understood. Even subsequent attempts to understand it in our own time have not met with much success. But if the scholars did not understand it those at Court seem to have found some practical value in it. Cecil declared it to be "of the utmost value for the securities of the Realme" and it seems apparent that Cecil and probably Elizabeth herself understood that Dee was employing ciphers to give certain information. In the *Monad* this was not the information of a spy, but of a scientist, but there was the underlying implication that secret intelligence could also be communicated by this means. A typical example of his technique was to employ alchemical symbols to convey scientific reality.

In fact Dee bamboozled most of his contemporaries by the complexity of his cipher-making. What appeared as the mumbo-jumbo of at least an eccentric alchemist and at worst the ravings of a black magician more often than not was the cover for a secret message. Trithemius's system had some advantage—that, by exercising some care, the existence of a coded message could be concealed so that the "clear" was in one language, while the message was in another. The basis of this system was the substitution of words or phrases for actual letters, giving a wide choice of phrases for each letter. Thus the word "bad" could be enciphered either by "Phallas is blessed of charm," or "you are admired by women, Astarte", or "A God of grace enthroned". It is easy to see how this method could be applied to disguise messages in the form of innocent sounding tales or myths, though its great disadvantage was that the enciphered message was so much longer than the "clear" that it took a long time to decipher.

How much Dee actually achieved in the realm of cryptography remains to a large extent a mystery. That his studies of cryptography on the Continent and elsewhere were of tremendous importance to Walsingham and Burghley (and possibly even to Elizabeth herself) there is no doubt whatsoever. That he himself used ciphers of various kinds both for his diaries and letters is proved by much of what is extant in his manuscripts in the British Museum and the Bodleian Library at Oxford. But a very great deal of his manuscripts still baffle the most enthusiastic searcher for hidden ciphers. In following Trithemius and attempting to seek the perfect cipher, Dee in many instances has puzzled posterity and the abstruseness of his codes may have exasperated his contemporaries in times of crisis.

Yet there is impressive evidence that Dee passed on a wealth of Intelligence gleaned on his Continental journeys and secret missions by means of his "angelic conversation". Only a portion of these still remain and they are contained in his *Libri Mysteriorum* in the Sloane Mss. The "angelic conversations" are a record by Dee of "conversations" and visions which he claimed to have when crystal-gazing with the help of his confederate, Edward Kelley. When these manuscripts were first examined by scholars they were generally dismissed as "unprofitable reveries of the occult sciences" or as "dablings in black magic".

In fact Dee was not a "black magician", though he might, by the standards of the Renaissance, have been termed a "white magician" who applied a scientific mind to the occult mysteries. It was Dr. Robert Hooke in the following century who first sought for a cryptographical explanation of the "angelic conversations", or, to be more precise, to analyse Dee's recordings of what the angels told him, and their replies to his questions, put to them by his scryer, Edward Kelley. Hooke, in an address to the Royal Society, declared that "the greater part of the book—especially all that which relates to the Spirits and Apparitions, together with names, speeches, clothing, prayers, etc., are all cryptography . . . he [Dee] made use of this way of absconding it that he might more securely escape discovery, if he should fall under suspicion as to the true designs of his travels, or that the name should fall into the hands of any spies as such might betray him or his intentions."

Hooke claimed to have discovered various hidden messages in the "angelic conversations" and other researchers have in recent times unearthed other clues.[3] These revelations provide not only a remarkable picture of Dee as a roving secret agent, but show how his erudition enabled him to unravel the most complicated plots. Dr. James Welwood, writing a century later on the Spanish Armada, described how Walsingham obtained information about Spanish plans. Welwood claimed that Walsingham heard from Spain that Philip had dispatched a letter to the Pope, telling him in detail of his war plans. Walsingham then sent orders to "one of his spies in Rome" to procure a copy of it. The spy persuaded a gentleman of the Pope's bed-chamber to take the letter from the Pope's cabinet and copy it out. There is no contemporary evidence to support this story directly, but as Dee was supplying a good deal of Intelligence on Spanish affairs at this time, it is possible that the true story is that he obtained this information from the notorious double-agent, Francesco Pucci, in Cracow. One of the allegations made against Pucci by the Vatican authorities was that he had attempted to steal some Papal correspondence with Philip of Spain. Dee was in close contact with Pucci during this period.

Indeed, even before Walsingham launched his *Plot for Intelligence out of Spain* in 1587 he had received from Dee vital information about Spanish intentions. This intelligence was that the Spaniards knew that England was committed to building new and bigger warships and that the only way they could check this was by attacking England's timber supplies. In those days the Forest of Dean was the nerve centre of English ship-building, for most of the timber for Elizabethan dock-yards came from this royal forest. And Dee's message, conveyed in the form of a conversation with an angel named Madimi, was that a small party of Frenchmen, acting as agents of the Spaniards, was going to the Forest of Dean to persuade and bribe certain of the foresters to burn down the trees.

It was a daring plan and if Dee's message had not enabled the Verderers to be alerted to watch for the Spanish agents, serious damage might have been caused. When the agents were caught it was learned that they had claimed squatters' rights in the forest and were planning a series of simultaneous fires in key points of the area.[4]

Possibly the warning of this plot to strike a blow inside England convinced Walsingham that an attack would be launched by Spain sooner or later. In 1588 Anthony Standen went himself to Madrid and advised Walsingham of Spanish plans direct from the Spanish capital.

As the news from Spain became more disturbing so Walsingham increased the number of his agents. It was like a game of poker played with rock-like nerves and with Walsingham gambling his own money to convince his Queen of the threat to her realm. The English Governor of Guernsey was instructed to send back details of all gossip that could be picked up by Breton ship's masters who had visited Spanish ports. Even the offices of the Portuguese Ambassador in London (Dr. Hector Nunez) were sought in an effort to establish a spy ring in Lisbon and Nicholas Ousley, one of his bravest and most assiduous agents inside Spain, was supplying information from Malaga as late as April 1588.

Walsingham knew he had to play for time: the Armada must be delayed at least by a year from sailing against England. Not only were England's preparations to meet the invader far from complete, but Elizabeth herself had yet to be fully convinced of the dangers. Even then, in 1587, when he had finally convinced her of the Spanish threat, he had still not succeeded in persuading her to confront it boldly. Elizabeth was by nature a temporiser, though not lacking in courage when completely convinced of the wisdom of a particular form of action. And Walsingham's task was not made easier by the firebrands in the "war party" who were all for instant action before England was fully ready.

As the Spanish threat grew it was soon apparent to Walsingham that the defence of England depended chiefly on his own wealth of intelligence. From this it was possible for a much smaller fleet and far fewer military forces to prepare effectively against and ultimately to match the might of Spain. He had accurate reports that gave him not only the numbers of the Spanish fleet, but its dispositions, tonnage, munitions, soldiers, sailors, provisions and even the numbers of its galley-slaves. Walsingham knew, too, of the Pope's willingness to co-operate in the Spanish attack on England, as well as the Duke of Parma's plan to launch a force of flat-boats across the Channel from the Low Countries as soon as the Armada gained control of the English Channel.

It has been a feature of the British Secret Service throughout its history that it attracts writers to its ranks. While in the Armed Services there has been traditionally a marked distrust and even revulsion from writers (typified by the Duke of Cambridge's comment when he was told that a certain officer was also a writer: "I always knew there was something wrong about the chap"), in the Secret Service writers have been welcomed and encouraged. One can turn at random to any age and find a writer playing a key rôle inside the organisation: in the seventeenth century Daniel Defoe; in the eighteenth century the playwright Leonard MacNally; in the nineteenth Sir Richard Burton and in the present century Somerset Maugham. In the sixteenth century the most celebrated writer to spy for Walsingham was Christopher Marlowe, a poet and dramatist. His actual rôle in espionage is still wrapped in mystery to some extent, but it was an important and patriotic, though somewhat cynical and Machiavellian enterprise.

Marlowe's career as a spy began as a young student from Cambridge. In the years immediately following 1580 Walsingham recruited many promising young men from Cambridge, some of them on the advice of John Dee, himself an old Cambridge scholar. There is proof of this from enemy sources, supplied by Father Robert Parsons, the Jesuit agent who escaped to Rouen after Father Campion's arrest. In one of Parsons' reports to the Jesuit headquarters in Rome, dated 26 September 1581, he stated: "at Cambridge I have at length insinuated a certain priest into the very university under the guise of a scholar or a gentleman commoner and have procured him help from a place not far from the town. Within a few months he has sent over to Rheims seven very fit youths."[5]

Here was espionage and enemy counter-espionage inextricably inter-woven. Parsons was a virulent opponent of Walsingham, who while admitting that he "maintained the reputation of an honest man", declared that he was "violently carried away by the folly of the Calvinists . . . assisted Leicester in all things, but chiefly in two; the one when it was in question to proscribe, to kill, to imprison, or to ruin the Catholics; the other when he wished to control the affairs of neighbouring states or to sow wars and dissensions among them. . . . He dressed this news, true and false, with such sauce as to please the Queen's taste."

It was sometime between February and July in 1587 that Marlowe was most active as a secret agent. It would seem that he served his country by pretending to be a Catholic sympathiser and probably he was one of the "seven fit youths" who were lured to Rheims by Father Parsons. At any rate he went to Rheims and was given hospitality by the Duc de Guise, leader of orthodox Catholicism and ally of Philip of Spain, because of his professed fondness for Roman Catholic ritual. There seems to be no doubt that Guise hoped to use him and other young Englishmen in plots against Elizabeth. But it is equally clear that he went abroad with the connivance of the English authorities to spy upon the Catholic conspirators by posing as one of their allies.

In fact Marlowe was but one of a number of young writers who turned spy under Walsingham's direction. Others who joined the Secret Service were Matthew Roydon, a friend of Marlowe and a writer of exquisite prose, Anthony Munday, actor and playwright, who went to Rome to keep a watch on the English seminary there and William Fowler, the Scottish poet. Apart from these both Philip Sidney and Ben Jonson were believed to have indulged in some espionage operations, though in the case of Jonson the evidence is only circumstantial.

Walsingham's counter-espionage against the Catholics was ruthlessly efficient, but there is some evidence that on occasions personal vendettas and religious bigotry were allowed to interfere with the tasks on hand. Sometimes Walsingham can be criticised for using downright ruffianly rascals to spy on Catholics. One such was Thomas Rogers, alias Nicholas Berden, who wormed his way into the confidences of many leading Catholics and obtained not only details of their plans, but dossiers on every known priest in the country. Berden was a particularly vindictive agent who was given excessive powers, including those of recommending what should be done with imprisoned priests. His marginal comments on the lists of such priests testify eloquently to his attitude towards them: "I return his honour's note", he wrote to Thomas Phelippes, Walsingham's chief decipherer and added "which I have well perused according to my knowledge and intelligence. Such persons as I have noted to be hanged are of most traitorous minds and dispositions. Such as I have marked for banishment are most meet for the said purpose, for that they are exceedingly poor and contentious. . . . And it might stand with the pleasure of his honour, it were meet they should all be hanged."[6]

However Berden was never one to allow his hatred of Catholics to deter him dealing out mercy when obvious rewards were obtainable. He was capable of being bribed and it is hard to believe that Walsingham was unaware of this. Perhaps Walsingham accepted corruptibility as part of the game, perhaps he thought it was an essential part of counter-espionage that in allowing one priest to go free for a bribe, information could be obtained which would enable him to catch three other more dangerous priests. As to Berden's corruptibility, his correspondence with Thomas Phelippes bears this out: "If you can procure me the liberty of Ralph Bickley at his Honour's hands, it will be worth £20 to me, and the liberty of Sherwood, alias Carlisle, will be worth £30. . . . The money will do me great pleasure, being now in extreme need thereof, neither do I know how to shift longer without it."[7]

Yet despite all the evidence of plots against her person and of the Spanish invasion plans Elizabeth still hesitated to provide the funds for repelling an attack. Walsingham must have been near to despair in the latter part of 1587 and the early part of 1588: "the manner of our cold and careless proceeding here in this time of peril and danger", he wrote to the Earl of Leicester, on 12 November 1587, "maketh me to take no comfort of my recovery of health, for that I see apparently, unless it shall please God in mercy and miraculously to preserve us, we cannot stand long".

John Dee had put his scientific studies to good effect by making careful calculations of weather prospects for 1588. He had consistently warned that violent and abnormal storms were to be expected in 1588 and that these should be taken into account when preparing to resist the invasion. There warnings were to some extent borne out by other astrologers and weather prophets and they were also exploited by propagandists. Throughout

Europe there had been warnings of impending disaster linked with devastating storms. The propagandists of each nation interpreted these dire prophecies according to their own prejudices and national policies. In Amsterdam and in Paris prophetic almanacks poured off the presses, foretelling violent tempests, terrible floods, hail and snow in midsummer and convulsions of earth ocean. In Spain recruiting was affected by the prophecies, there were desertions from the Fleet and in Lisbon an astrologer was arrested for "making false and discouraging predictions".

These warnings were cleverly exploited by the English Secret Service and especially by John Dee. As to whether he believed all he forecast is another matter: the prophecies of violent storms when the Armada sailed were completely borne out. But there is some evidence that Dee and others in the Secret Service indulged in psychological warfare by their astrological forecasts, hoping that enough gloom and despondency would be spread around to cause the Armada's sailing date to be delayed still further. In his "angelic conversations" Dee had given the Emperor Rudolph of Bohemia and King Stephen of Poland the most foreboding accounts of freak storms which would cause the fall of a mighty empire in 1588. Rudolph, who believed in astrology, certainly passed on these warnings to the Spanish Ambassador and to the Papal Nuncio, who in turn relayed them to the Vatican. Dee had good reason to make use of Rudolph for spreading this news, for the Emperor communicated with a wide range of astrologers as far away as Sicily, Spain and Denmark, often using a special courier to carry his intelligence on such matters.

Now those experts who read the weather according to the stars would have been certain to confirm Dee's forecasts of exceptionally bad weather in 1588 and this would have given credence to the other reports of the destruction of a mighty empire. It is also not without significance, when one considers this subtle form of psychological warfare, that the English authorities intervened with the printers to prevent the publication of prophecies which would spread woe and despondency. Walsingham, having had reports of how the warnings were having effect abroad, would not want Dee's psychological warfare to boomerang against the English people and cause despondency at home. For the agents who spread these rumours were clever enough not to name

Spain, or any other empire, as the one likely to suffer. A certain vagueness was much more effective.

One of Dee's crystal-gazing narratives at this time referred to a vision of castles rising out of the waves, with their raised drawbridges pointed in one direction, but with "the inhabitants therein intent upon procedding elsewhere and presenting a threat thereto. Theyr navigation shud be disregarded for they shall go not whence they seem and they will not be diverted from their real purpose until the angels from the watch-tower . . . mak the sign Ohooohaatan."[8]

"Ohooohaatan" was the name in Dee's secret code language, Enochian, for one of the four great Elemental Kings.[9] This was the King of Fire. Superficially this narrative would appear to be nothing more nor less than the kind of abstract symbolism of Cabbalistic ramblings which was a feature of the "conversations" with the angels through Dee's shew-stone, or crystal. But there could also be a clue here to some intelligence which Dee had obtained about the Duke of Parma's intentions. Later the Duke tried to mislead the English by putting out reports that the Armada would not be heading for England, but preparing for an attack on Walcheren. Dee was probably warning Walsingham of this ruse and begging him to avoid a trap. He was also urging that the English fleet should employ their fire-ships against the Armada, which was exactly the policy they adopted.

The stresses and strains of espionage and counter-espionage took their toll in agents and on many occasions valiant and loyal agents suffered because even in Whitehall malicious reports against them were accepted. This perhaps was truer of Burghley than it was of Walsingham. The latter was prepared to overlook a great deal, even reports of corruption and double-dealing, provided that he obtained intelligence which in his opinion outweighed any other disadvantages his agents might possess. This was as true of Dee as it was of Berden. Yet Dee was himself often under suspicion, though more of being a black magician than on any other grounds. Marlowe's death still remains a mystery. Frizer, his killer, was given a free pardon and nobody has ever explained satisfactorily what Robert Poley, a known spy in the Secret Service, was doing in an upstairs room at the Deptford tavern where Marlowe was stabbed to death. Poley had been a steward to Lady Sidney, Walsingham's daughter, and was a key figure in the espionage network. Somebody may have wanted to liquidate Marlowe, possibly because he was notoriously outspoken and unguarded in his conversation. Marlowe would have risked his life to make a dangerous epigram, for there is no evidence that he was disloyal.

On the other hand Dr. William Parry, Member of Parliament, paid for his double-dealing with his life. Both Walsingham and Burghley knew him as a convicted criminal, a fortune-hunter and a double-agent, but, as his information was valuable, they retained his services. But with singular ruthlessness Burghley schemed to get rid of him. Acting under instructions as a *provocateur*, Parry suggested a plot to assassinate Queen Elizabeth to a Roman Catholic, Edmund Neville. Neville mistrusted Parry and reported the conversation to Burghley, who pretended to believe in the plot and as a result had Parry arrested and executed.

4

Sir Henry Wotton and Thomas Chamberlain

WITH THE death of Sir Francis Walsingham in 1590 the English Secret Service lost its true pioneer, and there was nobody of the same calibre to take his place. A Spanish agent wrote to Philip of Spain to acquaint him with the news: "Secretary Walsingham has just expired, at which there is much sorrow." "There, yes!" wrote the Spanish monarch in a marginal comment on the letter, "but it is good news here".[1]

But the tradition of espionage which Walsingham had so patiently built up was carried on, though in rather more orthodox form than previously. In short, the English returned to the pre-Walsingham tradition of relying for the bulk of their Intelligence on their ambassadors, which was the policy which Spain, hitherto England's chief rival, had followed. Spanish agents were to be found in every European court, always under the cover of diplomacy, and at one time there were four Spanish ambassadors in Vienna, each supplied with letters of credit.

England continued to regard Italy as the best listening-post in Europe and Venice as of paramount importance. So it was not surprising to find that the supreme example of Intelligence organisation masquerading under a cloak of diplomacy was to be found in James I's reign at Venice where Sir Henry Wotton was ambassador.

Sir Henry was quite blunt about this. In the album of a friend at Augsburg he wrote: "An ambassador is an honest man sent to lie abroad for the good of his country."[2]

Sir Henry Wotton (1568–1639) was born at Boughton Malherbe in Kent, which was the home of the Wotton family for more than four hundred years. Courtier, diplomat and poet, he achieved as much success in literature as in diplomacy. Indeed, his poetry was often used in the cause of diplomacy as in his ode to Elizabeth of Bohemia:

So, when my mistress shall be seen
In form and beauty of her mind,
By virtue first, then choice a Queen,
Tell me, if she were not design'd
Th'eclipse and glory of her kind.

In Boughton Malherbe Church lies Sir Leonelle Sharpe, who was chaplain to Queen Elizabeth's favourite, Essex, and who after Essex had lost his head became chaplain to the Queen. A lucky escape. And Wotton was equally fortunate, for he was secretary to the Earl of Essex but had the good sense to leave the latter before he was disgraced.

Wotton went to Venice where in 1602 he undertook his first mission in espionage. Disguised and using the name of Octavio Baldi, he was sent by the Duke of Tuscany to warn James VI of Scotland of a plot against him. Wotton had his reward a year later when a grateful James VI of Scotland became James I of England and made him English Ambassador to Venice.

It was a difficult and frequently dangerous post for any ambassador. Under James I Wotton received £3 6s. 8d. a day and an additional sum of £400 to cover couriers and Secret Service work. Not a large sum when one considers that he had to support his staff as well as his family. In Venice any official seen conversing with a foreign minister was liable to be punished with life imprisonment, so Wotton had to play the diplomatic game with great caution. It was a situation in which bribery had to be employed, for nobody in such conditions of service would take risks unless paid for doing so. Wotton himself accepted a pension from the Duke of Savoy. The practice of bribery was widespread as a method of diplomacy.

Talented, artistic, with a gift for epigrams, Wotton was the secret agent-ambassador *par excellence*. Enjoying the confidence of his king, he built up his own Secret Service which, in effect, was for some years the most powerful England had, even though it was master-minded from Venice. He attracted the underworld of diplomacy to his embassy and openly professed that rogues were far more useful than honest men when it came to the more practical aspects of diplomacy. He regarded the truth with cynicism: "Always tell the truth", he advised a young diplomat on one occasion, "for you shall never be believed; and by this means your truth will secure yourself and will put your adversaries to a loss".[3]

Sir Henry was also adept at supplementing his own Secret Service funds by selling some confidential information to other friendly governments. He gave the Venetian Government intelligence about the Jesuits' activities at the same time that he passed it on to James I. He set up agents in Rome, Turin and Milan as well as in Venice and robbed the posts and stole the Jesuits' correspondence. His organisation was superb, for he made a study of the seals used by the Jesuits on their mails, found out the identities of their couriers and the methods they used for communications. And always his sense of humour lightened even the most dangerous acts of espionage. "I must confess myself to have a special appetite for the packets that pass to and from these Holy Fathers." Once he had intercepted the packets, read the contents and had them copied, he allowed the mails to go to the addresses intended.

James I was uncertain in his heart about his own religious preferences and even less sure about what his people wanted him to be. The son of a Catholic, Mary Stuart, and himself an indifferent Protestant, James decided that espionage must decide whether he should keep his lines of communications open with the Catholics on the Continent who might be his potential allies, or whether he must be perpetually on the look-out for Jesuit plots.

Sir Henry Wotton undoubtedly played along with his sovereign in the early days, for the Grand Duke Ferdinand of Tuscany had been an influential Catholic and a mediator between Henri IV of France and the Pope. But the requirements of the Secret Service were such that the rules were to communicate with Catholics, but not to make any commitments with them. Only so skilled an operator as Wotton, himself a Protestant, could have negotiated the pitfalls of Venice where he was surrounded by Catholics. When Wotton had arrived in that city as ambassador, the Pope had warned Catholic envoys to have no dealings with him: "I promise you that, if you let the English open a change house in Venice, I will never submit to it, even though I ended by being flayed alive in that city."[4]

It was under James I that England first became aware of the need for a form of commercial and industrial espionage. James was afraid that the growing power and commerce of the Dutch would seriously undermine the trade of England. Thomas Phelippes, Walsingham's former decipherer, developed a commercial spying agency on a modest scale and this was extended from the Low Countries as far afield as Sweden and Russia. Sweden was at that time of special interest to British merchants and manufacturers, notably in connection with the Swedish iron industry which had suddenly become highly competitive.

In the Swedish army at the time was an English officer, Captain Thomas Chamberlain, who had become embroiled in commercial espionage. A number of other English traders in north Russia persuaded Chamberlain to present a petition to James I, asking him to accept the Muscovite throne, as the Czar was dead and the boyars were not only searching for a new ruler but had taken an oath to choose a non-Russian. Some of these Russian nobles were prepared to accept James as their ruler.

Chamberlain, who was well versed in the commercial and financial advantages to be gained if James should agree to accept the Russian throne, saw Lord Dorchester, Principal Secretary of State, and described in extravagant terms the wealth of Muscovy and said that the offer of the czardom was "the greatest and happiest overture that ever was made to any King of this realm since Columbus offered King Henry VII the discovery of the West Indies".[5]

The prospect of increased trade for England as a result of acceptance of this offer greatly tempted the English merchants, whose personal meddling in espionage had helped to bring this about. It was indeed a splendid opportunity, but there no longer existed in Russia the same efficient liaison between the government and Secret Service as there was under Walsingham. John Dee had been so successful in penetrating Czarist circles that he had even received an offer of employment by the Czar; however, he had refused. And on this occasion in James's reign there was a sad lack of foresight by the English agents themselves. They neglected to maintain liaison with the boyars while James was considering the offer. James had been sufficiently impressed to send two agents to Russia to discuss matters further, but by the time they arrived a new Czar, Mikhail Romanov, had already been elected in March 1613.

A more successful, if unusual, effort in espionage was that undertaken almost single-handed by one Richard Foley, who was engaged in iron manufacture near Stourbridge. He saw the supremacy of his own and other English ironmasters threatened by the competition of Swedish ironworkers who had discovered a new process known as "splitting". The full details of Foley's enterprise will probably never be known, so much of it is woven into legend and gossip that it is not easy to separate fact from fiction. Legend has it that Foley, who had been a village fiddler before he set up his ironworks, went to the Continent, disguised as a minstrel, and wandered from city to city in Belgium, Germany, Italy and Spain, secretly collecting information about the techniques of ironmasters. What is certain is that he went to Sweden, where, posing as an ironworker, he obtained work in various factories and so discovered the secret of the "splitting" process. Returning home, he persuaded some friends to join him in building machinery to operate the new process. Foley failed in his experiment, but, undeterred, went back to Sweden to seek more information. His second experiment succeeded and a "splitting" machine was successfully introduced at Stourbridge and laid the foundations of the Foley family fortune. Within a few generations the Foleys were among the landed gentry in Worcestershire and had entered the peerage. Richard Foley died in 1657 at the age of seventy-five.[6]

The case of Richard Foley is worth mentioning if only to show that under James I (and indeed for that matter under Charles I, too) private enterprise in espionage was often more effective than that of the official Secret Service. Perhaps the factor which reduced the effectiveness of the Secret Service in James I's reign was the weakness and unreliability of the King himself. The "wisest fool in Christendom" not only vacillated in his policy-making, he ruined the chances of his agents by frequently double-crossing them and by promising to pay out sums of money and then reneging on his promises. He was mistrusted by foreigners and his own diplomats alike, not merely for his parsimony but for his indiscreet gossiping and inability to keep a secret. Least of all could James keep a State secret. Whatever he was told on matters of Intelligence, he unfailingly passed on to the Spanish Ambassador in London, and not surprisingly many of the secrets his Intelligence service procured for him were relayed back to the continental courts.

It was not surprising that with the rise of such an astute a manipulator of intelligence as Cardinal Richelieu in France, England's powerful espionage network, built up so ably and carefully by Walsingham, slipped back into the disorganised, haphazard system of the early Tudors. The Stuarts had also reduced diplomatic contacts with the Continent to such an extent that Walsingham's efficient secret communications system had been allowed to lapse. In consequence cryptography in England declined in use at the very time that it was being revolutionised and developed on the Continent, by the Gronsfeld system in Germany and by Rossignol in France.

On the other hand English cryptography still owed much to its amateur innovators who, eschewing any complicated systems, were often able to baffle decipherers by the simplicity of their methods. In the Civil War the need for cryptography once again became of paramount importance and the amateurs came into their own. When Sir John Trevanion was imprisoned in Colchester Castle during the Civil War for siding with the Royalists, execution faced him as almost a certainty. Consequently he was closely guarded and all his correspondence was carefully examined by decipherers before he was allowed to read it. One innocent looking letter was examined and passed on to him. It read:

"Worthie Sir John: Hope, that is the beste comfort of the afflicted, cannot much, I fear me, help you now. That I would saye to you, is this only: if ever I may be able to requite that I do owe you, stand upon asking me. 'Tis not much I can do: but what I can do, bee you verie sure I wille. I knowe that, if dethe comes, if ordinary men fear it, it frights not you, accounting it for a high honour, to have such a rewarde of your loyalty. Pray yet that you may be spared this soe bitter cup. I fear not that you will grudge any sufferings; onlie if bie submission you can turn them away, 'tis the part of a wise man. Tell me, as if you can, to do for you any thinge that you wolde have done. The general goes back on Wedmesday. Restinge your servant to command.

R.T."[7]

Sir John spent the day quietly in his cell. At night he asked to go to the chapel to pray. It seemed a reasonable request, as the chapel had only one door and narrow windows situated high up on the walls. Escape seemed an impossibility. So Sir John was left alone, praying in front of the alter. The warders waited outside the door, but after an interval of an hour they became worried and went in to see what he was doing.

Sir John had vanished. The innocent-looking letter was a prearranged cipher, based on a well-known system which would certainly not have baffled Walsingham's cryptographical experts. The clues lay in the punctuation, which, as can be seen, was very odd in places (indeed, it revealed all the traces of hastily contrived and not very clever cipher-making). The third letter after each punctuation mark spelled out the message: "Panel at east end of chapel slides."

It may seem surprising that such a cipher should be described as simple in the age of the Stuarts. But one must bear in mind that deciphering in the Renaissance period generally and in the Elizabethan age in particular had been brought to a high standard of efficiency. Walsingham had broken most of the known ciphers of the period and it was only because the expert deciphering organisation he had set up had been allowed to disappear and the system he introduced had been neglected that England was left in so weak a condition in Intelligence matters.

The earlier years of James I's reign were marked by an intensive drive against witchcraft and Secret Service agents found much of their time occupied in tracking down witches and warlocks. The King was determined rigorously to root out witchcraft in all its forms and tended to view "natural magic" and even some philosophical-scientific modes of inquiry as suspect. To be fair, there was some excuse for this. As a young man James had been the target of a series of plots linked with witchcraft and some plots against his life had been based on occult practices. There was the case of a witch named Agnes Sampson, who was ordered by Bothwell to kill James by bewitching him. There was also a secret society practising black magic as a weapon against the King and Dr. Fian, an Edinburgh schoolmaster, was the secretary and registrar of a group of witches who used a church for their nocturnal meetings and plottings.

Many of these incidents were described by James I in his *Three Books on Demonology*, which he based his personal examination of witches who had confessed to malpractices. Some of this evidence revealed that Dr. Fian had made a pact with the Devil to cause the King's ship to be struck by a storm on his voyage to Norway.

To enable his secret agents to bring suspected witches to trial James I persuaded Parliament to pass a Witchcraft Statute in 1604 to "uproot the monstrous evils of enchanters". Despite some hesitations among the Bishops in the House of Lords, who thought the statute was "imperfect", the bill was rushed through Parliament and put on the Statute Book within three months.

In the Elizabethan reign the Secret Service was mainly seeking to trap the Papists and at least these activities led to the unmasking of serious plots against the realm. But when under James I they turned their attention to witches and warlocks there was a great deal of unnecessary persecution, often of innocent people, the victims of malicious slander, and producing no worthwhile results.

England's interest in Russia fitfully reappeared from time to time and so encouraged the Secret Service to maintain close links with that country. This interest began when Queen Elizabeth conducted a lengthy correspondence with Ivan "The Terrible", Czar of Russia, culminating in the conclusion of a commercial treaty between England and Russia, and the sending out to Ivan of Robert Jacoby, one of Elizabeth's own physicians. The idea of a marriage between Elizabeth and the sinister Ivan had actually been mooted, not perhaps ever seriously entertained by the Queen, but cautiously broached by some merchant-adventurers who were known to have friends in Burghley's Intelligence organisation. Indeed the proposal to marry Elizabeth off to Ivan IV had been put forward before she was Queen.

In James I's reign, as we have seen, the question of James becoming Czar had been openly touted by English agents in

Sweden and in Russia. But if the English interest in ties with Russia waned somewhat after the accession of the Romanovs, the notorious hypochrondia of the latter caused them to retain a lively interest in English doctors. In 1621 the Czar, Mikhail Fyodorovich Romanov, asked the English court to recommend him a physician. The name put forward was none other than Arthur Dee, son of Elizabeth's astrologer. Like his father, Arthur Dee was a dabbler in magic and alchemy and when he went to Russia as the Czar's personal physician he became a close confidant of that monarch. There is some suggestion that Arthur Dee was in reality a spy. Whether suspicions about this in Russian circles was the cause is not known, but in 1634 he lost favour at the Russian court and returned to England. There he served as physician to Charles I.[8]

5

John Thurloe: Cromwell's Spy-Master

RIGHT THROUGH the Civil Wars England's Intelligence system dwindled, and indeed as far as obtaining worthwhile information from the Continent was concerned almost ceased to exist. By the time Cromwell had installed himself in power there was need for drastic action in this field, for England was seriously threatened again by enemies outside the realm.

Cromwell apparently realised the importance of a radical overhaul of national intelligence and did not stint the Secret Service of funds as had Elizabeth and the Stuart kings before him. According to Samuel Pepys, the Lord Protector spent £70,000 a year on Intelligence.[1] Cromwell adopted the principle of paying by results and, when those results were good, the payments to agents were exceptionally generous.

The Lord Protector, like the first Elizabeth, was above all else a realist. He did not allow his strong religious prejudices to interfere with his foreign policy. This greatly strengthened his hand not only in the diplomatic field but in espionage as well. His military organisation was disciplined and efficient, his armies well trained, sober and well-officered, and quite a few European countries, more out of fear than respect, sought to have alliances with him.

And, just as Elizabeth found in Walsingham the Intelligence genius which the hour demanded, so Cromwell brought to power in the person of John Thurloe a Secret Service chief who must rank as one of the greatest in the history of that organisation. A quietly spoken, modest Essex lawyer, Thurloe achieved power with the minimum of publicity and fuss. His assurance undoubtedly stemmed from the absolute trust Cromwell had in him.

Thurloe was given twenty-times as much money for his Secret Service work as Elizabeth gave to Walsingham. Without question these large sums enabled Thurloe to make the English Secret Service the most efficient in Europe in the space of a very few years. It was a remarkable achievement, built up in the first place through Thurloe's office as Postmaster-General. He intercepted a vast amount of correspondence, mostly that of Royalists, or Royalist sympathisers, and soon set up agents in every court and an extensive network of spies at home. As his Secret Service grew so Thurloe extended his powers by acquiring new offices. At one time he was not only Secretary of State, but Home Secretary, Chief of Police, head of the Secret Service, Foreign Secretary, War Secretary and Councillor of State.[1]

It was not surprising that with such a powerful organisation behind him Cromwell was able to speak so forthrightly to foreign diplomats as he did to a French envoy who called on him, remarking that he would come to France in person "with 40,000 foot and 12,000 horse, if necessary".

Thurloe was able to snuff out any plots against the régime hatched abroad because he had many agents who held the confidence of Stuart supporters. Cardinal Mazarin, himself an adept in the organisation of intelligence, frequently confessed himself baffled because when the French Cabinet met behind locked doors their secrets inevitably leaked out to Thurloe within a few days. Nor was this an isolated view of the efficiency of the English Secret Service. Sagredo, the Venetian Ambassador in London, wrote to the Council of Ten that "there is no government on earth which divulges its affairs less than England, or is more punctually informed of those of the others".[2]

Not a little of the credit of this success must be attributed to the manner in which Thurloe revived the art of cryptography and set up a deciphering organisation in London under the control of Dr. John Wallis, of Oxford. Wallis had the reputation of being able to "break" any code or cipher. Another man who played an invaluable role in Thurloe's cryptographical department was John Wilkins, Bishop of Chester. Though he later swore allegiance to Charles II, Wilkins was a Parliamentarian under

Cromwell and gave Thurloe the benefit of his personally written manual of cryptography.

Wilkins was so far in advance of his time that he even produced plans for the construction of a submarine boat. The cryptographical system he introduced was known as the "Pig Pen System", as it was comprised of dots and squares. It is a tribute to Wilkins that his system was still in operation in the American Civil War and is even today practised by schoolboys. It was a system that was simple, yet made for speed in an age that had not completely appreciated the need for high-speed communications. His manual of cryptography described some simple methods of transposition, a suppression-of-frequencies cipher of the less complicated style, the Bacon bilateral system and a method of double substitution.[3] Bacon had laid down as the main principle of his system that the perfect secret code was one which did not appear to be a code and, taking advantage of the invention of printing, his method of achieving this was by the use of two founts of type in printing a text which should contain a secret message. Thus the ordinary system would think that the typesetting had gone astray and would not suspect a code. It was because of Bacon's bilateral system and certain typesetting oddities in the text of some Shakespearean plays that scholars developed the theories that Shakespeare put codes into his plays and the converse theory that Bacon wrote Shakespeare's work.

Copies of many of the letters sent to Thurloe by his agents still exist. A volume of these, covering the period of November and December, 1656, from agents in France, Belgium, Holland and Germany, was recently quoted in a catalogue of manuscripts for sale. No item of intelligence was considered too trivial for Thurloe. There was a letter from a Hamburg agent stating that the English community in Hamburg thought there would always be a King and the protectorate would be successive with the Cromwell family. A correspondent in Bordeaux mentioned a peace treaty between the Kings of France and Spain and a French ordinance forbidding their ships of war from seizing private vessels.

Peter Fernando Montero wrote from Portugal with information about the massing of Spanish ships which were "intended to attack England when strong enough". John Butler in Flushing wrote reporting support for the Royalist cause: "Charles Stuart leavies are increased to 6 Thousand men. They flock to him out of England." A number cipher was obviously used at the time in the originals, for though most of the words have been decoded all persons' names, including those of some agents and others, are coded. For example, one message read: "to induce the 175 to submit to 141 all his right and pretence upon 141 wch would be to the satisfaction of 141 and then again to induce the 141 to quit the 176 wch would be to the satisfaction of 175. . . ."[4]

Thurloe provided an excellent example of his views on the efficacy of spending large sums of money on espionage in a letter of instructions to his agent in Leghorn. "Concerning a good correspondent in Rome", he wrote, "I doubt not to effect it to content when I shall know your resolution what you intend to spend therein. These people cannot be gained, but by money, but for money they will do anything, adventure body and soul, too. . . . Such intelligence must be procured from a Monsignor, a secretary or a Cardinal. . . . I should say 1,000 pounds a year were well-spent, with 500 pounds pension and now and then 100 pounds gratuity."[5]

Thurloe, rather like Walsingham, reversed the trend to rely on ambassadors for espionage, and pinned his faith in secret agents, arguing that ambassadors were vulnerable to bribes and were in any case too obviously likely to be suspected as spies and therefore too closely watched. The result was that, again like Walsingham, Thurloe was able to smell out any plot against the Lord Protector and, despite the fact that Charles Stuart in exile had offered a knighthood and £5,000 to anyone who would assassinate Cromwell, his agents knew all about the plots every time there was a volunteer for the job of killer. In one instance Thurloe was warned by one of his agents not to let Cromwell read any more foreign letters as some of them might be impregnated with poison. It was Thurloe's counter-espionage service which discovered Sir John Packington smuggling in arms under the guise of wine and soap shipments; they, too, unmasked the Penruddock rising in Wiltshire and the "Sealed Knot", a secret society of Royalist plotters, though he never succeeded in completely rounding up this formidable and agile band of conspirators. But

Thurloe was constantly on their trail and once when one of his agents followed a "Sealed Knot" member to Cologne, Charles Stuart was found there with a servant, but the elusive King in exile once more escaped the net.

Thurloe's ability to divorce his job from his Puritan prejudices stood him in good stead. He was one of the first to appreciate the value of Jews as secret agents and to develop their talents in England's favour. In this he was fully supported by Cromwell himself, for the Lord Protector encouraged the migration of Jews to England. It was a Jewish merchant, Antonio Fernandez Carvajal, who was given permission to settle in England and who offered the Commonwealth Government the services of his correspondents on the Continent. Another Jew, Simon de Caceres, passed on to Thurloe plans for an expedition against Chile and for the fortification of Jamaica.[6]

Historically, the attitude of both Cromwell and Thurloe to the Jews was of long-term importance to England. Hated and persecuted by the Spaniards and by many other European nations, the Jews turned to England as a protector and in return gave many centuries of valuable assistance to the Secret Service, certainly in much greater proportion than to any other foreign power. While there is no doubt from Cromwell's own pleading on behalf of the Jews that he took a genuinely liberal view about them—"is it not the duty of magistrates to permit the Jews . . . to live freely and peaceably among us?"—financial considerations also weighed with the Commonwealth on this subject. When on 5 January 1649, a petition was presented to Fairfax and the Army Council by two inhabitants of Amsterdam for the repeal of the banishment of the Jews the official view was that "if there may be a toleration of a synagogue of the Jews, they will give 60,000 or 80,000 pounds for that freedom, it will bring all the Portugal merchants from Amsterdam".

Sagredo, the Venetian Ambassador already quoted, seems to have made a careful study of English espionage under Cromwell. He comments, too, on the way in which England guarded her own secrets: "they meet in a room approached through others, without number, and countless doors are shut. That which favours their intent best is that very few persons, at most sixteen, meet to digest the gravest affairs and come to the most serious decisions. To keep them the more secret they pass through the head of a single secretary, who superintends political affairs and criminal as well. . . . To discover political affairs of others they do not employ ambassadors but use spies, as less conspicuous, making use of men of spirit but without rank unlikely to be noticed. . . . Thus by their money and bribes they have found a way to use the forces of Rome (i.e. the use of Jesuits as spies) and draw profit from their enemies, as they call the priests in London. . . . In France, Spain, Germany and at Venice they also have insignificant persons who from time to time send important advices, and, being less under observation, penetrate everywhere."[7]

Some of the more abhorrent features of a dictatorship were apparent in Thurloe's development of the Secret Service. He created a new form of police force, a militia, serving at home and employed for the purposes of a secret police force, under the control of Army officers. This militia was divided into eleven districts, each one commanded by a major-general. Some of the latter abused their position as spy-masters and, not content with revealing the presence of spies, sometimes used their powers to hunt down innocent victims of the Civil Wars and to close down ale houses and maintain a rigid enforcement of the Sabbath. The militia borrowed the language of modern totalitarianism and referred to their task as taking England into "protective custody".

Like Walsingham, Thurloe used his network of spies to keep a close watch on Spanish Fleet movement and it was as a result of intelligence passed to him by a Jewish agent in Jamaica that Admiral Blake captured the Spanish Plate Fleet at Teneriffe. English squadrons waited for the fleet for six months until the detailed information about the Spaniards' movements was borne out by their appearance on the horizon.

Thurloe firmly believed that, given time, almost any Royalist agent would crack and confess without his being apprehended. He seemed to have an astute gift for observing the psychological weaknesses of enemy and Royalist agents. In 1655 several arrests of Royalists were made in London following a search of houses where they had been hiding. This was due entirely to the information given to Thurloe voluntarily by a young man named

Henry Manning, who had arrived at Charles' Court in exile early in the year. Like many other of Charles' lesser supporters he had found himself without funds and with no prospect of receiving any, so he had decided to obtain money by writing to Thurloe. So desperate was Manning that he took the risk of writing to Thurloe before he had been given a cipher.

Manning was not admitted to the secret counsels of Charles' Court, but what he passed on to London was of immense value. He reported the general outline of Royalist plans against the English Government and gave the fictitious names which some of them used when hiding out in London. Thus in the first week of June 1655 several leading Royalists were arrested, and within a few days Lord Willoughby of Parham, Lord Newport of High Ercall, Geoffrey Palmer and Henry Seymour were sent to the Tower. Following further information from Manning, the Earl of Lindsey, Lord Lovelace and Lord Falkland were arrested in Oxfordshire. By the end of June it was clear from Manning's detailed letters that there was a Royalist plot to assassinate the Protector and that this was to be followed up by a rising against the Government. To counteract this, orders were then given to banish from London and Westminster all who had adhered to the Royalist cause in the past whether or not they were now under suspicion.

Thurloe's greatest gift as a Secret Service chief was his ability to draw out information from the heart of the enemy's camp, to give the enemy's agents encouragement and confidence to betray plots to him and, more important, to know which Royalists were most likely to be suborned. These tactics had been adopted before, but never on the same scale or with such devastating results. That Manning's Intelligence was undoubtedly accurate cannot be doubted. If Thurloe had been in doubt, he found ample confirmation of the reports when he obtained a copy of a letter to Charles Stuart from the Duke of York which read:

"... a proposition has been made to me which is too long to put into a letter, so that I will, as short as I can, let you know the heads of them. There are four Roman Catholics that have bound themselves in a solemn oath to Kill Cromwell, and then to raise all the catholics in the City and the army, which they pretend to be a number so considerable as may give rise for your recovery, they being all warned to be ready for something that is to be done, without knowing what it is. They demand 10,000 livres in hand and, when the business is ended, some recompense for themselves, according to their several qualities and the same liberty for Catholics in England as the Protestants have in France. I thought not fit to reject this proposition, but to acquaint you with it, because the first part of the design seems to me to be better laid and resolved on than any I have known or that kind; and for the defects of the second, it may be supplied by some designs you may have to join to it. If you approve of it, one of the four, entrusted by the rest, will repair to you, his charges being borne, and give you a full account of the whole matter."[8]

About the middle of November 1655, Richard Talbott and James Halsall were arrested in England on suspicion of being concerned in a plot to kill the Protector. But while there was little doubt that the two men were implicated in such a plot, the Government failed to obtain satisfactory evidence against them and after long interrogation they succeeded in escaping to the Continent. This was one of Thurloe's relatively few failures. The reason for it was that Manning had been trapped by the Royalists. In writing so frequently to London, often not even in cipher, he had taken too many risks and suspicions had been aroused. He was arrested and, though he pleaded that he had only given useless information to Thurloe, his inquisitors paid no heed to him. He was sentenced to death by the Royalists. The Elector of Cologne refused to allow the execution to take place on his territory on the grounds that he had committed no offence against the realm in which he was residing and that Charles exercised no sovereignty over the land from which he came. So the plotters took the unfortunate Manning across the border into the Duchy of Juliers and there he was shot in a wood.

Thurloe's system of lavish payments for good results in espionage paid off over the years. He survived Cromwell and the Lord Protector's son, Richard, who succeeded him, retained his services as Secretary of State. One of his last coups was to bribe Sir Richard Willis, a member of the "Sealed Knot" society. But by this time Thurloe's Intelligence service was already being undermined by the Royalists who saw that the prospects for

Charles's return to London were brighter than they had ever been. Just as Thurloe had infiltrated the Royalist ranks so the Royalists began to infiltrate the English Government's Intelligence service. Cromwell's Resident in Holland, George Downing, who had long been a loyal and able organiser of Intelligence for the English Government, astutely diagnosed that there was a strong current of opinion in favour of the restoration of the monarchy in England. Realising that his future might well depend on his attitude towards Charles Stuart in this critical period, Downing sent Charles a secret warning that Willis had been bribed. As a result Thurloe's coup miscarried.

Thurloe was succeeded as head of Intelligence, or Number One Argus, as that office was named, by Thomas Scott, who had been one of his chief Intelligencers, as well as Member of Parliament for Chipping Wycombe. Scot was paid £800 a year "to manage the Intelligence both at home and abroad for the State".[9]

6

From Secretary Morrice to Matthew Prior

THE METAMORPHOSIS which overcame England at the Restoration was no less visible in the field of espionage than elsewhere. In 1668 Samuel Pepys was noting in his diary that "Secretary Morrice did this day in the House, when they talked of intelligence say that he was allowed but £700 a year for intelligence whereas in Cromwell's time, he [Cromwell] did allow £70,000 a year for it; and was confirmed therein by Colonel Birch, who said that thereby Cromwell carried the secrets of all the princes of Europe at his girdle."[1]

Obviously after eight years of Stuart rule again there was some disquiet about the state of national Intelligence, as the criticism implied. Three days later Parliament once again debated the subject, but according to Pepys' diary for 17 February 1668, the amount of money given to Morrice was increased by only £50.

Clearly Members of Parliament had no qualms about openly criticising the Intelligence organisation, for Pepys recorded that "they did here in the House talk boldly of the King's bad counsellors, and how they must all be turned out, and many of them, and better, brought in: and the proceedings of the Long Parliament in the beginning of the war were called to memory: and the King's bad Intelligence was mentioned, wherein they were bitter against my Lord Arlington, saying among other things, that whatever Morrice's was, who declared he had but £750 allowed him for intelligence, the King paid too dear for my Lord Arlington's in giving £10,000 and a barony for it."[2]

The foregoing quotations may appear to confuse the issue. What was the true state of Intelligence under Charles II? Was the

Christopher Marlowe, who spied for England in France

Sir Francis Walsingham, 'father' of the modern Secret Service

Matthew Prior, poet-diplomat, in charg
of espionage against the exiled James I

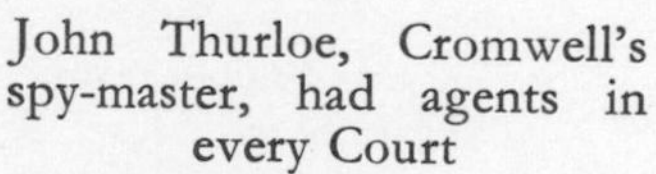

John Thurloe, Cromwell's spy-master, had agents in every Court

Secret Service vested solely under Morrice who was denied adequate funds, or did the real power in espionage organisation lie with Arlington, or even with Charles himself? The truth is that after the Restoration the Secret Service ceased to be centralised; it was split up into various independent entities, Morrice never being allowed to acquire anything like the power of Thurloe, and with the King himself often playing off one organisation against another and quite often running an Intelligence service of his own.

This was understandable to some extent. Charles' long period in exile had made him realise that few men were to be trusted, least of all his own supporters. So Charles would keep a wary eye on all sources of intelligence and check and double-check reports he received from one quarter by those supplied by another. It was an empirical form of intelligence, not markedly efficient, often resulting in much duplication of activities and information and rather typically English in its haphazard approach to Intelligence. Inevitably it bred mistrust, the mistrust of one section of Intelligence of another, and the assessments made were distinguished rather by cynicism than good judgement.

Charles II was from his accession to the throne desperately in need of money. Not that this deterred him from maintaining a lavish Court and large number of mistresses. But it made him dependent for funds on sources other than the English Parliament. His other main source was the French King, Louis XIV, and thorughout his reign he played off Parliament against Louis and vice versa, drawing funds from each in turn.

Being in the pay of Louis XIV, Charles' Intelligence system was to a large extent conditioned by this fact. As both the English and French courts were notable for the influence of royal mistresses, it is clear that espionage in the royal bedchambers and boudoirs became the order of the day. While Parliament watched suspiciously and with increasing dismay the series of imbroglios in which Charles and Louis indulged, the real power in Intelligence was more often to be found among the courtesans than the courtiers. If the official Secret Service was denuded of funds during Charles II's reign, one must look elsewhere for the missing money. A clue was provided when in 1968 a sale took place at Sotheby's in London of a number of "Secret Service Papers of

Charles II's reign". Those papers revealed that the phrases "Secret Service" and "Secret Service funds" were for matters which did not exactly cover Intelligence but were meant to conceal payments to the King's mistresses. Nevertheless, some of those mistresses were spies in the King's service and a few were agents of Louis XIV.

Despite the superficially friendly links between the English and French courts, each spied on the other and each sought to seduce their respective agents. The French diplomat, d'Estrades, came to London, bribed the wife of the Duke of York, daughter of Lord Clarendon, "with clock dials set with diamonds and other precious stones" and paved the way for the purchase of Dunkirk from England with a sum of 5 million francs. Meanwhile the French King's main aim was to encourage any move which would bring Charles II into conflict with his Parliament and thus make the "Merry Monarch" more dependent on Louis. Indeed when Charles II dismissed his protesting Parliament, Louis sent Ruvigny to London with funds to enable the King to maintain himself against Parliament.

Attacks on the Intelligence service, or rather on the lack of an adequate organisation, increased. Andrew Marvell, the poet, led a Parliamentary battle against the Secretary of State Arlington with the comment that previous Secretaries of State had enabled the Government to obtain "letters of the Pope's cabinet" and, he added, now "the money allowed for intelligence was so small, the intelligence was accordingly". While Morrice had £750 a year for intelligence, between 1666 and 1667 the Exchequer paid over £24,145 for "Secret Service", for purposes known only to Arlington and the King himself. Much of this money went to the royal mistresses.[3]

Of those undoubtedly the most costly and the one who benefitted most from "Secret Service funds" was Louise de Kéroualle, a dark-eyed beauty despatched from Louis XIV's Court to that of Charles II, partly as a spy and partly to win favours for the French King. She became Duchess of Portsmouth as well as Duchess of Aubigny and her behind-the-scenes intrigues were in no small measure to bring about the disastrous Treaty of Dover, which in return for an annual subsidy of 3 million francs and the acquisition of Walcheren imposed on Charles II the price of abandoning the Triple Alliance and allying himself with France against the Dutch.

Yet at least King Charles bestowed on the Secret Service a new cipher which bore his name. This was the cipher he had used when in exile in the Netherlands. An elaborate cipher, in which 70 was ab, 71 ad, 72 ac and very common words had special code numbers, it shows some indication of French origins and probably was in fact adapted from a French cipher of the period.[4] But from the time of his accession to the throne Charles II did little to encourage any development of the cipher system and, though the Secret Service methods of Thurloe had been studied, little was done to maintain an effective espionage system abroad. The Secret Service concentrated largely on watching for agitators and dissenters in England. Ambassadors abroad ceased to have any dealings with the Government secret agents and their reports home contained little worthwhile intelligence. An example of this lack of intelligence is to be found in the correspondence of the Secretary of State with Sir George Etherege, the dramatist, appointed by Charles as Ambassador to Regensburg, seat of the German Imperial Diet, in 1685:

"I hope", wrote the Secretary of State, "in a little time we may hear something of your diversions as well as your business, which would be much pleasanter and perhaps as instructive." What a change from the sobriety of Cromwellian diplomacy and espionage with its constant probings and demand for worthwhile intelligence.

Etherege, a rake-hell and wit who must have been bored to distraction by the solemnity and pomposity of the German Court, replied by sending in reports about the mistresses of German courtiers. Of one he said: "She wants not her little arts to secure her Sultan's affection, she can dissemble fondness and jealousy and can swoon at pleasure."

Etherege was unhappy among the prim and ponderous Germans and irked by the formality of the Court and the tedious recreations of the Regensburgers. He shocked Court opinion by consorting with an actress and wrote home in another report that he sighed for "the kind nymphs of the Thames. . . . I have only a plain Bavarian with her sandy looks, brawny limbs and a brick complexion."[5]

Thurloe had used the Post Office as an integral instrument in his Secret Services, but this royal monopoly under the control of the Secretary of State was neglected in Charles II's reign, and the indolent administration failed to take advantage of its facilities for keeping watch on the mails. The French Ambassador, Comignes, as was natural for a logical Frenchman, just could not believe that the powers-that-be did not use the services of the Post Office for counter-espionage, for he warned his Government that the English Government had "tricks to open letters more skilfully than anywhere in the world".

For nearly two centuries the Pepys diaries, which had lain neglected in the Library of Magdalene College, Cambridge, baffled all attempts at deciphering. Samuel Pepys had himself been mixed up in Secret Service work and certainly knew a great deal about its workings. Having himself suffered from accusations of treason, which he luckily was able to refute, it is not surprising that this Commissioner of the Admiralty decided to commit his innermost thoughts to code. In the early nineteenth century Lord Braybrooke undertook the task of trying to decipher Pepy's manuscripts and diaries written in a tiny cipher design which was difficult to see under a microscope, let alone solve.

Braybrooke was looking for a precise cipher, such as was used in the Stuart period, and he could not understand why Pepys' signs were so vague and imprecise and bore evidence of having been written in haste. It had always been an essential condition of any code or cipher that it should be clearly and deliberately written. At length he and a divinity student who had studied cryptography came to the conclusion that the writing was not cryptographical at all. They hesitated to think it could be a form of shorthand, as the signs bore no resemblance to any known modern form of shorthand. But, delving into the history of shorthand, they found that in Charles II's reign a Mr. Shelton had invented tachygraphy, an abbreviated, coded handwriting which had been approved by the University of Cambridge.[6] The Secret Service, as far as is known, made no use of tachygraphy, but Pepys, a bold innovator, enthusiastically adopted and adapted it for his own purposes and for the private espionage service in which he himself indulged when at the Admiralty. Indeed there is some reason for believing that Pepys was the founder of an unofficial Naval Intelligence Department. To complicate things further Pepys had first put some of the messages and notes into foreign languages, spelled phonetically, then enciphered and finally written out in his adapted form of tachygraphy. But it was a measure of the indolence and indifference of the age that instead of making the fullest use of this new form of communication Pepys chiefly employed this mode of writing for recording everyday chit-chat and casual amorous encounters.

This failure to keep abreast of the latest cryptographical developments and other code devices might easily have changed the course of history. When Charles II died and James, Duke of York, succeeded him on the throne, it very nearly did so. James was hated by a considerable section of his countrymen as a Papist and a would-be tyrant, and the Duke of Monmouth, an illegitimate son of Charles II, had been exiled to Holland because of the rôle he had played in trying to keep his uncle from the throne. Monmouth, a Protestant, sought as an ally the Earl of Argyle, who had also been exiled for his part in a Covenanter uprising. Their joint aim was that with the aid of Dutch arms and ships they would sail homewards, Argyle to Scotland and Monmouth to England, and raise the standard of revolt.

Every precaution was taken to keep this project secret and all messages sent back to Britain were in cipher. Needless to say it was a cipher of which the English Secret Service, such as it then was, had no key and no skilled men to tackle its unravelling. By a mischance one of Argyle's messengers was caught and his papers, all in cipher, were sent to London. There was panic when the men in Whitehall saw the jumble of words and failed to understand their meaning. For so many days were they baffled that their panic spread outside Whitehall and whispers went around that a serious plot was afoot, but that the authorities did not know the details.

Then somebody noticed by chance that by transposing some of the words he obtained a sentence which made sense. The Earl of Argyle had set out his message in columns of 256 words, writing the first word in the first column, then the last in the same column, the first and last in the second and third columns and in subsequent columns, and, finally, back to the second and last but one of each. Eventually the message was deciphered more by luck and feverish pertinacity than by skill or professionalism and it revealed that Argyle intended to land on the west coast of Scotland, Monmouth following him within a week by landing on the west coast of England, the object being to avoid the English ships watching the east coast.[7]

The driving force behind this amateurish attempt to decipher the vital messages was James's head of Secret Service, Sir Leoline Jenkins. As a result of the capture of the incriminating documents the Secret Service ordered the round-up and arrest of all suspected persons in the area where the Earl of Argyle planned to land. Thus when the Earl arrived he was able to muster only about two thousand unequipped ghillies and peasants and was immediately confronted by the King's forces. Monmouth's uprising, though it met with considerable popular support, was short-lived, as the Government forces were ready for him and it was ruthlessly crushed and Monmouth himself executed. James II was able to remain on his throne, but not for long. A few years later he had ignominiously abdicated. But this incident—serious warning though it was for the need for an efficient cryptographical department—did not lead to any action in this section of the Secret Service. Indeed the situation there had become so critical when William III came to the throne that in desperation that monarch asked Dr. John Wallis in 1699 to train a young man in the arts of deciphering "that they may not die with you". Wallis was somewhat pessimistic: "all persons are not qualified or capable of acquiring the art of deciphering," he said, but he promised to do his best "to set matters so that the security of the State will not again be imperilled".

William III was as painstakingly efficient and systematic as the Stuarts had been careless and erratic in administration and espionage. He reconstructed the diplomatic service and removed the Secret Service from the control of the Secretaries of State. As he remained the Dutch sovereign as well as being King of England, he spent half of the year out of the country and in his absence vested great powers in the hands of William Blathwayte, his Secretary of State of War. All intelligence reports, and indeed all diplomatic despatches from ambassadors, were sent to Blathwayte direct.

The principal target for the Intelligence service was now the same as in Cromwell's day—the Royal House of Stuart in exile and the sympathisers and active supporters of James II. This meant maintaining a special espionage section to keep an eye on James's activities in France, where in exile he was aided and abetted by Louis XIV. And once again a writer was put in charge of the espionage section directed against James—the poet-diplomat Matthew Prior, who had been appointed secretary to the English Ambassador in Paris. Prior had entered the diplomatic service in 1690 at The Hague and had won as much respect for his gifts as a negotiator as for the wit and grace of his amorous odes.

In Paris, Prior built up a small but effective spy-service to keep a constant watch on James, mainly using people who had contacts with the servants and minions around him. Here again was an instance of the Secret Service playing a more important rôle in the shaping of political policies than history officially gives credit. Trevelyan, in his *England under Queen Anne*, pointed out that "the secret negotiations between England and France that resulted in the Peace of Utrecht have always been associated in the world's mind with St. John, Lord Bolingbroke . . . in fact he had nothing to do with the affair until it had been going on for nine months". But preparations for just such a deal had been going on continuously from the reign of William III and Mary. Matthew Prior, who had had a hand in the negotiations for the Peace of Ryswick in 1697, had always been scheming towards the broad aims of the Treaty of Utrecht. When he left Paris and returned to London in 1699 he was rewarded for his services by being appointed Under-Secretary of State. He left behind in Paris a record of the spies he had employed for the benefit of his successor. Apt comments on each were put alongside the names.

They were a motley crowd of rogues. There was a man masquerading under the name of Baily as a clergyman, but whose real name was Johnston—"a cunning fellow, and true debauchee", was how Prior described him, adding that he was paid two louis a week. Brocard, an Irishman, who posed as a business man, was paid rather better at about two hundred pounds a year and a widow named Langlois and her two daughters ("the old woman is a cunning jade as lives") supplied him with a variety of gossip about the life in exile of James II.[8]

Prior summed up James's "court" as being melancholic and ineffective: "their equipages are all very ragged and contemptible".

In 1711 Prior's mastery of intelligence paved the way to the finalising of the Treaty of Utrecht. He was at this time working closely with Bolingbroke and he was smuggled into the gardens of the Palace of Versailles where he secretly met Madame de Maintenon, Louis XIV's mistress. She arranged for him to have secret talks with the aged King in the gardens and it was as a result of these that Louis sent Mesnager to London. Thus the vital preliminary work for the Treaty which was not signed until a year later was largely carried out by Prior himself.

Perhaps Prior's greatest asset apart from his charm and his taste for Secret Service work was his ability to mix in all classes of society. He possessed a considerable talent for mixing Bohemianism with the official life and was just as at ease in a royal boudoir as in a tavern. His writings reveal an amused tolerance of low society, though he moved among the nobility without effort and with influence.

7

Daniel Defoe

For a Dissenter to be found in the hierarchy of the Secret Service would have been something of a sensation in the nineteenth century. For such a thing to happen in the early days of the eighteenth century was almost unbelievable. Yet Daniel Defoe, author of *Robinson Crusoe* and *Moll Flanders*, rebel, revolutionary pamphleteer and Dissenter, admitted that he had been employed by Queen Anne "in several honourable, though secret services".[1]

One of the curious features of the various biographies of Defoe is the inability of each writer to be really objective about this many-sided character. To some of his contemporaries Defoe was the Devil Incarnate, to others he was a great patriot. These attitudes have been re-echoed by his biographers, as one of the more recent of them—James Sutherland—has shown. "Scoffed at by his political opponents as 'a mean mercenarie prostitute, a state mountebank, an hackney tool, a scandalous pen, a foul-mouthed mongrel, an author who writes for bread and lives by defamation'," writes Sutherland, "he was not always content to smile patiently, or to suggest that such reports were exaggerated. He had a pharisaic habit of turning up the whites of his eyes and protesting that he had always remained absolutely true to his principles, that he had never equivocated, that he had always sought to avoid quarrels and to promote peace. . . . His biographers, accepting the challenge, have been too willing to assume that Defoe was either a cunning and quite unprincipled opportunist, or else an upright and consistent gentleman shamefully abused by his contemporaries."[2]

Similarly, in writing of his Secret Service work, historians have been equally contrary in their verdicts. Some have ignored this work and given him no credit for it; others, such as R. W.

Rowan and R. G. Deindorfer, have described him as "one of the great professionals in all these centuries of secret service . . . in himself almost a complete secret service".[3]

Daniel Defoe was the son of James Foe, a Presbyterian tallow-chandler of Cripplegate, London, and the name Defoe was perhaps an affectation, a combining of the signature "D. Foe" into a single surname, while retaining the first name Daniel. The truth is that Daniel the rabble-rouser and Dissenter was also somewhat of a snob and in his *Tour Through England and Wales* he mentioned "the antient Norman family of the name of De Beau-Foe", hinting that he was descended from it, for which there is no evidence at all.

Educated at Newington Academy, Daniel had early on in life a lesson on the dangers of supporting upstarts and pretenders to the throne: three of his school friends were executed for their part in the Duke of Monmouth's uprising. From that day he decided, not openly, but inwardly with great conviction, that he would pave his way to success by always supporting the winning side in government. But while one can sometimes criticise Defoe for his humbug in spouting principles, but relying on expediency and compromise to decide his course of action, one cannot deny that during his career he took some risks, as a result of which he was twice imprisoned and once put in the pillory. For in his writing and his pamphleteering Defoe seemed to forget the caution he showed in other walks of life. He was in many respects a creature of contradictions. Though a Dissenter and a Puritan in upbringing and by pretension, he had a passion for horse-racing; though in his books and everyday talk a preacher of virtue in sexual matters, he had a weakness for women of easy virtue and rogues (even Jack Shepherd the highwayman) fascinated him. As a journalist Defoe was almost the first crime reporter; in *Applebee's Journal,* a weekly newspaper, he published a series of articles on the lives of notorious criminals and he actually interviewed Jack Shepherd and gave an account of his escapades.

Similarly, he made a worldly and respectable marriage to the daughter of a City merchant who brought with her a dowry of £3,700 and then, at the age of twenty-five, became involved in the Duke of Monmouth's rising. But, as has already been mentioned, the execution of his old school friends and the fact that he himself escaped arrest taught him the wisdom of avoiding quixotic adventures in lost causes. As a business man he was a failure and his efforts led him into bankruptcy. In 1702 he published anonymously his pamphlet, *The Shortest Way with Dissenters*, which he wrote, so he said, to prove that the Dissenters "ought to be destroyed, hanged, banished, and the Devil and all". How came the Dissenter Defoe to be penning virulent diatribes against his own kind? His own excuse was that by exaggerating the language of the High Tories in their diatribes against Dissenters and in going even further in attacking them than the Tories would have dared, he would show up the extremism of the High Churchmen. But this kind of double-talk is apt to lead to the opposite from what is intended. The extremists among the Tories unthinkingly applauded the pamphlet and were hugely delighted with its language, and the Dissenters were not unnaturally dismayed. It has never been exactly clear what Defoe's true purpose was in writing such a tract. He may have hoped that by parodying the language of Tory extremists he would cause a split between these people and the moderate Tories.

But on reflection the Tories saw that in all probability Defoe was satirising them and on 3 January 1703, the Earl of Nottingham issued a warrant for his arrest, for it had soon been found out that the author of the anonymous pamphlet was Daniel himself. An advertisement was published in the *London Gazette*, offering a reward of £50 to anyone who would give information leading to his arrest. Defoe went into hiding, but had the impudence to send a letter to Nottingham, suggesting that "if her Majestie will be pleased to order me to serve her a year or more at my own charge, I will surrender myself a volunteer at the head of her armies in the Netherlands to any Coll of horse her Majestie shall direct . . . and if my behaviour I can expiate this offence, and obtain her Majestie's pardon, I shall think it much more honourable to me if I had it by petition".

But Nottingham was not influenced by this appeal, so Defoe offered to put himself at the disposal of Robert Harley, Earl of Oxford, but the latter was equally unable to change Nottingham's mind. Meanwhile Defoe was found in the house of a French weaver and taken off to prison.

It is by no means certain how long Harley had been a patron of Defoe and in his confidence. Some indeed assert that Harley had urged Defoe to write his pamphlet as a subtle attack on the Tory extremists. But there is a clue to their long-standing and confidential relationship in a poem in which Defoe wrote:

> *Ah, Sir! before your great deserts were known*
> *To th' Court the S*[*tat*]*e, the Country or the Town;*
> *When you and I met slyly at the Vine,*
> *To spin out Legion-Letters o'er our wine . . .*
> *My Legion-Letters scattered up and down . . .*
> *My step to th' P*[*illor*]*y,* The Shortest Way,
> *These were the useful flame and shams, thou know'st,*
> *Which made thy passage easy to thy post.*[4]

Daniel Defoe owed his ultimate release from prison to the good offices of Harley, and the Harley Papers make it abundantly clear that for most of Queen Anne's reign Defoe had been acting as a Secret Service agent under both Harley and Lord Godolphin. Indeed, when Lord Godolphin was forced out of office by Queen Anne in 1710, he personally recommended Defoe as a reliable secret agent to his successor, Harley. Defoe had been so efficient in smelling out the hiding-places of Jacobites in Scotland under the Whigs that the Tories, putting aside their prejudices, were only too glad to give him further employment in the same field. Here was one of the earliest examples of a leading member of the Secret Service being used by rival parties and governments diametrically opposed in their aims. This in itself is a tremendous tribute to the success of Defoe in his Secret Service career.

But it was Harley who was Defoe's chief protagonist. Of Puritan stock, good-tempered, a wine-bibber and an adroit statesman, Harley maintained links with both the two great political parties of his day. Because of this Harley the moderate Tory found no difficulty in making friends with Defoe, the Whig Dissenter. Similarly, Defoe found it comparatively easy to salve his conscience in making an alliance with a moderate Tory on the grounds that in such company there was more practical hope for national unity than under an extreme High Tory such as Nottingham, or under the more extremist of the Whigs. Defoe summed up his attitude politically in the preface which he wrote to the seventh volume of his *Review*:

"I have always thought the only true fundamental maxim of politics that will ever make this nation happy is this, That the Government ought to be no party at all . . . Statesmen are the nation's guardians. Their business is not to make sides, divide the nation into parties and draw the factions into battle against each other. Their work ought to be . . . to keep a balance among the interfering interests of the nation. . . ."

Of course there was a more urgent and practical consideration which must have been uppermost in Defoe's mind when he sought Harley's aid from prison. In one of his letters to Harley in 1703 he wrote: "Seven children whose education calls on me to furnish their heads if I cannot their purses, and which debt if not paid now can never be compounded hereafter, is to me a moving article and helps very often to make me sad."

But if Harley was determined that Defoe should realise that he alone had enabled the pamphleteer to gain his freedom and that he should always be in his debt for this service, it was left to Godolphin to persuade the Queen to give Defoe his pardon. From then on Defoe's letters to Harley were sometimes signed in his own name, more often under those of "Claude Guilot", or "Alexander Goldsmith". One of these letters in Defoe's own handwriting stated a case for the establishment of a new secret service for England, by which the Queen's Ministers could be provided with detailed intelligence from all parts of the realm so that it could easily be ascertained at any given moment exactly how each city and district was disposed towards the Government of the day. It was vital, declared Defoe, that the Government should know all about the character and morals of the Justices of the Peace and the clergymen and leading citizens in every town and parish, that they should know for which party they were likely to vote. Defoe proposed something very like a modern public opinion poll, but based on individual assessments, not on random soundings. There should be a "settled intelligence" in Scotland and an army of confidential agents throughout Britain.

Harley was impressed and in the summer of 1704 he sent Defoe on a tour of the country to gather what intelligence he could. Defoe was to be a principal secret agent, travelling on horseback, to sound out the views of his countrymen. "I firmly believe this journey may be the foundation of such intelligence as never was in England," he wrote to Harley in July, 1704.

And he travelled incognito, on this occasion as "Alexander Goldsmith". It was work in which Defoe, with his love of intrigue, delighted, and his letters were full of exuberant touches as though he revelled in the secrecy of his mission and the danger attached to it. But, like most secret agents, he was frequently short of funds and needing more money: "the magazine runs low", he complained in a letter from Bury St. Edmunds, "and is recruited by private stock which is but indifferent." It was Defoe's mildly humorous, somewhat rueful way of indicating that the next remittance from Harley would be much appreciated. On other occasions the reminders that he needed money were rather sharper. For the British Secret Service then, as in more recent times, was markedly churlish towards its agents. The funds which reached Defoe were usually intended to cover expenses incurred several months beforehand: "treat 'em mean and keep 'em keen" was Harley's motto and he behaved in a manner which suggested he wished Defoe to remain in a state of uncertainty as to his future prospects and to remind him that Harley was his sole paymaster. But, money and Harley's parsimony apart, the two men enjoyed a relationship which was thoroughly rewarding and mutually satisfactory. Both Harley and Godolphin relied on Defoe's judgement and in the negotiations which finally resulted in the Union of England and Scotland they were mainly guided by the reports which Defoe sent in. For Defoe was much more than a mere supplier of intelligence. Whereas previous agents, even those in the higher echelons of the Secret Service, had been content to supply information, Defoe co-ordinated that information and phrased his reports so that he summarised the lessons which should be learned from it. He was above all a political animal, with a keen facility for observing political trends and interpreting them. "The Whigs are weak," he wrote to Harley, "they may be managed, and always have been so. Whatever you do, if possible divide them, and they are easy to be divided. Caress the fools of them most, there are enough among them. Buy them with here and there a place; it may be well bestowed."[5]

In return Defoe received the protection of the authorities against further legal action. Lord Chief Justice Parker checked further proceedings against him and formally subscribed to the view that Defoe was a loyal supporter of the Crown. It was just as well that Defoe had this discreet official protection in the background for the nature of his work often led to the risk of his arrest. At Weymouth he was forced to flee when a message to him was intercepted by a suspicious local bureaucrat and at Crediton a Justice of the Peace actually issued a warrant for his arrest only to find that Defoe had left the district before it could be put into effect. Writers of any kind were apt to be regarded with suspicion of being propagandists in those days and Defoe combined espionage with writing and on his journeys across Britain gathered material for his latter-day work, *Tour through England and Wales*.

In the summer of 1706 Harley sent Defoe to Edinburgh in connection with the negotiations for the Union of the English and Scottish Parliaments and on this mission he was given a brief which far exceeded that normally given to a secret agent. Apart from obtaining intelligence, Defoe was charged with playing an active rôle in bringing about the Union by seeking to persuade the Scots that this was the best possible solution for Scotland: no easy task. His brief also included undermining the influence of the enemies of Union and convincing the Scots that England did not mean to interfere with the Scottish Kirk. This all-embracing task had to be carried out not in the rôle of a negotiator with full powers, but as a casual visitor to Scotland, voicing his private opinions and giving these such weight and credence as he could.

Harley was still apt to be dilatory in making payments to Defoe, as is shown by a letter the latter wrote to him: "As to family, seven children, etc. *Hei mihi* . . . thus, sir, you have a widow and seven children on your hands." It was an obvious hint by Defoe as to what might happen to him and the responsibilities that would devolve upon Harley.

Defoe's biographer, James Sutherland, stated that Defoe's "work in Scotland in the winter of 1706-7 was the most satisfactory achievement of his oddly private and obscure public life. That it was begun and carried on in an atmosphere of deceit need not detract from the value of the work done." There is no doubt that while in Scotland Defoe lied his way through all difficulties, was all things to all people and the plausibility of his tongue carried him through. But he did a good job from his country's standpoint. "I am writing a poem in praise of Scotland," he wrote to Harley, ". . . but my end will be answered. . . . All conduces to persuade them that I am a friend of their country." This from a man who referred to the Scots as "a hardened, refractory, terrible people, a fermented and implacable nation."[6]

Defoe pretended he had come to settle in Edinburgh to start a glass factory or a salt works. Later, when this story wore a little thin, he said he was writing a history of the Union and a new version of the Psalms. "I act the old part of Cardinal Richelieu," he told Harley. "I have my spies and my pensioners in every place and I confess 'tis the easiest thing in the world to hire people here to betray their friends. I have spies in the Commission, in the Parliament and in the Assembly, and under pretence of writing my history I have everything told me."[7]

Eventually, on 18 January, 1707, the Act of Ratification of the two Parliaments was passed and in March the Queen gave her consent to the Union. Defoe felt his mission had been accomplished and that some recognition of the part he had played was due to him. At the same time he was somewhat apprehensive: ". . . everybody is going to solicit their own fortunes and some to be rewarded for what I have done—while I, depending on your concern for me and her Majesty's goodness, am wholly unsolicitous in that affair."

But Defoe appears to have been rather deliberately overlooked, for even in the following July he was complaining to Harley that he regarded himself as one forgotten: "It is now five months since you were pleased to withdraw your supply, and yet I had never your orders to return."[8]

It was not until November of that same year that Defoe received funds again, this time a bill for £100, upon receipt of which he set off to London again. It may well be that Harley was intent on keeping him waiting in order to press for more information.

Daniel Defoe worked in such original and devious ways that it is not easy precisely to sum up in any dramatic or simple terms what he did or what he achieved. In some respects he was spymaster and spy combined. Technically he was employed as a spy and paid on results, but as he also co-ordinated the results of other people's espionage and often of his own accord tried to formulate policy it could be said that he assumed the mantle of spymaster, which was one reason why, quite wrongly, he has been described as the head of the Secret Service in his day. When Harley went out of office he advised Defoe to continue in Government service under Godolphin and the latter was glad to re-employ the secret agent. In 1709 Godolphin was concerned about Jacobite activities in Scotland and he despatched Defoe to Edinburgh to report on the situation. But gradually Defoe's confidence in his ability to influence situations caused him to suggest bolder and more original measures to the authorities. One such idea, based on his observations as an agent, was for "a Court of Appeal for all the injured and oppressed, whether they are Princes or People that are or ever shall be in Europe to the end of the world." In effect it was a proposal remarkably like Woodrow Wilson's original concept of the League of Nations. In addition he used his pen increasingly as an espionage and counter-espionage weapon. It was a deliberate attempt to influence policy in the subtlest way. Thus in 1716 Defoe the Dissenter became a "Tory" editor for Viscount Townshend, Whig Secretary of State under George I. The aim was to produce a Jacobite newspaper "to keep the party amused" and to forestall the Jacobite launching one that might be much more dangerous.

Defoe was well aware that his devious methods might be misconstrued and boomerang against him. "I may one time or other run the risk of fatal misconstructions," he wrote. "I am for this service posted among Papists, Jacobites and enraged High Tories—a generation who, I profess, my very soul abhors; I am obliged to hear traitorous expressions and outrageous words against His Majesty's person and government and his most faithful servants and smile at it all as if I approved of it; I am obliged to take all the scandalous and, indeed, villainous papers that come and keep them by me as if I would gather materials from them to put them into the news; nay, I often venture to let things pass which are a little shocking, that I may not render myself suspected."[9]

The Public Records Office Secret Service Accounts reveal that in the first half of 1714 Defoe was paid £500 out of Secret Service funds. The payments were entered as having been made to "Claude Guilot", which, as has been seen, was one of Defoe's pseudonyms.

Needless to say, during all these years the Secret Service had to be concentrated almost entirely on watching Jacobite activities and the supporters of the House of Stuart. In 1715 the Jacobite Rebellion was defeated and Defoe's behind-the-scenes work again played an invaluable rôle in bringing this about. In taking over and toning down *Mist's Weekly Journal*, he succeeded in making it less violent and less of a menace to the Government while yet maintaining its popularity and a circulation of ten thousand copies a week. And it seems certain, incredible as it may sound, that Mist himself had no idea what Defoe was up to. Mist was content to rely on the judgement of a good editor and an entertaining writer, though he always denied that Defoe had anything to do with the paper. Later, when Mist got into trouble for publishing a letter which criticised foreign policy, he did not hesitate to blame Defoe. But fortunately for Defoe the authorities turned a blind eye to this indiscretion; they realised that his partial control of the paper was vital to the Government and that any action would cause them all sorts of embarrassments.

It was, as one wit put it, that Defoe "delighted to encircle himself in a mist". He revelled in the intrigue and declared his secret purpose as follows: "By this management, the *Weekly Journal* and *Dormer's Letter*, as also the *Mercurius Politicus*, which is in the same nature of management as the *Journal*, will be always kept (mistakes excepted) to pass as Tory papers, and yet be disabled and enervated so as to do no mischief or give any offence to the Government."[10]

8

The Drive Against Jacobite Espionage

FOR PRACTICALLY the whole of the first half of the eighteenth century the English Secret Service's main task was to contain and keep in constant check the machinations of the Jacobites. Ever since James II had abdicated, the threat of a Stuart revival and restoration of one of this royal house to the throne of England had from time to time become rather more than a possibility. The Jacobites were numerous, well organised in various secret societies, obstinate and competent in the arts of intrigue.

The long underground battle which the English Secret Service waged against the Jacobites often took the form of a direct confrontation with its opposite number, for the Jacobite Secret Service was no less adept in infiltrating England and Scotland with its own agents and creating counter-diversions. The archives of this "secret service" at Scott's College, St. Germain, provide ample evidence of this. It is, for example, evident that Charles Edward Stuart, the "Young Pretender", paid at least one or two secret visits to London without being discovered, as Compton Mackenzie reveals in his book *Prince Charlie and His Ladies*.

Thus for almost fifty years the English Secret Service became almost entirely a domestic agency, concerned with combatting the Jacobites in England and Scotland and far less a Continental-wide network of spies such as had been established under Walsingham and Thurloe. The French Government also used Jacobites as spies against Britain through the Intelligence service set up by Maurice de Saxe, an organisation that reached its peak of efficiency about two years before the 1745 Rebellion, the Young

Pretender's last gallant attempt to win back the throne of his ancestors.

Yet despite this activity espionage lost much of its professionalism during this century. Bribery and corruption had become part and and parcel of every establishment in Europe, diplomatic ethics were non-existent and the double-dealing of statesmen and diplomats, of Kings spying upon their servants and negotiating behind the backs of their own Ministers, affected the whole field of Secret Service work. Every Foreign Office set aside funds for bribery and it would be no exaggeration to say that bribery for many years did the work which previously had been tackled by secret agents.

Of course bribery had always been an essential part of Secret Service work, but in the past it had been controlled bribery, practised by the professional heads of espionage sections and used for employing the able, the brave and intelligent. The few secret agents who shone in this age were mainly gifted amateurs and eccentrics—men such as the charlatan astrologer, Cagliostro, the roving profligate, Casanova, and the mysterious figure of the Chevalier d'Eon.

As an example of how Secret Service work was superseded by bribery one can point to the experience of Sir Robert Murray Keith, who as English Minister in Russia was given by the Foreign Office the sum of £100,000 "only for such gratification as I may judge it necessary to make, from time to time, to particular persons".[1]

But this was rather a special case, though it fitted into the general pattern of diplomatic espionage. The cost of the British diplomatic service, excluding the pay of consuls, cost on an average some £70,000 during the 'fifties of the eighteenth century. A large percentage of this was spent on bribery, as records of the period show only too clearly. D. B. Horn, writing on "The Cost of the Diplomatic Service, 1747-52", in the *English Historical Review*, revealed something of the widespread, systematic bribery in the service—items such as "wines and liqueurs for General Apraxin and the Archbishop of Troitza", "shaving equipage mounted with silver" for the "Master of Ceremonies", "drinks and snuff for the State dames of the court", a violin for the Chancellor, "a gold sponge box in the form of an egg at

Easter" for Grand Duchess Catherine. These were just some of the bribes totalling £1,500 paid out by the British Ambassador to Russia, Lord Hyndford, between 1745 and 1749.[2]

It was, in fact, a strangely incongruous picture which the pattern of espionage presented in this era. On the one hand, for the first half of the century, the Secret Service was concentrating almost entirely on Jacobite espionage on British territory while neglecting to set up a foreign network. On the other were vast sums of bribery spent by diplomats but achieving results often worthless and rarely more than of marginal value. Spies were greedy and demanded excessive sums for those days; the average request for a foreigner who wanted to work for the English was £400 a year plus travelling expenses. With genuine, unselfish patriotism sadly lacking, with cynicism and venality dominating the minds of the governing classes, the only surprising thing about the eighteenth century is that revolution came only to France: it would be no exaggeration to say that large areas of Europe were so slackly administered, so corruptly governed that the whole continent was ripe for revolt. Only expediency and compromise among the ruling classes and leaderless apathy among the masses averted elsewhere the upheaval which came to France.

Britain, however, achieved a few notable successes, though most of these were obtained through the services of enthusiastic amateurs. Falconnet, a double spy, was in the pay of the British as well as the French and the gold the British paid him gave them the advantage. The result was that when the French Minister, D'Affray, negotiated with Falconnet he was provided with bogus plans and messages. France had only one resident spy in England, as far as is known, for many of these years, a Dr. Hensey. His reports seem to have been ineffectual and he was eventually arrested and brought to trial in 1758. His fate is wrapped in mystery, though the report of his trial records that he was sentenced to be hanged. The British authorities were prepared to make an example of Hensey and thus avoid a blunder of some years earlier. In 1755 two French agents, Maubert and Robinson, had been sent to London to start a run on the Bank of England by circulating forged notes. Maubert escaped and Robinson, though captured, was kept in the Tower of London for only six months and then released. So when Hensey was caught the authorities were determined to make an example of him. There were protests against the sentence of hanging and it may be that Hensey was surreptitiously released after a long term of imprisonment, but though the records are not absolutely positive it would seem that the sentence may have been carried out in secret.

A new type of amateur spy became evident in the middle of the eighteenth century, similar to the Elizabethan scholar who travelled widely and sent back intelligence reports to his country. But in the eighteenth century such matters were relatively worse organised than in the sixteenth century and the impetus for such efforts came from the travellers themselves rather than from the Secret Service in London. The new amateur spy was the young aristocrat or scion of the upper middle classes who made the Grand Tour of Europe to complete his education. It was an age in which secret societies and clubs sprang up all over England. As the brothers Goncourt wrote in the same century, "if two Englishmen were to be cast aside on an uninhabited island, their first consideration would be the formation of a club". This was the golden age of clubmanship and the clubs ranged in style from the Chocolate House Club to the Kit Cat, founded by one Christopher Cat, a cook better known for his mutton pies than his social aspirations.

Many of these clubs took on a definite political hue, some were even bigotedly political in their choice of members, while there were a few devoted to subversive activities which attracted the attention of the Secret Service. There was the October Club, a High Tory organisation, while the Calves' Head Club, not disbanded until 1734, had been established for the sole purpose of deriding the memory of Charles I. But perhaps the most remarkable of all these clubs and certainly the one which enjoyed the greatest notoriety was that entitled the "Knights of Saint Francis of Wycombe", often erroneously referred to as the "Hell-Fire Club".[3]

This club was founded by the squire of West Wycombe, Sir Francis Dashwood, a rake-hell and flamboyant character who, for a brief period, was Chancellor of the Exchequer. At one time some of the most influential of Cabinet Ministers were members of this strange club which used to meet first in Medmenham Abbey on the Thames and later in caves carved out of West Wycombe Hill underneath the church. They included, apart from Dashwood himself, John Montagu, Earl of Sandwich, who was First Lord of the Admiralty, Thomas Potter, Paymaster-General, the Earl of Bute, Prime Minister, and several members of Parliament, among whom were John Wilkes and George Selwyn.

It was not until John Wilkes was prosecuted for the obscene libel of his *Essay on Woman* in 1763 that the biggest political scandal of the day was unearthed. A shocked public learned that its political leaders had for years been masquerading in the semi-ruined Abbey of Medmenham. Not only had they dressed up as "monks" and indulged in mysterious rites, but they had admitted to their strange society masked and hooded women whom they were pleased to call "nuns". When the secret of Medmenham became known, this rakes' club transferred its headquarters to caves cut deep into the heart of West Wycombe Hill. Thus posterity has come to know the originally styled Knights of Saint Francis of Wycombe as the Hell-Fire Club and the caves themselves, which are open to the public today, are known as the Hell-Fire Caves.

Most of the legends surrounding this club—that its members practised black magic and celebrated black masses in Medmenham Abbey and in the caves—are quite erroneous and the result of malicious propaganda by political opponents of its leading members. Not that the club was in the remotest sense respectable in a conventional way; it was used for wining, dining and wenching and for harmless play-acting and dressing up, as well as for Rabelaisian practical japes and jokes. But there is no doubt at all that it was infiltrated by secret agents, both British and foreign, because it made an admirable listening post. The British agents used it as a club where valuable intelligence could occasionally be obtained when the wine flowed freely and also to exploit the club for political ends. Foreigners used it because they felt sure that a club which was situated in dark and damp caves in an English hillside, whose members included Cabinet Ministers, must surely be the headquarters of political schemers.

Four members of the club were undoubtedly mixed up in espionage and gained much of their intelligence through belonging to it. Almost certainly several of the other members were at one time or another working for British Intelligence. The four were John Wilkes, that rascally though likeable Radical whose place in history is still somewhat underrated; the Chavalier D'Eon de Beaumont, a French diplomat, Sir Francis Dashwood himself and, surprisingly enough, Benjamin Franklin, the statesman and philosopher. An oddly assorted quartet to be members of the same club.

Dashwood was one of the many scions of noble families who made the Grand Tour of Europe and found himself drawn into Secret service work during this period. The conventional classical education of the day at Charterhouse was rounded off by a tour of the continent which some of the less fair of his biographers have described as "fornicating his way across Europe". In his youth Dashwood had a passion for travel much in excess of that of most of his compatriots. He visited Russia and is said to have masqueraded at St. Petersburg as Charles XII of Sweden, the great adversary of Peter the Great. But as Charles had been dead for many years one cannot altogether accept this version by Horace Walpole of what happened at the Russian court. It would be in keeping with his fondness for amorous adventure that he used this disguise to seduce the Czarina Anne, a liaison which is said to have been maintained for some months. But one must sometimes take Walpole's statements guardedly. He seems to have been both fascinated and repulsed by Dashwood, noting the latter's amorous affairs on the Continent and commenting that "he has the staying power of a stallion and the impetuosity of a bull".[4]

It was, however, the ability of Dashwood to make friends with the females at the Russian court which enabled him to set up what until then London had lacked, agents in St. Petersburg who could supply intelligence. He wormed his way into the confidence of the Grand Duchess Catherine, thus paving the way for further consolidation of Anglo-Russian relations by Ambassador Sir Charles Hanbury-Williams. There are also indications that Dashwood was active as a British spy in Italy, though Horace Mann, the head of British espionage in Rome, sent home reports complaining that Dashwood was "a Jacobite agent", alleging that he had written to the Young Pretender, telling him that the

British Prime Minister was about to fall. But Mann, like Walpole, and like many other spy-master before and since, tended to send home reports which denigrated rival intelligence sources and gave the kind of information which he thought Whitehall would like to hear. His reports were frequently erroneous, as for example when he wrote describing the Young Pretender as "no longer any threat . . . a moral and physical wreck". This was certainly belied by the '45 Rebellion and by the fact that Prince Charles Edward Stuart lived until he was sixty-eight and never had a breakdown in health until his very last days.

It is more likely that Dashwood was playing a double game, gaining the confidence of Jacobites and obtaining information from them which he passed back to London. On his return to London and before entering political life seriously in 1751 Dashwood made a curious and ostentatious disavowal of Jacobitism.

Sir Charles Hanbury-Williams achieved considerable success in organising a secret service section of his own in St. Petersburg. He decided to follow in Dashwood's footsteps on the grounds that the ladies of St. Petersburg were so bereft of intelligent and cultured male company that they were natural targets for an Ambassador searching for secret allies. The Grand Duchess Catherine described the Russian court of this period as a "desert in which the art of conversation is unknown, where hatred is mutual and sincere, and where the slightest serious word was a crime and treason".

Russia was then a nation with a very thin veneer of civilisation imposed on a semi-civilised and partly Asiatic conglomeration of peoples, almost completely cut off from the influences of European society outside court circles. King George II wished to win Russian goodwill because he suspected that France and Prussia were secretly plotting to gain control over his native state of Hanover. Thus he offered the Russian Chancellor Bestucheff a sum of half a million pounds in exchange for some sixty-thousand Russian peasants to serve him as soldiers, obviously intended to defend Hanover. Hanbury-Williams went out to Russia to carry this arrangement a stage further, the idea being to obtain a secret agreement by which Russia would send men to the aid of Britain or Hanover whenever required to do so. The

Ambassador soon became a close friend of the Grand Duchess Catherine, while the Marquis de la Chétardie, the French Ambassador, wooed the Grand Duchess's mother. But in the matter of obtaining intelligence the British Ambassador always had the edge on the Frenchman. It was not merely King George's gold which turned the scales, it was the skilled seduction of the ladies of the court by Hanbury-Williams and the manner in which he used them to win the Grand Duchess as "an adherent and spy of London" and Bestuchev as a regular informer. Bestuchev intercepted the despatches sent to Paris by the French Ambassador and passed them all on to Hanbury-Williams.[5] In the British State Papers of this period there are twenty-seven volumes of "intercepted despatches" for the years 1756-63.

All this paved the way to an alliance between Britain, Russia and Austria against Prussia.

It was against this background that in 1755 the Chevalier Charles d'Eon de Beaumont was sent to Russia as an envoy of Louis XV, not under his own name, but in the guise of Mademoiselle Lia de Beaumont, an attractive young lady of a noble French family. Without question the Chevalier was the most successful female impersonator who ever lived; in modern times he would have made a fortune on the stage. As will be seen later the secret of his true sex was never firmly established until after his death and throughout his life by his intrigues and sometimes pranks he had people guessing as to whether he was male, female or hermaphrodite.

When he was four years old the Chevalier's mother is said to have arranged a special ceremony for her young son to be consecrated to the Sisterhood of the Virgin. Whether or not this tale is true, history at least records that from the age of four to seven, on his mother's instructions, he was dressed in girl's clothes and this must have conditioned him for the rôles he was later to play in female impersonation. But it must not be thought that d'Eon de Beaumont was a namby-pamby, mincing, unmasculine character. Though slight of build, frail in appearance and with a soft, somewhat girlish complexion, he demonstrated his masculinity by his skill and fearlessness as a fencer. So adept was he with foils and rapier that he was elected *grand prévôt* of the *salle d'armes*. This talent, allied to his scholarship—he took his degree as a doctor of civil and canonical law at an early age—drew upon him the attention of Louis XV.

His mission to Russia was to establish contact with the Czarina Elizabeth and to persuade her to enter into secret correspondence with Louis. From then on the story of this extraordinary Chevalier of France sounds more like fiction than fact. Posing as a shy, demure young woman, d'Eon de Beaumont so won the hearts of the Russian court that painters competed with one another for the honour of doing portraits of the beautiful "Mam'selle Lia". These paintings exist today to prove the story of the mission. Before long the Chevalier was appointed a maid of honour to the Czarina.

From the point of view of the British Secret Service the Chevalier's activities were a matter of some concern, for Louis was using his envoy to pursue a deliberately anti-British policy. Mid-eighteenth century diplomacy had been influenced by the rise of Prussia and Russia as powers to be reckoned with, and for the first time the shadow of German militarism appeared on the European horizon. The German contempt for treaties and agreements of any kind, their double standards in diplomacy which have characterised their nation for more than two centuries was even then aptly and cynically expressed by Frederick Wilhelm I: "I know from experience that people of position and merit are not fit for business. They entrench themselves behind their point of honour. . . . This does not suit me and for the future I prefer taking yelping dogs, whom one can order about without their being sulky, who must do whatever I wish. . . . Treaties are made to be broken at one's convenience."

The French Ambassador's despatches, when revealed to the Czarina after the Russians had opened them (and passed them on on to the British) revealed a campaign of calumny against the Czarina. As a result Chétardie was ordered to leave St. Petersburg and Russia allied herself with England and Austria against Prussia. But, through incompetence in the British Government and Austrian mistrust of British intentions the effectiveness of this alliance was slowly undermined. Hanbury-Williams did his utmost to make the alliance work by bribes and espionage, giving the Russian Chancellor Bestuchev alone £10,000 and lending a similar amount to the Grand Duchess Catherina for "use in the

King's service". The Grand Duchess not only supplied the British Ambassador with a steady stream of intelligence reports that told him all that was going on at the Russian court and the details of French plots, but on one occasion, it is recorded, she "sat up all night to translate a despatch from Constantinople out of the Russian language".[6]

If Hanbury-Williams had been supported by firm, consistent and resolute action by his government in London, the shape of Europe might have been changed for centuries to come. But a pro-German party in Britain achieved a sudden reversal of policy. Just when Hanbury-Williams had succeeded in establishing firmly a basis for a permanent alliance with Russia, even gaining the support of Shavalov, the Czarina's lover, news came from London that crushed his hopes: Britain concluded an alliance with Prussia in 1756. The Czarina detested the tyrannical King of Prussia and from that moment she regarded Britain as an enemy and Hanbury-Williams as a spy in the midst of the Russian court. At the same time the Chevalier d'Eon de Beaumont had regained French influence in St. Petersburg. The British Ambassador had to be recalled to London.

When the Chevalier returned to France honours were showered on him and he received an annual pension of 3,000 livres. He continued to alternate between the rôles of the swashbuckling fencer who sometimes served in the French Army (he was aide-de-camp to the Duc de Broglie, who was head of the French Secret Service) and the delectable, entrancing Mademoiselle Lia. Next he was sent to London, officially as secretary to the French Ambassador, but in fact as a spy. As such he was again highly successful, intercepting vital documents from the British Foreign Office, making a study of the English home counties to work out a plan for the best routes for a French Army to take when it invaded England.

But the French, instead of rewarding this invaluable, indeed inimitable secret agent, blundered incredibly. Having made him a minister plenipotentiary in London, they appointed to England an enemy of d'Eon's who was obviously intended to supersede him. Enemies of the Chevalier at the French court had intrigued to destroy him and he was ordered to return to Paris, one such communication peremptorily reminding him how he had served

Louis XV "in women's garments" and advising him to put on such attire once again. It was more than a snub; it was a calculated insult.

Perhaps d'Eon's enemies thought he really would return and accept this humiliation. If so, they reckoned without the high spiritedness of the Chevalier. France's loss became Britain's gain and d'Eon asked for sanctuary in London. It was a calculated risk for the havoc d'Eon had wrought in Britain and his purloining of State documents could easily have resulted in his being kept in confinement, or even sentenced to death. But the British, true to their tradition of giving sanctuary to the persecuted, welcomed this surprise acquisition.

John Wilkes, the Radical Member of Parliament, took up d'Eon's cause and became one of his closest friends. Probably he introduced the Chevalier to the secret society which conducted its revels and meetings at Medmenham Abbey and the caves under West Wycombe Hill. "Saint Agnes", one of the "nuns" installed in the caves, eventually married Léon Perrault, an associate of d'Eon. One cannot say for certain that the Chevalier was a member of the "Inner Circle" of the society, but he certainly attended their meetings. It may even have been that he became acquainted with the Knights of Saint Francis of Wycombe before he sought sanctuary in England. Among that strange confraternity he was undoubtedly a double-agent, anxious during his period of sanctuary to please the authorities by giving them a certain amount of intelligence. Certainly he liked England and the English and he was immensely popular over here, even among the masses where his name was a legend. John Wilkes, who was himself a spy, probably recruited him to the English Secret Service, though there was never any positive evidence that he was a traitor to France. Wilkes himself always declared that one reason why d'Eon sought sanctuary was because he declined to revert to his rôle as a female impersonator. D'Eon's only visit to Medmenham Abbey had nothing to do with the Franciscan society. This was on 24 May 1771, when he was examined there by a jury of aristocratic ladies in order that judgement might be pronounced on his sex. The ladies, after "a most thorough investigation", returned a verdict of "doubtful", a finding that by no means pleased those who had placed bets amounting to more than

£100,000 in the hope of obtaining a positive decision one way or another. Six years later these bets resulted in a law-suit and a new jury found that d'Eon was a female, after which the Chevalier spent the remainder of his days dressed as such. Yet when he died a doctor ruled with equal emphasis that he was "without any shadow of doubt a male person" and he was buried as a male at St. Pancras in 1810.

D'Eon's association with the secret society at West Wycombe is interesting but confused. Mlle. Perrault of Paris, a descendant of the man who married "Saint" Agnes, writes that "there is no evidence that I know of that in any way links the Franciscans [Sir Francis Dashwood's society] with the adherents of the Young Pretender. In fact, quite the reverse. The Chevalier d'Eon was asked by the French Government to inquire into the 'political purposes' of the Franciscans and (according to Leon Perrault) he had to report that there was nothing in the society to warrant investigation and that the reports of Jacobitism were utterly unfounded."[7]

This rather suggests that by this time at any rate d'Eon was already playing some subtle game with the English, for it is certain that any serious agent of the French who had penetrated the society would have informed his Government that the Franciscans, even if not pro-Jacobite, were a plentiful source of intelligence. The French were furious at d'Eon's refusal to return. There were two attempts by them to poison d'Eon and several attempts to kidnap him. Egged on no doubt by Wilkes and stung by the attempts on his life, d'Eon hit back. He wrote letters to the British press denouncing his French enemies and proceeded to protect himself by raising a private army of friends, former agents and French deserters in England, suborning the latter to win popular support in London. He had taken the precaution of keeping letters sent to him by Louis, instructing him to spy out the English defences, documents which could easily have provoked war at a time when Louis was certainly not ready for it. On the strength of these he hinted that he would not hesitate to blackmail the French King if the French authorities continued to pursue their campaign against him. Both Louis and his mistress, Madame de Pompadour, who was an instigator of plots against d'Eon, tried to buy back the letters. D'Eon ignored the offers disdainfully and even published a few of the King's letters, containing all manner of indiscreet remarks.

Yet though Britain gave him sanctuary there were many in official circles who failed to appreciate the prize that lay within their grasp. Had it not been for the support of John Wilkes, d'Eon might not have survived French pressure for him to be arrested and handed over. Officialdom had learned of d'Eon's exploits in Russia against the British and feared he was not to be trusted. But though the value of defectors was not fully appreciated in those days the Secret Service ultimately made some use of him and found him to be a remarkably helpful interpreter of French intrigues as well as telling them where to set their hands on French agents in London. He remained faithful to the British and not only rejected a French offer of £12,000 a year if he would consent to spy for them again but, when a certain M. Norac was sent over to seek a secret interview with him, revealed to the British the identity of his visitor. The latter was none other than Caron de Beaumarchais, who wrote *The Barber of Seville* and *The Marriage of Figaro*.

The French even went so far as to engage an English chimney-sweep to hide in the chimney of d'Eon's London home and to make loud groaning noises to suggest the house was haunted. Their aim was to make d'Eon imagine the place was inhabited by a ghost and then to report him to the authorities in the belief that the latter would have him put away as insane. But d'Eon was not so easily trapped; he immediately suspected the presence of an intruder, thrusting his sword up the chimney and threatening the chimney-sweep with death unless he came down. The sweep, covered with grime, climbed out of the chimney, an abject, shivering figure, confessed that he had been hired by the French and was allowed to go. D'Eon's revenge was to publish more revelations about the private life of the French King. This time he told how one of the inmates of Louis' harem in the Parc aux Cerfs had discovered the identity of her royal lover and how Louis to silence her had declared her insane and had her shut up in an asylum.[8]

9

William Eden Re-organises the Secret Service

THE ELDER Pitt did much to improve the British Secret Service. It was his boast that not a shot should be fired anywhere in the world without the British Government knowing why. It was he who saw most clearly that Britain as a nation depending on sea power and with an increasing number of overseas possessions depended for her security on a well organised world-wide secret service.

Pitt took a personal hand in re-organising the Secret Service and in utilising the Diplomatic Service as a weapon of espionage. His prime aim was the interception of diplomatic correspondence. This was particularly effective throughout the Seven Years War and France's plan of naval and military strategy at the outbreak of this war was soon ascertained in London. At this time France was seeking an alliance with Sweden and the Swedish envoy in Paris was given details of French naval dispositions which he passed on to Stockholm. From there the plans were passed on to a British agent who returned with them to London. Stockholm, it would seem, was then London's chief source of information in Europe, for Pitt also obtained from there correspondence between the French and Spanish courts. This was all the more remarkable an achievement in view of the fact that from 1746-1766 Britain and Sweden had no diplomatic relations.

In 1767 Lord Chatham organised the theft of French military plans for an invasion of England. The French had made a most detailed survey of the coast of the south of England and had been assisted in its compilation by a Colonel Grant of Blairfindy,

Right, Daniel Defoe; *below, left,* Mlle. de Beaumont, or the Chevalier D'Eon; *right,* William Eden, 1st Baron Auckland. All worked for the British Secret Service

Left, Double agent, Sidney Reilly; *below, left,* Sir Richard Burton; *right,* Lord Baden-Powell

a Scotsman who was a secret agent of France. He had revealed to the French the exact number of landing places which would be available to their troops. Once they had landed the French forces were to rendezvous inland and march in two columns on London. In the estimate of this over-optimistic agent "four thousand French grenadiers could beat all the militia of England".[1]

When the American colonies sought their independence from Britain in 1776 the British Secret Service faced a new and totally unexpected situation. For the American colonists, even before the Declaration of Independence in July of that year, had started to set up their own secret service.

Its organiser was an able and original character named Arthur Lee, who revelled in the rôle of intriguer. On 3 June 1776, he set up the Committee of Secret Correspondence and worked out a cipher which was to be used by it. Lee's cipher was a new development in the history of cryptography. It depended on each party carrying on correspondence having in their possession a particular edition of a dictionary—in Lee's case he laid it down that it was to be Entick's *New Spelling Dictionary*. The person sending a message had to transmit a series of reference numbers giving the page and line on which would be found the word he wished to indicate. Then the person receiving the message merely looked up these numbers in his dictionary and read the message.[2]

But Lee's fame was not confined to the invention of ciphers. The following year he arrived in Berlin as the representative of the American Colonies in Europe. His aim was to win the support of the Emperor Frederick for the American revolutionaries. Consequently the British Government instructed Hugh Elliot, their twenty-five-year-old Ambassador in Berlin, to keep a close watch on Lee.

Elliot bribed a servant of the Hotel Corzica where Lee was staying and obtained from him the keys to Lee's room and to his desk. When Lee was out of the hotel Elliot, taking a great risk for an Ambassador in a country which was hostile to Britain, entered his room and stole Lee's papers. These were taken back to the British Embassy and copied. When this task was completed the papers were smuggled back to Lee though not before he had discovered his desk had been tampered with. He reported the theft to the Prussian authorities who immediately suspected Elliot.

The British Ambassador, who had already despatched the copies of Lee's papers to London, maintained absolute calm. He listened to the Prussians' accusations with equanimity, apologised profusely and said that a servant of his had committed this "unwarrantable action" and that as soon as he discovered it he had returned the papers to Lee. "I assure you my Government had absolutely nothing to do with this affair and were in ignorance of it," he added, "and if His Prussian Majesty so desires, I am ready to ask for my recall to London."

Frederick was very angry and denounced Elliot as a man for whom "Englishmen ought to blush for shame that they sent such an Ambassador abroad". But he did not press for Elliot's removal. King George III, with typical hypocrisy, called a Cabinet meeting to express his "dissatisfaction with the conduct of a Minister whose zeal in the public service is as little doubted as his ability, and who . . . had been induced to swerve from that discreet regard to his own situation and the dignified principles of his court".[3]

But Elliot's services were not forgotten; he was given £500 by a grateful Government. Lee, however, eventually gained his revenge on the British. In due course he went to London as representative of the American Colonies and immediately set up contacts with the French and with John Wilkes, a supporter of revolution wherever it was to be found. Wilkes introduced him to d'Eon de Beaumont whom he found still occasionally dressing up in woman's clothes to baffle the British public, who seemed to love him as much for his eccentricities as for his diatribes against the French. Lee made friends with both British Radicals and French agents in London and made a deal with the latter for the supply by the French of arms for the Colonist rebels.

Blundering British generals in America had clumsily turned a revolt into a war and thereby precipitated a revolution. It was left to the British Secret Service, now master-minded by the Honourable William Eden, to try to retrieve a situation which the military had created. In the end this effort met with no success, but a vast sum of money in bribes was poured out to try to put matters right. Eden, afterwards Lord Auckland, was an able administrator and he acquired more detailed information on America's relations in foreign courts than Washington himself received. In many respects this was one of the most successful periods of British espionage and it was no fault of Eden's that Britain failed to regain her colonies.

Eden's vast collection of papers, documents and manuscripts which in 1889 the British Government released to F. B. Stevens, an American scholar in London, testify eloquently to the range and extent of his espionage system. Twenty-five volumes of these papers include the reports which Eden received from informers and British agents and those gathered in by Lord Suffolk, the Colonial Secretary responsible for Secret Service operations inside the American colonies.

Research into these papers shows that many men who have hitherto been held up as American patriots were in fact agents of the British Secret Service. Such infiltration of the American diplomatic and other services was carried out in the face of a well equipped Intelligence service organised by General Washington himself and headed by the very efficient Major Benjamin Talmadge. Between 1776 and 1781 Washington spent more than ten per cent of his military budget on Intelligence operations. But perhaps the greatest surprise is that Benjamin Franklin himself became a tool of the British Secret Service.

American historians tend to be still too shocked by any such suggestion to be able to view the facts objectively. Similarly the suggestion that Franklin was a member of the Knights of Saint Francis of Wycombe has equally been received by them with loud noises of outraged indignation. Intensive research by various American university professors was carried out some years ago with the aim of refuting this thesis, but they failed to reach any firm conclusion in the matter and preferred to let it rest there. But the evidence on this side of the Atlantic points strongly, if not absolutely conclusively, to his membership of the society. But, if he joined, it must have been long past the heyday of the club and in a period when the membership had dwindled to only a few of Dashwood's personal cronies, of whom Franklin was unquestionably one.

Franklin's early background encourages rather than precludes the belief that he could have been a member. Though of Presbyterian stock and of a normally sober and scholarly disposition, he was strongly anti-clerical in his young manhood and in 1745 spent a whole year of bawdy revelry in the taverns of Philadelphia, drinking rum and Madeira and writing verse of a type common to the Franciscans of Wycombe:

Fair Venus calls; her voice obey;
In beauty's arms spend night and day.
The joys of love all joys excel
And loving's certainly doing well.

Franklin was a regular visitor at Dashwood's home, West Wycombe House, where he stayed in the summers of 1773 and 1774, and he refers to a sixteen-day visit there in July 1772 which is significant in that it was in the months of June and July that the Chapters of the Brotherhood were held at West Wycombe. But the most conclusive evidence of Franklin's membership, or at least of his association with this mysterious society, is contained in his own writings. In a letter he sent to a Mr. Acourt, of Philadelphia, Franklin mentioned "the exquisite sense of classical design, charmingly reproduced by the Lord le Despencer [Dashwood's later title] at West Wycombe, whimsical and puzzling as it may sometimes be in its imagery, is as evident below the earth as above it". This must surely be a reference to the caves and one can only assume that some of the statuary from Medmenham's gardens found a resting place in the subterranean headquarters of the Franciscans.

There is a curious story told about a visit paid by Franklin to West Wycombe in 1772. Accompanied by Dashwood and others Franklin paid a visit to some grottoes nearby when Franklin offered to perform a "miracle of bringing peace to stormy waters". Franklin led the way from the caves up some steps to a crevice to look down on a subterranean stream and, raising his stick and pronouncing some mumbo-jumbo, astonished his companions when the water suddenly became strangely still. He explained to them afterwards that all he had done was to secrete some oil which he had allowed to trickle down to the stream. There is a subterranean stream in West Wycombe Caves.

But it was when Benjamin Franklin was at the American Embassy in Paris that the British Secret Service achieved its most conspicuous successes. Inside this Embassy was a cell of British Intelligence organised by Edward Bancroft, Franklin's friend and chief assistant, passing on all information he obtained from his master straight to the British. Not only did Britain learn all the American secrets but many items of French intelligence as well, for the French trusted Franklin and gave him a great deal of information. The kindest deduction one could make from all this was that Franklin was duped by his assistant and, from a security point of view, was utterly incompetent. But a close examination of the facts by no means suggests that this was the case. Franklin was widely travelled, an efficient administrator, a man of the world, fully cognisant of intrigues and highly intelligent. It is unthinkable that he did not know something of what was going on. And when Arthur Lee confronted him with the charge that Bancroft was a spy in the service of the British and actually gave proof of this, showing how Bancroft's links with the British Secret Service had been uncovered and how when he visited London he was in touch with the Privy Council, Franklin stubbornly refused to accept the evidence. Franklin countered by denouncing Lee and insisted that Bancroft's visits to London produced worthwhile intelligence for America. The truth was that all Bancroft brought back from these trips was false information provided by the British. It is worth noting that when Franklin returned to America from France, a Congressional Committee was appointed to examine his accounts which showed a deficit of £100,000. Asked to explain this, Franklin enigmatically replied: "I was taught as a boy to read the Scriptures and to attend to them, and it is said there 'Muzzle not the ox that treadeth out his master's grain'. "[4]

During the French Revolution the British Government had to step up its espionage activities to match those of the Revolutionary Government. The latter had swiftly organised a comprehensive Intelligence service which was in effect a weapon of terror and the French central espionage bureau was set up in the Ministry of Foreign Affairs. Britain's problem in combatting the "French menace", as the revolution was then regarded, was to pay subsidies to Prussia in the hope that the latter would use them to fight the French. In fact the Emperor Frederick Wilhelm used these funds for invading Poland. The British, disgusted with Prussian perfidy, decided that revolts against the French revolutionaries might be started by agents operating outside France. With this aim in view the British Government decided that Switzerland was an ideal centre for espionage and they despatched to that country William Wickham for the purpose of fomenting a Royalist uprising in France. It was a somewhat complicated procedure for it meant first of all seeking out French exiles in Switzerland and linking them up with British agents on the continent. Lord Grenville assured Wickham that this was "an honourable task and not simply a form of spying, for the aim of His Majesty is only to see a government established in France as may lead to the permanent establishment of general tranquility".

Wickham's official position in Switzerland was that of *chargé d'affaires* and as such he was the paymaster of the British spy ring, travelling around the cantons, making contact with Royalists and French *émigrés*. At last he had won the support of sufficient enemies of the Revolution to make plans for an invasion of France through Lyons, to be linked up with an Austrian invasion through Piedmont.[5]

It was a bold, imaginative plan, but for its success it depended upon support from inside France, which was not forthcoming. Wickham reported back to London that he needed sufficient cash to bribe key revolutionaries to come over to his side. Wickham must have made out a plausible case for he obtained £29,214 from Pitt and immediately used some of this money to finance the secret activities of a bookseller of Neuchâtel named Louis Fauche-Borel. The latter was a snob, a romanticist and a man of burning ambition and he had been promised that if the monarchy was restored to France he would be awarded the Order of St. Michael, the office of Inspector-General of the Libraries of France and paid a sum in cash into the bargain. His task was to suborn the Republican General Charles Pichegru.

Fauche-Borel, utterly inexperienced in the world of espionage and diplomatic intrigue, nevertheless entered into his rôle with a confidence and optimism that were overwhelming. His self-assurance succeeded where a diffident amateur would have failed completely. He used his funds to pour out gifts of food and drink to the ill-fed soldiery of the Republicans. Pichegru was irked by the bookseller's persistence so that he told his aide in front of Fauche-Borel one day, "Next time this gentleman calls on me, you will oblige me by having him shot." Yet Fauche-Borel was undeterred; he persisted in pestering the General and before long put Pichegru in touch with Wickham to whom the General gave assurance of his "determination to attempt something whenever a favourable opportunity shall offer".

Pichegru conducted a correspondence with Wickham under the pseudonym of Baptiste, despite the fact that by this time the Republican Government suspected treachery. Fauche-Borel in his amateurish way had succeeded where a professional might well have failed. And it was a very considerable success for the winning over of Pichegru was a tremendous prize. He was not only general in charge of the French Army of the Rhine but one of the ablest military leaders in the French Republic.

In selecting Pichegru as their target both the British and the French Royalists had chosen wisely, for he had already become dissatisfied with his lot and disillusioned with the Republicans. When the campaign against him went badly and he lost two battles and the fortress of Mannheim, Pichegru signed a six months' armistice. This he did almost in desperation when his own somewhat *opera bouffe* methods of fulfilling Wickham's requirements proved futile. Brilliant as Pichegru might have been as an officer, he was inept as a tool of the plotters, brave as he might be in action, he was feeble as a plotter. Wickham had constantly to admonish him and urge him to greater effort: "Have courage," Wickham told him, ". . . and at the same time do not trust your enemies who are sharp, clever, united and audacious."[6]

Thus on four occasions Pichegru gave the Austrians an opportunity to defeat him in the field; each time, he complained, they had blundered and not taken advantage of the chances he had given them. "If the Austrian generals had had the spirit," he told Wickham, ". . . the whole might and probably would have been destroyed."

In the end an armistice was the only move he could make. Immediately the French Directory recalled Pichegru and replaced him with another general, Moreau. When General Moreau reached the battle-front he found the armistice was not yet being carried out, so he ordered a series of cavalry raids into Austrian territory. As a result of these the baggage train of General Klinger of the Austrian General Staff was captured. Among the papers found was a packet in cipher.

The cryptographic device employed was one of the simplest and most obvious imaginable—the Julius Caesar Cipher. When deciphered the papers did not incriminate Pichegru, but they made mysterious references to "the affair of General Pichegru", enough to make the Republicans take notice. They dared not bring Pichegru to trial without further evidence, as his popularity was tremendous, but they warned him he was not to leave Paris.

Instead of being thankful that he had had a lucky escape and being more cautious, Pichegru continued to plot against the Republic. What was worse he still used the same cipher and ultimately a letter from him was discovered in which he agreed that when he had command of an army again he would use it to overthrow the Republic. He was thrown into prison where he died, whether by his own hand or by those of his jailers is not clear.

Through the discovery of Pichegru's treachery the French learned of Wickham's large-scale espionage and the French Government made such strong protests to the Swiss that they were forced to expel the Briton.

It is sometimes erroneously assumed that the coming to power of Napoleon Bonaparte destroyed the achievements of the French Revolution and turned the Revolution away from its original purpose. But it was Britain, not Napoleon, which struck the deadliest blow at the Revolution and thereby set the clock back for the forces of democracy. To understand the workings of the British Secret Service in this period one must appreciate that the purpose behind the struggle between Britain and France was essentially a class struggle, however much the masses in Britain may have been duped into believing otherwise. On the one hand was Britain, dominated by an aristocratic ruling class and a growing industrial capitalist society, on the other, France who, despite all the evils and brutalities of the Revolution, was devoted to the ideals of democracy and a new form of government. As to Napoleon, though a dictator and a military leader with ideas of spreading his power across Europe, he was a child of the Revolution, eager to preach its ideals and lessons and, above all, he detested capitalism and financiers and considered trade was largely "legalised thievery". When he called the British a "nation of shopkeepers" he was using the phrase almost in a Marxist sense.

Because of this conflict of class interest and democracy versus capitalism, the Secret Service increasingly used reactionary aristocratic allies abroad both as instruments of intrigue and as agents to provide information. Thus much of the intelligence gleaned was prejudiced and inaccurate, coloured by partisan thinking, and much blundering in high places resulted from using agents who indulged in wishful thinking rather than practical, objective observation. The Prime Minister, Pitt, was at loggerheads with his own Foreign Minister, Grenville, and the Foreign Office was so slothful, so inefficient that many intelligence reports went unread for years. When the Whigs formed a government in 1806 they found despatches of twenty years earlier still unopened. Certainly the British Secret Service, despite some of the improvements brought about, was in no way a match for the brilliant espionage force which Fouché had created for Napoleon. Where the British had been amateurish, haphazard and empirical in their espionage the French had been methodical, disciplined and ruthless. The reason for these contrasts was not difficult to find: whereas in the London set-up of the Secret Service even good work in the field was ruined by incompetence and divided authority in London, in the French Intelligence everything was geared to one man—Fouché himself. Fouché's aim was to maintain himself not merely as the sole arbiter of the Secret Service but to make that service so efficient and indispensable that Fouché himself would be indispensable. What made the system even more effective was that Napoleon revelled in Intelligence reports and insisted on spending at least three hours each day poring over them.

But in one respect the British Secret Service gained an advantage over the French. As we have seen it was dependent on the forces of class and capitalism and as such made the fullest use of the instruments of capitalism. In communications the British found that security was best served by using the continental banking houses for transmitting letters and reports.

One of the most fascinating incidents in which the British Secret Service had a hand in this period was what is still known as "The Mystery of Tilsit". On 25 June 1807, Napoleon met the Czar Alexander on a raft moored in the Miemen River and here was drawn up the Treaty of Tilsit, the terms of which remained a secret for eighty-four years. The gist of the treaty was that France and Russia agreed to support each other in every war in which they might engage against any other European power (this was obviously directed against Britain) and Denmark, Sweden and Spain were to be forced to close their ports to British ships. France and Russia between them were to be the masters of Europe and together destroy the might of the British Empire.

Somehow the British Secret Service obtained the terms of this treaty, though exactly how this was done is still to some extent a matter of surmise. There are, however, certain clues which point to a concentrated effort in espionage which wiped out many of the blunders and errors of earlier years. On the day after the meeting at Tilsit a letter was sent from Memel, close to Tilsit, to the British Minister at Copenhagen. This was forwarded to London to George Canning, then Foreign Secretary. Whatever was in that letter—and it is almost certain it made some reference, if only in speculation, about the Treaty of Tilsit—Canning acted swiftly: he ordered the British Fleet to demand assurances from Denmark.

But Canning also received another letter on the same day, this time from Garlike, the British Minister in Copenhagen, which told of French troops being massed near Holstein. And the following day Mackenzie, a British secret agent known to have been stationed in Tilsit at the time of the meeting of Alexander and Napoleon, arrived in London. There is also some evidence that Canning had information from the Count d'Antraigues, a French exile in London who had been known to sell secrets to Britain as well as to Russia. The basis for this belief is that the Count was dismissed from the Russian Secret Service shortly afterwards and at the same time was granted a pension of £400 a year by Canning.[9]

As a result of this intelligence from a variety of sources, which left Canning in no doubt as to the very real threat posed by the Tilsit talks, Britain was able to thwart Franco-Russian plans. She first demanded the handing over of the Danish fleet and then, when the Danes refused this blunt and brutal request, the British fleet bombarded Copenhagen, sailed in and towed away the Danish ships. It was a ruthless, outrageous action even by the standards of the times and many Britons criticised it, Lord Malmesbury, Under-Secretary of State, resigning in protest; even George III was shocked. But Canning would have been failing in his duty to his country if he had not acted swiftly and effectively checked France and Russia from dominating the Baltic.

It has long been one of the puzzles of history how the British Secret Service saved Britain from disaster following the Tilsit Treaty. Contemporary historians, and even those of fifty years later, critical of Canning, hinted that he had merely speculated on what secret clauses the Treaty might contain and gambled his political future on sabre-rattling action. One could answer this by saying that the Secret Service's reports were evidence enough of a Franco-Russian plot, but the truth is that Canning must have had detailed information about the secret clauses which no mere spy could have obtained. For example he instructed Arthur Paget to go to Constantinople to warn Turkey that "His Majesty's Government have received the most positive information of Secret Articles being annexed to the Treaty [of Tilsit], from the tenor of which . . . it is the contemplation both of Russia and of France to expel [Turkey] from all the Territories which it at present possesses in Europe." The full text of the Treaty of Tilsit was not published until more than eighty years after this date and it proved that Canning must have had detailed knowledge of its contents.

It now seems certain that the Secret Service had won over the Russian Ambassador to London, Vorontzov, as an ally. No historian has ever mentioned Vorontzov in this context and all those who have written the history of this era seem to have been singularly blind in not noticing that the evidence points in his direction. There is no doubt that Vorontzov knew what was happening at Tilsit, for on 14 July 1807, less than a month after the Treaty had been signed, the Russian Ambassador wrote to his son: "My spirit is disquieted by the news which arrives from all sides, announcing that the Emperor was going to make peace with Bonaparte, that he had an interview with that monster." Two days later Canning knew all about the Treaty.

Now Vorontzov was a close friend of Canning and he is known to have had correspondence at this time with Sir Robert Wilson, a British secret agent who was also a close friend of Vorontzov's son, Michael, an officer in the Russian Army who was actually aboard the raft during the meeting of Alexander and Napoleon. Did Michael pass information to Wilson who relayed it to London?

Prince Czartoryski loathed Napoleon and belonged to the pro-British party in Russia. He wrote Vorontzov a letter on 2 September 1807, which is even more revealing, mentioning in it that "Wilson, who carries this letter, is already known to you; he is an excellent young man, beloved by our whole army. . . . Wilson is filled with zeal for the good cause. He will inform you of a thousand details which would take too long for me to write. . . . God give that we avoid a rupture between Russia and England."[8]

Probably the full truth will never be known. Canning protected the Russian Ambassador so effectively that he was never even suspected of informing the British. As to the terms of the Treaty, Alexander's copy of it was published in 1891, but Napoleon's copy which was lodged in the Ministry of Foreign Affairs in Paris mysteriously disappeared in 1815.

10

Wellington's Intelligence Service

DURING THE prolonged war with Napoleon British Intelligence depended increasingly on the Navy and the Army. Previously almost all worthwhile intelligence had come through diplomatic or civilian channels; now the Services developed their own branches of secret service.

The rôle of the Navy in this respect was the most vital it had played since Cromwell's time. Nelson used his frigates to keep watch on neutral harbours suspected of sheltering hostile ships and the scouting frigate became a prime weapon in British espionage, passing on warning signals to other vessels.

One of the most enterprising agents used by the Royal Navy in the Napoleonic era was John Barnett. He persuaded the Admiralty that the best method of finding out Napoleon's plans was by playing on the latter's weakness for women and using female spies to worm their way into his confidence, or alternatively to suborn those women who currently enjoyed Napoleon's favours. Barnett, who stationed himself aboard H.M.S. *Lion*, when that ship was cruising off the Egyptian coast in the Mediterranean, made occasional trips ashore at night in a fast but tiny craft which was kept at his disposal especially for such a purpose. Disguised, Barnett paid a number of visits to Cairo where he began to organise a small but efficient spy network by bribing both French clerks and Egyptian servants and guides. In a remarkably short time he had obtained a detailed picture of Napoleon's mode of life and learned the name of his latest female favourite, a Madame Fourès, wife of a young Gascon officer.[1]

Madame Fourès,—"*la blonde Bellitote Fourès*", as she was

known by the troops—had attracted attention to herself by the manner in which she arrived in Egypt. The wives of officers had been forbidden to accompany their husbands to Egypt, but Madame Fourès had smuggled herself aboard a troopship in masculine attire. Napoleon came to hear of this ruse, intended sternly to reprimand her and then, having seen her blue-eyed beauty for himself, decided to allow her to stay. Soon Napoleon and the Gascon officer's wife were lovers.

But the presence of Fourès himself was an embarrassment and an excuse was found for his recall to Paris on the grounds that there were important dispatches to take to the capital. Fourès was told that the dispatches were of vital importance and top secret and that he must not allow himself to be taken prisoner; also his wife must not return to France with him as if she were captured by the British they might use her as a bargaining counter for Napoleon's despatches.

Fourès suspected nothing and embarked in the French sloop *Chasseur*. Meanwhile Barnett had learned of Napoleon's new amorous conquest and the reason for Fourès' return to France. From French clerks whom he had bribed Barnett also learned that the despatches were of no great importance and had merely been an excuse for getting Fourès out of the way. It was then that the perhaps over-imaginative and certainly over-sanguine Barnett hit upon the idea of turning Fourès into Napoleon's assassin.

It was the kind of plan that might well have worked. Napoleon took appalling risks in choosing the wives of his officers as paramours: there was always the chance that one of them would seek revenge. And Fourès was known to have a fiery temper. So Barnett informed the commanding officer of H.M.S. *Lion* that Fourès was sailing in the *Chasseur* and had the sloop intercepted soon after she put to sea. Fourès was arrested and taken aboard the *Lion* where, however, he was treated as a guest of honour and entertained in style. Barnett played his cards remarkably well. He acquainted the Gascon officer with Napoleon's perfidy, told him the true reason why his wife had not been allowed to return to France with him and finally showed the young officer copies of the unimportant despatches he was bearing to Paris. Fourès begged the British to allow him to return to Egypt to "avenge his honour" and the implication was that he was prepared to confront both his wife and Napoleon and that, if he found the British allegations were correct he would kill Bonaparte.

Fourès was smuggled back to Cairo and, on his return he must have discovered that Napoleon and his wife were now openly living together. But whether caution superseded anger, or whether the call of patriotism on reflection outweighed personal emotions one cannot say, but Fourès, who had given every indication of intending to kill Napoleon, made no attempt to carry out his threat. All he did was to resign his commission and return to France, a move which suited Napoleon admirably.

The Duke of Wellington had his own espionage service that was almost self-sufficient. He even possessed the key to the French cipher. Much of his intelligence was obtained cheaply, a very great deal of it at no cost at all, for the Spanish peasants, who loathed the French, voluntarily brought in information and for good measure intercepted French despatches. Frère, the British Minister in Lisbon, testified that there was "no beggar so poor that bribery could induce him to carry French despatches. These were brought to our officers to an extent incredible to those who have no experience of a war carried on against the national feeling."[2]

But apart from the Spanish peasants in the Peninsular War the Duke of Wellington had a secret service which contained some of the ablest agents in Europe, men such as Major Colqhoun Grant and James Robertson. It was with considerable truth that Wellington was able to say years later when speaking of the Peninsular War, "I knew everything the enemy was doing and planning to do."

Major Grant was Wellington's most trusted Intelligence officer in the Peninsular. Even when captured by the French and in confinement he managed to smuggle out items of intelligence which were sent back to British headquarters. Later, when sent to France under escort, Grant escaped, secured an American passport and posing as an American sent Wellington reports on Napoleon's plan for his Russian campaign. Eventually he escaped to England in a fishing boat and Wellington was so impressed with his services that he made him a colonel and gave him the task of heading his Intelligence service.

During the Waterloo campaign the British Secret Service was directed by a Colonel Hardinge whose headquarters were in Brussels. Here he managed to win the services of at least two members of the staff of the French War Ministry. Working closely with these Frenchmen British agents were able to provide Hardinge with a relay of messages which gave advance notice of French intentions. Thus, on 6 June 1815, such a message reached Hardinge in Brussels:

"... The Emperor will go in person to Avesnes with the intention of carrying out a feigned attack from the Maubeuge side upon the Allies, while the main attack is to be made on the Flanders side between Lille and Tournay, in the direction of Mons."[3]

In this way Hardinge acquired the most detailed reports on Napoleon's forces, his positions and order of battle. He was also informed that French morale which on the surface appeared so good was in reality poor. The élite of Napoleon's army were dedicated and disciplined, but the National Guard lacked enthusiasm for battle and had to be induced to fight only at the point of a bayonet. Wellington then knew that if he could only contain the reckless, courageous charges of the French spearhead, victory was his. But, as he said afterwards, "it was a dam' close run thing".

Wellington was also fortunate in having an ally in the Foreign Office in the Earl of Wellesley, his brother, for the latter made a point of watching out for recruits for the Wellington Intelligence service. One such was "Brother James", alias James Robertson, who had spent most of his life in the Scottish Benedictine monastery in Regensburg and who spoke German fluently. Robertson was recommended by Wellesley for secret service in Germany.

On this occasion, however, Robertson was chosen to work under the Foreign Office's orders, his mission being to make his way to North Germany and to find out what had happened to some 15,000 Spanish troops believed to be stranded in Denmark. The Foreign Office had been particularly interested in the fate of the Spaniards for some time. The story of how they came to be in Denmark was yet another example of Napoleon's wiles. Before Bonaparte launched his attack on Spain he had cunningly persuaded the Spaniards to despatch some of their best troops to

Denmark on the grounds that that country was threatened by Britain. Now the Spanish forces, under the Marquis de la Romana, were trapped somewhere in Denmark or in the islands off the Danish coast. The British aim was to enable them to escape by ship.

Robertson went first of all to Britain's recently acquired possession of Heligoland, where the British Secret Service had already set up a listening-post and centre for gathering intelli gence. From here he was smuggled in a small craft up the mouth of the River Weser into Germany. Once arrived in Bremen—he made the journey on foot—Robertson took on the identity of one Adam Rohrauer. After many inquiries which took him from Bremen to Hamburg, Robertson learned that the Spanish forces had been split up into small groups to render them ineffective and were more or less marooned on various small islands off the Danish coast.

Deciding boldly to take a risk and to rely on his Catholic contacts to keep his secret, Robertson discovered a Spanish chaplain who knew all about the forces of La Romana and where the Spanish general was stationed. So he confessed to the chaplain the secret of his mission and his trust was not betrayed. The chaplain told him how to reach La Romana. Travelling via Copenhagen the gallant Scottish monk crossed to the island of Funen where La Romana was kept in isolation, being neither allowed to send nor receive messages or letters. The resourceful Robertson bought a large quantity of cigars and chocolates and, posing as a commercial traveller, sold his wares to the Spanish soldiers. In this way he met the Spanish general and passed on the British Government's message of help.

The problem was how Robertson could inform the British frigate sailing in the vicinity that he had found the Spaniards and to let them know the latter were prepared to be rescued. The British authorities had bungled badly in not making any arrangements for signalling, nor had they given Robertson signalling equipment. Perhaps they feared that if Robertson was caught with such equipment in his possession his mission was doomed in any event. More probably the Foreign Office had only the faintest hopes that Robertson would discover the whereabouts of the Spaniards, for the evidence is that Canning was extremely doubtful about the wisdom of employing a supposedly unworldly monk. But amateurish though Robertson might have been, his courage, his pertinacity and his resourcefulness carried him through; no doubt patriotism also played a part. In a desperate attempt to draw attention to himself one day when a British frigate was sailing close inshore he waved his handkerchief from a clifftop. A Danish soldier patrolling the shore noticed him and promptly arrested the monk. Robertson claimed he was a commercial traveller, that he had sold wares to the Spaniards and he had hoped to do some trade with the British ship, too. The soldier was suspicious because Robertson did not speak Danish, so he took him before the Danish commanding officer. Fortunately for Robertson the officer spoke German and, noting that the monk spoke perfect German, was soon convinced that Robertson really was Adam Rohrauer.

After many adventures Robertson was able to get a message across to Heligoland to inform Admiral Keates to be ready to take off the Spanish troops within a few days.

The Royal Navy acted promptly. Admiral Keates sailed with his ships to Nyborg and La Romana gathered his troops together on the pretext that they were to swear allegiance to their new King, Joseph Bonaparte. It was a ruse that worked and never aroused the suspicions of the Danes. Some nine thousand of the fifteen thousand troops were embarked in British ships and taken back to Spain where they took part in the Duke of Wellington's campaign.

All this time Colin Mackenzie, the agent who brought the news from Tilsit to Canning and so warned the British of the secret Franco-Russian agreement, was the dominant figure in coordinating British espionage in the Baltic and indeed over a wide area of Europe. Quite frequently he went on lone missions himself, taking care to tell nobody in advance and to make no record of his exploits. This is one reason why his true rôle at Tilsit still remains somewhat of a mystery. Whereas even Robertson wrote an account of his adventures,[4] Mackenzie left behind no memoirs at all. He was the organising genius behind the espionage network at Heligoland and worked very closely with the British fleet.

Secret communications became very difficult during the Napoleonic wars and though banking houses were frequently made use of effectively in getting messages to destinations on the Continent relatively close to London, the Secret Service was forced to find other and more devious routes for despatches to far off places. When Austria was defeated by Napoleon and ceased to be a British ally, British agents, supplied with cash, had to be sent to Prague and Carlsbad to organise espionage centres and to act as a post-box for intelligence. The sending of messages into and out of Vienna was an extremely hazardous operation, but it was helped by the fact that Metternich was persuaded to maintain secret relations with the British and the Secret Service rather cleverly persuaded Count Hardenberg, the Minister for Hanover in Vienna, to act as an intermediary. He sent British Intelligence messages to London through the Austrian Ambassador in Berlin.

Often the most roundabout routes had to be taken by agents carrying messages. Ports of call of the British Fleet such as Gibraltar and Malta were used as post-boxes and agents collecting messages from Malta would travel across the Mediterranean to Constantinople and then to Leucadia in Albania, where the British had established another listening-post, to Vienna. Fishing vessels of neutral powers were sometimes used to carry secret messages and one ship's master charged as much as £7,000 a year to smuggle dispatches to and fro.

No doubt this hard-won intelligence helped to give the British an inkling that, despite their secret understanding, both France and Russia were preparing to make war on each other. But the real clue which London received on this subject was contained in an apparently innocuous list of books which arrived on the Earl of Wellesley's desk from Colin Mackenzie. The list contained books dealing with such subjects as the topography of Lithuania, an account of the campaigns of Charles XII in Poland and Russia, geographical books on various Russian provinces, maps and atlases of Livonia, Riga and the Baltic provinces of Russia.

No other information was contained on the list, but Wellesley needed no more. He knew that the books listed had been recently purchases by Napoleon through a Paris bookseller who was in the pay of a British agent. From the list the Secret Service was able accurately to deduce that Napoleon was planning to invade Russia.

11

Thomas Beach: Double-Agent in America

In the eighteenth century the British Secret Service had to contend with a slowly but surely growing menace near home—that of Irish insurrection. The American revolution and the War of Independence had brought home to British governments the need to check subversive movements at their birth and the French Revolution only served further to underline this problem.

A branch of the Whitehall Secret Service was set up in Dublin Castle in the latter part of the eighteenth century. If there was no money to be spared for the Irish people's needs, there was never any lack of cash to be doled out to informers in Dublin. To this centre of British Intelligence came a steady stream of information, some of it factual, much of it fanciful and a great deal more simply malicious. This service depended on Irish informers—"Irish patriots", as the British called them, "traitors" as the Irish rebels dubbed them. Their purpose was two-fold: first, to find out about plots formulated by Irish insurrectionists, second, to keep a watch on Irish links with French espionage, something which had been causing concern to the British authorities for years.

The system of paid informers undoubtedly enabled the authorities in London to keep rebellion in check, to snuff out countless plots and for more than a hundred years to retain control of a country which gave itself over increasingly to lawless secret societies whose aims were assassination and war on the hated English. It may seem remarkable that in a country which came to develop a high sense of patriotism so many informers flourished. For the answer to this poser one must study the Irish character.

For it was not always the need for money that caused these informers to betray their fellow-countrymen, more often it was that innate love of intrigue and double-dealing which drove them into espionage. If successive British governments showed a dismal and crass lack of understanding of the Irish problem, their executives in Dublin at least fully grasped the psychological quirks of the Irish mind and comprehended the deviousness of the Irish temperament, which they fully exploited for their own ends.

The Irish revolutionary societies were founded in the eighteenth century, the Irish Volunteers, who were the forerunners of the Irish Republican Army, being formed in 1779. From the outbreak of the American Revolution Irish rebels fixed their hopes on every adversary of Britain which appeared on the horizon. First it was the American rebels, among whom there were many Irish immigrants anxious to strike a blow for the "auld country"; then Napoleon himself became a hero of the Irish revolutionaries and the great Fouché himself was not slow in coming to terms with the Irish intriguers and recruiting them in his own ranks. On the other hand the British took considerable pleasure in noting that some of Fouché's more zealous police-spies quite often arrested the Irish as British spies as soon as they landed in French ports. How were ordinary French *gendarmes* to know the difference between an English and an Irish accent? One such Irishman was Hamilton Rowan who, having escaped from Newgate Prison where he had been committed after being sentenced for sedition, arrived in France and was immediately arrested and lodged with galley slaves in Brest.[1]

Among the most prominent of the early informers in Dublin was Samuel Turner, who was so valuable to the British that he was given a pension £300 a year. Turner was perhaps the supreme example of the arch double-dealer, the Philby of his day in the manner in which he posed as the very opposite to what he was. Turner, the agent of the British, kept the secret of his perfidy from almost everyone, even the other Irish informers. He posed as a rebel, defiantly wearing green, and even pretended to be hiding from the British for a long period. All the time he was in the confidence of the conspirators he was passing information about them to the British authorities. Eventually Turner fled to the Continent, a move which must have seemed suspicious to the British, but Pitt's secret agent, George Orr, appears to have been satisfied that only fear of assassination drove him there.

Perhaps Turner could not resist double-dealing; possibly intrigue and the strain of living a Jekyl and Hyde existence became too much for him so that he was promiscuously loyal to both sides. One cannot really be sure, for he turned up in Hamburg where he was known as the chief agent of the United Irish Rebels and a close friend of Lady Edward Fitzgerald into the bargain. How much he aided the Rebels is a matter of conjecture, but it is certain that the British owed him an immense debt. He informed against Father O'Coigly, who was condemned and executed on his evidence. And even then another spy, Thomas Reynolds, was blamed for the death of O'Coigly.

Turner was a barrister and it was in this capacity that he gained much of his intelligence for the British. Other legal men who were informers for the Secret Service were James McGucken, the Belfast attorney, and Leonard MacNally, a lawyer who betrayed his partner and clients for handsome rewards. Possibly MacNally was the most rascally of all these informers and the one for whom cash counted for most. Records of Dublin Castle show that MacNally received regular sums of a hundred pounds at a time and it is almost certain that the pseudonym of "Robert Jones", for whom £1,000 was paid for the betrayal of the rebel Robert Emmett, masked the identity of Leonard MacNally. The evidence points strongly in this direction as "Robert Jones" was obviously a code-name and MacNally's partner, Curran, had a daughter who was engaged to Emmett, and, most damning of all, MacNally himself visited Emmett in his hide-out at Harrold's Cross shortly before the British police arrived to arrest Emmett.

In his way the rascally MacNally was as bold a poseur as Samuel Turner. He had the impudence to make fervent speeches denouncing the British authorities and then sent reports to these same authorities to give lists of names of the people attending his meetings. MacNally even had the audacity to volunteer to defend Emmett at the latter's trial, thereby ensuring his conviction. Poor Emmett, never for a moment suspecting the treachery, thanked him profusely for all he had done and kissed him farewell.[2]

In this manner the tradition was laid of a ruthlessly efficient British Secret Service in Dublin, built on treachery and double-dealing and creating an instrument of oppression that for a whole century kept Irish terrorism under control without ever destroying it.[3] As the nineteenth century progressed so this Secret Service gathered in strength until more professional and perhaps more trusted British agents could take the place of the Irish informers. Of all the purely British agents working in Ireland in the middle of the nineteenth century the master-mind was Thomas Beach, an officer born in Colchester who eventually became Major Henri Le Caron, agent of the British Government in the camps of American Fenianism.

The Fenians, the Irish Republican Brotherhood, were an Irish-American revolutionary movement founded in the United States in 1858 by John O'Mahony. The Fenians' aim was to free Ireland from British rule and to set up a republican type of government. In the year 1865 a number of Fenians crossed to Ireland from America to attempt a rising, but it proved a complete fiasco. For a time the Fenians considered seriously a diversionary movement—"the invasion of Canada" became their motto and they pinned their hopes on setting up an Irish-in-exile government in Canada, believing that from such a base they could dictate terms for Ireland.

Thomas Beach had served in the American cavalry and played his part in the American Civil War, enlisting as a private soldier and finishing his career in the Army as a major. In 1865 Beach came across a strange-looking twenty-dollar bond with the words "The Irish Republic" stamped across it. He discovered that this was one of the methods being used by the Fenians to raise funds. These bonds were given in exchange for ready money to simple and gullible Irish immigrants (and anyone else for that matter) who believed in the possibility of an Irish republic. To a large extent these bonds were financed by poor Irish servant girls in New York and other large northern cities.

The United States authorities appeared to take no action against the initiators of this fraudulent bonds project, nor for that matter did the government of President Andrew Johnson try to clamp down on the Fenians' agitation to invade Canada. Beach made inquiries about the Fenians, amassed quite a lot of information on them and mentioned this in letters written to his father. The latter, without referring to his son, immediately handed the letters over to his Member of Parliament, who, in turn, showed them to the Home Secretary.

From this moment Beach was quite by chance brought into the orbit of the British Secret Service. The Home Secretary told Beach's father to ask his son to send further details. On the morning of 1 June 1866, Beach's forecast of the invasion of Canada by the Fenians was borne out. But the attempt was an utter failure. The Fenians were driven out of Canada, sixty of them being killed and two hundred taken prisoner with the loss of only six Canadian lives.

The following year Beach returned to Britain and after consultations with the authorities it was agreed that he should become a paid agent of the British Government in order to infiltrate the Fenian ranks. In his book, *Twenty-five Years in the Secret Service*, Beach mentioned that this proposition was put to him at a meeting with Government officials at 50 Harley Street. He returned to the United States and offered his services "as a military man in case of active warfare" to the Fenians. He was accepted under the name of Major Henri Le Caron and immediately organised a Fenian camp in Lockport, Illinois, where, as commandant, he received all official reports and documents issued by the Fenian hierarchy.[4]

In due course, having carved out a considerable reputation for himself in the Fenian ranks, Le Caron was appointed Military Organiser of the Irish Republican Army at a salary of sixty dollars a month with seven dollars a day expenses. His job was to organise the various military bodies attached to the rebel society. "To my unhappy amazement," he wrote in his autobiography, "I learned that I was, while engaged on this work, to address public meetings in support of the cause. . . . I was in a regular mess, for if called on to speak—as I feared—I should be found absolutely ignorant of Irish affairs."

Nevertheless Le Caron performed his speech-making to the satisfaction of all and without arousing suspicions. In 1868, in company with O'Neill, another Fenian, he had an interview with President Andrew Johnson at the White House. This provided an enlightening insight into American Presidential thinking and into Johnson's biased interpretation of the Neutrality Laws in Ireland's favour. Referring to the invasion of Canada by the Fenians, Johnson said, "Your people unfairly blame me a good deal for the part I took in stopping your first movement. Now I want you to understand that my sympathies are entirely with you, and anything which lies in my power I am willing to do to assist you. But you must remember that I gave you five full days before issuing any proclamation stopping you. . . . If you could not get there in five days, by God, you never could get there; and then, as President, I was compelled to enforce the Neutrality Laws, or be denounced on every side."[5]

Le Caron was promoted to the rank of Inspector-General of the revolutionary forces and in this capacity was sent from time to time to the Canadian border to locate arms and ammunition dumps. He found an excuse to visit Ottawa where he established a system of communications with the Chief Commissioner of Police, Judge M'Micken, as well as with Lord Monck, then Governor-General. As a result of the intelligence Le Caron gleaned, the Fenian organisation was largely disrupted by 1870. But not before a second invasion of Canada had been planned. This time security was stricter and the plans were carried out in the utmost secrecy. Needless to say Le Caron knew all about the plan. The object of this second invasion was to obtain possession of Canada, not as the permanent seat of an Irish Republic but as the only possible point of attack—the base for operations against Britain. O'Neill, who was the organiser of this coup, was ambitious enough to visualise the Fenians obtaining control of ports and shipyards in Canada from which they could send pirate ships to prey on British shipping, aiming at the same time to get belligerent rights from the United States.

After the interview with President Johnson, previously recorded, it can be understood that the Irish had some reason for optimism about getting belligerent rights from the U.S.A. This single fact gave Whitehall a great deal to think about and from this moment until the present time the British Secret Service has always been conscious of the need for detailed espionage Intelligence reports from the U.S.A. Governments may pretend that the two countries are Allies and that spying on one another is unthinkable, but the need for inside information of Presidential and State Department thinking (not to mention in modern times the perpetual nightmare of the Pentagon) has been as vital on such occasions as the Anglo-French campaign at Suez and the Berlin crisis of the late 'forties as at the time of the planned invasion of Canada and the uneasy neutrality in World Wars I and II.

The second invasion also fizzled out ignominiously. Le Caron had passed on information to the right quarter and this time, as he records, "General Foster, who, acting with that precision so peculiar to General Grant's administration, when contrasted with that of Andrew Johnson's, had, in consequence of the information furnished, arrived on the scene of the battle immediately after I left and arrested O'Neill for a breach of the Neutrality Laws."

Despite these serious setbacks for the Fenians, Le Caron still had much subversive activity to contend with. There was the "Knights of the Inner Circle", essentially a secret society and therefore all the more difficult to penetrate. This society paved the way for the establishment of the Fenian organisation in Britain as an underground movement under the title of the Irish Republican Brotherhood, but though established in 1870 it was not until 1873 that it was fully developed. A Masonic form of ritual was developed and all the paraphernalia of a secret society, with passwords, solemn oaths and penalties for giving away information which included the death sentence. As to just how treasonable this society was from the British viewpoint may be gauged from its constitution: ". . . it shall prepare unceasingly for an armed insurrection in Ireland".

In code were references in written documents to the "Jsjti" and "Jsjtinfo"—the Irish and Irishmen, a rather obvious cipher, substituting the letter following each letter which formed the actual word. Le Caron was one of the Knights of the Inner Circle, notwithstanding the fact that some Fenians still felt he was partly responsible for the disastrous second Canadian invasion. Not that they suspected him of treachery, but they believed he had rashly urged the leaders to go ahead with the plan.

By 1876 the revolutionaries had a membership of more than 11,000, including such prominent rebels as Alexander Sullivan, O'Donovan Rossa and Colonel Clingen. Le Caron saw every document issued by the headquarters of the movement and passed all information on to a "Mr. Anderson in London".[6]

His reports throw a very different light on the whole question of Home Rule for Ireland. It can still be argued with some logic that if Ireland had been given Home Rule in the 'eighties of the last century, she might still be part of the Commonwealth and that the Irish problem would have been solved. But this thesis only holds if it can be proved that the moderates, the Parnellites and their allies, would have won the day. Le Caron's reports must throw grave doubt on whether by the 'eighties the revolutionary forces were not already too strong for the moderates to have withstood their pressure. Even in the 'seventies it was quite clear what would happen if Britain was once again engaged in a major war:

"Old Europe is threatened with a general convulsion," was the theme propounded by the Fenians in a document dated 21 April 1877. "War on the most tremendous scale cannot much longer be staved off by all the artifices and subtleties of all the diplomatists in the world. Russia and Turkey are equally resolute to fight the inevitable fight. . . . The rest of the Great Powers of Europe will be drawn by an irresistible force into the arena. England, above all, whether she likes it or not, must draw her sword once more or meanly confess herself a third-class power. . . . England's difficulty then has all but come; in other words, 'Ireland's opportunity'. Is Ireland prepared to seize that opportunity? . . . We propose forthwith to create a 'Special National Fund' to aid the work of Ireland's deliverance."[7]

The revolutionaries were certainly enlarging their horizons and shortly after this Le Caron learned of moves by the revolutionaries to enter into negotiations with the Russian Government. "Wild and absurd as the idea at first appears," wrote Le Caron, "these negotiations were in the end completed and developed to the stage of a regular diplomatic compact at headquarters in Russia." Relations between Britain and Russia were strained between 1876 and 1880 and war between the two nations often seemed imminent. The Russians responded to the revolutionaries' overtures, doubtless impressed by the fact that they were operating in the United States and backed by American money. Dr. Carroll, one of the rebel leaders, was put in touch with the Russian Minister in Washington by Senator Jones of Florida and discussions were started on the question of the Irish intervention on the side of Russia should war break out.

This was but one of many plots, each more sensational than the other, from the plan to assassinate Queen Victoria to the kidnapping of the Prince of Wales and an attack on Portland Prison to rescue Michael Davitt. But Davitt was released before the last-named plan could be set in motion. It is significant that he sailed for America immediately.

At about the same time the rebels launched a scheme for building a submarine torpedo boat which was intended to destroy the Royal Navy. It was quite the most ambitious scheme which the rebels had devised and as the Royal Navy had not yet even considered the idea of a submarine it could have had lethal effects. According to Le Caron, the craft was actually built "on the Jersey side of the North River at a cost of some 37,000 dollars, but nothing ever came of it, for it was apparently completed only to be towed to New Haven where it lay", presumably until it rotted.[8] Le Caron's report was of the utmost value to the authorities, but they seem to have acted on it belatedly. It was passed on to the Admiralty, but only at the turn of the century did a naval engineering expert act on it, see its revolutionary possibilities and press the authorities to build a British submarine based on the Fenian project. When Britain acquired her first submarine in 1901 it was entirely due to Le Caron's report of earlier years.

On routine intelligence concerning Irish terrorist and revolutionary organisations there is no doubt that le Caron was of immense value to the British authorities and a prime factor in keeping terrorism at bay. Nevertheless, despite the fact that the British Secret Service had successfully infiltrated the Fenian ranks, the organisations continued to function: they were never broken up, at the best they were merely contained. While the Secret Service had the necessary information, they seemed sadly to lack the political know-how to exploit their knowledge and to use it to destroy, or at least divide the often uneasy coalitions of warring temperaments within the revolutionary ranks.

The reason for this is not hard to find. Too much reliance was placed on the political judgement of the secret agents, most of whom were so vehement in their hatred of the revolutionaries that they were apt to regard any Irishman who wanted independence as a traitor or a revolutionary. Le Caron provides an enlightening example of this. When he returned to Britain in the 'eighties he was asked by the British to gain the confidence of Charles Stewart Parnell, the leader of the Irish Party in the House of Commons. In his assessment of Parnell, Le Caron seems to have got right out of his depth and merely to have provided ammunition for the politically blinkered who wished to see Parnell destroyed. But first let us turn to Winston Churchill's assessment of Parnell, written after the latter's death:

"He was the reverse of a demagogue and agitator. . . . Assassination he abhorred. He was too practical to harbour Fenian dreams of insurrection against the might of Britain. As his authority grew, Fenians and Invincibles stayed the bloody hand for fear of a Parnell resignation."[9]

Le Caron on the other hand gave a very different picture of Parnell based on his own interviews with the Irish leader, interviews which he had in his capacity as an envoy of the revolutionaries. Parnell, he said, "saw no reason why, when we were fully prepared, an open insurrectionary movement could not be brought about. He went carefully into the question of resources and necessaries." And, added Le Caron, Parnell stated that "he had long since ceased to believe that anything but the force of arms would accomplish the final redemption of Ireland."[10]

In short Le Caron sought to convince the authorities that Parnell was the ally of the revolutionaries and terrorists. This, of course, would suit perfectly the aims of those who opposed Home Rule. For without Parnell Gladstone would never have attempted to support Home Rule. Parnell was the one moderate, the last great leader who could use his authority over the whole of Ireland, Catholic and Protestant. Therefore to destroy all hopes of Home Rule the enemies of Irish independence had first to destroy Parnell. Did the Secret Service do what secret services have so often done before and since—tell their masters what their masters wished to know? There is a great deal of evidence that the Secret Service at this time, far from being an objective body as far as Ireland was concerned, was used as an instrument for destroying the Irish moderates and in particular blackening

Parnell's character. Consider the evidence. With the Treaty of Kilmainham and Gladstone's support for Parnell, terrorism suddenly ceased; the Dynamite Campaign was brought to a close and even the wildest of the Irish-American revolutionaries had their hands stayed on Parnell's orders. In the previous five years the Dynamite Campaign had threatened to terrorise the cities of Britain. The Dynamitards, as they called themselves, had travelled over from America and, using the Charing Cross Hotel as a headquarters, established a nitro-glycerine factory in Birmingham. From here large quantities of liquid were despatched to various points in London in rubber bags and rubber shooting-stockings. But through the Secret Service having been tipped off the plotters were arrested and the whole of the nitro-glycerine seized. Le Caron stated that "what the actual designs of this dynamite band were, are not, and probably never will be known. Quite sufficient for the public must be the fact that so enormous was the quantity of nitro-glycerine discovered that, according to experts, it was quite equal to the blowing up of every house and street in London, from one end to the other."

But all this had ceased completely. Britain and Ireland were on the threshold of a new understanding: the peaceful co-existence of the two countries seemed at last a political reality. But the enemies of Home Rule would not have it. They sought for trumped-up evidence that would destroy Parnell and Home Rule. And there is not much doubt that the Secret Service played a somewhat discreditable rôle in helping to manufacture the evidence they required.

The Times began to publish in 1887 a series of articles under the heading of "Parnellism and Crime". To support the charges of criminal terrorist links between the extremists and Parnell a facsimile reproduction of a letter purporting to be in Parnell's handwriting was published. This letter directly associated the Irish leader with the assassination campaign. The facts of the "Parnell Letter" and the Special Commission which was appointed to investigate the allegations are well enough known. It will suffice to remind readers that *The Times* had obtained the letter from an unscrupulous, broken-down journalist named Richard Pigott who lived in Dublin, a man who eked out a living by selling pornographic books and photographs. A mysterious intermediary had offered Pigott a guinea a day, hotel and travelling expenses if he could produce incriminating documents to show Parnell as the ally of the terrorists. The manager of *The Times* paid £2,500 for the letters, a huge sum in those days, and it seems possible that the Secret Service provided at least a part of these funds. For who was the man behind this strange affair? None other than Henri Le Caron, described by Churchill as "a strange figure . . . in the deep-hidden employ of the British Government".[11]

Le Caron himself makes it quite clear that this was the year—1888—when he finally left America. Following the Special Commission he could hardly return to the revolutionary ranks for that would have meant certain death. "I had twice written to Mr. Anderson, offering my services in connection with the Special Commission," he wrote, thus clearly implicating the Secret Service in the "Parnell Letter" plot. But there must have been some who were doubtful of the wisdom of letting this affair develop, for Le Caron added that "nothing had come of my proposal, and I had no idea that anything would happen in connection with the matter. My idea was . . . that the Government were really prosecuting the Parnellite party, and I could not understand how all the information which I knew them to be possessed of was not appearing."

There is no doubt that the Secret Service did not want to have Le Caron as a witness. Anderson insisted that "he had no intention of giving up such a useful informant on his own initiative". But events moved too fast for the authorities. Le Caron's evidence of terrorist activities became vital for the authorities to build up their case against Parnell. Prudently Le Caron insisted on the Secret Service bringing over his family to Britain and to safety before he went into the witness box.

Le Caron gave evidence of terrorist activities, but the climax of the case was reached when Pigott himself was put in the witness box. He was asked to write down the words "likelihood" and "hesitancy" which were misspelt in the notorious letter. Pigott repeated the misspellings. The fact of forgery was established: the whole case against Parnell was a fraud and an invention. Pigott fled the country and finally blew out his brains in a hotel in Madrid.

That was the end of Le Caron's work for the Secret Service. Yet he referred afterwards in eulogistic terms to Pigott and seemed to have no remorse about the forgery incident. His chief tribute in his book, however, was reserved for his director in the Secret Service, Anderson: "For twenty-one years I served under this gentleman in the Secret Service, and no greater honour can I pay him than to say that during all this time I was never discovered. . . . To him, and to him alone, was I known as a Secret Service agent."[12]

Yet maybe there were others in the Secret Service who took a different view of Le Caron, alias Thomas Beach, and who suspected his motives. Le Caron admitted that if his identity remained undiscovered it was "not for want of attempts on the part of colleagues of Mr. Anderson to find it out". So determined was one official of the Secret Service to discover Le Caron's identity that, having in some way found out that his first name was Thomas, and assuming it to be his surname, he sent a detective to Chicago to discover the man called Thomas in the organisation there.

"When this attempt failed, communications were sought to be opened up with me by the same official through Sir John Rose and Judge M'Micken, with whom I had acted at the time of the Fenian raid of 1870. So strong, indeed, was the pressure brought upon Judge M'Micken, that the old gentleman travelled specially to Chicago to see me on the point."

Le Caron, like many of the informers on Irish terrorism in the British ranks, was often criticised for his extravagant expenditure. He admitted as much: "Many a lecture did I receive on the subject of spending. . . . The expenditure of money among the Irish patriotic class was an absolute necessity for my purpose, and consequently I could never put any money by, but rather lived up to, if not, indeed, at times beyond every penny of my income."

Le Caron, indeed, complained bitterly of "the miserable pittance doled out for the purpose of fighting such an enemy as Clan-na-Gael". He referred to the fact that Gallaher, one of the Dynamite Gang, had £1,400 on his person when arrested in 1883, and that Moroney, when sent from New York in 1887 in connection with the Jubilee Explosion Plot, carried £1,200 with him.

"How on earth can the English police and their assistants in the Secret Service hope to grapple with such heavily financed plots . . . on the miserable sums granted by Parliament for this purpose? . . . America is called the Land of the Free, but she could give England points in the working of the Secret Service, for there is no stint of men or money."

The case for larger spending by the British Secret Service on a terrorist organisation as well financed as the Irish American Brotherhood or the Fenians may well have been made out. But the payment of £2,500 for a forged letter by a man like Pigott, deliberately concocted to ruin the one great and moderate leader Ireland had in that stormy period, is another matter altogether. It remains a permanent stain on the tradition of the British Secret Service and one which brought it into the greatest disrepute abroad for many years to come.

In fact the revelations of the Parnell Letter case did much to harm British influence and relations abroad. They achieved in one day the winning of widespread sympathy for the Irish cause in America so that even Americans who had been well disposed to Britain switched their allegiance to the Fenians.

12

The Great Eccentrics: Kavanagh, Burton and Reilly

IT WAS sometime during the middle of the nineteenth century that the tendency grew in Britain for the Secret Service to be regarded as something which was not mentioned in polite society. Le Caron, in his biography, hinted at this tendency, mentioning that he had often heard it urged that "the thought of Secret Service is repugnant to the British heart".[1]

Suspicion about the Secret Service was certainly considerable even as early in the century as 1829 when, under the leadership of the Duke of Wellington, Sir Robert Peel planned the organisation of the policing of Britain. Because Wellington supported Peel's scheme he was, according to a contemporary, suspected of plotting to "seize supreme power and usurp the throne". The cry of "police spies" went up from the masses as they howled down the "Peelers" (as they contemptuously called the new police); they believed that Peel's scheme was none other than an extension of the Secret Service to make the nation a police state. The appointment of an Army officer, Sir Charles Rowan, a close associate of Wellington at Waterloo, as head of the new police force convinced people that Wellington wished to raise a body of uniformed men to keep permanent watch on them, enter their homes at will and so to enslave the nation. From being a national hero the Duke found himself an object of hatred.

These suspicions and beliefs were, of course, quite unjustified and the newly created Police Force, possibly because of the criticism it originally aroused, went out of its way to avoid being suspected of being involved in espionage, or in any sense prying on ordinary law-abiding citizens. This was amply borne out in

1851 when the head of the Prussian espionage service visited London for the World Fair. The Emperor Friedrich Wilhelm of Prussia lived in constant terror of agitation among the masses and saw revolution and subversion in the smallest incident. His spy chief, Wilhelm Stieber, made the London visit an excuse for investigating the activities of Prussian radicals living in London and, above all, to spy on Karl Marx himself.

Stieber, who was also editor of the Prussian police journal, confidently expected to gain the full co-operation of the British police and was sadly disappointed when he found that his espionage was not only frowned upon in London but was actively discouraged and even frustrated. The London police chiefs disliked Continental police methods and left Stieber in no doubt of their disapproval.[2]

The Secret Service in London acquiesced in the Police dislike of Stieber's methods. They were only really interested in Irish terrorists and one cannot help wondering whether in concentrating so heavily on Irish terrorism in this century the Secret Service did not lose sight of other and equally important matters. For there is a good deal of evidence to show that in this period—the middle of the century—Britain lost ground in both counter-espionage at home and espionage on the European continent and in the Far East. Ireland seemed to be a special case, but while the Intelligence Service relentlessly tracked down Irish terrorists, they too often turned a blind eye to French, German and Russian espionage inside Britain. The truth was that, Ireland apart, the official view had tended to regard spying as something indecent and out of character with British traditions.

The military blunders and scandals of omission of the Crimean War revealed the poverty of Britain's military intelligence. Most of the catastrophes of that campaign were due to an almost total lack of information about the enemy. As a direct result of this a Topographical and Statistical Department was established at the War Office in 1855. This was a very modest beginning in creating an Intelligence department, but at least it attempted to provide maps and topographical studies of foreign countries, something which had been totally lacking in the previous twenty years.

From the somewhat desultory and unambitious attempts to

map the outside world in terms of military information reforms slowly but surely emerged. One of the first officers to serve in the Military Intelligence Division was a young captain, H. M. Hozier, later to be knighted and father of the future bride of Winston Churchill. In the early eighteen-seventies—there seems to be some confusion about the exact date—the department was re-organised under the title of the Intelligence Branch. Sir George Aston gives the date as 1873, but according to Major-General Sir John Ardagh a nucleus of the new organisation was started at Queen Anne's Gate in 1871. The first premises of the Intelligence Branch consisted of a house in Adelphi Terrace and an abandoned coach-house and stables near the Government offices in Whitehall, a typical example of bureaucratic meanness in matters of Intelligence at the time. In 1874 a more permanent home for the organisation was found at Adair House, near Nell Gwynn's old home in Pall Mall.

It was a tradition in this period that for some obscure reason artillery officers were recruited for intelligence work and the first Director of Military Intelligence was one of them—Sir Henry Brackenbury. He was succeeded by Lieut.-General E. H. Chapman and in 1884 the Intelligence Branch was moved back to Queen Anne's Gate in a secluded and shuttered house which had all the ambiance of the fictional secret hide-out of an Intelligence service.

Yet even when Major-General Sir John Ardagh took charge of the Branch in 1896 the functions of the organisation, while clearly defined, were still extremely limited and lacking in imagination. They were set out as follows: "the preparation of information relating to the military defence of the empire and the strategical considerations of all schemes of defence; the collection and distribution of information relating to the military geography, resources and armed forces of foreign countries and the British colonies and possessions; the compilation of maps and the translation of foreign documents."

There was inadequate communication between the Intelligence Branch at Queen Anne's Gate and the War Office and the Branch itself was ridiculously undermanned to cope with its requirements. One section comprising two officers and a clerk had the task of covering the Russian empire, almost the whole of

Asia, including China, India and Japan. Curiously, this was the most efficient of all the sections, probably because after the Crimean disasters a major effort was made to seek intelligence on Russia and territories adjacent to her.

The tendency to rely on the brilliant amateur lasted until towards the end of the Victorian era, mainly, it must be admitted, because intelligence was wanted on the cheap and this could best be achieved by employing adventurous Britons with ample private means whose sense of patriotism prevented them from accepting payment.

But while some such Britons were brilliant, many more were merely incompetent and often blundering amateurs and in the early 'nineties it was realised with some consternation that the Secret Service depended too much on the brilliant amateur and that there were too few of them. Desperation leads to ruthlessness and later the Service was to show that it had recovered some of the tough, professional approach to the task of its Elizabethan and Cromwellian predecessors. Meanwhile two facts should be taken into account. First of all there was in Britain a marked distaste for Continental police methods. There was abundant testimony to the scourge of police rule and Secret Service terror throughout Europe. In France the employment of the police as a section of the Secret Service had survived the Revolution and continued with all its abuses unchecked. The French Emperor had his own army of spies, the Prime Minister had another Intelligence service and the Prefect of Police and the Empress each had spy organisations of their own. Often these various services spied on one another. The British public was fully aware of this comic opera form of espionage which vitiated France just as that of the Prussian Emperor was well known to the authorities in London as a singularly clumsy and brutal instrument of intelligence.

The other fact, no less important in the light of history, was that the British Secret Service even encouraged the disaffected emigrés from various parts of Europe to settle in London. They were actually welcomed as refugees, in keeping with the British tradition of providing a sanctuary for the victims of political persecution. By the late 'sixties there was a growing feeling of stability in Britain; it was felt that prosperity was increasing, that a tradition of law-abiding citizenship had been well and truly laid and that whatever Continental countries might think, the revolutionaries of other nations held no particular dangers for the British. Perhaps the authorities were right, perhaps they were wrong: but gradually London became the sanctuary for all kinds of frightened and hunted Continentals, from anarchists and Radicals to terrorists and criminals. On the whole they created very little trouble, they formed their own societies and kept to themselves. Anarchy was plotted behind closed doors in comparative respectability, not in the streets or in open-air meetings.

What could be argued is that the Secret Service might have made more use of these foreigners. But the only use that was made of them to any marked degree was to keep a long-distance check on the activities of Russia. Britain's chief concern about Russia was the ever-present fear that that country had predatory designs on India and this was the reason why more attention was paid to Russian espionage than to that of other European countries.

The Secret Service had another reason for being cool towards Wilhelm Stieber. Even as early as 1851 there had been rumours in London that Stieber was a freelance spy rather than a patriotic Prussian. The British Secret Service believed he had links with the Czar at the same time that he was serving the Emperor Friedrich Wilhelm.[3]

The authorities in London were well advised to be chary of Stieber's proposals and approaches. The Prussian's tactics were to win the confidence of other European Secret Services and by giving them lists of dangerous Radicals (often the people they listed were more mad than Radical) and urging them to assist him by refusing to grant these people political asylum. Stieber liked to feel that his tentacles reached out into every capital and that by using other Secret Services he could control Prussian nationals abroad. In some European capitals his tactics succeeded, but in London the view was taken that Stieber was prepared to sell his services to any country which would subscribe to his theories, and that the wares he had to offer were simply a list of relatively harmless anarchists and Radicals. As far as the first part of this view was concerned the British authorities were right, though Stieber was a man who deep in his heart put Prussia before anything, however much he might proffer his services elsewhere. But the British may have underestimated the anarchists and Radicals, as some of the latter were later to provide them with useful information on Stieber's strategy which, as far as intelligence went, gave Britain an advantage over the French.

For the London rumours about Stieber proved in the long run to be accurate. When the Emperor Friedrich Wilhelm was pronounced insane Stieber lost favour and was removed from office. He then disappeared to St. Petersburg where he began to reorganise the Czarist Secret Service. To have acquired such influence in the Russian court so swiftly Stieber must have maintained secret links with the Russians over many years.

It was only then, when they received confirmation that Stieber was working with the Russians that the British began belatedly to realise that the fugitives from Russian persecution in London's East End might become an asset to the Secret Service. Though the British authorities regarded most of these fugitives as both harmless and useless, thereby losing some potentially good agents in their midst, slowly they came to the conclusion that the Russian immigrants at least were worth cultivating. This change of mood was due almost entirely to the machinations of Stieber. When the Prussian Intelligence chief became the effective founder of the Ochrana, the dreaded Russian secret police, the immigrant Russians in London warned the British Secret Service not only that Russian agents were being sent to London to track them down but that Stieber had by no means severed his links with Prussia. London noted with some relief that as far as Russia was concerned Stieber was not much interested in military espionage, or for plots against India, but that his aim was merely to develop a foreign espionage service to hound the enemies of the Czar outside Russia. At the same time Stieber continued to pass information about Russia on to the Prussians and it soon became clear that he was using the Ochrana as much in Prussian as in Russian interests. Indeed, later Stieber proved to be indispensable to Bismarck and did more than any man to plan carefully the campaign against France, culminating in the invasion of 1870. Stieber was *par excellence* the meticulous Teutonic genius who invented the espionage of co-ordinated facts and figures, collecting details of every factory, every bridge, every arsenal and fort, every barracks and military stores depot in France.[4]

The East End of London even in the 'fifties and 'sixties of the nineteenth century had become a hide-out for all manner of foreign refugees from persecution and tyranny. Most of these were Poles, the Russians followed somewhat later. The British people had evinced a strong sympathy for Polish refugees from tyranny in their own country. Henry Mayhew tells us that "to be a Pole and in distress was almost a sufficient introduction, and there were few English families who did not entertain as friend or visitor one of these unfortunate and suffering patriots. So excellent an opportunity for that class of foreign swindlers which haunt roulette tables . . . 'the destitute Pole', with false military documents and stories of miraculous escapes from Russian prisons, became a feature of the underworld."[5]

Later more Russians than Poles flocked into the East End. They had been disregarded by the police—foolishly, as it transpired—and allowed to form clubs of their own in Whitechapel, Houndsditch, Stepney and other centres where they established compact political organisations. Anarchism, that political theory which propounds that any form of government is bad, had found its chief propagandist in Proudhon, and his ideas had been enthusiastically adopted by such Russian thinkers as Bakunin and Kropotkin. In the first place no doubt the Secret Service authorities and the police were wise not to curb these people, or to interfere with their rights as individuals and the justice of this policy was demonstrated by the fact that a majority of them settled down as peaceful, hard-working citizens. But the criminals, the *agents-provocateurs* and secret agents who followed, created a problem which was not fully realised until the next century.

Theoretical anarchism had been superseded in Russia at least by the doctrine of "propaganda by deed", on the principle that the more dastardly the deed the more effective the propaganda. From about 1883 onwards most European countries had passed severe repressive measures against anarchists, but Britain had taken no action, with the result that London's East End became the safest refuge they could find.

Yet though on the surface one gets a picture of a tolerant officialdom turning a blind eye to anarchist plotters in its midst, this is by no means an accurate impression. The Secret Service had infiltrated the ranks of these revolutionaries from Russia and in some instances used some of the anarchists as British agents. In the 'eighties there were at least seven revolutionary clubs in East London. One, named the Jubilee, and founded under this innocuous title in 1887, was the centre of the Anarchists; it also had a West End headquarters known more romantically as the Bohemian Club.

Curiously enough it was the series of sadistic, sexual murders in the East End of London in the late 'eighties, popularly known as the "Jack the Ripper" crimes, which brought to light a good deal of the information which we now have on the prevalence of Russian secret agents in London. William Le Queux, who helped the British Government with Secret Service work both before and during World War I, declared that the Kerensky Government in Russia handed over to him in confidence a great quantity of documents found in the safe of a cellar in Rasputin's house after the death of the strange *moujik* monk who had intrigued his way into the Court of the Czar. The Kerensky Government were only too anxious that Le Queux should write a damning biography of the amorous charlatan.

"Among this mass of letters," wrote Le Queux, "I found a manuscript entitled *Great Russian Criminals*, written in French, a language which he [Rasputin] knew slightly, typed under dictation." Long after he wrote his book on Rasputin, Le Queux made use of some of this material in *Things I Know*, published in 1923. In it Le Queux alleged that "the true author" of the "Jack the Ripper" crimes "was disclosed by a Russian in London named Nideroest, who was a member of the Jubilee Street Club, the Anarchist Centre in the East End of London".[6]

According to Le Queux, Nideroest was given this information by an old Russian Anarchist, Nicholas Zverieff, who declared that the "Ripper" was Dr. Alexander Pedachenko, who had lived with his sister in Walworth. Zverieff's story was that Pedachenko sallied forth at night from Walworth, took an omnibus across London Bridge and walked to Whitechapel, where he committed the murders. Le Queux quoted from Rasputin's manuscript:

"The report of Nideroest's discovery amused our Secret Police greatly, for, as a matter of fact, they knew the whole details at the time, and had themselves actively aided and encouraged the crimes in order to exhibit to the world certain defects of the English police system, there having been some misunderstanding and rivalry between our own police and the British. It was, indeed, for that reason that Pedachenko, the greatest and boldest of all Russian criminal lunatics, was encouraged to go to London and commit that series of atrocious crimes, in which our agents of police aided him.

"Eventually, at the orders of the Ministry of the Interior, the Secret Police smuggled the assassin out of London and, as Count Luiskovo, he landed at Ostend and was conducted by a secret agent to Moscow. While there he was, a few months later, caught red-handed attempting to murder and mutilate a woman named Vogak and was eventually sent to an asylum where he died in 1908."[7]

Superficially William Le Queux's story has an air of some of the more extravagant stories of Baron Munchausen about it. Even Le Queux seems to have had some misgivings because he omitted any reference to the alleged Rasputin manuscript in his *Minister of Evil*, published five years earlier than *Things I Know*. However, he explained this omission by saying that he had "only recently discovered that a doctor named Pedachenko actually lived in Tver, the place named by the Rasputin manuscript, and that in this area his homicidal tendencies were well known. And he added that he had further ascertained that a man named Nideroest was a member of the Jubilee Street Club and was "known in connection with the Anarchist affray at Tottenham and also with the Sidney Street affair".[8]

This diversion into the realms of crime detection does revea something of the complicated and often obscure relationship between British police, Secret Service and Russian agents and freelance Anarchists in London in this period. Nideroest was not a figment of Rasputin's or Le Queux's imagination. But he was not a Russian, he was Swiss, though he was a member of the Russian and Lettish Socialist Club in the East End. Chief Inspector McCarthy gave evidence in 1909 that Nideroest was not an Anarchist, but had been selling information to the newspapers about bombs made in Whitechapel which the police found to be untrue.

Yet in June 1915, Nideroest was brought up at Bow Street and deported as an undesirable alien.

Margaret Prothero, in her *History of the C.I.D.* at Scotland Yard, referred to the anarchist propaganda circulating among the poorer classes in London at the end of the last century. "In 1894," she stated, "Anarchists and Nihilists from Russia were at work in England."[9] They had, in fact, been active in London for the best part of twenty years prior to this date and it was long after this that Scotland Yard realised the extent of their intrigues. Sir Basil Thomson declared that "the East End of London ever since the Jack the Ripper murders had become a city of refuge for aliens whose countries had become too hot to hold them".[10]

But the Secret Service were partly to blame for this. They deliberately witheld much information from the police and regarded these aliens as being solely within their own province, usually taking the view that it was better to tolerate them and know what they were doing than to blunder into premature action and lose much useful intelligence.

Once a Secret Service starts to play a lone game on its own territory against foreigners it invites the intervention of other Secret Services. And so it was in London: while Scotland Yard could hardly differentiate between one set of foreign revolutionaries and another, between Anarchists and Socialists and the early bolsheviks, a new force arose in the East End, a counter-revolutionary, or more exactly a counter-espionage organisation financed by the Czarist Government and aimed at discrediting and unmasking the Anarchists. A typical example of the counter-revolutionary agents was Serge Makharov, alias Ivan Nikoliaieff, who, years later, according to Soviet sources, was the original "Peter the Painter" of the Sidney Street siege. Makharov, who belonged to an aristocratic but impoverished family, first entered the Russian Army, and then, following a duel with a brother officer, resigned his commission and served with the Secret Police. He was then assigned to the task of spying on revolutionary Russians in Paris, London and elsewhere.

The methods adopted by Makharov are of special interest. His instructions were to locate the revolutionaries, who were mostly in London, to compromise them and find some means of involving them in trouble with the British police. The object of this was to create a public demand for their expulsion from Britain. That these were the permanent tactics of the Secret Police over many years is made abundantly clear not only in the records of the first Soviet Government, but in documents obtained from Czarist sources and from British police records.

Of course it would have been far simpler and much less costly for the Czarist Government to make representations to the British Government for the deportation of the revolutionaries. But the Czarist Government was just as secretive as Soviet Governments have been and just as reluctant to discuss internal problems with foreigners. Apart from this even unofficial representations to Britain on this very subject had been unsuccessful. While the Czarist régime had succeeded in persuading European governments to ban Anarchists, London was still regarded by the British authorities as a natural and perfectly legal sanctuary for them. Thus London became the focal point of all Anarchist activities and the only chance the Russians had of changing this situation was to discredit the revolutionaries and hope that public opinion would demand their removal.

Makharov and other agents so compromised certain Anarchists that the latter had to leave London to avoid arrests on criminal charges. The revolutionaries, who were men not usually engaged in criminal pursuits, were tricked by Makharov into lending their names to criminal enterprises in the belief that they were really waging war against the Romanovs, and, in doing so, were providing the sinews of war for the revolutionary cause at the expense of the Czarist régime.

As a result of the Russian counter-espionage activities in London to discredit the revolutionaries a curious new situation arose. The police, who were not told of these activities by the Secret Service, were generally hostile to all foreigners in the East End of London and came to look upon the Anarchists as criminals. The Secret Service on the other hand were generally sympathetic to the Anarchists and hostile to the Russian government agents, regarding the activities of the latter as an illegal intervention on British soil. There was also another reason for this sympathetic approach: belatedly the Secret Service had realised that there were serious gaps in their network and that recruitment of new agents was essential. The view was—and it should be stressed that this was the view of the Secret Intelligence Service and not of the Service intelligence organisations—that the need for new agents was so acute that they should be sought for among foreigners and especially refugees from other lands.

This was a sound enough policy up to a point because Britons are notoriously bad linguists and most would-be agents, however courageous and willing, frequently failed to make the grade because they lacked the ability to speak two or more languages convincingly enough to be mistaken for nationals of other states. What was deplorable in this change of policy was that there was a total lack of liaison between the Secret Service and the police in this period. The Secret Service, of course, discouraged police action against the Anarchists on the grounds that this would be playing into the hands of the Russian Government agents and make fools of the police. True enough, but the Secret Service might more usefully have indicated who the real culprits were: as a result of this lack of co-operation between the Intelligence services and the police many real criminals were allowed to escape the police net while *agent-provocateurs* continued their work more or less unhindered. One of the foreign criminals who almost certainly escaped arrest was the man responsible for the "Jack the Ripper" murders.

Yet where the police could have helped even more, in the absence of any professional counter-espionage organisation except that of the Irish branch of the Secret Service, would have been in vetting foreigners who were potential recruits for the S.I.S. Some double-agents, if not potential enemy agents, were recruited by mistake in the latter part of the nineteenth century, sufficient to make the Military Intelligence Branch highly sceptical of the S.I.S.

Major-General Ardagh has given one example of the development of the telegraph service in the field of intelligence. When there was a revolt among Sudanese troops in Uganda on one occasion a telegraphed report received by the Foreign Office was passed to Military Intelligence at 5.30 p.m. with a request for an immediate verbal opinion as to the action which ought to be taken. Intelligence made their assessment, gave their opinion and before 7 p.m. the same day it was telegraphed to Simla by the Secretary of State for India. Troops were immediately dispatched in compliance with the orders and Uganda was saved from massacre and anarchy. Ardagh was the first to realise the vital importance of cable and telegraph communications and he decided that these must be planned with intelligence requirements borne in mind and controlled accordingly. He refused sanction for any new cable cable lines which did not favour the interests of the state.

Much money was expended on gathering information by such Ministries as the India Office and the Colonial Office, or even by indirect means by various societies which provided funds for exploration in remote parts of the world. Much that was contributed towards the cost of obtaining intelligence came, sometimes unrequested, from the pockets of private individuals whose motives were either purely patriotic, or those of unbridled curiosity. This was the golden age of the amateur in all walks of life and the great eccentrics of the Victorian era played a remarkable rôle in providing intelligence as free-lance agents, acting on their own initiative. Sometimes, too, even Consuls and Vice-Consuls, Colonial officials in distant places and officers in the Indian Army financed their own secret missions. Whereas the Prussians had made espionage a question of serious-minded professionalism and the French and Russians had come to regard any form of intelligence as a commercial commodity that must be bought, Britain had once again reverted to her traditional amateur status, never officially spending too much on what was looked upon as something foreign to British instincts, but contradictorily and quixotically allowing full play to any amateur who lusted after information for information's sake. It is easy to be flippant about this attitude to intelligence, but it is also extremely unwise. Britain's greatest eras in her Secret Service history have been marked by brilliant amateurs, eccentric individualism and imaginative projects often arising from the absurd to the professionally sublime. Who in the sphere of espionage can say for certain where absurdity ceases and genius emerges? Espionage for the most part is a painstaking business: to be drearily mundane it is simply an infinite capacity for taking pains to ascertain the truth. Yet in Britain where intelligence work has through the ages been so dominated by the amateur, a romantic, almost a schoolboyish and irresponsible approach to the subject, while sometimes causing the Secret Service to plummet to the depths of absurdity has also made it shine with a brilliance that seems magical. Indeed, the word magic is not misplaced, for what else but this masked genius has caused other powers even in the present century to suspect that the British Secret Service has sometimes invoked the supernatural.[11]

The intelligence gleaned in the nineteenth century may have been casual, haphazard, fortuitous, irrelevant and often unprofessionally obtained. Yet it was acquired by individual effort more often than not; frequently it was the by-product of some individual or organisation having no connection with the Secret Service. It was also obtained by persons unhampered by inhibitions and possessing most of those talents which the most cliché-minded writers have attributed to every race but the British. Only now does one begin to appreciate the superhuman qualities of the great Victorian eccentrics and their gratuitous efforts on behalf of the Secret Service. Richard Burton, Doughty, Wilfred Scawen Blunt and Arthur McMorrough Kavanagh all provided examples of the freelance volunteer to the Secret Service. Historians and biographers may have dismissed them and continue to dismiss them as of little consequence in the history of their country. But, more often than not, they were all in an unofficial capacity among the ablest secret agents of their day.

Richard Burton and McMorrough Kavanagh will suffice as two examples of this type of freelance agent in this century. Each in his way was in the tradition of what Wilfred Noyce described as the "lodestone seekers". Burton, says his biographer, Byron Farwell, "was an adventurer in the purest sense of the word . . . what made him different from most others . . . was that he extended his exploration to the realms of the intellect and the spirit."[12] And, though this exploration in quest of information was frequently eccentric, often showing an obsessive interest in sexual phenomena and customs and in much else that seemed pointless, Burton in the course of his many journeys in Africa and Asia and the Middle East unearthed much that was of value to the gatherers of intelligence. Certainly when the British captured Sind his ability to provide brilliantly detailed intelligence reports was soon demonstrated to Sir Charles Napier, the Commander-in-chief. As a young subaltern Burton, disguised as a native and speaking their language, opened three small shops in Karachi, selling cloth and tobacco for a few rupees and a mass of information. He made notes of a wide range of subjects from the weapons and armour and methods of fighting used by the natives, to Indian aphrodisiacs, talismans, sexual habits and even the underclothing worn by the Sindi Women.

Whether the report on pederasty in Karachi which he was asked to make by Sir Charles Napier was a cover for rather more practical intelligence one does not know. Staining himself with henna and posing as Mirza Abdullah of Bushire, Burton disappeared into the male brothels of Karachi night after night. He was so skilful in disguising himself as an Indian that he often passed his Commanding Officer without being recognised.[13]

McMorrough Kavanagh never achieved the same fame as Burton, but he was even more remarkable as a man who triumphed over great odds. Born in Ireland without either arms or legs—his mother had had German measles prior to his birth—he nevertheless succeeded in doing rather better than most men the things which normally-limbed men do. Kavanagh started his journey through life as he intended to continue it, relying on nobody but himself to help him over his disabilities. Thus he learned to ride, even as a child, strapped into a special cradle-saddle, to write and paint with pen and brush between his teeth, to fish and to shoot, using a sawn-off shot-gun, with the trigger-guard removed, nudging the gun from under his right arm stump across his left stump, supporting the stock on a wall and touching the trigger with his other stump. Lord Morton, who accompanied him on shooting expeditions, said that he "has shot a great many wild geese, ducks and snipe. His shooting is quite as wonderful as his riding."

As a youth in 1848, while staying with his great-aunt, the Dowager Marchioness of Ormonde, at Garryricken, he volunteered as a Government scout to patrol the mountains on horseback at night in search of Smith O'Brien's Irish rebels. Then for some mysterious reason—a youthful romance was said to be the cause—young Kavanagh was sentenced to banishment from home for two years by his mother. Together with his elder brother and the family chaplain, Arthur Kavanagh went on one of the most extraordinary tours that any disabled man can ever have undertaken. He spent many months abroad, travelling across Scandinavia, Russia, Kurdistan, Persia and India, often under harsh and dangerous conditions. Kavanagh narrowly escaped death more than once and spent some time immured—delightfully, it seems—in a Persian harem. Yet the ardours of their travels took toll of the party. Kavanagh's brother and his chaplain died and the limbless young man alone survived. He hunted and killed tigers in the jungle and then, left alone in India with none but the friends he had made himself, and with only thirty shillings in his pocket, he had to earn a living. This he did by becoming a dispatch rider for the East India company.

All these adventures Kavanagh recorded in his diaries which, fortunately, were preserved for posterity, though the personal diary covering this period of his life was lost in a river while carrying dispatches. But, the records of the East India company show that he was later accepted in the Survey department of the Poona District. It was during this employment that Kavanagh volunteered his services to the Secret Service. He even offered to travel to Persia to make a report on Russian intentions towards India. When the authorities declined his suggestion, he asked to be allowed to obtain a report from his friend, Prince Malichus Mirza in Tabriz.[14]

Until 1886 Secret Service funds were partly allotted to members of Parliament for services given in support of certain bills, such as the Finance Scheme of Burke. In 1886 these funds were dissociated from the Civil List and included in the ordinary grant for the Civil Services, the amount being £65,000 per annum. This sum was about on a par with what the Germans were then spending on Secret Service, but far less than the huge sums the Russians spent on espionage. Some estimates show that Russia was paying out more than a million pounds a year on espionage in the 'seventies and 'eighties. Certainly at the turn of the century this sum was approaching £1,700,000 a year, a total which was actually reached by the year 1910.

Yet, as may be surmised from the facts given in the earlier part of this chapter, the Russians' spending on espionage indirectly helped the British. Through having so many exiled Russians, hostile to the Czarist régime, in London and other parts of Britain, the British Secret Service was able not only to keep a watch on

Russian counter-espionage but to learn a good deal of the very intelligence the Russians themselves were so expensively obtaining.

Liberalism may not often pay dividends to spy-masters; more often it may actually thwart them. But in the liberal, tolerant London of the latter half of the nineteenth century intelligence could frequently be obtained either cheaply or at little cost from the polyglot community of Anarchists, revolutionaries, Liberals, socialists and cranks who, sometimes even without passports or immigration visas, had flocked to the capital. Thus Alexander Herzen, illegitimate son of a Russian aristocrat, revolutionary in search of "the mighty, titanic poetry of 1793,"[15] came to settle in London and to publish in a back-street off the Caledonian Road the first independent Russian newspaper ever published. Not that he was particularly grateful for the sanctuary and freedom which London gave him: "Life here is as boring as that of worms in a cheese," he wrote. But if any nation had the opportunity to learn exactly how a revolutionary movement was slowly gathering force, it was Britain. The Secret Service had all the evidence. Yet it failed to make use of that evidence until it was almost too late. On the other hand its experience over more than half a century enabled it between 1917 and 1922 to combat an attempt to mount a revolution in Britain itself. History has so far minimised the attempted revolution of those five years and indeed has often suggested it existed only in the minds of a few reactionaries obsessed by Bolshevism to an insane degree. It is easy to minimise what never happened. But the Secret Service must take credit for the fact that this revolution was crushed before it began, though not until long after it had been plotted.

One man who helped to thwart revolution and might even have defeated it in Russia between 1917 and 1920 was in the service of British Intelligence as early as 1895. In many respects he is a symbol of what this chapter is about. He is a typical recruit of the foreign refugee who, in the late 'eighties and the early 'nineties, Britain was beginning to use as a spy. He exemplified the change in the mentality of the Secret Service chiefs from the deprecatory attitude to spying of the middle of the century to a bolder, more ruthless approach to the quest for intelligence in the 'eighties. Again he marked the growing preoccupation of the S.I.S. with Russia and their fondness for Russian immigrant recruits. Above all his employment marked the gambling instincts of S.I.S. chiefs and that lack of co-operation with the police when vetting foreigners.

Had Sidney Reilly been considered by the S.I.S. today for employment as an agent, it is almost certain that M.I.5 would have rejected him out of hand. In 1895 there was no M.I.5 and no Special Branch, but had the police been consulted there is little doubt that they would have given a very poor report on the man.

As Sidney Reilly played an important rôle in the Secret Service for a period of thirty years—a remarkable longevity for any spy—he must inevitably play quite a rôle in this book. He was without question the greatest and most influential secret agent in the whole history of the Secret Service and he wielded more power, authority and influence than any other spy. That influence extended long after his presumed death and, like a time-bomb set for ten years later, was to create a series of explosions in the Secret Service in 1935, 1951 and 1960. For this reason it is worth taking a close look at his origins.

It is still a subject of some controversy as to who Sidney Reilly really was. Robin Bruce Lockhart has stated that he was born "in South Russia, not far from Odessa, on 24 March 1874. His mother was Russian of Polish descent; his father apparently a colonel in the Russian army with connections at the court of the Tsar."[16] At the age of nineteen Reilly discovered he was not his father's son at all but the product of an illicit union between his mother and a Jewish doctor from Vienna and that his real name was Sigmund Georgievich Rosenblum. It must have come as a terrible shock to the boy to realise that his Catholic origin was spurious (he had been brought up in the faith) and that he was, as his uncle brutally put it, a "little Jewish bastard". It is not surprising therefore that on various occasions, like many other secret agents in history unable to resist creating a mystery about his antecedents, Reilly told different stories about his origins even to people who thought they knew him well. Once in Prague, where he was on a mission with General Spears, Reilly went to the British Legation to a lunch party. Here he regaled the company with stories of his childhood in Odessa. Later, when he took his passport to have it endorsed, he was asked, "How comes it, Mr. Reilly, that your passport gives your birthplace as Tipperary, when at lunch you yourself admitted several times that you were born in Odessa?"

"There was a war and I came over to fight for England," replied Reilly, completely unshaken. "I had to have a British passport and therefore a British birthplace, and, you see, from Odessa, it's a long, long way to Tipperary!"

Reilly's favourite story was that he was the son of an adventurous Irishman whose escapades sounded not unlike those of Baron Munchausen. But the clue to much of the mystery which Reilly in later life used to encourage about his family background was to be found not so much in shame as in the difficult position in which the Jewish people found themselves in Russian Poland, even more than in Russia itself. The Czarist régime was very anti-semitic and Reilly, acting for a foreign power, would have had to be very careful to cover his parentage to protect his family.

Reilly left his family after the discovery about his true parentage and stowed away on a British ship bound for South America. For a time he had a variety of jobs, as a docker, a road-mender and a plantation worker. His first real break came when he secured the job of cook to a British exploration party in Brazil. It has already been noted in this chapter that exploration parties frequently undertook espionage tasks for Britain in this century and it so happened that Major Fothergill, the expedition leader, was a permanent member of the Secret Intelligence Service. Reilly proved to be not merely a good cook but the most useful member of the party. When the party lost their way it was Reilly who guided them to safety, when they were attacked by natives it was he who, almost single-handed, and with superb revolver marksmanship, picked off the assailants one by one. In acknowledgement of his services Major Fothergill gave him a cheque for £1,500 and fixed him up with a free passage to Britain.

Thus it was that the exile from Russia was asked to work for the British Secret Service, and by 1897 Reilly was working for them in Russia, his particular mission being to find out Russian plans concerning oil discoveries in Persia. While in Russia he met a Nonconformist minister, the Rev. Hugh Thomas, and his wife.

The former was over sixty, dour and forbidding, the wife was twenty-three, gay, amorously inclined and a most attractive red-head. Reilly, who all his life was an inveterate womaniser, was soon having a secret *affaire* with Mrs. Thomas. He returned to London with the Thomases and immediately asked for prolonged leave from his Secret Service work, without giving any reason for this. Then, when Hugh Thomas became ill, Reilly, who claimed that he had a great knowledge of medicines, not only prescribed for the sick minister, but brought the medicines along for him and dismissed the doctor. Shortly afterwards the Rev. Hugh Thomas became decidedly worse and was persuaded by his wife and Reilly to make a will in his wife's favour. Very soon afterwards Thomas died and within a year Reilly and Margaret Thomas were married at a register office in Holborn.

At last Reilly was able to enjoy something approaching wealth, for Hugh Thomas left his widow considerable funds. For a whole year he did no work at all and the Secret Service must have begun to wonder whether a promising recruit ought to be written off. Then suddenly he reappeared and said he was ready to work for them again.

It seems incredible that the Service should have accepted Reilly in the first place for, by all accounts, he declined to give them any details about his origins and was very vague about his associations with Russia. But it is even more remarkable that they should have again taken him on so confidently after he had disappeared for a whole year. On the credit side was the report that they had of his behaviour, resource and initiative on the British expedition, the fact that he was brave, a crack marksman, spoke several languages and had done good work in Russia. On the debit side was his refusal to give adequate details of his origins and early life, that he was a womaniser who had acquired at least four mistresses in three years (one of them a prostitute), and that he had declined to work for them on his return to England. An agent who is not available for work when asked to do it is usually an unreliable spy.

The answer to the poser of why the Secret Service re-engaged him is probably that they were short of good agents and that Reilly's charm and plausibility won them over. He made no secret about his marriage to Margaret Thomas and had the impudence to explain this away by claiming that by acquiring a British wife he was linking himself more closely with Britain, and at the same time providing himself with private means because, without access to money, he could not afford to work for a Secret Service which paid so badly! For good measure he added that he had now given himself legally the name of Sidney Reilly, an Irishman, pointing out that as such he could even pose as being anti-British if that became desirable in the course of his work.

Reilly had, however, won for himself one strong ally in the Secret Service—Sir H.M. Hozier, the father of Winston Churchill's wife-to-be. It was an alliance which several years later was further strengthened by a personal relationship with Churchill himself. In the Secret Service, British or otherwise, despite what may be said, rogues are frequently tolerated if they produce results and it could be said that in some circumstances their selection may be justified. The British Secret Service had used rogues in the rumbustuous distant past and was to use them again in the twentieth century, but at the time of Reilly's selection they had little experience in handling such a type. It is questionable whether such a risk ever pays off for more than a relatively short period. Sidney Reilly was one exception to the rule. Yet the implications of the mysterious death of the Rev. Hugh Thomas should have raised doubts in the minds of the hierarchy. The circumstantial evidence was suspicious to say the least. It is extremely odd that there was no inquest and one cannot help wondering whether Reilly deliberately removed the risk of having one by persuading Thomas within a few days of his death to travel to the Continent. As it happened they only reached Newhaven, but that was far enough away from gossiping neighbours who might have gone to the police.

In later life Reilly was a skilled operator with poisons and rarely travelled without such sinister aids to espionage. It is almost certain the man who was re-engaged by the Secret Service was a cold-blooded murderer and that his wife was an accomplice.

13

The Origins of M.I.5

Cryptography developed very slowly indeed in the early part of the nineteenth century. When the revolutionary changes came about they eventually received their impetus from two factors, the first being M. Chappe's "lightning telegraph" and the second the rising literary interest in cryptography.

M. Chappe had introduced in France a series of tall semaphore posts, with two arms, along all the main roads leading from Paris to the frontiers of France; these had enabled messages to be passed at far greater speed than by couriers. Intelligence reports to London on this development enabled the Royal Navy to adapt this system for their own use by using hoists of coloured flags at intervals from London to Portsmouth. It was not until the 'fifties that S. F. B. Morse's electric telegraph completed this revolution.

But interest was mainly revived and an impetus given to the stagnant cryptographic departments of all the powers by the attention paid to ciphers by various writers. If this had more effect in Britain than elsewhere, then it can only be attributed to the fact that most of these articles and books were written in the English language. In 1819 there appeared in Rees' *Encyclopaedia* an article on ciphers that attracted much attention in London intelligence circles and then came the influence of Edgar Allan Poe. Admiral Sir Francis Beaufort, who was himself a great influence in developing and modernising cryptography for Naval Intelligence, wrote: "Poe has been of more help to British Intelligence than the whole pack of informers we employ. He has thrown an entirely new light on ciphers both from the point of view of creating new ones and of deciphering those of the enemy. I find him of more use in this respect than Balzac who has even managed to fox his French readers by his ciphers."[1]

All of which may seem somewhat obscure. Balzac had put a cyptogram into his *La Physiologie du Mariage* and been greatly amused that not a single cipher expert in France in his own time had been able to find a solution to it. Beaufort, however, came to the conclusion that the cryptograph was an elaborate fake, carefully compiled with all manner of false clues, a conclusion eventually reached by Commandant Bazeries but Beaufort warned that such a technique needed to be guarded against as its use could waste the time of deciphering departments indefinitely.

Cryptography had a fascination for Poe and he proceeded to make a thorough study of the history of this subject. On the strength of his study he wrote an article in a Philadelphia weekly magazine in 1840 stating that there was no such thing as an unsolvable cipher and offering to solve any cipher message sent to him. He received about a hundred ciphers and solved all but one and that one he denounced as a fake intended to deceive him. One of the messages sent to him was from a young naval officer, Lieutenant R. P. Cator, who had devised a system of his own. But Cator submitted his cipher not under his own name but through an intermediary. This cipher message was published in an article by Poe in *Graham's Magazine*, 1840. Poe commented that it was an extremely difficult cryptogram, requiring a great deal of time to solve and possessing many unique features. What impressed Poe was that anybody who actually had possession of the key to this cipher would have had almost as much difficulty in making out the meaning as he did. This was because the text of the message was overloaded with unusual words.

Lieutenant Cator paid attention to Poe's findings. While encouraged by the tribute Poe had paid to his cipher-making, he was even more impressed by Poe's criticisms. Cator was after all only an amateur in cryptography. He had had no training in ciphers other than the basic instruction given to most young officers and there was then no Intelligence section at the Admiralty. Poe had succeeded in proving to him that what he thought was an original trick—the attempt to deceive decipherers by use of unusual words—was a very common practice among amateur cryptographers. So the persevering Cator spent another ten years evolving one which was harder to decipher but quicker to write and read once one had the key. Poe had advised him to study

French ciphers, claiming that the French were more advanced than the British in this respect, and urging him to study the Vigenère method. Blaise de Vigenère had been a cipherer as long ago as the reign of Henri III of France.

So Cator adapted the Vigenère cipher by placing the index letters of the right instead of the left, completely reversing the Frenchman's encipherment process. This may seem a purely academic change in cipher-making, but it marked the beginning of a cryptographical war between the Intelligence services of Britain, France and Germany. Poor Cator does not appear to have been given the credit for his initiative and perseverance. He achieved the rank of captain, but what success came to him was as a seaman, not as a cryptographer. For years his papers on the subject lay in an Admiralty pigeon-hole until in 1887 the Admiralty set up a department for collecting intelligence on foreign navies and defence. Admiral Sir George Tryon appointed a Foreign Intelligence Committee with a naval officer as chairman to assist the Admiralty. The first Director of Naval Intelligence was Admiral Beaumont, who immediately set about re-organising the cipher system. He discovered Cator's work on the subject and compared it with the well-known Vigenère system. The task of developing ciphers, however, was passed to Admiral Sir Francis Beaufort whose attention was attracted by the fact that all modern systems of encipherment as used by the orthodox intelligence services were to some extent based on the principles of Vigenère and that this could mean that in future no cipher secrets would be safe from a potential enemy.

It is true that both the French and Germans were coming to much the same conclusion, but Admiral Beaufort was well ahead of them when he created the Beaufort system which was really a modification of Cator's. Beaufort, in his own words, made the following discovery: "My system has a complement in the Vigenère system, that is to say, in deciphering a message which can be identified as a double substitution of the Vigenère cipher, the whole mode of deciphering can be speeded up by drawing up a table of these complements. Thus, when deciphering, all that needs to be done is to set down the resulting letters and its complement, as either the one or the other will give the right solution."

Various tricks were played by the Secret Services in developing what came to be known as the war of the cryptographers. Reversed or "disordered" cipher alphabets were used to multiply the amount of work which a decipherer had to put in before breaking the message. But it was soon realised that delaying tactics still did not prevent ciphers from being broken.

When the Boer War started somebody in Whitehall recalled that the briefest and most effective cipher message on record had been sent from India by Sir Charles Napier—"*Peccavi*". Translated, it meant "I have sinned"; spoken aloud it gave another meaning: "I have Sindh" and it dawned on the War Office that Sir Charles had captured Sindh. So in the Boer War it was decided that the use of Latin for ciphers would be doubly effective on the grounds that all British officers were grounded in Latin, whereas the Boers in the main were entirely ignorant of the language. But at the best Latin was only a stop-gap as long as the element of surprise was present.

By the end of the nineteenth century the British Secret Service was not so much in the doldrums as frantically trying to catch up with the other powers. At the best it took third, if not fourth place *vis à vis* France, Germany and Russia, and in some respects the Intelligence Service of the United States had begun to make great strides. Ireland and the Irish rebels still bedevilled Whitehall and the best resources of the Secret Service were still concentrated on giving warnings of all plots by Irish rebels against Britain.

Admiral Coustance had taken over from Admiral Beaumont as Director of Naval Intelligence and by this time the Navy had the best Intelligence service in the Armed Forces, while that of the Army was still lagging behind. During the Boer War the Military Intelligence Branch was accused of having failed to assess correctly the numerical strength of the Boers, of being ignorant of their armament and neglecting to fathom the Boers' offensive designs on Natal. These criticisms were not altogether fair: Major-General Ardagh had given warnings of the Boers' intentions, but these had either been ignored or simply not passed on. The improvement in military intelligence which came about towards the end of the Boer War was in great measure due to Ardagh's efforts. What he had to fight was not so much the enemy as the total lack of appreciation by the War Office of what the Intelligence Branch had been doing. Up to the time of the Boer War, maps and reports from the Branch had not been seen in Downing Street, or studied by the Cabinet simply because the War Office merely regarded the Intelligence Branch as—to use Ardagh's own words—"a useful reference library".

Ardagh pressed hard for an overhaul of intelligence and for proper recognition of his department's functions. When intensive mapping needed to be done during the war he did not wait for a Treasury grant but went right ahead with the task. He was also responsible for sending George Aston to undertake secret service work in South Africa, watching German activities during the Boer War. Aston remained with Military Intelligence until 1913 when he was transferred from the War Office to the Admiralty.

The first real attempt in the Army to introduce a system of personal observations by professional Intelligence officers was made by General Sir Henry Wilson when he was commandant of the Staff College at Camberley. Wilson not only gave lessons on how and what to observe but encouraged his own officers to make holiday trips to the Continent for the purpose of espionage. Believing in practising what he preached, Sir Henry went on a cycling tour in Germany and from the information he secured worked out the principles of the Schlieffen Plan.

This was a start in the right direction, though continental armies had long ago trained their officers in the arts of what was euphemistically called "personal observations". But the Boer War quickly put a spotlight on the shortcomings of Intelligence in the British ranks. At the start of that war military intelligence in South Africa was little more than an unorganised trickle of haphazard information. Just how desperately short the intelligence services generally were both in agents and in quantity of information can be surmised from the fact that when Reilly was re-engaged one of his first tasks was to go to Holland, posing as a German, to report on Dutch aid to the Boers.

Gradually, however, the British talent for improvisation began to produce results. Kaffirs and Zulus were engaged by the British to act as spies and ciphers were dispatched by native runners. The experience of officers from India was useful in devising new methods of cryptography, a cipher being compiled in the Hindustani language, spelled out in a Roman script. African spies were taught to smoke pipes and given two each, one containing a secret message hidden underneath the tobacco, with instructions to light up the pipe and burn the message if capture seemed imminent.[3]

The British called upon their experience both in the Far East and the Far West and knowledge of the Red Indians' use of fire and smoke signals was passed on to the African natives so that they could keep the British informed of Boer movements and the numbers of their troops. It soon dawned upon the Army that as far as the Secret Service was concerned nobody had done their homework in South Africa. The entire task of developing an effective Intelligence system developed upon the Army, for neither the Secret Service nor the Colonial Service was able to help.

Two names stand out in the development of a military intelligence system in Southern Africa—Lord Kitchener, who was chief of staff, and General Sir Robert Baden-Powell. Both men were closer in spirit to the tradition of the great nineteenth-century eccentrics than to the changing age in which they were operating, yet the quality of serendipity which each possessed was of the utmost value in the intelligence field. Kitchener had been in the habit of making solitary trips around the Middle East as a young subaltern to train himself for intelligence work. In South Africa he now applied himself to the task of developing projects to strengthen British intelligence. But Kitchener's eccentricity proved his downfall in at least one of these projects. He caused a "Peace Committee" to be organised, comprising among others a sprinkling of dissident Boers. The committee was not intended so much to campaign for peace—that might have boomeranged against the British—as to spread despondency among the Boer ranks and to provide intelligence. The Boers, however, soon realised the true significance of the "Peace Committee" and set out to break it up. On 13 January 1901, they published a despatch which marked the end of Kitchener's ruse: "The agents sent by the Peace Committee of Boer Prisoners in Pretoria were captured by De Wet on the Tenth of January. One of the emissaries, a British subject, was shot. The other ten were flogged."

Baden-Powell was more successful than Kitchener. He was always an embarrassingly eccentric officer with a penchant for dressing up, playing charades and indulging in disguises and practical jokes. Sir Winston Churchill, describing his first meeting with Baden-Powell at Meerut, said he was struck by the quality of a vaudeville show given by an officer of the garrison and a young lady, declaring that the "performance certainly would have held its own on the boards of any of our music halls." That officer was Baden-Powell and in retrospect Churchill thought that the promotion which B-P certainly deserved might have been withheld because of eccentricities such as this—"a senior officer kicking his legs up before a lot of subalterns".[4]

This may have been true when Baden-Powell was passed over for senior command postings, but his eccentricities bore fruit in the intelligence field. Once when he had been asked to obtain details of the guns in the Dalmatian fortress of Cattara, Baden-Powell went there as an entymologist, taking pains to learn entymology and how to handle a butterfly net before he set out. He was quite a skilled artist and prior to his mission he made coloured sketches of butterflies he would be likely to encounter. These he took with him. Into the wings of those sketched butterflies he drew the outlines of the fortifications and details of the armaments. On another occasion he posed as a drunk, and, having soaked his clothes in brandy, staggered off in the direction of a secret German military installation. He was, of course, swiftly discovered and arrested, but, believing him to be hopelessly drunk and incapable to finding out any secrets, the Germans sentries let him go.[5]

In South Africa he was a given a solitary reconnaisance mission into the Drakenberg Mountains to obtain intelligence. It was just the type of work in which B-P revelled. He disguised himself in torn civilian clothing, grew a beard and set off with two horses, one for riding and the other for carrying his rations and blankets. Some nights he slept out under the open sky and his biographer, William Hillcourt, writes: "he used as his excuse for travelling about in this fashion that he was a newspaper correspondent seeking information 'with a view to recommending the country for immigration'. He met a number of Boer farmers on this journey and got on friendly terms with them. . . . While surveying and sketching the territory, B-P discovered that the maps he had brought with him were inaccurate in many respects. He made the necessary corrections as he went along."[6]

Baden-Powell's wiles were of vital importance in the defence of Mafeking. He recruited Zulus for scouting activities and trained them in the use of disguise. He himself, with typical modesty, gave most credit to a Zulu assistant named Jan Grootboom. B-P was convinced that throughout Southern and East Africa the British were fighting not merely the Boers but the Germans. He failed to convince the British Secret Service of this fact and even Military Intelligence was inclined to pooh-pooh the idea. Baden-Powell was certain that the Germans were running their own espionage service in Africa in training for an eventual confrontation with the British. Perhaps they thought this was just another example of this gallant officer's quixotry, but they probably forgot that as far back as 1886 he had risked being arrested as a spy when he posed as a drunk to find out about German armaments at Spandau. He had, in fact, throughout his entire military career, often while on leave, indulged in espionage, not only in Europe but in Algeria, Tunisia, deep into the heart of the Sahara and in Turkey. While snipe-shooting he had watched the manoeuvres of Spahis and Chasseurs d'Afriques, and sent many reports and sketches back to London. In 1891 he had attended the Austrian military manoeuvres as a military correspondent accredited to the *Daily Chronicle*. Always he had his sketch book with him and once when officers saw him painting and wondered what he was up to he showed them a water-colour of the mountains which, by reason of its excellence, dispelled any suspicions and aroused nothing but admiration. But all the time B-P was noting the numbers of troops, their methods of signalling and transport and the guns and supplies they carried. Between 1880 and 1902 Baden-Powell was perhaps the most active freelance spy the British possessed.

The talent among agents was there, but the rigidity of the higher authorities and the politicians' mistrust of secret service work generally prevented the best use being made of much of this information. The Secret Service was far more concerned with the Irish troubles and the possibility of a Chinese rising than with events either in Africa or Germany. Even in those days in intelligence circles France was still regarded as more of a threat than Germany.

Of course Baden-Powell was right. In the first place the Germans from Kaiser Wilhelm downwards had encouraged the Boers to resist and had offered key men in their own intelligence system to teach the Boers espionage. Understandably the Boers had accepted the offers and so the Germans were able to infiltrate and to some extent control and use for their own ends the Boer system of intelligence. Dr. Leyds, the Boer Secret Service chief, brought many Germans into the country, and it is almost certain that he himself was a paid agent of the German Government.

"These men will ultimately be fighting against us in Europe itself," warned Baden-Powell, and nobody perhaps bore out this warning more positively than Frederick Duquesne. This dangerous secret agent spied against Britain three times, in the Boer War and in both World Wars. Duquesne started his spying career as a youth of seventeen. He was supposed to have developed a fanatical hatred of Lord Kitchener, whom he swore to kill. He had a variety of aliases from Fritz Joubert Duquesne to Frederick Fredericks and he was also known under the names of Captain Stoughton of the "West Australia Horse" and Piet Niacoud. During World War I he offered his services to the Germans and was implicated in the sabotage of the British ship *Tennyson*. Arrested in the United States, Duquesne feigned paralysis for seven months before making a dramatic escape. In 1932 a book entitled *The Man Who Killed Kitchener* was published under the name of "Clement Wood": in fact it contained Duquesne's own version of his career. He described how, posing as a Russian liaison officer, he managed to get aboard the cruiser *Hampshire* in 1916 on the eve of Lord Kitchener's departure in that ship for Russia. Kitchener was then War Minister and, because of the famous recruiting poster which bore his picture, the best-known figure in Britain. Duquesne then described how he used an "electric torch" to signal for a German submarine to fire a torpedo at the cruiser. The sequel to this imaginative fantasy was that Kitchener went down with the ship while Duquesne himself, braving the raging seas, kept afloat until he was rescued by the German submarine to return to Germany as a hero.

Certainly the *Hampshire* was sunk off the Orkneys one June

evening in 1916 and Kitchener went down with her. But though there was a great deal of mystery about the whole affair there was more incompetence on the British side than brilliant intelligence on the German side to account for it. In any event the *Hampshire* was destroyed by one or two mines, not by a torpedo. However, impudent and fraudulent as this story undoubtedly was, Duquesne was without doubt a clever and dangerous German agent. Only blundering incompetence by British Military Intelligence saved him from being shot as a spy during the Boer War. Even in the years before World War II American Attorney Harold Kennedy described him as "the master-mind of the German spy ring in the United States". In 1941 he was arrested again in connection with a plot to blow up a big factory in Schenectady with a time-bomb.[7]

But at the turn of the century German spies were still being disregarded with an almost criminal indifference by Britons in high places, both among politicians and Secret Service chiefs and those who, like Baden-Powell, tried to convince the authorities of the new threat to Britain failed lamentably. This was partly due to the fact that for the best part of half a century the Secret Service had been dominated by anti-French personnel who tended on account of this to be pro-German. It was a tendency which unhappily remained even after World War I.

In part this was due to a peculiarly British tendency to sympathise with the underdog and also, more cynically, to a belief that Britain needed to support the less powerful nations to preserve the balance of power. Thus France was regarded as being a power colonising in Africa and the Far East at the expense of Germany, entirely missing the point that France was merely indulging in carving an empire in the undeveloped and to a large extent still unexplored parts of the world, like Britain herself, whereas Germany's intentions, as had been clearly indicated by the Franco-Prussian war of 1870, were to establish a military hegemony in Europe. Similarly in the Far East the "Yellow Peril" in China was regarded as the real threat, while, quite complacently, Britain openly backed "little" Japan and hung back from any alliance with Russia.

It must not be thought that the Secret Service was not obtaining information in these years prior to the First World War. On the contrary Britain was not only acquiring a great deal of intelligence but was at last spending more on Secret Service work than Germany, though probably not as much as France and certainly not as much as Russia. But just as Russia was extravagant in the amount of money she devoted to espionage, so that her spy chiefs had no disciplinary hand to ensure they spent effectively, so Britain was often getting the wrong kind of information from the right places and the right kind from the wrong places. She had neglected Germany and concentrated more on Russia: this was an error at a time when Russia was slowly moving close to Britain and Germany heading for a direct confrontation. On the other hand in the long-term it meant that Britain easily had the best intelligence service of any foreign power inside Russia during World War I and immediately afterwards. Also Britain was lamentably late in organising a spy network in those areas where oil was to be found and thus was singularly ill-prepared for the power battle in the oilfields which began to be waged in the early part of the century. It was Sidney Reilly who first pointed out this defect after his visits to Russia and Persia.

But where Britain lagged behind her rivals most was essentially in the sphere of counter-espionage where in previous centuries she had often been supreme, the sole exception being in the matter of combating the Irish revolutionaries.

Sidney Reilly's next assignment was in the Far East. He went to Port Arthur where he registered a timber firm in the name of Gruenberg and Reilly. Eventually he became a director of the *Compagnie Est-Asiatique*, all the time obtaining plans of Russian defences and details of naval armaments. At this time his wife was drinking heavily and becoming a liability to him in his job, so he sent her back to London. Once again Reilly behaved in an odd and unpredictable manner. He had engaged the services of a commercial adviser and one night he discovered in this man's desk a cipher-code and a half-finished dispatch and he quickly realised that his adviser was a key figure in the Russian counter-espionage service. The manner in which he exploited the situation was typical. He knew that if he was to exploit his discovery, the Russian agent must never guess what had happened, therefore if he was to leave Port Arthur he must have an alibi that would not be suspected. So, always one who believed in combining the business of spying with the pleasure of dalliance, he made love to a woman with whom he had been casually flirting and persuaded her so eloquently that the very next day she eloped with him to Japan, where he received a large sum of money for the information he brought with him.

There is no doubt that even at this time Reilly was playing a very strange game and also working as a double agent. He certainly sold information to the Japs as well as the British. No doubt both benefited equally well and Reilly could, of course, salve his conscience by the fact that an Anglo-Japanese alliance had been concluded in 1902. Yet at this very time that he was supplying information to the Japs he informed his chief in London that he wanted leave of absence because he did not want to be embroiled against Russia in the Russo–Japanese war that was even then imminent, and that he was afraid any information he gave London might be passed to the Japs. Then he disappeared for several months into China, living in a lamaserie in the province of Shen-Si and becoming a Buddhist. This story of a Jewish bastard brought up as a Catholic eventually becoming a Buddhist has a remarkable parallel with the career of Trebitsch Lincoln, whom in some ways Reilly resembled and about whom more later.

Yet despite twice having disappeared on "private business" and without having given any account of his activities, Reilly was still used by the Secret Service. He had not only proved that he was a first-class agent who could deliver intelligence that the average agent could not get, he had also shown that his forecasts of what would happen in various parts of the world were unerringly accurate.

Germany, however, with far less to spend, was developing an effective and economical spy service overseas. Colonel Walther Nicolai, the General Staff Officer in charge of the German Secret Service, confessed after World War I that "it only gradually dawned on the General Staff how defective the Intelligence Service of the Government actually was . . . a very different picture from that which was presented by the Intelligence Service under Bismarck".[8] That may well have been, but the men in Germany who at the turn of the century were organising their Secret Service on a war basis had concentrated their attention on spying against Britain and by doing so had stolen an advantage in the espionage game. The director of this branch of German Intelligence was Gustav Steinhauer, who had previously been a private detective for the famous Pinkerton Agency of America. He described himself as the "Kaiser's Master Spy",[9] but it was not the assessment of his own superiors when war broke out. Steinhauer was probably a moderately good amateur spy-catcher, but he lacked the professionalism which stamps the efficient spy chief, he had little grasp of military matters and, gravest fault of all, cared little for the fate of the spies he employed. Indeed, he took no steps to give them adequate protection.

It was not particularly clever of Steinhauer to have put so many spies into Britain in the early part of the nineteenth century. That he succeeded was due mainly to the laxity of the British authorities and their pig-headed refusal to take allegations of German espionage on their own territory seriously. All that can be said is that the inefficiency and indifference of the British caused both the spies and their master to be careless.

It was incredible that the British were so dilatory in appreciating the threat which German spies posed to the nation, for it was known in official circles that Steinhauer had paid a number of visits to Britain at a time when the Secret Service at least was well aware of his status. But because of the state of the law, argued the politicians responsible for security, nothing could be done about Steinhauer. From time to time warnings were given in the press about the presence of spies in Britain, but people who volunteered information on the subject were liable to be treated as at best nuisances and at worst as obsessed lunatics. For a long time there was a lone voice in Parliament who protested about the lack of action against potential spies—that of Colonel A. R. M. Lockwood—his criticisms were brushed aside by Ministers. Even Lord Haldane, the War Minister in the Liberal Government, told the House of Commons that "officers of all nations, when abroad, look about for useful information. . . . That is a different thing from coming as spies".[10]

Haldane may well have had cause to regret this statement as much as his other indiscretion when he declared that Germany was "my spiritual home" when, after the outbreak of war in

1914, the vicious press campaign which dubbed him as a "pro-German" forced him out of office. The campaign was, of course, grossly unjust to one who was probably the greatest War Minister of the century, a man who was too contemptuous of hypocrisy to pretend that our own as well as potential enemy officers did not seek "information" when abroad, and one who could still pay tribute to German virtues while unostentatiously planning against German aggression. But Haldane, like most other Britons of his era, whether Liberal or Tory, had not yet realised that espionage was a deadly peril.

Oscar Wilde once said that the man who could call a spade a spade should be compelled to use one. But the refusal to call a spy a spy was the real reason for the ostrichism of those controlling Intelligence in these years. Fortunately when the Committee of Imperial Defence was set up in 1902 after the South African War some of the planners began to realise that the Boer War had revealed the poverty of British counter-espionage at the same time that it began to be realised that a European power struggle was becoming inevitable. A sub-committee of that body recommended the establishment of a new intelligence organisation on the military side which would supplement the activities of the Naval Intelligence Department.

The idea was approved, but not with a great deal of enthusiasm. Nobody appeared to set great store in the proposed new department except the originators of the idea. There was no suggestion that it should be a department with any special powers, or that much money should be spent on it. It was as late as 23 August 1909, that the new department was formed, and even then, at a date when Germany was hell-bent on war preparations and had a team of spies inside Britain, the job of organising it was given to a mere captain. This officer was given a small room, which became known as M.O.5 in the War Office, but literally no staff at all. For several months M.O.5, or M.I.5 as it later came to be known, comprised one man who was told to keep his expenses to a minimum.

It was a small and almost laughable step in the right direction, but in one respect it brought immediate results, for the most important brief which was given to M.O.5 was that the new department should co-operate with Scotland Yard. Thus the military were put in touch with the very problems that had been worrying the police for years—how to cope with potential spies. The Yard had a list of suspects and a great deal of information of which the military were blithely ignorant. For the first time the co-operation of police and military became an established fact, a combination which ultimately was to thwart the German espionage machine.

But though the chief of M.O.5 was only a captain he was an experienced officer, widely travelled, a brilliant linguist and one who had a considerable knowledge of the requirements of intelligence in all parts of the world. Captain Vernon Kell, of the South Staffordshire regiment, was no ordinary soldier of limited vision. He came from a cosmopolitan background, for though his father had been in the same regiment as his son, his mother was the daughter of a Polish count with a wide circle of friends throughout Europe and gregarious tastes. Thus young Kell had grown up among continentals and as a boy had learnt French, German, Italian and Polish. He had made full use of his talent for languages while in the army, studying Russian in Russia, Chinese in China and passing his examinations as an interpreter in each language. He had seen service in the Boxer Rebellion in China and had been made Intelligence Officer on General Lorne Campbell's staff in Tientsin. But ill-health had interrupted his military career and in 1904 Kell's prospects for future service must have seemed grim indeed because of recurrent outbreaks of asthma, the effects of dysentry and pains in his back which were so acute that for the rest of his life he could barely sit upright in a chair, though few would have guessed it from his upright carriage when walking.

Kell was made a staff captain in the German section of the War Office in 1902, a post he held until that day four years later when he was officially retired from the Army but given the job of organising M.O.5. Kell himself was in some doubt as to whether to accept the new post, but his wife persuaded him that he would make a success of it. The man who suggested Kell for the job was Colonel James Edmonds, a member of the sub-committee which had recommended the creation of the new department.

"The job will be a secret one," Edmonds told Kell, "and you will have to give up your Army career. As the work will be secret there will be no public recognition of it, but I do assure you it could be a job of vital importance to the country."

Kell had some very clear ideas of his own about the task before him. Probably, due to the fact that he had been in the German section of the War Office and had worked on the secretariat of the Committee of Imperial Defence, he had had an opportunity of realising the extent of the German menace. At least he was one of the few, even among serving officers, who regarded war with Germany as inevitable. In 1908 he had paid a visit to Germany and been depressed by what he heard and saw.

Yet, as is often the case with all new departments in the Services, M.O.5 was treated as a veritable Cinderella of the War Office. A lesser man than Kell might have lost heart in the first six months of his job. He was told to keep his expenses down to a minimum and when he asked for a clerk there were immediate protests. Eventually, however, he was given one assistant and gradually as he produced a mass of impressive and disturbing reports much greater attention was paid to his suggestions. He soon proved to General Ewart, the head of Military Intelligence, that Britain urgently needed a well organised counter-espionage unit.

Kell's greatest initial success was in winning the co-operation of the police and of working effectively with Scotland Yard. He asked the Yard to provide him with regular information on all suspected spies in Britain and with the help of Superintendent Patrick Quinn learned all about the mysterious underworld of London. Realising that spies were spread over the whole of Britain he travelled frequently to all parts of the country, investigating reports personally and training himself to be a counter-espionage agent.

He quickly found that the biggest obstacle to spy-catching was the outdated Official Secrets Act. He pointed out to the War Office that in case after case Germans had been found gathering information about ships, factories and harbours, but that nothing could be done to check this because in law the spies were committing no offence. Vigorously he pressed for changes in the law.

Resistance to changes in the Official Secrets Act was, however, much stronger than Kell had expected. It was not merely the defenders of the liberty of the individual who resisted change;

the establishment and even the legislative were just as obstructive. Apart from that there was appalling ostrichism in high places and a pretence by those who should have known better that spying was something abhorrent to all civilised governments. Nothing better illustrated the credulity and obstinacy of this type of mind more than the comments of the Lord Chief Justice, Lord Alverstone, when sentencing one German spy to the mild sentence of eighteen months' imprisonment. He declared that relations between Britain and Germany were "most amicable" and gratuitously and quite unnecessarily added that he was sure nobody would condemn the "practice of which the prisoner had been found guilty more strenuously than the leaders of Germany".

But Kell was undeterred by preliminary failures to persuade the authorities to change their minds and give him the powers he required. The man who described his hobbies and recreations in *Who's Who* as "fishing and croquet" was made of exceptionally tough moral fibre. As one of his colleagues put it, he "could smell a spy like a terrier smells a rat". He thrived on danger and excitement; these ingredients took his mind off his pains. Above all he was flexible and adaptable in his approach to the spy game. He may have been an officer of the old school on the surface, but in his intelligence work he had no prejudices about employing men who belonged to the criminal fringes of society. He used to jest that he was "a master forger without equal in England", and added on one occasion that "only this week I have forged letters in seven languages, including Arabic". In fact he was exaggerating for he employed a team of skilled forgers, some of whom were criminals who carried out their work for him inside cells in Parkhurst Prison.

14

The German Spy Menace: 1902–14

In the years between 1902 and 1910 a number of changes were made in the intelligence world which immensely strengthened the whole field of secret service in Britain. The truth was that the Boer War had shown up the deficiencies of secret service and the need for improvements.

One key appointment was that of George Kynaston Cockerill, an officer who had served with the Royal Warwickshire Regiment in South Africa as D.A.A.G. on the lines of communications. During the operations in Cape Colony he was responsible for the administration of martial law. On returning to Britain he was appointed in 1902 to the newly created Special Section of the Intelligence Division of the War Office and four years later was put in charge of it. In this position he was responsible for various branches of the Secret Service, the study of ciphers and for plans (which when war came were put into operation) for the organisation of cable censorship and the military side of press censorship.

Meanwhile there had been an attempt to reorganise naval intelligence which had begun to lag behind the military efforts and lacked an effective centralised co-ordinating body. The armaments race between the great powers forced the Admiralty to take action, for the free-and-easy methods of obtaining information through the reports of naval attachés who visited foreign arsenals and dockyards and secured information largely on a *quid pro quo* basis were now obviously inadequate. The Naval Intelligence Department had consisted of a ridiculously small staff and two equally small rooms. One of its directors had been Captain William Henry Hall. Twenty years afterwards Hall's son, then

Commander William Reginald Hall, began to take an interest in intelligence matters. He was convinced that Germany was building a navy to challenge Britain's supremacy on the seas and, being appointed in command of the cadet training ship, H.M.S. *Cornwall*, he decided to set off on a training cruise visiting German ports. He took with him a lengthy questionnaire on German activities. He was impressed by the fact that German security was much better than our own and he found police guarding all German forts and dockyards. But he employed the tactics of a spy to gain the information he needed. The Duke of Westminster was at Kiel in his large motor-boat and Hall borrowed the boat from him. Dressing up as an engine-room artificer, he went up Kiel Harbour at a speed of forty knots as far as the dockyard, photographing the slips through the conning-turret.[1]

It gives a clear idea of the inadequacy of naval intelligence at that date that Hall discovered that existing Admiralty Charts of this region and intelligence information were hopelessly out of date and that their only knowledge of the Frisian Islands was obtained from *The Riddle of the Sands*, by Erskine Childers. Hall returned to the Admiralty and immediately impressed on his superiors the need for a drastic overhaul of the intelligence system.

As a result of this permission was given in May 1910, for two Marines officers, Captain Trench and Lieutenant Brandon, to make a tour of the German sea-coast defences and especially on the Frisian Islands. Armed with cameras and note-books, Trench and Brandon obtained a good deal of intelligence, but unfortunately both men were caught and arrested. Each was sentenced to four years' imprisonment, though seventeen months before the end of their sentence they were pardoned by the Kaiser to mark King George V's visit to Berlin. Astonishingly, the two Marine officers were shabbily treated on their return. The Admiralty wanted to have nothing to do with the whole business and even refused to meet some of the heavy financial loss which the officers incurred through their purely patriotic venture. It was suggested to the officers that they had been making a pleasure trip while on leave and that whatever happened to them was entirely their own fault. Yet this was a complete distortion of the true position, for Trench and Brandon had been asked to undertake this mission by Captain Regnart, of the N.I.D.

Hall was furious. He wrote to Trench to say: "The only objects I have in view are to see you and B. righted and then to make sure that such things cannot happen again."[2] But it was not until Hall himself became Captain in charge of Naval Intelligence that he was able personally to put matters right and to recompense both men.

Hall's chance to check this kind of nonsense in the intelligence system did not come until 1914, but the Admiralty had in the intervening years paid some attention to the revision of ciphering procedures and, more important, to the interception and interpretation of German ciphers and codes. This came about quite by chance when Admiral Fisher asked Alfred Ewing, then a professor of mechanical engineering at Cambridge, to become Director of Naval Education. Fisher and Ewing immediately struck up a close relationship and it was as a result of this that Ewing developed ideas of his own on the organisation of a code and cipher-breaking department. As a result of Ewing's initiative when war came in 1914 the nucleus of a cipher section was already supplying the Operations Division of the Admiralty with intercepted German naval wireless signals and had discovered the German method of ciphering.

It was about this time that George Aston joined the N.I.D. and he found his work singularly frustrating at first. When in South Africa he had thought that carrier pigeons might be used for intelligence, but he found the Admiralty totally opposed to the idea, despite his warning that "pigeon post" might well be effective when wireless broke down, or in areas not covered by wireless. There existed in the Admiralty, as Hall himself found in the early days, a mentality that actually despised the N.I.D. If any member of the N.I.D. made a boob, the obstructionists would exploit such a situation to the detriment of the department. The chief of the obstructionists were the civilian staff at the Admiralty. The French at this time had discovered a new explosive called *mélinite*. Aston heard that a book bearing this name was being published in France. He ordered a copy and found it was a novel bearing a picture of the heroine, whose name was Melinite, on the cover. The Assistant Secretary at the Admiralty found the book and in scathing terms sent out a departmental memo asking "Does this sort of information come within the scope of the new intelligence officers?"

But it was on the home front where changes were required most and these were held up as much by the politicians and public opinion as anything else. Not even the reports from the Secret Service and from Captain Kell in his one-man office in Whitehall that Gustav Steinhauer was paying frequent visits to the country induced the authorities to take action. Kell, however, had the good sense to realise that the best method of pressing for changes in the law and the increase in his own establishment to make it an effective counter-espionage bureau was more likely to be achieved with the co-operation of the police than without them. For the vital department which must agree to the changes in the laws was the Home Office, under which the police came.

Superintendent Quinn, who proved to be Kell's best ally, reported to M.O.5 about a barber named Karl Gustav Ernst, who had a shop in the Caledonian Road. Nothing was known against Ernst, but Quinn had been quick enough to notice the significance of one small incident. A senior officer in the German naval intelligence service had visited this barber and, so Quinn argued, a man in such a position would be hardly likely to go to the Caledonian Road to have his hair cut. Quinn felt that it might be worth while having the barber watched, but he had insufficient men to spare for this job, so he asked Kell for help. Kell agreed with alacrity and was quickly convinced that this barber was linked in some way with the German intelligence system. With Quinn's support Kell applied to the Home Secretary for permission for Ernst's mail to be intercepted. Much red tape had to be cut before this permission was granted and when Kell eventually saw Sir Alexander King, the Civil Servant in charge of the G.P.O., he was told that two members of the Post Office staff must be present when the mail was examined.

The suspicions of Kell and Quinn were quickly justified. There were letters from a Fräulein Reimers in Potsdam and from Steinhauer himself. It was obvious that the barber was acting as a "post office" for the German espionage machine. Kell was still not powerful enough in his own field of counter-espionage to take full advantage of this discovery. But he found another ally in

Captain Mansfield Cumming, a naval officer who had become head of the Secret Service spy system overseas—Cumming was able to corroborate that Steinhauer was the director of German espionage in England. That much he had ascertained from his own agents on the Continent. What was more he revealed that Steinhauer's real name was Reimers.

Incidentally there has been a mistaken idea that the heads of M.I.5 and M.I.6 always take the code initial by which they are known from the first letter of their names. This was true of Kell, who was referred to on official documents as "K" and it was also true of Cumming, who was referred to as "C". It is also true that Sir H. M. Hozier, whose rôle in intelligence was somewhat vaguely defined, though in an unostentatious way he was extremely efficient, was known as "C". But it was not true of Sir Stewart Menzies, a later head of M.I.6, even though Ian Fleming in his Bond stories referred to the head of M.I.6 as "M". The truth is that the head of M.I.6 is still known as "C" regardless of the first letter of the name of the occupant of the post.

Kell soon realised from the interception of letters that the ramifications of the German spy system extended all over Britain and was especially strong in the sea-ports. But his policy was to compile a detailed dossier on them and to try to find out every German spy who existed on British territory. To attempt to catch one or two would only alert the others and enable them to escape or go to ground. By playing a waiting game Kell was able not only to find out what letters were coming into Britain, but what was going out. Two German agents, Karl Muller and John Hahn, used invisible ink and felt certain they were operating with complete safety. Kell intercepted their letters, read them, turned the ink invisible again and sent them on to Germany. Long after Muller had paid the penalty in the Tower, his letters continued to be sent to the continent: they were, of course, cunningly concocted and forged by men in Kell's own department.[3]

For gradually Kell won his battle to extend M.O.5. He was given the services of Captain Frederick Clark and Captain R. J. Drake and Inspector Melville from Scotland Yard as well as a barrister, Walter Moresby, who handled the legal side of the department's work. In 1910 Lieutenant Siegfried Helm, a German Army officer, was caught sketching the defences at Portsmouth harbour and making notes of guns and fortifications even down to the positions of searchlights. He was prosecuted by the Attorney General himself, then Sir Rufus Isaacs, who, after making out his case against Helm, stressed the fact that the German had already spent four weeks in prison before being released on bail. This was tantamount to suggesting that Helm had already paid sufficient penalty for spying. Also, considerable play was made in the court both by the defence and the prosecution that this was the first time that a foreign officer had been charged under this Act. Not surprisingly, after this submission by the Attorney General. Helm was bound over and discharged.

This was Kell's chance. He made the most strenuous representations that this kind of treatment of a blatant spy, this softness by officialdom was calculated to hold Britain up to ridicule abroad and to encourage the Germans to be even bolder in their efforts to secure our secrets. In this action Kell was strongly supported by Scotland Yard. However, although there is little doubt that people in high places were singularly lax in tackling the problem of German spies, there is evidence that there was rather more behind Sir Rufus Isaacs' remarks than generosity to the prisoner. For, unknown to Kell, pressure had been exercised by Captain Cumming of M.I.6 for Helm to be dealt with leniently. No doubt the plea by M.I.6 was passed on to the Attorney General himself.

The truth was that the Secret Service desperately wanted to let the German intelligence believe that their spying efforts in Britain were not taken seriously. A harsh sentence at this stage might have had the reverse effect; at the best it would alert all spies in Britain to the need for caution, at worst it might even cause Germany to withdraw some of her agents from Britain before the authorities could trap them. For years the Secret Service had underestimated German espionage in their midst; now that they had begun to realise the full danger they made amends by keeping their heads. Until the outdated Official Secrets Act was amended they realised they would only be able to catch blatant and obvious spies such as the crude amateur, Lieutenant Helm. And they wanted to be able to catch the whole pack of spies at the right moment.

Here was another example of Britain being slow to act, but ruthlessly efficient once she had realised the need to act. The following year the Official Secrets Act was amended. It was fortunate that Kell, as head of M.I.5, as it now was, had arrived at more or less the same conclusions as Cumming in M.I.6. By giving German agents in Britain full scope for their intrigues, by not making any moves which might cause suspicion, Kell ensured that when war came he would be able to put his hands on every German agent in the country.

Nevertheless there had to be exceptions to this generally accepted rule that German spies were merely to be watched and left undisturbed. If the authorities had carried this policy to extreme lengths, then even the slow-witted Teutons might have suspected what the British game was. So, in a few other cases of blatant spying, arrests had to be made. Max Schultz, an Ober-Leutnant of the German Hussars, was arrested at Plymouth in August 1911; Heinrich Grosse was tried at Winchester in February 1912. Schultz had asked a Plymouth solicitor, Samuel Hugh Duff, to find correspondents in Britain to work for the German News Agency. The fact that he was offering salaries of £1,000 a year—a large sum for pre-1914 Britain—immediately aroused suspicion, as did the fact that Schultz made it clear that only naval and shipping news was required. The solicitor immediately went to the police. Schultz was sentenced to twenty-one months' imprisonment, a very light sentence. The other agent, Grosse, was caught through the interception of correspondence going to the barber's shop. Mention had been made of a "Hugh Grant" living in the Portsmouth area. Inquiries by M.I.5 revealed "Hugh Grant" was Heinrich Grosse, an officer on the German Naval Reserve. The contents of Grosse's correspondence made it imperative to take action, however much Kell would have preferred to leave Grosse alone for a little longer. For in one of these letters was a mass of information about gunnery range-finding systems used by the British, how the latest submarines were being fitted with guns, which ships had wireless telegraphy and details about dockyard supplies.

As will be seen from the cases of German spying in Britain already mentioned, there was nothing particularly clever about its organisation and some of the agents were downright careless to the point of criminal negligence as far as their country's interests were concerned. The fault seems to have been that they were directed by a man who, far from being the "Kaiser's master-spy", as he called himself in his own biography, was only of the calibre of a small-time agent. A director of spies does not normally play the rôle of an agent as well. But Steinhauer could never resist doing this, though rarely at any risk to himself. This was probably because he had for so many years acted as an agent of the German political police under Von Tausch. One of his more amusing escapades was when he hid under the bed occupied by a Captain Scholtz, of the German Army, and a French spy named Jeanne Durieux, as a result of which Scholtz was sentenced to six years' imprisonment. But Steinhauer's own account of his activities is boastful, inaccurate and often a complete distortion of the facts. He claimed, for example, that he had known that some of the correspondence of his agents in Britain was being opened by the authorities and that one such agent had been warned by "one or two postmen" that his mail was being read by the authorities. If Steinhauer knew this, why did he not warn his agents to go to ground and start a new spy chain in Britain? There was a half-truth in this story of Steinhauer's: at least one postman did warn a German agent, but only because he believed the man was running a secret betting business and that all the authorities were doing was to seek evidence for a prosecution against him on these grounds. And Steinhauer with somewhat typical naiveté had thought this to be the truth.

It was years later that the Secret Service realised that their methods of intercepting mails were not nearly secret enough and that far too many people inside the Post Office knew what was happening. The blame for this can be placed on Sir Alexander King's insistence on following Civil Service procedure in the opening of letters. King had insisted that the man responsible for sorting all the mail for any areas where correspondence was to be tapped must be let into the secret, as well as insisting that another Post Office official from headquarters staff must be present when the letters were opened.

By this time it was quite clear to Kell that the Germans had a spy-network in Britain comprising some Reserve German officers, mostly naval (for the Royal Navy was much more the target for espionage than the Army), waiters, a barber, a baker, at least one doctor and some small tradesmen. This network covered the north of Scotland as far as Scapa Flow, Glasgow, Liverpool, Belfast, Cardiff, Portsmouth, Plymouth, Newcastle and Grimsby as well as London. But while M.I.5 could trace these spies, they could not, of course, arrest them: any arrests had to be made with the co-operation of Scotland Yard. Because of this it was decided that the Secret Service needed a key man in the Yard, one who could mould the recently created Special Branch into an equally effective counter-espionage unit.

The man chosen for this post was the son of an Archbishop of York, Basil Thomson, a remarkable enigmatic character of considerable force and drive who had already had a varied career in many parts of the world. Educated at Eton and Oxford, he had started his career as a farming pupil in Canada. After a year on the prairies he returned to England and was nominated to a cadetship in the Colonial Service in the newly acquired colony of Fiji. He had a natural gift for native languages and for acquiring the confidence and respect of the native peoples and instead of having to wait two years for confirmation like his fellow cadets, he was at the end of three months made a magistrate with extended powers.

Thomson was renowned in later life for his cynicism and this quality revealed itself early on when he said that "my first native friends were cannibals, but I learned very quickly that the warrior who had eaten his man as a quasi-religious act was a far more estimable person than the town-bred, mission-educated native".[4] Then, at the age of twenty-eight he was made Prime Minister to the ninety-two-years-old King of Tonga. When his period of service in Tonga came to an end he became chief-of-staff to Sir William McGregor, Governor of British New Guinea, where he was involved in native wars. He returned to Fiji to find himself Native Commissioner.

Quite possibly Basil Thomson was by this time already marked down by the authorities at home as a prospective recruit for the Secret Service. At any rate he was abruptly summoned home to undertake a most unusual job, that of the education of the sons of the King of Siam. During this period he qualified as a barrister, training which was to prove invaluable later when he went to Scotland Yard. Then the Home Office offered him the post of Deputy Governor in the Prison Service, which shortly afterwards was followed by promotion to Governor of Dartmoor Prison. There had been disturbances in this prison and Thomson's reputation as a riot-breaker was such that he was later sent to put down a mutiny at Wormwood Scrubs.

Already Thomson was being groomed for Secret Service work, for his qualities as a gatherer of intelligence in the Colonial Service had not gone unnoticed in Whitehall. When he was moved into the Home Office he paid particular attention to the Anarchist movement in the East End of London and when in 1913 he was appointed head of the Special branch at Scotland Yard, this was mainly on account of his handling of the problem of foreign immigrants and his detailed knowledge of the habits and methods of habitual criminals.

The years 1907–9 marked the gradual diminishing of the activities of the Anarchists and a corresponding rise in those of the Bolsheviks. For perhaps a period of ten years between 1903 and 1913 there was an overlapping of the activities of both sets of revolutionaries and this often led Scotland Yard to confuse the Anarchists with the Bolsheviks and *vice-versa*. One cannot blame Thomson for this state of affairs, for it was not until 1913 that he had any real opportunity of making a detailed study of the situation in the East End and even then the problem of Russian Anarchists was secondary to that of German spies. But long before this the situation had been further confused by the existence of a third body, financed by the Czarist Government and aimed at discrediting and unmasking the Anarchists. To understand this one must examine the set-up of the Ochrana (Russian Secret Police) and their use of *agent-provocateur* tactics.

Azeff, the Ochrana's mentor, used these tactics in a different manner from any previous Secret Service. Azeff started life as a plotter in the Social Democrat circle. Then, in 1893, he wrote to the Ochrana, offering to sell his comrades' secrets and to spy upon their revolutionary activities. His offer was accepted and he became the supreme *agent-provocateur* of the age. Thus, while posing as a revolutionary, he travelled from Moscow to Karlsruhe and to Zurich in quest of information for the Czarist Government. He even married a young revolutionary. His policy went far beyond mere spying: it can be summed up very simply—to provoke revolutionaries into committing acts of terror and then to crush them.

Azeff, however, carried his play-acting just too far. When the Grand Duke Sergius was bombed, it was Azeff who was acclaimed by the underworld of revolutionary plotters and again when Plehve, the Minister of the Interior, was sent to his death. Azeff was responsible. Before long Azeff was exposed as the brains behind the bombings and terrorist attacks and his exposure recoiled upon the Ochrana when it was realised that one of their own spies had plotted the assassination of the Czar's uncle and of the head of all the police.[5]

These tactics had in the 'nineties and in the early part of the twentieth century been adopted by the Ochrana all over Europe, but more especially in London, the Russian revolutionaries' chief sanctuary. When one considers how such tactics often baffled the Ochrana, or at least led them into ridiculous blunders, it is easy to see how the British Secret Service must have found it difficult to assess who among the Russians was working for one side or the other. An example of this confusion in the police ranks is provided in *Lost London*, by Detective-Sergeant B. Leeson, whose work had taken him among the Anarchists in the East End. Leeson told how in 1908 occurred "the great strike of Jewish dockers in the Whitechapel district, organised by one Perkoff, perhaps Russia's first *agent-provocateur*, to operate in London. It was a strike organised on Chicago racketeer lines, a method to which the Anarchists were very partial."[6]

This statement is full of inaccuracies. Perkoff, as has been shown in a previous chapter, was not the first Anarchist leader to operate in London and certainly not the first *agent-provocateur* sent by the Russians. He was not really an Anarchist—not, at least, in 1908—but a Bolshevik and he belonged to the same revolutionary group as Stalin.

The fact was that the Secret Service at this time was not sufficiently well informed on Russian activities in Britain, much less well informed than they had been in the 'eighties. This, of course, was partly due to the need for concentrating on German espionage and, to a lesser extent, because of the alliance of Britain with France and Russia. It was not so much that the Secret

Service did not possess ample information about these various Russian organisations operating in Britain, but that they had no expert to interpret them properly. It was not until ten years later that Basil Thomson himself was to tackle this problem and assess the information properly.

The perfect example of the counter-espionage technique used by the Russians was provided by the events which led up to the Siege of Sidney Street. A police sergeant, investigating a report of "strange noises" coming from a house in Sidney Street, Houndsditch, called there and was shot dead. When other police surrounded the house and demanded that the occupants surrendered, they were met by a barrage of fire from automatic pistols. Two more police were shot dead and Sir Winston Churchill, then Home Secretary, ordered out the Scots Guards to assist the police. For five hours one thousand police with the Scots Guards, personally supervised by Churchill, kept up a fire on the house, which was eventually burnt down.

The relevant facts of the Sidney Street affair are still confused. It is definitely established that the Sidney Street gang was recruited from a small colony of about twenty Letts from Baltic Russia, but the identity of their leader was never officially confirmed. This mysterious character was known as "Peter the Painter", and long afterwards the Soviet Government alleged that he was Serge Makharov, the Czarist *agent-provocateur,* mentioned in chapter twelve. Mr. Gerald Bullett, who delved into this story at some length, stated that there was a "certain amount of corroborative evidence that Peter the Painter so far from being the leader of the gang, was in fact an agent of the Russian Government, entrusted with the delicate and dangerous task of posing as a comrade of the anti-Tsarist conspirators, and of persuading them to engage in criminal activities such as housebreaking, which would attract to them the attention of the London police and ensure their ultimate deportation to Russia.

"This, I think, is by far the likeliest explanation of the mystery of Peter the Painter. . . . In all probability it was Peter the Painter, *agent-provocateur,* employed by the police of Tsarist Russia, who by elaborate trickery encompassed the defeat and dispersal of the Houndsditch murderers. It was at his instigation, I suggest, that the jewel robbery was planned."[7]

In explanation of this theory it should be stated that the immediate cause of the Sidney Street Siege was the planning of the burglary of a jeweller's shop in Houndsditch. It should perhaps be mentioned that an ex-officer of the old Russian police had stated that the jeweller in question had been entrusted with the safe custody of treasure belonging to the Romanoffs. That this statement is a distortion of the facts is more than likely. The explanation is possibly that this is the sort of story the Czarist agent would invent in order to incite the revolutionaries to burgle the jeweller's premises.

Peter the Painter has been variously identified as Serge Makharov, Jacob Peters, Fritz Svaar, Jacob Vogel and Peter Straume. In 1918 it was reported that Jacob Peters, a man responsible for the execution of hundreds of victims of the Bolsheviks was Peter the Painter. It was then stated in the press that Peters came to England in 1910 and secured employment as a presser with a firm of wholesale second-hand clothes dealers in North London. On December 22 1910, Peters was arrested on suspicion of being concerned with a number of others in the murders of the three policemen in Sidney Street. At the trial the defence suggested that this was a case of mistaken identity and that Peters was mistaken for his cousin, Fritz Svaar, who had lost his life while resisting the police during the siege. Peters was acquitted and remained in Britain until April 1917. On May 1 of that year he was sent to Russia by the Russian Delegate Committee in London. Soon after his arrival in Moscow Peters became a Bolshevik and later achieved notoriety as President of the Committee for Combatting Counter-Revolution and Sabotage. Certainly *Pravda* printed an order by Peters for the arrest of the wives and grown-up children of all officers escaping to the anti-Bolsheviks and another order later forbidding all citizens to walk the streets without passes.

A. T. Vasil'ev, one-time head of the Police Department of the Czarist Ministry of the Interior, stated that when Rasputin's house was searched for documents after his death they found information showing that a man named Nideroest, a member of the Russian Socialist Club in London, had helped "Peter Straume, a Latvian in Whitechapel, to escape to Australia . . . later I was able to confirm from independent sources that this was indisputably correct".[8] The only British police chief to mention Straume was Basil Thomson, who, in *The Story of Scotland Yard*, named Peter the Painter as "Peter Straume, a Latvian living in Whitechapel, who, it is believed, escaped to Australia and died in U.S.A. in 1914".

Detective-Sergeant Leeson, who was badly wounded in the Sidney Street affair, wrote afterwards that Peter the Painter "fled to Australia". Sometime later Leeson went on a convalescent trip to Australia and encountered Peter the Painter in the booking-hall of Sydney's Central Station. Leeson had by that time ceased all connection with the police, though doubtless Peter thought he had come to arrest him. "That was the last of him so far as I was concerned," wrote Leeson, "until I received a letter from his brother saying he had died in America in 1914".[9]

Though the statements of Leeson, Basil Thomson and Vasil'ev all tally, only the last-named asserted that Peter was a Czarist agent. Mr. Gerald Bullett, however, suggested a possible answer to the question of why Peter was not arrested—"that he escaped with the other inmates, *and with the knowledge of the police*, before the firing began". The suggestion here is clearly that the British police connived at the activities of the Czarist counter-espionage in order to trap the real Anarchists.

Again, this is an over-simplification of a complex case. But there is no doubt that the siege of Sidney Street was a menacing problem for the British authorities, involving questions of those strange *quid pro quo* arrangements in the field of Secret Service in which governments undoubtedly engage. It has been suggested that Winston Churchill went to Sidney Street himself because he could not resist the challenge and excitement of such an affray. It is far more likely that he knew all about the ramifications of counter-espionage which this siege involved. What is quite clear is that the Secret Service was caught seriously napping on this occasion, whether from commitments secretly made to the Russian counter-espionage in Britain, or from lack of detailed knowledge of the real motives of the culprits.

15

A Formidable Trio: Mansfield Cumming, Basil Thomson and "Blinker" Hall

UNDER THE direction of Captain Mansfield Cumming M.I.6 began to extend its activities deeper into the heart of Germany. To be more accurate M.I.6 was then known as M.I.1.C. It had grown rapidly since the early days of the century and Cumming had established important key posts for his aides in U.S.A., Russia and Switzerland.

Cumming was a legendary figure, much less in the limelight than Admiral Hall, but nonetheless an almost picturesque character about whom many stories were told in the S.I.S. He was in effect the founder of the modern Secret Intelligence Service as it is constituted today and his organisation methods in M.I.1.C. certainly outlived him—perhaps for too long. He was in his mid-fifties when he took charge of the S.I.S. and still possessed the reputation of being somewhat of a womaniser, a quality he shared with Sidney Reilly. Prior to Cumming's arrival the Secret Service hierarchy had been somewhat stuffy and pompously military in outlook and they very much frowned on agents who philandered unless there was a very sound Service reason for the philandering. Cumming changed all that: he rather liked his agents to be gay dogs.

A curious feature of Secret Service executives is that a majority of them have a passion for speed and for fast cars or, as in the case of T. E. Lawrence, fast motor-bicycles. Cumming was no exception and he often terrified his agents by taking them on hair-raising drives. Speed had brought tragedy to his life. He lost his leg in a car accident when he was driving. Various stories are told of this crash: one is that his son was trapped under the car and, in an attempt to reach him, Cumming cut off his injured leg with a pen knife, but the son died before he could reach him. He had a wooden leg to which he was always drawing attention by striking matches on it, or, rather more alarmingly, by tapping it with a paper-knife while interviewing people.

As a selector of personnel he was not in the same class as Hall and he looked for quite different qualities in his agents. While Hall inclined towards the academician, the stockbroker or the man of letters, Cumming looked for what he called "the cut of the gib of an alert agent". Perhaps his best selection was the very one in which he made a Hall-style choice—that of Sir William Wiseman, his No. 1 man in the United States during World War I. Wiseman, educated at Winchester and Cambridge, was a baronet who had one of the keenest, most analytical minds in the espionage game. Officially Wiseman was head of the British Purchasing Commission in the United States, but in effect he controlled all Cumming's agents in U.S.A. and kept a close watch on all German activities from his office in New York.

Of all the agents he employed Sidney Reilly was the one about whom Cumming had doubts from his very first interview, though he fully admitted that he was a brilliant agent. But as Cumming told a friend, "by the time I joined the S.I.S. Reilly was not only an agent of long standing, he had made himself almost indispensable. You just couldn't sack an agent who was so deeply entrenched as he was. He had guts and genius, but was too much of a politician, the last thing a good agent should be."

Reilly had indeed done brilliant work on the continent. He had even obtained a job as a welder at Krupp's works in Essen, posing as a German under the name of Karl Hahn. In stealing plans of this arms factory Reilly was believed to have killed two watchmen before he made his getaway. It was not the first time Reilly had murdered to carry out Secret Service work, nor was it to be the last. Of all British agents who had what James Bond would have called "a license to kill", Reilly was the one who used it most frequently and in a singularly cold-blooded and professional manner. Whether by poisoning, stabbing, shooting or throttling, he was an adept at murder.

"Reckless Reilly", as his colleagues in the Secret Service called him, next turned up again in Russia, swiftly gaining for himself an extensive social circle in the brittle, feverish, hedonistic St. Petersburg of the pre-war era. He was a prominent member of the most exclusive club in the capital, the Koupetchesky, where he was known as a skilled, if lucky gambler in a nation long notorious for producing the most dedicated gamblers in Europe. Unlike most spies, Reilly never worried about attracting attention; he relied on his extrovert qualities to destroy suspicion and revelled in ostentation as a means of disarming the wary. His flat was more of a museum than a home; it contained many superb examples of Renaissance art and his library of first editions totalled more than three thousand books. He also drove his own sledge, drawn by reindeer, when he went to the Ice Hills for an evening party. Though he maintained various businesses from patent medicines to aircraft and had a wide range of commercial interests, one cannot help thinking that Reilly drew funds from more than one espionage service. Almost certainly he was a double-agent, though it would still seem that the British had by far the best of the deal.

As a result of the St. Petersburg Flying Week that he organised Reilly obtained information on German aircraft developments. By getting the job of sole agent in Russia for the German firm of Blohm and Voss of Hamburg, the naval builders, he managed to see all the blueprints, plans and specifications of the latest developments in German naval construction. All these were passed back to Britain. It was really a fantastic piece of espionage which must have made Germans and British equally suspicious. The Germans did not know he was a British agent, but they were sufficiently suspicious of his name to have him watched day and night, yet he still secured copies of the plans. Meanwhile he was providing Russia with orders from a German firm which he might more easily have obtained for a British firm, and indeed when the British colony in St. Petersburg heard about the British subject who was so vigorously winning orders for the Germans some of them protested to the British Ambassador about him. The S.I.S. must have had anxious moments, too, for Reilly was drawing large commissions from the Germans.

Reilly's reply to this was that he was saving the Secret Service the cost of his salary!

On top of all this Reilly's love life also gave the Secret Service a headache. He had always insisted that his wife Margaret, hysterical alcoholic though she was, need never be a hindrance to his work. This was perfectly true as long as she was living away from him, but one day she turned up in St. Petersburg. He offered her a large sum of money to divorce him. When she refused he must have made some threat to her because she immediately left the country. The S.I.S. feared that a scorned and angered wife, however frightened, might make trouble and upset all their plans for Reilly. However, there was worse to come: Reilly proposed to marry bigamously the divorced wife of a naval officer in the Russian Marine Ministry.

Yet still they retained their brilliant, if erratic rogue of a spy.

The discovery that Karl Gustav Ernst was the "post office" for the German Secret Service in London proved to be the most valuable find that Kell had made as war approached. It is a measure of how sure the British Secret Service was that war was coming that no attempt was made to arrest the suspects until the very last moment. Kell wanted to be in a position to catch every German spy in the land the moment war was declared. He felt certain that premature action would rob his newly formed department of the one advantage they had already gained.

The Germans were not paying much for their spy service. Despite the grandiose offer made to the solicitor in the West country if he could find correspondents to provide naval information—a stupid blunder guaranteed to arouse suspicion—Ernst was only given a pound a month for what was a dangerous and responsible task. German intelligence, not for the last time, completely underestimated the efficiency of British counter-espionage in the risks they ran. For example letters of instructions to spies were sent to Ernst in envelopes which already bore British postage stamps. Ernst's job was to post them as soon as they arrived. Replies came back to him and he forwarded them either direct to Germany, or sometimes to a neutral country. Thus it was an easy task for M.I.5 to open and read this mail and to have a clear picture of all that was going on both as regards incoming and outgoing mail.

Slowly at first, then much more regularly, reports from British citizens reached Kell's desk. It was in this way he was put on the track of Dr. Armgaard Karl Graves, who had posed as a Dutchman. Graves was not a professional spy and he had bluffed his way into working for the German intelligence by claiming, without any justification whatsoever, that he knew how to find his way around the port and harbour areas of Scotland. The amateurish fashion in which he set about spying in Edinburgh soon aroused attention and Kell had him watched. For a long time Kell was not particularly worried about his activities; then he learned that he had made friends with an employee of a Glasgow arms firm. Immediately he gave orders for Graves to be arrested.

In Graves' room were found messages in code from Amsterdam, notes he had made of arms firms in the area, pictures of the Naval base at Rosyth and maps, as well as details of a new gun being manufactured by William Beardmore of Glasgow. Graves was sentenced to eighteen months' imprisonment in 1912, but within four months he was released on specific instructions from Kell and given a free passage to America.

This was one of the few gambles which Kell made which did not quite come off, though a strong case can be made out for it. Kell had learned that Gustav Steinhauer did not put too much trust in Graves and had in fact decided to liquidate him, even going so far as completely to disown him. And Graves, once he was in prison, immediately sought interviews with the British Secret Service, claiming that if he was set free, he would be prepared to work as a double spy. All he asked for was a free passage to the United States and a certain amount of cash.

Kell should have realised that Graves was an incompetent amateur and that, even if he could be trusted, he was unlikely to be any more successful on behalf of the British than he had been for the Germans. The truth was that, though he boasted of a great deal of knowledge of German Intelligence, he knew hardly anything at all about them. But Graves never had any intention of working for the British; he never sent in any reports from America, but spent his time there writing a book entitled *The*

Secrets of the German War Office. It was published less than two months before war broke out and had quite considerable sales.

Unfortunately for Kell newspaper inquiries were made in 1913 as to when Graves was due to come out of prison, and it created an instant sensation when it was realised that he had long since left his cell. Questions were asked in the House of Commons and the then Home Secretary, Mr. McKinnon Wood, parried them with the quite deliberate misinformation that he believed Graves was in a poor state of health.

Dr. Page, the American Ambassador in Britain during World War I, wrote: "One of the most curious discoveries and one that casts an illuminating light on the German simplicity is the confident belief of the German Government that its secret service was in fact secret. The ciphers and codes of other nations might be read, but not the Germans'; its secret methods of communication, like anything else German, were regarded as perfection."[1]

Confident they may have been, but it was not long before their confidence was utterly destroyed by the naval Intelligence Department under Captain Hall. Sir Alfred Ewing, who had been called in to examine batches of German naval signals which had been intercepted, insisted on the immediate setting up of a special team to work on them. Luckily for the Admiralty, Ewing had made a study of ciphers years before as a hobby, but his team had to be trained in the whole complicated procedure of ciphers and de-ciphering. He selected amateurs from various walks of life, concentrating wherever possible on amateur wireless fans. He was fortunate in that two such amateurs came to him of their own accord, Russell Clark, a barrister, and A. J. Alan, later to be a well-known B.B.C. broadcaster and story-writer. They claimed that they had been getting German messages on their receiving sets and that, given better facilities and equipment, they thought they could intercept a good deal more.[2]

Nevertheless the Admiralty had left it dangerously late to implement an organisation which could cope with the interception and deciphering of German signals. Even as late as July, 1914, this organisation was not operational. But again luck played a useful rôle for the British. On 20 August 1914, the Russians were engaging German warships off the Gulf of Finland.

The German light cruiser Magdeburg ran aground during a fog and, as the German captain saw the Russian fleet bearing down on him when the mists cleared, he sent a ship's officer out in a rowing boat to drop the secret naval-code books in deep water, but, in doing this, the officer was swept into the sea. The Russians closed in on the ship, fired a number of broadsides and caused a considerable loss of life. But the Russian captain ordered as many as possible of the German bodies in shallow water to be recovered so that they could be given a proper burial.

In this case a virtuous deed had its own reward. Among the bodies recovered was that of the officer with the lead bindings of code-books in his arms. The Russians reasoned that the code-books could not be far away, so they sent down divers to recover them. Then, surprisingly for a nation so suspicious as the Russians, they passed the books on to the British. The books not only furnished the code then in use, but, with the diligent prying of Ewing's team and a certain amount of paper work, the key to the whole system on which German naval codes were based. They were all dictionary codes, consisting of a series of parallel columns, and from the disordered arrangements of the code-words it was obvious that they were so planned that codes could be changed from time to time.

Ewing's experts noticed that though a code-group might signify different words on different days, or even different hours, the same sequence of code-signs always stood for an alphabetical sequence of words. This was of the utmost significance: it meant that if a single code-sign could be identified with a clear word, after keys had been changed, all the code-signs in that column could be identified by setting down the opposite signs in the column German words in alphabetical order. The result was that, despite the fact that the Germans changed their keys frequently, their radio messages could still be read and understood by the British. It was a discovery of tremendous importance that gave Ewing's team a swift advantage after starting off at such grave disadvantages. More than once the British learned in advance plans for raids by German ships across the North Sea and were easily able to thwart them. From this chance bonus of war-time, considerably enhanced in value by the feverish home-work done by the cipher team in Room 40 at the Admiralty, British battle cruisers won the day at the Battle of the Dogger Bank and even as late as the Battle or Jutland the German Fleet was trapped because their signals had been read correctly.[3]

The Germans learned one major lesson from their activities prior to World War I, but they were not able to benefit from it until the early days of World War II, a quarter of a century later. Then, as will be seen later, they proved they had assimilated the lesson with devastating effect, so much so that in a single day they brought about a revolution in British intelligence methods and a complete overhaul of Secret Service personnel. Prior to 1914 the Germans—and especially their intelligence service—had spoken in terms of *Der Tag*. The day that war was declared was to be the day when victory was compounded. But in their preparations on the naval side they completely overlooked the importance of Scapa Flow, then—and until 1939—the British Navy's proudest and most impregnable citadel. Possibly the German intelligence organisation was deceived by the glib talk of such agents as Dr. Graves. But the fact is that, despite intensive efforts to gain information on the more southerly ports, they neglected those of the north. It was not until July 1914, within a month of the outbreak of war that Gustav Steinhauer realised this omission and, posing as a fisherman, went to Scapa Flow, and, fishing with a knotted line, took soundings of the naval anchorage. This alone suggests that the German Admiralty did not then possess accurate charts of the area and it was not until the end of July that they were aware that the largest of British battleships could anchor safely in Scapa Flow. It was about all the information of any value that they secured at this stage about this vast anchorage, though later German submarines and neutral fishing vessels enabled them to obtain detailed intelligence not only of Scapa Flow, but of the minefields, approaches and swept passages leading to and from it.

By the end of 1913 both the Special Branch at Scotland Yard, under Basil Thomson, and M.I.5 were in a state of readiness for the day war was declared. In one sense these two sections of intelligence were complementary, in another, mainly due to Thomson's ambitious nature, they were rivals. Thomson had already decided to go beyond the normal bounds of counter-espionage and to enroll the services of agents outside the country.

He was determined to have a spy service as well as a counter-espionage organisation so that he should not be too dependent on M.I.5. Kell's department had now been enlarged to include four officers, one barrister, two investigators and seven clerks. This team had built up immense files on spies and suspected spies and they needed more space. So their offices were transferred from the War Office to the basement of the Little Theatre in John Street, off the Strand. This move by M.I.5 was accomplished with the maximum amount of discretion and secrecy, but inevitably in the early stages it brought Kell into touch with people in the theatrical world. One of these was an actor-manager named Maundy Gregory who lost no time in offering his services to Kell. Normally Kell would probably have been suspicious of an inquisitive outsider with a somewhat inauspicious background. But Gregory played on the fact that his father had been a vicar in the Southampton area—Kell was a deeply religious man—and that, having fallen on hard times in the theatre, he had started up a hotel detective agency which could be most useful to British intelligence because of the information he had gleaned on undesirable foreigners in London. Thus it was that Arthur John Peter Michael Maundy Gregory—to give him his full names—came to work for the Secret Service. As soon as he had gained Kell's confidence he made similar overtures to Sir Basil Thomson and became rather closer to Thomson than ever he was to Kell. Later he was to use his influence in the Secret Service as a means to becoming the most rascally tout in the sale of honours ever known in Britain.

Kell had made it the policy of his department that once a spy, or a suspected spy, had been located, a permanent watch was to be kept on him. Thus it was that in 1911 he had learned that a certain Frederick Gould, who was the landlord of the Queen Charlotte public house in Rochester, close to Chatham's naval dockyard, was born Frederick Adolphus Schroeder. Kell had ordered that Gould's mail was to be intercepted and it was found that he was passing information to the continent. Anything of vital importance in these letters was skilfully altered so that a completely erroneous picture was conveyed. Similarly the replies that Gould received were also doctored by British intelligence before the latter read them. It was soon noticed that Gould was paying periodic visits to Ostend and that from there he went on to Cuxhaven where he received payment from the Germans. From this correspondence it became clear that in February 1914, Mrs. Gould was to make a trip to Brussels and deliver some important information to a German agent there. Mrs. Gould was arrested in the train before she left these shores and inside her bag were found plans of anti-submarine defences, a gunnery manual, plans of a cruiser and charts showing minefields. They also found the name and address of the agent she was to contact in Brussels.

Kell dared not play a waiting game any longer. Both the Goulds were taken into custody and sent to trial at the Old Bailey in April 1914. But, curiously, while Gould was sent to prison for six years, to be followed by his deportation, the prosecution against Mrs. Gould was withdrawn and she was discharged. Perhaps Kell felt that if Mrs. Gould was allowed to go free, she might lead his investigators on the track of other spies. It transpired that Gould himself had been working for the German Naval Intelligence Department since 1902 and that they had given him a thousand pounds to become landlord of the public house at Rochester. For twelve years he had been supplying the Germans with information and as a lone agent he had probably been their most effective spy in Britain.

Much of the credit for the efficiency of M.I.5 must go to Winston Churchill during his period of office as Home Secretary before he went to the Admiralty. In his book *The World Crisis* he wrote: "I inquired further about sabotage and espionage and counter-espionage, and I came in touch with officers working very quietly and very earnestly, but in a small way and with small means. I was told about German spies and German agents in the various British ports."[4] Where Churchill helped was in waiving the normal rules after Kell had made an appeal to him. Until 1911 each time Kell's section wanted to intercept mail they had to obtain a special warrant from the Home Secretary. This wasted valuable time and prevented M.I.5 from keeping abreast of all the spy correspondence coming in and going out of the country. Churchill gave permission for all letters sent or received by people who were listed by Kell to be opened on a general warrant.

As a result of this, when war was declared on 4 August 1914, Ernst, the barber who acted as "post office" for the German intelligence, and twenty-one other German spies in Britain were rounded up and by the morning of the fifth were safely under arrest. Even while allowing for the fact that stupidity on the part of the Germans and the bungling amateurism of many of their spies made things easier for M.I.5, the feat of this junior branch of intelligence was considerable. It meant that for the best part of a year Germany was without any effective spy service inside Britain. It took almost as long as that for the Germans to create a new network.

The round-up of German spies caught Berlin completely unawares and enabled the British Expeditionary Force to cross the English Channel without their movements being reported to the enemy. As a result British troops arrived at the front in time to support the French before Von Kluck and Bulow could trap them.

Sensational stories in the press, some of them no doubt engineered by the counter-espionage services, telling of German spies in Britain and alleging that more were coming over in the guise of Belgian refugees, helped to create a spy hysteria in Britain the like of which has never been witnessed since. Reports of spies—most of them wildly inaccurate and without any foundation—flooded in to the police and military and wasted so much time that the Home Office was forced to put out a statement. In this, for the first time, the existence of military and naval counter-espionage units were admitted:

"It was clearly ascertained five or six years ago that the Germans were making great efforts to establish a system of espionage in this country, and in order to trace and thwart these efforts a special intelligence department was established by the Admiralty and the War Office, which has ever since acted in the closest co-operation with the Home Office and Metropolitan Police and the principal provincial police forces.

"In 1911, by the passing of the Official Secrets Act, the law with regard to espionage, which had hitherto been confused and defective, was put on a clear basis, and extended so as to embrace every possible mode of obtaining and conveying to the enemy information which might be useful in war.

"The Special Intelligence Department, supported by all the means which could be placed at its disposal by the Home Secretary, was able in three years from 1911 to 1914 to discover the ramifications of the German secret service in England. In spite of enormous efforts and lavish expenditure of money by the enemy, little valuable information passed into their hands.

"The agents . . . were watched and shadowed without in general taking any hostile action, or allowing them to know their movements were watched. When, however, any actual step was taken to convey plans or documents of importance from this country to Germany, the spy was arrested, and in such case evidence sufficient to secure his conviction was usually found in his possession."

The statement went on to indicate the number of spies who had been arrested on the outbreak of war, adding that "This figure does not cover a large number, upwards of 200, who were noted as under suspicion or to be kept under special observation. The great majority of these were interned at or soon after the declaration of war. . . . Although this action, taken on 4 August, is believed to have broken up the spy organisation which had been established before the war, it is still necessary to take the most rigorous measures to prevent the establishment of any fresh organisation, and to deal with individual spies who might previously have been working in this country, outside the organisation, or who might be sent here under the guise of neutrals after the declaration of war. . . . The Home Office and War Office have now the assistance of the cable censorship and postal censorship, which has been extremely effective in stopping secret communications by cable or letter with the enemy."

It was a long statement, and the latter part of it was intended mainly to soothe public fears and to check spy hysteria. There was also a warning of the harm which purveyors of spy scares could do: "In carrying out their duties the military and police authorities would expect that persons having information of cases of suspected espionage would communicate the grounds of the suspicion to the local military authority or to the local police, who are in direct communication with the Special Intelligence Department, instead of causing unnecessary public alarm, and possibly giving warning to the spies, by public speeches or letters to the Press.

"In cases in which the Director of Public Prosecutions has appealed to the authors of such letters and speeches to supply him with the evidence upon which their statements were founded in order that he might consider the question of prosecuting the offender, no evidence of any value has as yet been forthcoming."

There were some criticisms that the tone of the statement was somewhat too complacent and indeed the mood of the people was such that they continued to bombard the police and their members of Parliament in some instances with stories of suspected spies in Britain. That this is no exaggeration can be gauged from the official figures given by the then Lord Chancellor, Lord Haldane, on the activities of the authorities in investigating espionage cases. "Over 120,000 inquiries have been carried out; enemy aliens numbering 342 who have been suspected as dangerous have been interned. . . . 6,000 house searches have been made."

Official references to a "Special Intelligence Department", of course, are misleading. This was a blanket term used, as far as counter-espionage was concerned, to cover the Special Branch under Basil Thomson, the Naval Intelligence Department under Hall and M.I.5 under Kell. The heads of these three departments worked extremely closely together, very much better than was the case in World War II, though this was probably partly due to the fact that each section was then much smaller.

Of these three organisations the Naval Intelligence Department was by far the most important as war progressed and also the most powerful. One reason for this was Hall's drive, energy, ruthlessness and purposeful character. He was without doubt the ablest intelligence officer which World War I produced. Dr. Walter Page, the astute American Ambassador in London, no mean source of intelligence himself, wrote to President Wilson about Hall on 17 March 1918: "I do study these men here most diligently who have this vast and appalling War Job. There are most uncommon creatures among them—men about whom our great-grandchildren will read in school histories; but, of them all, the most extraordinary is this naval officer—of whom, probably, they'll never hear."[5]

The other reason for N.I.D.'s supremacy was that, unlike M.I.5, it organised spying overseas as well as undertaking counter-espionage. Hall, as Director of the Department, had very positive ideas on this subject: his overall view was that the N.I.D. must have agents in all parts of the world so that the maximum amount of intelligence not only on all fronts and oceans, but in neutral lands and places outside the sphere of the war. For this reason he brought civilians into the N.I.D.

Hall had a theory, which ultimately became almost accepted practice in the Department, that the City of London was a particularly good place in which to seek a personal assistant. He chose Claud Serocold, a stockbroker, to become his number two. Others he recruited were James Randall, a City wine merchant with considerable contacts on the Continent, Thomas Inskip, who later became Lord Caldecote, Algernon Cecil, an historian, and Sir Philip Baker Wilbraham, Fellow of All Souls, Oxford. These were the men who assessed the stream of intelligence flowing into Room 40, as the nerve centre of the N.I.D. was designated, and compiled reports on them. Hall was anything but hidebound in his attitude to the organisation of naval intelligence and he followed up his move to bring civilians into the N.I.D. by allowing women into the Department as well. This aroused some opposition in the Admiralty itself, but Hall refused to listen to the usual clichéd comment that "the Navy was going to the dogs". His rules for would-be female recruits were simple enough: they must be daughters or sisters of serving naval officers, know at least two languages and be able to type. They became known as "Blinker's Beauty Chorus", "Blinker" being Hall's nickname.

Whereas Kell was quiet, modest and very much a patiently tenacious intelligence chief, Hall was forceful, impatient and eager for greater powers because he realised he would never bring the N.I.D. to a pitch of superb efficiency unless he achieved a completely free hand. He was quick to note that Basil Thomson was a man of ambition and in a key position. With Thomson as an ally he believed he could achieve still greater authority. There is no doubt that Hall, even at this stage of the war, saw himself as the real power in British secret service. He persuaded Basil Thomson to let him sit in at the interrogation of all naval prisoners. The combination of Hall and Thomson as a cross-examining team was formidable indeed. Sir Basil Thomson himself described his cross-examining technique as follows: "There was in my room an ugly and uncomfortable armchair with remarkably short legs. In peace time no one ever sat in it, but in war time it was always wheeled up to my table for the suspected spy. We noticed that the people who sat in it at once became communicative, and that whenever a specially awkward question was put they would raise themselves a little by the arms as if to bring their faces up to the level of the questioner. So we tried an experiment. I sat in the chair and my colleague, now an eminent K.C., assuming an expression of ferocious severity, began to question me. I noticed immediately the enormous advantage he had from sitting at a higher level."

Hall's first battle with the authorities was on the subject of censorship of mail and cables. He suspected that the methods being used to carry this out were slow, thus giving rise to suspicions in foreign and neutral countries that letters were being intercepted, and inefficient to the extent that much mail simply escaped unopened. When he visited the sorting office at Mount Pleasant in London his opinion was confirmed. He found piles of letters, awaiting attention by the censors, and many bags which had not been examined at all.

Control of the censorship of mails was in the hands of Brigadier-General George Cockerill and Hall felt that too much attention was being paid to those members of the Cabinet who actually favoured ending all forms of censorship of civilian mail and not enough to the requirements of wartime intelligence. Hall was determined to take a hand in the matter. He saw Cockerill and pressed on him the view that only about five per cent of the outgoing mails were being examined, and insisted that all foreign letters should be opened. Somehow, despite the fact that there had been complaints from neutral countries about lengthy delays in the mail from Britain, Hall got his way—unofficially, at least.

The N.I.D. coped with the extra work involved by opening more of the foreign correspondence and all went well until one of the examining staff foolishly left a departmental headed leaflet in one of the letters. It was a foreign letter addressed to a Member of Parliament who immediately complained to the Home

Secretary, then Reginald McKenna. The Home Secretary carpeted Hall and pointed out somewhat pompously that tampering with the mails without official permission was a serious offence, carrying a sentence of two years' imprisonment. Hall strenuously defended his action and then sought an interview with Asquith, the Prime Minister, who, without much further discussion, gave Hall permission to carry on his work, but with the proviso that in a short time a new department, a War Trade Intelligence Department must be set up to handle this work in collaboration with the Admiralty and the War Office.

Meanwhile much progress had been made in tackling the problem of invisible inks used in letters, a technique which was constantly being improved by the enemy. A chemical laboratory was established for this purpose, as some of these inks called for a special developer. In many cases these inks were used not by spies, but by commercial firms in neutral countries who were sending cargoes destined for Germany. One of the greatest hauls which the N.I.D. made out of the censorship of all foreign mail was information about cargoes intended for Germany in advance of their dispatch. By this means naval ships could be warned to intercept the ships involved. In the opinion of the Ministry responsible for the blockade of Germany the combined efforts of the N.I.D. and the War Trade Intelligence Department did much to *suppress* enemy trade and the information gathered was invaluable in detecting enemy merchandise carried as neutral goods in neutral ships.

After the war Brigadier-General Cockerill was able to tell his staff in a farewell message that they had stopped "enemy remittances to the value of about seventy million sterling and you have completely destroyed the enemy's overseas communications, so far as they were vulnerable.

"Through your essential assistance in preventing speculative transactions in raw materials, controlling prices, and estimating available supplies of vital war commodities, you have saved the country vast sums, amounting in the case of a single transaction to £1,500,000, and at a moderate estimate approximating in the aggregate to £200 millions."[6]

16

Vernon Kell, 'Father' of M.I.5

"During the war," wrote Basil Thomson, "the Germans seldom employed spies who undertook the work from motives of patriotism. They preferred the hireling, and they chose him very badly. These were artists, musicians and even the lower sort of criminal—persons who were quite untrained for gathering information of any practical value. A few of these undertook the work from a love of adventure, but the majority for what they could make out of it. Only a few were Germans; the rest belonged to neutral countries."[1]

If the men who were sent out prior to the war to spy in Britain were of poor calibre, those who followed were worse. When the first batch of spies were rounded up in 1914 it was several days before the German Intelligence realised that their network had been destroyed and then, in a mood of panic, they sent amateur replacements.

One of these was a Naval Reserve lieutenant, Carl Hans Lody, completely inexperienced in espionage, but a volunteer which was a factor that counted in his favour. Lody knew Britain well, having been a tourist guide for the Hamburg—America shipping line. As his English, which was fluent, had an American accent, he was sent to Edinburgh in September 1914, carrying a forged passport in the name of an American tourist, Charles A. Inglis.

Lody's trouble was his enthusiasm for the job. He asked far too many questions, especially about the naval station at Rosyth. He also aroused suspicion by sending a telegram to Adolf Burchard, of Stockholm. This was followed by various letters to the same address. In one of these letters he revealed the poverty of his qualifications for espionage: he repeated a rumour that had for weeks been circulating all over Britain—that a Russian army had landed in Scotland to be transported to France to fight on the Western Front. The only detail which he omitted and which later went down in history as one of the great jokes of the war was that the Russians had "landed with snow on their boots." But what had really made the intelligence service suspicious of him was when he cabled his Stockholm contact to say "hope we beat these damned Germans soon". For an American to waste space in a cable to express such sentiments in a war in which the U.S.A. was not yet involved seemed highly unlikely. It could only have been used by someone who wanted the censorship authorities to think he felt this way, presumably to mislead them.

The story of the Russians arriving in Britain was supposed to have originated in a query which a porter made to some Scottish soldiers when their train halted in a small English station. The porter wanted to know where they came from. The soldiers replied "Ross-shire". The porter thought they said "Russia" and possibly mistook their broad accents for a foreign language.

The porter passed on his story and soon it swept the country and people not only swore they had actually seen the Russians, but that they had long, black beards (it was always assumed that Russians had long, black beards) and that they had even noticed the snow on their boots. In fact the story was deliberately circulated as propaganda by Secret Service agents partly in the hope of misleading the enemy, partly to bolster morale at home.

Lody was shadowed by the Secret Service from Edinburgh to London and on to Liverpool, Holyhead and Dublin. They could afford to concentrate all their attention on him for he was the only German agent in Britain at that time. The fact that Lody was moving about all over the country and not staying in one place was full proof of this. For when M.I.5 made their round-up on 5 August 1914, they caught spies in London, Newcastle, Portsmouth, Sittingbourne, Brighton, Winchester, Southampton, Weymouth, Falmouth, Warwick, Barrow-in-Furness, Padstow and Mountain Ash. Eventually Lody was arrested by the Royal Irish Constabulary on the instructions of Scotland Yard, tried and sentenced to death, being shot at the Tower of London, on 6 November 1916.

Yet despite all his failures and blunders Lody, ironically enough, was taken most seriously by the Germans on the subject of his most foolish report, the arrival of the Russians. On the strength of this news received from Sweden the Germans detached two divisions to guard the Belgian coast against the possible invasion by the Russians. The loss of these two divisions from the main Western Front probably cost the Germans the vital Battle of the Marne. Officially the use the Secret Service made of the porter's story about the Russians has been denied. It was denied for a very good reason: intelligence services have long been aware that the Germans are apt to believe the most fantastic rumours and to admit that this penchant had ever been exploited by the British could have done untold harm.[2]

The counter-espionage teams were confident that the Germans' next effort to infiltrate the country with spies would be to send them in under the cover of Belgian refugees. Consequently Basil Thomson insisted on the most rigorous questioning of all refugees coming into the country. They did not have long to wait. A steady flow of would-be agents came in as refugees, or alien neutrals and in one particularly impudent case as a German offering to help the Allies. On 4 November 1914, the Germans sent in a replacement for Lody. He was Horst von der Goltz, who again had a forged American passport in the name of Bridgman Taylor. He immediately presented himself at the British Foreign Office and offered to supply information about the projected German air raids, the source from which the *Emden* obtained her information about British ships she raided on the high seas, and how Germany got her coal supplies. The Foreign Office sent von der Goltz to Basil Thomson, who found him "ingratiating, cunning and thoroughly unconvincing".[3] Nor was Thomson impressed by the information which the man offered: he knew it was intelligence of a type which could not possibly be obtained by an American. Relentlessly Thomson pressed the cross-examination, brutally rejecting the offer of assistance, and at the end of half an hour he had obtained von der Goltz's confession that he had left valuable papers in a safe deposit in Holland. Thomson obtained the key from him and three days later British intelligence found the papers which were of no importance whatsoever. Thomson was sure the man was a spy, but had insufficient proof to bring a charge; however he was able to charge him with failing to register with the police and for this offence von der Goltz was sentenced to six months' imprisonment and recommended for deportation.

But the von der Goltz story did not end there. The German military and naval attaches to the United States, von Papen and Boy-ed, after having abused their diplomatic immunity by practising spying in the U.S.A. were recalled at the request of the American Government. They were accorded a safe-conduct by the Allies for the Atlantic crossing, but Thomson's training as a barrister made him aware that the safe-conduct applied to their persons and not to their papers. Consequently, when their ship arrived at Falmouth, on 2 January 1916, in spite of von Papen's protests, their papers were examined under orders from Thomson himself. Among those papers was a cheque on the Riggs National Bank, dated 1 September 1914, in favour of "Mr. Bridgman Taylor" for two hundred dollars.

Von der Goltz was then serving his sentence at Reading Prison. He was sent for and again taken before Basil Thomson who this time obtained a complete confession that he was a German who had been a soldier of fortune in the Mexican Army. From the German point of view he was a thoroughly unsatisfactory agent who readily told the British authorities all he had done, even admitting that he had been employed by von Papen on dynamite outrages in the United States, giving the names of all his fellow-agents in America, including that of Hans Tauscher, Krupp's chief agent in the United States. Eventually he became the chief witness against Tauscher at the latter's trial in America. Unfortunately von der Goltz made as poor an impression on the jury as he had on Thomson and as Tauscher's counsel was able to produce damaging evidence about von der Goltz's character. Krupp's agent was acquitted.

But Thomson, while regarding von der Goltz as a most inept spy, stated afterwards that "we must not forget that it was partly owing to von der Goltz's evidence and still more to the behaviour of von Papen himself that America joined the Allies when she did. We owe them both a debt of gratitude that calls for no repayment."[4]

Still the spies came over. There was a young Norwegian,

Alfred Hagn, who had written a novel, painted Futurist pictures and composed *avant-garde* poetry without succeeding in selling his talents to anyone. He went to America to peddle his paintings, but returned penniless in the autumn of 1916. A German painter named Lavendel, who was a friend of his, suggested he might make some money by offering his services to the German intelligence as a spy. Thus he came to Britain as the correspondent of a Norwegian newspaper, an assignment he had obtained only because he asked a ridiculously low fee for it. But not only was Hagn as incompetent as his predecessors, but the Germans seem to have realised this and kept him short of money.

Astonishingly Hagn was caught solely because a fellow-lodger in the Tavistock Square boarding house where he lived thought he was so abnormally quiet that he was probably a spy. In nine cases out of ten such a report would merely have been a wasted errand for the police. But such was the thoroughness of M.I.5 that they decided to make absolutely sure. Unknown to Hagn they searched his bedroom and found that the throat gargle on a shelf was, when tested, an invisible ink. When challenged, Hagn broke down and confessed everything.

So much has been written about the grossly over-romanticised and extremely inefficient spy, Mata Hari, alias Marguerite Zeller, who was caught and shot by the French, that it would be pointless to add much about her in this history. Suffice to say that had she heeded the stern warning meted out to her by both Basil Thomson and Hall, she might have saved her life. She was reported to the Naval Intelligence Department as having been consorting with suspected German agents in Madrid and when the ship in which she was returning to Holland put in at Falmouth early in 1916, Zeller was removed from it and brought to London to be interrogated. Neither Thomson, nor Hall had sufficient proof of her activities to take any action, though they were convinced of her guilt and before she was allowed to travel on to Holland they told her that she would be in trouble if she persisted in consorting with the enemy.[5]

From the end of May to the middle of June 1915, seven spies were caught in Britain. Most of these had been tracked down by Kell and his department and so well had M.I.5 carried out its work that from then until the end of the war Britain was never again seriously troubled with German spies.

One spy who was caught, Courtenay de Rysbach, was a little cleverer than the rest. A British subject with a naturalised Austrian father, a music hall artist who had been in Berlin when war broke out, he was a natural recruit to the German spy service. He obtained various engagements on the music halls and attracted no attention to himself until one day the postal censors opened a letter addressed to Zurich. Inside were the words and music of some songs written out on music manuscript paper and the letter was signed "Jack Cummings, Palace Theatre".

There seemed to be nothing particularly remarkable about the songs; on the other hand there seemed no thoroughly convincing reason for having sent them. It was the lack of planning on de Rysbach's part that proved his undoing. It is not merely the subterfuge which is vital in espionage, it is the whole story that must add up to a convincing reason for such enclosures that must be fool-proof. De Rysbach had not taken the trouble to provide a sound enough cover story. Yet a few years previously the innocent-looking sheets of music would probably have been allowed to go through the post without further query. But both M.I.5, the N.I.D. and the Special Branch had become acutely conscious of the fact that since the outbreak of war the enemy had introduced new techniques in secret inks, which called for a special developer to make them visible and made the work of detection that much harder. Thus it had become essential to conduct much closer examinations of letters for the presence of invisible inks. The Special Branch and the N.I.D. had ordered the setting-up of a research laboratory for the testing of invisible inks and this had enabled more messages to be intercepted. De Rysbach's song sheets were sent to the laboratory. When the song sheets were treated it was found that messages had been written in invisible ink between the bars of the music. Eventually the Austrian was arrested in Glasgow while he was appearing in a trick-cyclist act.

A friend once asked Vernon Kell what he regarded as his best achievement in World War I. Kell was taciturn, shy and extremely modest and, characteristically, with a twinkle in his eye, he pointed to an old-fashioned little two-seater car from which he was almost inseparable. He was such a martyr to pain in his back that he used it for the shortest journeys. "That car was certainly one of them," Kell replied. "The Germans did not know it, but they bought me that a year or so ago. They have maintained it for me ever since and I've found it enormously useful in laying others of their kidney by the heels."[6]

This was almost literally true, for Kell used this car to go on his various spy quests almost in the fashion of an invalid chair. The story of the car started with the arrival of a certain Dutchman who was sent to Britain by the German Intelligence. Messages from the Continent preceded his arrival; these were intercepted and the Dutchman fell straight into Kell's trap almost as soon as he arrived. Although there are always exceptions, the Dutch are, as the intelligence services of most of the great powers will still testify, highly vulnerable as secret agents. They are apt to fail in a crisis and have little stomach for the extreme tests of endurance to which a spy is often put. Consequently they are invariably unreliable. Kell knew this and he played on the susceptibilities of the Dutchman who swiftly proved that he could easily be bought and was almost eagerly prepared to betray the Germans and act for the British.

So M.I.5 used the Dutchman as a double-agent in a purely passive rôle. All he had to do was to acquiesce to his letters being sent on to Germany after they had been duly doctored by M.I.5 but being sufficiently accurate in some details as to lend some credence to their contents, while passing on a considerable amount of misinformation. The Germans were so delighted with these letters that they increased the Dutchman's pay and allowances. These, as they arrived, were confiscated by Kell and, as much as a joke as anything else, Kell used the funds to purchase and maintain his car.

There was one other remarkable man who spied for the Germans against the British, in many respects one of the most curious spies in history. If he was a failure, he never acknowledged defeat; if there was a reason for his failure it was his overconfidence and the extravagance of his ideas. Psychologically, he made a fascinating study and it may well be that the reason why he became a spy against Britain was that the British Secret Service failed to understand how to make use of him.

His full name was Ignatz Timotheus Trebitsch. He was born of devout Jewish parents in Hungary in 1879. His father wanted him to become a Rabbi and he was sent to a Jewish seminary in Hamburg. But young Trebitsch was irked by the fact that the students were not allowed to have female companions. He defied the ban and indulged in a series of secret affairs, finally becoming so fond of one girl that he announced his intention of becoming engaged to her. This marked the beginning of a break with his family, as, when he left the seminary, Trebitsch declined to enter the family business, which was boatbuilding, and went for a trip to England, where he abandoned his Jewish faith and became an Anglican.

Later he went back to Hamburg and was received into the Lutheran faith as a trainee for the ministry. About the end of the nineteenth century Trebitsch went to Canada with a Lutheran mission. There he married a girl of German origin and made a name for himself as a preacher. Yet in 1902 when his mission was taken over by the Anglican Church, he quite calmly reverted to Anglicanism and was consecrated a Deacon by the Bishop of Montreal. Shortly afterwards he sailed for England and in 1902 became a curate at Appledore in Kent.

A year later Trebitsch resigned his curacy, noting in his letter to the vicar that "today is 10th December 1903. Note the date. In seven years I shall be a Member of Parliament."[7] In fact Trebitsch was less than a month out in his forecast; he fulfilled his promise in 1910.

A man who can make a boast such as this, a man who was then not even a British subject, who spoke broken English, who had had no political experience or training, and who actually made good his words, must have had some sound reason for believing that he could achieve what must have seemed to the vicar an impossibility. For that reason one must probe a little deeper into Trebitsch's past. Of the many writers who have sought to plot Trebitsch's career too much attention has been paid to his time spent first as an Anglican, then as a Lutheran and after that as an Anglican again. In fact he travelled quite widely in intervals in this game of religious musical chairs. The probability is that Trebitsch entered the profession of espionage at a very early age and that religion was merely a rather curious cover for a long-term purpose. The young man who rejected the Jewish religion to chase young girls was hardly a natural convert to Anglicanism. Trebitsch had also visited South America and in the Argentine had made friends with a Welsh immigrant named Isaac Roberts who gave him a letter of introduction to Lloyd George. Trebitsch had acted for Roberts as an adviser on oil prospects in the Americas which suggests that at an early age he had his eyes on somewhat larger horizons than the Anglican Church. One of Trebitsch's churchwardens at Appledore in a local newspaper interview told how Lloyd George had more than once come to listen to the Hungarian curate preach and that Trebitsch had told him on one occasion that he was going to London to see Lloyd George, adding that "if the interview was satisfactory, Trebitsch said, he would leave the Church".[8]

Certainly Trebitsch must have had some rather special encouragement, for, when he gave up his curacy, he had no job to go to. He went to Hampton, changed his name by deed poll to Trebitsch Lincoln and was welcomed into the Liberal fold by Lloyd George himself. Then Mr. Seebohm Rowntree, the cocoa manufacturer and a philanthropist of the Society of Friends, engaged Lincoln as a research specialist, sending him all over the Continent to investigate the conditions of the labouring classes. Years afterwards Rowntree explained: "For three and a half years Lincoln was my head investigator in Belgium, France, Germany, Hungary and Switzerland. I chose him because he was an accomplished linguist, being able to speak ten languages, and also because of a personal recommendation from Mr. Lloyd George."

Nothing could have suited Lincoln's purpose better than these trips around the Continent with all expenses paid by Rowntree. Under the guise of a student of the working classes he was able to collect all sorts of information useful to him, not only to further his ambitions for a political career, but to establish business contacts, and, ultimately, for espionage.

When his naturalisation papers were adopted Lincoln was adopted Liberal candidate for Darlington in April 1909. Liberals looked askance at this black-bearded eccentric, but Lincoln attracted to his side the more advanced Radicals as he preached a fiery, left-wing brand of Liberalism. He was elected and soon important Liberals, stockbrokers and company promoters were flocking to the home of the new M.P.

Yet, just as he was on the very threshold to success, Lincoln was suddenly plunged into the depths of failure. The story was that he had been speculating wildly in the oil market and had landed himself in serious financial straits. When the next general election came Lincoln could not afford to fight his seat. Shortly afterwards he was made bankrupt.

There is no doubt at all that Lincoln acted as an adviser to Lloyd George on oil, a subject which always fascinated Ll. G. Not only did he prospect in the Galician oilfields, but in Algeria as well, and it is interesting to note that an official of the *Société d'Etude et Récherche du Pétrole,* who was asked to make a report on a British probe into Algerian oil prospects, stated: "We all knew about Trebitsch Lincoln. Both the *Deuxième Bureau* and private oil interests were watching his activities for we suspected he was a double-agent for Britain and Germany."[9]

Thus it is highly probable that Lincoln had been working for the German intelligence for many years, certainly in the period between 1911 and 1914, possibly while working for Rowntree. It may have been the bond of a German wife who drew him into the German network, or he may have been enticed into espionage when he was at the Jewish seminary in Hamburg. But one point which has never satisfactorily been answered is whether he was a double-agent, or if at one time he intended to throw in his lot with Britain. The French suspected he was working for Britain mainly because of his links with Lloyd George; they were alarmed when Lloyd George himself visited Algeria shortly after Lincoln had been in that country early in 1914. As the official of the *Société d'Etude et Récherche du Pétrole* put it: "We feared that Lincoln, with his known friendship for Lloyd George, was planning to divide up North African oil areas by working out concessions for Britain and Germany."[10] There was a more substantial basis for these French fears than either suspicion of Lincoln or anglophobia, for in 1915 Lloyd George (then Chancellor of the Exchequer) sent the Master of Elibank out to Algeria in quest of concessions. By then the French Government suspected that this was part of a deeply laid Government plot and they flatly refused to co-operate.

Two weeks after war broke out Lincoln applied for a post as censor of Hungarian and Rumanian mails and almost immediately was given the job. But this appointment lasted only a few months. Lincoln claimed he was dismissed because there was prejudice against his foreign origins; the truth was complaints had been made that he wrote indecent comments in the margins of letters addressed to women. That was the official version of the matter: there was also some suspicion that Lincoln might be using his authority as a censor to add code messages of his own to the letters.

Unabashed, possibly believing that boldness was the best policy when financial ruin and unemployment threatened him, Lincoln then offered his services to the Naval Intelligence Department. "When Hall interviewed him," wrote Admiral Sir William James in his biography of Hall, "he [Lincoln] produced some fantastic schemes for tempting the German Fleet into the North Sea, which, he claimed, could be implemented if he crossed to Holland and offered his services to the Germans at Rotterdam."[11]

This scheme of Lincoln's was ingenious, but it involved the loss of a number of British ships before the main task force of the German Fleet could be lured to destruction. Hall declined to have anything to do with the proposal, which involved Lincoln going over to Rotterdam and offering his services to the German Consul while in fact working all the time for the British. The plan was for him to tell the Germans that a small number of ships would be sailing into the North Sea at a certain time. The Germans would then send out a larger force and sink the British. This ruse would be repeated a second time but with a larger British force and then, on the third occasion, instead of a small number of ships the whole British Fleet would be waiting to destroy the Germans.

But, having had a refusal from Hall, Lincoln had almost reached the point of no return. If he played a cautious game and did nothing, he knew he was doomed to poverty and obscurity. So he travelled to Rotterdam on 18 December 1914, visiting Gneist, the German Consul, who was known to be an espionage agent. He returned to London and again went to the Admiralty, but the information which he claimed to have obtained from the Germans was of no value whatsoever. This time Hall called Lincoln's bluff, told him he was not wanted in this country and suggested that if he wished to escape imprisonment he had better leave on the next ship.

This was probably one of the relatively few errors which Hall made during the war. It would have been much less trouble in the long run to have waited until Lincoln could have been charged and locked up. Instead he was put on a ship leaving for the U.S.A. Once arrived in New York he lost no time in approaching the German Consulate. But while the Germans appeared to be doubtful of his value as a spy, they were in no doubt that he could usefully be employed as a journalist. So they encouraged his anti-British sentiments and the articles which he had published in various American newspapers. In these he gave what purported to be startling revelations about British espionage and diplomacy and hints about treachery in high places. He brought out his autobiography in which he hinted that a British Cabinet Minister had both before the war and since been secretly in league with the Germans and pursued a pro-German policy.

These ventures into authorship were probably more damaging to the British cause than actual spying: the innuendoes about unnamed Cabinet Ministers aroused doubts and suspicions on both sides of the Atlantic, for such news travelled fast. In America Lincoln's version of affairs caused considerable harm as the fact that Lincoln had actually been a British Member of Parliament gave more credence to his stories. Belatedly the Secret Service decided that Lincoln must be dealt with. But it was all rather clumsily contrived: it was suddenly "discovered" that years before Lincoln had forged a cheque in Seebohm Rowntree's name for £700 and had committed other frauds. On these grounds the British asked for extradition.

Why this action was not taken in 1914 will remain a mystery, but it is fairly certain that Lincoln had enough evidence to discredit a member of the British Cabinet—probably Lloyd George—and that further disclosures could not be risked. Lincoln, however, went into hiding and evaded his pursuers for some time. It was not until 1916 that Lincoln was shipped back to Britain, charged with fraud and sentenced to three years imprisonment.

But that was far from being the end of the Trebitsch Lincoln story. After leaving prison Lincoln returned to Germany to stir up trouble there. He became involved in the Kepp conspiracy which sought to stage a right-wing revolt and at the same time make a deal with the Soviet Government. When that failed Lincoln re-appeared in the guise of a Buddhist in the Far East and gave the Secret Service a headache for many years to come.

17

The Triumphs of Room 40

"In 1915 the enemy started his propaganda among us," wrote Adolf Hitler in *Mein Kampf*. "From 1916 onwards it became more and more intensive until finally by the beginning of 1918 it had swollen into a regular flood. Gradually the Army learned to think as the enemy wished."

Thus Hitler paid tribute to the British propaganda service in World War I and determined that he would borrow from its ideas when he launched his own drive across Europe. Purists may argue that there is a strict dividing line between Secret Service work and propaganda; in fact it is a very thin and barely definable line and the two must inevitably be closely linked in war-time, at least, if they are to be effective. The distinction that should be made is between straightforward propaganda such as is put out by Governmental information services and propaganda that is planned by the Secret Service to be used as a war weapon.

In World War I the new form of bloodless warfare in the propaganda which emanated from the Government Press Department was an invaluable complementary weapon to naval and military action. History has tended to suggest that our undoubted victory in the propaganda battle was won by the press lords in general who were mobilised to tackle this job and by Lord Northcliffe in particular. In fact Northcliffe only took over the task of propaganda on 1 September 1918, prior to which it had been mainly directed by the Directorate of Special Intelligence.

Both in the military intelligence sections and at the Admiralty skilled use was made of every means of propaganda to mislead the enemy. Admiral Hall, no lover of Northcliffe, was not slow in making use of some of Northcliffe's staff, including his friend,

Tom Marlowe, editor of the *Daily Mail*, and H. W. Wilson, a *Daily Mail* correspondent. Northcliffe himself was mistrusted by the professional intelligence services partly because it was well known that he lusted after political power and partly because his hatred of Germany was so obsessive that it verged on the paranoic, thus in the field of propaganda tending to make him unobjective.

A particularly brilliant example of Hall's skill in manipulating misinformation for the enemy was provided in the special edition of the *Daily Mail* which he caused to be printed on 12 September 1916. The situation on the Western front at that time was critical, with the Allies under such severe pressure that desperate measures were required to try to entice German troops away from the main front. The Secret Service decided that a diversion of some kind was necessary, but, with a grave shortage of man-power, the chances of creating even a minor diversion seemed negligible. Hall gave orders for the spreading of rumours that there was to be an expedition from Britain to land on the north Belgian coast. Using the Emergency Ward Code, which he had given to one of his own agents to sell to the Germans, he sent out signals stating that groups of ships would sail from Dover, Harwich and Tilbury. To clinch the authenticity of the story even further he asked Tom Marlowe to print the special edition of the *Daily Mail,* a mere twenty-four copies, six of which had a particular paragraph blacked out, and these blacked-out copies and some of the others were despatched to Holland. The vital paragraph read as follows:

"From Our Special Correspondent, H. W. Wilson,

"AN EAST COAST BASE, MONDAY.

"Everything here indicates the imminence of great events. I have today completed a tour of the eastern and south-eastern counties, and am able to say that very large forces are concentrated near the coast. In fact, the preparations are on such a scale that the public may expect something much more exhilarating than mere defence of the coast.

"The general commanding the southern group of armies has during the past few days paid numerous visits to the troops. New equipment has been issued to most of the units. There has been grumbling, mingled with a good deal of speculation, all leave having been suddenly stopped.

"I was struck by the number of large flat-bottomed boats lying in certain harbours, but was too discreet to ask any questions. Harwich and Dover are not healthy places today for a correspondent with an inquisitive mind."[1]

The ruse worked perfectly, for the papers found their way into the hands of German agents in Holland and German intelligence was convinced that somehow vital news had leaked into the *Daily Mail*[6] before it had been cleared by the censor. The result was that the Germans moved a large detachment of their forces to the Belgian coast. However, though the ruse had been successful, it had a delayed action result which gave the British something else to worry about. For the military intelligence in France reported back to London that the Germans' move towards the Belgian coast was in preparation to invade Britain. The N.I.D. were certain that this was not so, but, such is the rivalry between intelligence services, they did not inform the War Office of what had happened. The result was that plans were made for the evacuation of towns and villages in South-East England.

It was not surprising that the Americans gradually became to believe that the N.I.D. was the most effective instrument Britain possessed in the winning of the war. Admiral Hall's department had a hand in a wide variety of enterprises which extended to all parts of the globe, but the majority of which were directed to espionage or counter-espionage on the American Continent. While some of these activities were hailed as the work of a genius by pro-Allies factions, the isolationists saw Hall as a *bête noire*, bent only on bringing the United States into the war. The truth was that a considerable part of his work was devoted to this end.

Persuading Anthony Drexel, a well-known American sportsman, to allow his yacht to be used for espionage purposes was among the more original of Hall's feats, but one which brought him into serious conflict with his senior officers at the Admiralty. In this enterprise Hall was helped by Basil Thomson, who found a German-speaking "owner" to take over the vessel, *Sayonara*. The bogus "owner" was a Major Wilfred Howell, who had seen service in the Boer War and had been educated in Austria. Hall himself provided the captain, a young R.N.R. lieutenant named Simon. On Hall's instructions the cover story for *Sayonara*, was that she should be an American yacht engaged on a winter cruise to Bermuda. As soon as the yacht was well out at sea the captain read the Articles of War to the crew and swore the fifty naval ratings who had been taken aboard to secrecy.

Trouble began when the *Sayonara* put in at Irish ports and was suspected of being a German spy ship, despite her American flag. This was because both Howell and Simon, acting under orders, behaved as though they were both pro-German and pro-Irish Nationalist. Irate signals were sent by the Admiral commanding the Irish coast to the Admiralty complaining that the yacht was undoubtedly a spy ship, while reports also poured into the War Office from Ireland wanting to know why the ship had not been seized as those who landed from her during her calls at Irish ports had been openly associating with Sinn Feiners. One Irish peer was so furious that he travelled over to London and sought a personal interview with Hall, alleging that the crew of the *Sayonara* had been putting mines in Waterford harbour. When Hall tried to assure him that there was nothing to worry about, he threatened to raise the matter with Churchill at the Admiralty. To save the situation Hall had to take the peer into his confidence and swear him to secrecy.

One of the *Sayonara*'s chief missions was to link up with the Sinn Feiners, obtain details of their plans and, if possible, to learn where Sir Roger Casement proposed to land when he returned to Ireland from Germany to raise his Irish Legion. But Casement's return was postponed, though the *Sayonara* eventually came back to Portsmouth with valuable information about Irish Nationalist plots.

One of Hall's schemes was so outrageously ambitious that, had it had the backing it deserved, the whole Dardanelles and Gallipoli operation might well have been the turning point of the war and paved the way to victory by 1917. As Alan Moorehead, utilising Turkish sources for his book *Gallipoli*, showed, there is unimpeachable evidence that naval attack, if pressed by the Allies, would have succeeded in this theatre of the war. Yet there was a much more imaginative approach that provided an alternative operation, an alternative that Moorehead did not mention in his book. That alternative to a fully-fledged onslaught taking in Salonika as well as Gallipoli, was a peace offensive directed at detaching Turkey from the Central Powers.

Admiral Hall's policy was to attempt such a move, for he was well aware from his intelligence reports not only of the difficulties of the direct onslaught, but of the lack of enthusiasm which Lord Kitchener had for the Dardanelles project. To describe it as a peace offensive is not so contradictory as at first appears, for Hall with vigour, foresight and ruthlessness planned to use his agents to persuade Turkey to break with Germany and to promote revolution against Enver Pasha and the "Young Turk" party then in power, or at least to persuade the more moderate members of that party to make peace with Britain. Hall was probably far better advised on Turkish matters than the British Foreign Office, whose policy at that time was extremely timorous in the Balkans and Middle East and, what was worse, was seen to be timorous by Britain's enemies. One of these advisers was Gerald Fitzmaurice, an able young diplomat who had been attached to the British Embassy in Constantinople at one time, but who, prior to the war, had been brought home on the grounds that his activities had upset the Germans.

Hall also had the advantage of knowing that Lord Fisher, that unpredictable genius who was First Sea Lord at the time, was at best lukewarm and in his worst moments positively antagonistic to the Dardanelles plan. Yet he alone among soldiers, sailors and politicians had the sound sense to devise a sane alternative.

Hall was also helped in his aim by the receipt of a deciphered telegram which came from Room 40 at the N.I.D. This read:

"H.M. the Kaiser received the report and telegram relating to the Dardanelles. Everything conceivable is being done here to arrange the supply of ammunition. For political reasons it is necessary to maintain a confident tone in Turkey. H.M. the Kaiser requests you to use your influence in this direction. The sending of a German or Austrian submarine is being seriously considered."

This indicated quite clearly that the Turks were short of ammunition and Hall, knowing Fisher's doubts, reported the matter to the First Sea Lord. Meanwhile, acting on his own initiative and without telling the Cabinet, Hall had sent his agents a letter guaranteeing four million pounds for the success of a reconciliation plan between Turkey and Britain. Hall was prepared to pay £500,000 for the complete surrender of the Dardanelles and the removal of all mines. The Chief of Intelligence knew from his agents' reports that there were influential people in Turkey who were in favour of making peace with Britain. Fisher was at first enthusiastic when he realised the scope of Hall's intelligence network inside Turkey and that the Turks were short of ammunition, but he was appalled when he learned that the Director of Naval Intelligence had offered such vast sums of the Turks without first obtaining Government approval. Hall retorted that it was still a very small price to pay for winning over Turkey, shortening the war, or even for a guarantee of a free passage for the British Fleet through the Dardanelles. But Fisher, as unpredictable as ever and already showing signs of mental instability, suddenly changed from being a vehement opponent of the Dardanelles project to becoming its most formidable champion. He determined that the Dardanelles should be forced and ordered Hall to call off his negotiations. Thus, in a single interview, Hall very nearly brought off one of the biggest *coups* of the war, but Fisher ruined everything by stopping the talks at the very moment when they seemed most likely to succeed.

Meanwhile the cipher war was being waged as silently but as assiduously by all the powers involved as was the war on the Western Front. As soon as one side discovered the ciphers and codes of the other so each fed false information to the other. It was just such a move as this which, in part at least, led to the sinking of the cruiser *Hampshire*, with Lord Kitchener aboard, in June 1916.

The Germans, as well as the British, broke down codes and ciphers often enough to obtain accurate intelligence of what went on across the German Ocean, and Room 40, well aware of this, made every possible effort to mislead the Germans. In the Marine Section of Colonel Nicolai's Secret Service listening post at Neumunster in the spring of 1916 a Norwegian named Lange was employed in the small deciphering staff. He had originally been recruited because of his experience as a wireless operator and his knowledge of British shipping routes. He had also shown an exceptional talent at deciphering. On May 26 1916, only a few days before the Battle of Jutland, Lange made what proved to be the most remarkable *coup* of his career. He picked up a message which seemed to be relatively unimportant, but to Lange it appeared to be unusual. It was a message from a British destroyer to the Admiralty saying that a channel west of Orkney had been swept free of mines. Lange thought it was odd that the destroyer should report direct to the Admiralty and not to the shore station. Lange was persistent, if nothing else. He waited to see if the message was repeated. When he heard it being repeated four times in an hour he was convinced there was some urgency about this message. If somebody wanted the Admiralty to know that this area had been swept free of mines it could only be because the information was of vital importance to London. He suspected that the answer was that an important ship was to take this route and that the Admiralty had to be advised that it was clear of mines.[2]

Colonel Nicolai himself took notice of the message. He knew that this particular route was never normally used by shipping; he had heard also of Lord Kitchener's impending visit to Russia. On the strength of all this information instructions went out to the submarine mine-layer U 75, commanded by Ober-Leutnant Kurt Beitzen, to proceed at full speed to the west coast of Orkney to lay mines on the specified route.

It was one of the mines laid by U 75 which sunk the *Hampshire*. Controversy and mystery surrounded that tragedy for many years and it was not until ten years later that, after constant questioning in Parliament, a stubborn and evasive Admiralty in London eventually issued a White Paper on the sinking of the cruiser. It was really a white-washing Paper for it added little to what was already known and hid most of the facts. The most important of these hidden facts was that the Admiralty's right hand did not know what its left hand was doing: in the White Paper the Admiralty insisted that the mines were laid off Marwick by mistake, but they did not explain that the mistake was their responsibility.[3]

The truth was that there had been a lack of co-operation between the Naval Intelligence Division and the Operations Division of the Admiralty. Some senior officers in the Admiralty regarded Room 40 as a cell of amateur cryptographers and refused to allow them to pass on their own comments on signals to Operations. Hall on his side, a ruthless autocrat, had not always seen fit to pass on all he knew to his superiors at the Admiralty. The signal which the Germans had intercepted had emanated from the N.I.D. and was intended to mislead the Germans and cause them to lay mines in this area, where in normal circumstances they would have harmed nobody. But instead of misleading the Germans, naval intelligence had fallen into the very trap they themselves had set. No one had informed the Commander-in-Chief that mines might be laid in this area in consequence of the bait set for the Germans by the wireless message. The message was sent in cipher which the N.I.D. knew the Germans had obtained; it was repeated four times so that they should not miss it.

This is the explanation of the mystery of the *Hampshire*'s sinking; it also explains the Admiralty's reticence when pressed to reveal the secret report on the whole affair and the legend which persisted for many years that the British Secret Service had engineered Lord Kitchener's death.

In the field of intelligence it is easily possible to be too clever: power in the Secret Service may or may not corrupt, but it certainly tends, unless strictly controlled, to overreach itself. Filson Young has this devastating comment to make on this aspect of intelligence in the Navy: "in the little parish magazine of *Secret Intelligence*, that was served out to Commanding Officers afloat the [Admiralty] continued to report the *Audacious* as being with the Second Battle Squadron, although everyone in the fleet knew she had been sunk in November, and the fact had been published in the American press.

"It was a good example of the somewhat childish point of view of Intelligence, in which it seemed to be held a clever thing to tell a lie, in the general hope that someone might be deceived. It was one of the more innocent of the ways in which we tried to imitate the Germans. When they told lies it was with a definite purpose: we told them without any purpose at all."[4]

This may be a sweeping and even an unfair indictment, and the true purpose of intelligence is not always clear to the uninitiated. But the tell-tale message was certainly not particularly clever and, though it may have had a purpose, that purpose was comparatively unimportant and certainly not worth the risks involved.

But if an accident such as this caused the sinking of the *Hamp-*

shire, a rather more fortunate accident enabled the N.I.D. to solve the mystery of the incoherent gibberish signals which had for a long time baffled the cipher-breakers. The German radio station at Nauen followed its evening broadcast of the daily communiqué with signals sent out at such a speed that they provided no clue as to whether they were intended as messages, or if they were merely testing signals. One day in the wardroom of a British warship the officers had played the entire repertoire of the ship's gramophone records. But one of the more inexhaustible of the officers insisted that they should wind up with a record that had been made of what was known as "Nauen's ragtime gibberish". Perhaps he had had a little too much to drink, but, in putting the record on, he forgot to wind up the gramophone, and the result was that instead of the meaningless radio gibberish there came a series of deliberate cipher groups. Luckily a cipher officer was among those present and, impressed by this discovery, he checked with records and found that this was a message from German G.H.Q. to the German general commanding in German East Africa.[5]

The pre-war German Army cipher had been cracked by the British years before, but although the Germans knew all about this, they had been unable to get the new ciphers through to East Africa because of the blockade and other difficulties. For this reason they had adopted the device of sending out messages in the cracked cipher but at very high speed.

The British Secret Service not only showed initiative and enterprise in cracking enemy ciphers in Room 40, but they made many brave attempt to plant spies inside enemy territory in an attempt to obtain ciphers. To do this they had been bold enough to risk employing an Austrian national, a young radio expert named Alexander Szek. Wireless operators were still in short supply in these very early days of the development of radio and the Germans, when they learned of Szek's talent in this field, did not hesitate to employ him, failing completely to ascertain that his mother was English and that he himself was anti-German.

Admiral Hall has, somewhat unfairly, taken the credit for finding and employing Szek. In fact he was only at the receiving end of Szek's work and his own part in the affair is one of the less creditable aspects of Hall's sometimes ferociously ruthless handling of intelligence matters. It was Sidney Reilly who first gave the tip to one of Cumming's agents that Szek had been forced by the Germans to work in the radio station in Brussels, despite the fact that he was actually born in Croydon and probably had one British parent. Cumming passed the news to M.I.5 who swiftly tracked down Szek's family. Kell's plan was to tell the family that Szek was being forced to work for the Germans, that they must not worry about this and that M.I.5 would be glad to pass on any reassuring messages to Szek. This, Kell maintained, would not compromise Szek, would not reveal to his family that the S.I.S. wanted to use him as a spy and merely serve as a warning. But somebody else visited the family and adopted quite different tactics. This visitor obviously came from the N.I.D., for he mentioned the Department by name as well as attempting to blackmail Szek's family. "The Navy need the German cipher," he said, "and it is your son's duty to steal it for us. You must write a letter, telling him this, and one of our agents will see he gets the letter. If you refuse, then we shall have no alternative but to have you locked up in an internment camp."

Faced with this brutal threat the family had little choice but to agree to write the letter. The N.I.D. may have had a rap on the knuckles for being so heavy-handed for they were ordered to hand the letter over to Cumming's department and from that point the affair was handled by M.I.6. Szek was visited by a British agent and told he must obtain the cipher.

This was a formidable task, calling for that rarest and best combination of virtues in a spy—patience and courage. Szek had to work on the job for weeks, never being able to risk copying down more than a few words from the cipher-book each day in those comparatively few moments when he was unobserved, hiding them in tiny slips of paper on his person until he could go to the lavatory where he concealed them in his rectum. Cumming always maintained that because continentals used bidets instead of using lavatory paper they were "less likely to associate arse and paper" and he drilled it into all his agents that the rectum was a safe place for concealment when in Europe. But this particular ruse has long since been discarded as being too well known.

When Szek went home he passed the slips of paper on to the

British contact man. The whole job took months to complete Even then Szek was instructed to remain at his post so that there would be no suspicion on the German side that their ciphers had been broken. Here Hall again intervened with M.I.6 and insisted on the importance of Szek carrying on in his post and, in fact, countermanding the promise made to him that he would be brought safely home when the job was done.

Hall could, of course, claim that events had changed circumstances and that it was vital to preserve the secret of the stolen cipher at all costs, even a broken promise. For it was through this feat that the Secret Service and particularly the N.I.D. were able to manoeuvre the United States away from neutrality and towards their ultimate decision to enter the war on the side of the Allies. For one of the diplomatic messages picked up was the notorious "Zimmermann Telegram", as it came to be known.

Two amateurs were responsible for deciphering the message—one, Nigel de Grey, a publisher, the other, the Rev. W. Montgomery, of the Westminster Presbyterian College, Cambridge. The message read:

"BERLIN TO WASHINGTON. W 158. 16 January 1917.

"Most secret for Your Excellency's personal information and to be handed on to the Imperial Minister in (?) Mexico with . . . by a safe route. We propose to begin on the 1 February unrestricted submarine warfare. In doing this however we shall endeavour to keep America neutral . . . (?) If we should not (? succeed in doing so) we propose to (? Mexico) an alliance upon the following basis:

"(Joint) conduct of war (joint) conclusion of peace. . . . Your Excellency should for the present inform the President secretly (? that we expect) war with the U.S.A. (possibly) (Japan . . .) and at the same time to negotiate between us and Japan. . . . Please tell the President that . . . our submarines . . . will compel England to peace within a few months. Acknowledge receipt.

ZIMMERMANN."

Here was clear proof that not only was Germany intending to launch a campaign of unrestricted warfare against all shipping, Allied and neutral, but to bring Mexico into the war on her side, a move which challenged the policy of a neutralised American continent to which the United States was committed, on which, in fact, her whole foreign policy up to that time was based.

The poser for the N.I.D. was whether to keep this discovery secret and thereby hide the fact that the Germans' diplomatic cipher had been broken, or whether to publicise the Zimmermann telegram on the grounds that as propaganda it would do immense harm to Germany and possibly swing the U.S. over towards the Allies. Naturally Hall could not on his own account take action without referring the matter to the Foreign Office. Hall knew that the Foreign Office, then presided over by the wary philosopher, A. J. Balfour, would delay matters, so surreptitiously he took what action he could. Impatient at waiting for a Foreign Office decision, he gave details of the telegram and others similar to Edward Bell, of the U.S. Embassy in London. When Bell learned that Germany was supposed to be encouraging Mexico to capture the states of Texas and Arizona, his first reaction was one of anger at the impudence of the move, his second one of disbelief. He suspected the telegrams were either a hoax on the part of the Germans, or a concoction of allied intelligence. Hall's task now was one which called for the most skilled gifts of diplomacy; he had to persuade Bell that the messages were genuine and in this he succeeded, but while urging Bell to inform the American Ambassador, he had to beseech him not to pass on the information until the Foreign Office had decided what action to take.

Fortunately Dr. Page, the Ambassador, who was strongly pro-Allies at heart, was in no doubt what the best plan was. He urged that the Foreign Office ought to pass the texts of the telegrams to the President. Again, luckily for Hall, not only had the British obtained the German diplomatic code, but they had found another channel by which German secret messages were passed—via the Swedish Foreign Office cipher telegrams. In short, Hall had obtained abundant evidence in various quarters of the authenticity of the intercepted telegrams.

The American President was informed of the German plans, but he was also urged to accept the subterfuge that, when the news was released, it must be stated that the Americans themselves had intercepted and deciphered the telegrams. Perhaps bearing in mind what every schoolboy learns about George

Washington's traditional respect for the truth, Hall diplomatically suggested that the veracity of such a statement could become a reality if one of his deciphering team went to the American Embassy and showed them how to decipher the messages. Thus was the humbug of diplomatic honour satisfied and a false claim made into a half truth. Publication of the Zimmermann Telegram created a tremendous sensation in America and even though it was denounced as a forgery by the vocally strong, if numerically small pro-German faction in the United States, public opinion was swung over to the Allies at a vital moment of the war. But if the newspapers of the world were taken in by the story that the Americans had stolen the original text of a German diplomatic telegram, the Germans were quite certain that the British were the culprits and immediately ordered an investigation into the whole affair.

When the N.I.D. learned through M.I.6 that the German intelligence had started inquiries at the radio station in Brussels, they realised that it was time for Alexander Szek to be removed. But there seems to have been some controversy between the N.I.D. and the S.I.S. as to whether he should be removed to safety, or merely caused to "disappear", that sinister euphemism which Secret Services use for the wiping out of one of their own agents. Partly because there was disagreement and partly because the affair was undoubtedly somewhat discreditable, the fate of Alexander Szek remains to this day something of a mystery. All that is certain is that he left his job at the Brussels radio station and then disappeared. One story is that he was rescued by a British agent who smuggled him out of Belgium into France and arranged a passage to England for him. But Szek never reached England: that much is certain. French sources, who learned of the ruthless handling of this agent, stated that the British Secret Service pushed him off a ship in mid-channel to prevent his giving away the names of contacts if the Germans should ever trace him. Another British version of his fate is that the German Secret Service captured Szek before he made good his escape.

Neither of these versions is completely accurate. There seems to be no doubt at all that Szek was treated very shabbily by his British task-masters and the only excuse that could be made for their behaviour is that they might have discovered Szek was a double-agent. The truth as revealed to the author by a British agent who took part in the Szek affair is that Szek, knowing that sooner or later he would be trapped by the Germans if he remained in the radio station after the whole cipher was stolen, tried to strike a bargain with the British. He told his contact that he wanted the British to make good their promise to bring him back to England and that he would only deliver the final links in the cipher when he reached London. The S.I.S. seem to have behaved perfectly honourably in the matter. They agreed to the proposal as being perfectly reasonable, which indeed it was, bearing in mind that Szek was an Austrian and not a British subject. They smuggled him safely out of Belgium.

Now the N.I.D.'s story always was, as has been indicated earlier in this chapter, that Szek provided them with the whole cipher before they broke the Zimmermann Telegram. This was intended as a "cover" story for their own ruthlessness. Szek had helped them a tremendous amount, but they still needed the vital links. So they insisted on intervening and taking charge of the agent from M.I.6.

"We certainly kept our part of the bargain," the former S.I.S. agent told the author. "We understood that the N.I.D. were arranging for Szek to be taken to England by a naval ship. But a month later when I returned to Brussels I heard that he had been run down by a car in a side street not far from his lodgings. 'Accidental death' they called it. I am sure he was deliberately killed by another British agent and his body somehow smuggled back into Belgium. And I don't think the Germans were deceived for long. Perhaps it gained the N.I.D. a few more months of freedom from any suspicion that they had stolen the cipher, but no more."

Later Szek's relatives protested that their son had been double-crossed and murdered by the British. Hence the British cover story that the Germans had caught him and killed him. Not a very pleasant chapter in the annals of British intelligence. Hall, brilliant as he was, could be as ruthless in the underworld of intelligence as any Gestapo or Cheka spy chief, as the use he made of the notorious Casement diaries on the eve of Sir Roger Casement's trial fully demonstrated. Those dubious, controversial diaries of Casement's alleged homosexual adventures in South

America were deliberately released to the Americans to damp down the appeals for clemency for Casement. It was a nasty, disreputable propaganda effort by Hall, against all principles of justice, and totally unjustified even in the name of total war. If, as is still asserted by some, the diaries were forged, it is an even greater blot on Hall's name. Certainly the diaries bear all the signs of having been tampered with and of having salacious material inserted into them. One story is that Hall used Maundy Gregory to work on the diaries, Gregory, then working on behalf of M.I.5, being an authority on and a collector of pornographic private letters and diaries.

However, from a strictly historical point of view, what really mattered following the revelations of the Zimmermann Telegram was that President Wilson told Congress that the intrigues of the German Government had served "to convince us at last that that Government entertains no real friendship for us and means to act against our peace and security at its convenience".

A few days later the president signed a Declaration of War and Colonel House, the President's aide, wrote to Hall: "I cannot think of any man who has done more useful service in this war than you, and I salute you."[6]

18

Zaharoff: Agent Extraordinary

IN THIS terrible war of incessant deadlock on the Western Front, where initiative was stifled by the sheer necessity of grimly hanging on to trenches that had been dug, intelligence behind the lines was perhaps one of the few spheres of combat where there was scope for imagination and individualism.

It was, of course, a disciplined individualism: the free-lance spy of the nineteenth century with his flair and eccentricity had almost disappeared. But something of this spirit still occasionally flickered even in the most unlikely places. Sidney Reilly exemplified something of the spirit and he still insisted on having an informal relationship with the Secret Service, never being completely tied to the organisation. At the beginning of the war he had temporarily retired from the Service, moving between Japan and U.S.A. In New York he was soon competing with the Germans in buying arms supplies for the Russians. It was Sir William Wiseman, Cumming's man in New York, who persuaded him to take a more active part in the war and, as a result of the latter's plea, he joined the Royal Canadian Flying Corps, but in fact this was to be a cover for his returning to the Secret Service fold.

He arrived back in London early in 1917 and was then scheduled for a series of missions behind the enemy lines. Reilly was in fact one of the first to volunteer for the dangerous task of carrying out observation work behind the German lines after being parachuted from a plane, despite the fact that he was now in his forties. He made several such missions. Once he was dropped near the town of Mannheim, disguised as a German artisan and armed with papers to show he had been invalided out of the German Army. He spent three weeks in the district, picking up valuable information about the Germans' planned spring offensive of 1918, an offensive which might easily have won the war for the Germans if intelligence from the British side had not enabled counter-measures to be planned in advance. Reilly was picked up by a British plane attached to a bomber squadron which had made a raid on the Mannheim district.

For all these missions Reilly was awarded the Military Cross. It was a modest enough reward for an extraordinary one-man performance. For he not only operated behind the German lines, but deep into the heart of Germany as well. Emboldened by his own success, this reckless, though always astute agent actually joined the German Army as a private on one occasion and within a few days was made an officer. Robin Bruce Lockhart states that Reilly was "also in East Prussia, where, disguised as a German officer, he messed with German officers in Königsberg. With his flawless German and Russian, he could pass equally well as native of either country. He would cross through the German-Russian lines and report back information from both camps."[1]

According to Reilly's own version of his missions he also once met the Kaiser at German G.H.Q. and at a conference there learned the plans for a new submarine attack on Allied shipping, killing a German colonel, stripping him naked and dumping him into a ditch before donning his uniform and attending the conference in his place. Perhaps Reilly added some fictitious touches to this story, but whatever the facts, he undoubtedly obtained the information.

Another example of the initiative sometimes displayed by officers with training in intelligence occurred in February 1918 when the British Sixtieth Division was ordered by General Allenby to attack Jericho. In their briefing there were instructions to capture a small village named Michmash as a preparation for this attack. A brigade was ordered to detach itself from the main force and to storm the steep hill on which this village was sited.

The Brigade major felt that this was a difficult task, made even more difficult because of the scant information about the terrain. But, fortunately for his men, he knew his Bible and he recollected that Michmash was mentioned there. In Samuel I, chapters 13 and 14, he read:

"... the Philistines encamped in Michmash ...

"Now it came to pass upon a day, that Jonathan, the son of Saul, said unto the young man that bare his armour, Come and let us go over to the Philistines' garrison, that is on the other side, But he told not his father ... and the people knew not that Jonathan was gone.

"And between the passages, by which Jonathan sought to go over unto the Philistines' garrison, there was a sharp rock on the one side, and a sharp rock on the other side: and the name of the one was Bozez, and the name of the other Seneh.

"The forefront of the one was situated northward over against Michmash, and the other southward over against Gibeah. And Jonathan said to the young man that bare his armour, Come and let us go over unto the garrison ... it may be that the Lord will work for us: for there is no restraint to the Lord to save by many or by few.

"And that first slaughter which Jonathan and his armour bearer made, was about twenty men, within as it were 'an half acre of land, which a yoke of oxen might plow'."

Thus from his knowledge of the Bible the young major was able to glean vital intelligence about the approaches for Michmash and he was able to convince his brigade commander that they might follow Jonathan's example. What clinched the decision to do this was the discovery by the commander that the pass was exactly where it was described in the Book of Samuel. So the plan for the attack was changed and instead of making a frontal attack with the whole brigade, the commander sent a single company to tackle the Turks and take them by surprise.

The attack was a complete success with the minimum loss of life. This story is told by the young major himself, Vivian Gilbert in his book, *The Romance of the Last Crusade*: "we killed or captured every Turk that night in Michmash, so that after thousands of years, the tactics of Saul and Jonathan were repeated with success by a British force."[2]

The story about Major Gilbert may in a narrow sense be said to have nothing to do with Secret Service work, yet it does point a moral. It shows better than anything else that the whole field of intelligence is often dependent on the specialised knowledge of an individual outside its own ranks. Apart from this it reveals the lack of know-how of a military intelligence unit that had not done its homework on the subject of Michmash as well as the young major.

As these pages have already shown the place of the writer in the British Secret Service has always been rather a special one. Just as Marlowe and Defoe had played an important role in the sixteenth and seventeenth centuries so did such authors as Somerset Maugham, A. E. W. Mason work for the Secret Service in World War I. At first writers were recruited mainly for propaganda work and a special department was set up at Wellington House in London, including in its ranks such authors as Arnold Bennett, Robert Bridges, G. K. Chesteron, Conan Doyle, John Galsworthy, Thomas Hardy, George Trevelyan and Gilbert Murray. A. E. W. Mason, however, clamoured for rather more action than writing propaganda and it was not long before his plea was heeded. Though in his fiftieth year he joined the Manchester Regiment as an infantry officer after which he was called on to work for Admiral Hall.

One suspects that Mason drew on much of his wartime experience in espionage for the plots of three Secret Service short stories that he wrote afterwards. Each one is set in those areas in which Mason actually operated while working for the N.I.D.—Spain, Gibraltar and Morocco. He sailed in a yacht for a cruise around the Spanish and Moroccan ports and obtained much useful information about German ships and submarines which made use of Spanish facilities by surreptitiously re-fuelling in Spanish ports. In the early part of 1915 Lyautey, the French commander in Morocco, was busily engaged in trying to snuff out a rebellion engineered by the Germans among the Moors. Mason went to Morocco to report on the progress of the revolt and the best methods of checking it.

Hall's biographer, Admiral James, states that Mason "sent in a long report of what he found . . . and recommended that the best way to destroy the German influence was to discover and cut off the channel by which their money was flowing into Morocco. This he proceeded to do himself."[3] But Admiral James made no mention of how this was achieved.

There is, however, an amusing story of one of Mason's experiences in Morocco. Mason's biographer, Roger Lancelyn Green, states that Mason narrated in the last chapter of *The Winding Stair* how the centre of the pro-German movement in Morocco was finally destroyed. He writes: "One of the oddest of the many German moves to stir up trouble in Morocco was to spread the information that Bernard Shaw had declared the invasion of Belgium was a legitimate incident of the war and not its cause. Why the word of Shaw should have impressed the Moors it is difficult to see, but Mason was certainly convinced that it was having a bad effect in Morocco."[4]

When Mason returned to Britain he tackled Shaw on the matter. Despite Shaw's cynicism about the war, or about all wars for that matter, he readily agreed to co-operate in giving the lie to the German propaganda. Mason himself wrote about his asking Shaw for "a statement that he wished his own side to win. I received within two hours the most ample statement with not merely the wish that the Allies would win, but a statement that they would win, and a warning to all whom it might concern not to be led into any doubt of that."

This statement was given to Lyautey who, presumably, had it circulated among the Moors.

On a more serious note perhaps Mason's most important mission during his Secret Service work was one about which few details are available. It is referred to in Mason's notes as "Anthrax through Spain".[5] This cryptic reference was to a typically Hun-like operation which the Germans were planning, the spreading of an anthrax epidemic on the Western Front. The Secret Service received information about this plot and learned that two methods were favoured by the Germans: the first to infect shaving brushes which were to be imported for the French army via Spain and South America, the second by injecting anthrax germs into mules. Mason managed to intercept a consignment of the shaving brushes, but there is no indication of what happened to the mules.

Curiously, later in the war, when in Mexico, Mason emulated Sir Robert Baden-Powell's ruse when spying, of posing as a lepidopterist. Whether Sir Robert had borrowed the idea from Conan Doyle's villain, Stapleton, in *The Hound of the Baskervilles*. who also adopted the same tactics, is perhaps doubtful, but Mason admitted afterwards that he had got the idea from the book. In this disguise he discovered that German wireless officers from ships interned in the harbour at Vera Cruz were using the wireless station at Ixtapalapa every night. Mason himself wrote that at that time he had "working under him three Mexicans of worth; the first had been a prominent officer of President Madero's private police, the second had been chief of President Huerta's police, and the third was a young fellow with a great charm of manner who held one of the highest positions as a burglar in Mexico."

With the aid of this team Mason planned and brought off the *coup* of putting the wireless station out of action by destroying the audion lamps on which it was absolutely dependent. These lamps were extremely difficult to obtain.

Thus, as will be seen, Mason's rôle in the Secret Service was both versatile and considerable. But it went much further than this and had far-reaching effects which lasted throughout the Second World War as well. One advantage which Mason possessed was to be an Army officer working for naval intelligence. Thus his links with and influence in Army intelligence were considerable. He was able to persuade Colonel Thoroton, of the Royal Marines, of the importance of preserving a strong peacetime espionage service based on Gibraltar, an organisation which was to reach its zenith in World War II under the personal direction of the Governor, General Mason MacFarlane, and in Tangier where the network was presided over by Colonel W. F. Ellis. The Gibraltar–Tangier Secret Service network was a powerful factor in World War II.

More important than this Mason was entirely responsible for winning over as a spy for the British the head of a powerful smuggling ring operating in Southern Spain. This was Juan March who lived in Majorca and even then had a reputed income of more than £10,000 a year and who lived to become one of the most influential men in Spain and a millionaire. Juan March may have played along with the Fascists in his time, but he always remained a friend of the British Secret Service and was a great admirer of the Royal Navy.

Of the German espionage and sabotage ring in the United States in World War I and of the British success in combatting this much has been written both in Von Papen's Memoirs and in

Von Rintelen's *The Dark Invader*. Again this was largely a Naval victory, for Captain Guy Gaunt (later Admiral Sir Guy Gaunt), the British naval attaché in the U.S.A., himself organised an espionage system in Washington. Gaunt had spies in the Austrian Embassy who kept him well informed of what was going on. Among the men sent out to America by the Germans to organise sabotage in the arms factories was Captain Franz Rintelen von Kleist. He went to America under a forged Swiss passport in the name of Emil V. Gasche. For several months he recruited saboteurs from among the German-Americans, fomented strikes in factories and arranged for incendiary devices to be put in the holds of ships carrying munitions.

Gaunt quickly got on to Von Rintelen's trail and discovered not only the date on which the sabotage schemer was due to sail back to Germany, but also the ship he was in. This news was relayed to London and the ship was intercepted by a British patrol boat off Ramsgate and the indignant "Swiss", Gasche, was taken off for questioning. Despite grilling by Hall, Basil Thomson and Kell, Gasche insisted he was a Swiss and asked them to check with the Swiss Embassy. The Swiss authorities in London confirmed that he was one of their nationals. But M.I.5 had no intention of letting Von Rintelen go so easily. They asked the Swiss to check where Gasche was at that moment. Within a day back came the reply that he was safely in Geneva. Von Rintelen was immediately interned.

The story of this dangerous saboteur did not end there, however. When he returned to Germany after the war he found much that he disliked and was one of the first to see the menace of the rise of the Nazis. In 1926 he came to live in England and in 1931 he renounced German nationality. But he must have been singularly naïve if he thought that the British would forget and forgive quite so quickly. He met his old adversary, Admiral Hall, and the two became close friends. Hall, like one or two others in the N.I.D. in the inter-war years, was somewhat sympathetic towards ex-enemies as distinct from Nazis, and though no longer anything to do with the N.I.D. then, he thought his prestige and sponsorship should clinch Von Rintelen's application for British nationality. But even with so formidable a supporter as Hall the application was turned down and in 1940 Von Rintelen was interned in the Isle of Man. The Secret Service were furious with Hall and used every pressure to block Von Rintelen's application. When he was released from internment he was practically penniless and in 1949 he was found dead in a tube train in London.

By 1918 the ramifications of the intelligence services of Britain were so complex that it was, as often happens in war-time, difficult sometimes to know which section was fighting which war. There is no doubt that some of the more cosmopolitan figures who were used by the Secret Service indulged in power games of their own, if not actually working as double-agents. But in war the double-agent may sometimes be a necessary nuisance; often it is wiser to employ him than to ignore him.

One such man was the enigmatic Sir Basil Zaharoff, who claimed with considerable justification to be the Allies' chief munitions agent. Zaharoff was the living counter-part of Shaw's arms magnate in *Major Barbara*, Undershaft, whose gospel was "money and gunpowder, freedom and power. Command of life and command of death". Zaharoff's exact origins were even more uncertain than those of Sidney Reilly for he took great care to conceal them, sometimes producing forged documents to show he was a Greek born in Mouchliou, at others claiming to be the son of a Polish father and a French mother, while some claimed he was of Russian extraction and born in Odessa. At all events he spent his boyhood in Constantinople where he was a brothel tout and moneylender and later branched out as a munitions salesman, eventually becoming one of the most important agents for the firm of Vickers.

At the turn of the century he was earning vast sums from Vickers in commissions—£34,000 in 1902, £35,000 in 1903, £40,000 in 1904 and £86,000 in 1905. As war approached he had more than doubled his commissions.

Zaharoff had the most unsavoury reputation of not only using bribes to win arms contracts, but of actually inciting and fomenting wars by intrigue, propaganda and threats. He sold Greece one of the first submarines, swore them to secrecy, then informed the Turks and persuaded them to buy two submarines. In the nineties Zaharoff was involved in a no-holds-barred competition with Krupp for arms for Spain. Zaharoff won the day by an adroit oriental bazaar manoeuvre. He bought Krupp arms and then sold them to the Cuban rebels who were giving trouble to Spain. Then he betrayed the rebels to Spaniards in his pay and was able to convince the King of Spain that Krupp was siding with the enemy. In the Russo–Japanese war Zaharoff had made a fortune by selling arms to both sides. That he used bribery to achieve his ends is admitted in *Vickers: A History* by J. D. Scott: "There is evidence that on two occasions in Serbia in 1898, in Russia later, and probably in Turkey, Zaharoff paid secret commissions, or bribes, of sums running from £100 to possibly several thousands of pounds."[6]

From all this it will be seen that when war broke out, Basil Zaharoff was a key figure. Not only did he possess the know-how to obtain munitions and the supplies of vital raw materials for making munitions for the Allies, but he also knew the enemy's sources of munitions and how to forestall Germany in getting supplies. Long before the war his aim had been to infiltrate the armaments firms of Europe, not only those of the *Entente*, but of the Central Powers as well.

It was perhaps not unnatural that the paths of Basil Zaharoff and Sidney Reilly had crossed during the intense competition for arms contracts that was waged in Russia in the years preceding the war. For it was Sidney Reilly who achieved what no man before him had succeeded in doing, to get the better of Zaharoff and win for Blohm and Voss the very contract which Zaharoff hoped to get for Vickers. The story is that Zaharoff then tried to get Reilly to join Vickers as an agent and that Reilly refused. It is said that from that day Zaharoff was determined to have his revenge on Reilly.

Clearly it was the task of the Secret Service to see that so cosmopolitan and shifty a character as Zaharoff remained on the Allies' side and to ensure this they needed to keep him within their own orbit. His activities must have puzzled and worried them for it was never quite clear what subtle, long-term game Zaharoff was playing. Often it seemed as though he saw the war as something to be run in his own interests first and those of the Allies second. Thus the Secret Service needed to spy on Zaharoff just as much as they needed his services to spy for them. In Paris, where he mainly lived, he had his own intelligence headquarters, popularly known as "*Le bureau* Zaharoff", and that was to a limited extent at the disposal of the Allies.

Of course, with Zaharoff, the supremely important thing was to ensure that all the factories and arms plants in all countries in which he had an interest remained intact at the end of the war. He was greatly helped by the British Foreign Office which in 1913–14 considered it part of its duty to ensure that Vickers and Armstrong (later the two firms were combined) secured munitions orders from foreign countries and in this way the power of the armament-makers became paramount. Zaharoff had insisted right up to the end of 1914 that it was important for the Allies that he should maintain underground links with certain enemy firms. No doubt these links proved of assistance to the Secret Service, but information obtained in this manner was often at too high a cost in warfare itself. For example right through the war no offensive action was taken by any of the Allies against blast furnaces and arms factories at Briey and Thionville, both of which were in German hands and were of vital importance to the Germans for mineral supplies.

These arms factories and blast furnaces had been created by the French *Comité des Forges* and Zaharoff was an intermediary between French and German interests in obtaining tacit agreement to an extraordinary arrangement by which, at the outbreak of war, French forces were withdrawn to a distance of twenty-two kilometres behind the frontier, leaving this plant in German hands. Yet on 10 October 1917, the newspaper *Leipzige Neuste Nachrichten* stated: "If in the first days of the war, the French had penetrated to the depth of a dozen kilometres in Lorraine, the war would have ended in six months by the defeat of Germany."

Zaharoff was undoubtedly responsible for one of the more unsavoury of British Secret Service ploys in Greece when the aim was to use agents to discredit the King, Constantine, and to pave the way for a *coup* by Venizelos, the pro-Allies Greek politician. The notorious *Agence Radio*, a propaganda wireless station which Zaharoff financed, was part of this plan and, according to the official report of the Prefect of Police in Athens, the list of Zaharoff's own agents, who were certainly linked up with the

British Secret Service, totalled "160 persons, including twenty-seven convicted thieves, twenty-one professional gamblers, twenty-seven white-slavers, ten smugglers and eight men suspected of murder."

Compton Mackenzie has described something of Secret Service machinations in Greece in World War I in his book, *Athenian Memories*. He was appointed head of the Anglo-French police in Athens, accepting this post with considerable enthusiasm for he had very definite ideas of his own about what British policy should be in the Balkans, and was anxious to see a Greek crusade against both Turks and Germans. Unfortunately for Mackenzie he was blamed for many of the outrages perpetrated by Zaharoff's thugs and some grossly inaccurate and wildly extravagant stories were told about him in Athens. He was even alleged to have made an attempt on King Constantine's life and to have tried to surround the palace with fire so that there should be no possible escape for the inmates.

Reggie Bridgeman, who was then first Secretary at the British Legation, wrote to him on 23 December 1916, to say:

"For the last ten days the Athens newspapers have been writing about a proposed plot to poison King Constantine. . . . The Greek Government do not at all like your capture of the Islands. You have annexed a splendid lot of them!"

And Bridgeman added: "The Minister spoke to the Prime Minister on the subject of the newspaper article on the matter. Before doing so again he will be glad to know whether Tucker ever did employ an agent called N——— and if so what instructions were given to him."[7]

British Ministers in the Balkans and the Middle East spent a good deal of time in World War I either trying to explain or excuse what British secret agents had done, or to make vigorous denials of what they were alleged to have done. In either case they were nearly always inconvenienced by the fact that they never could be quite sure what the Secret Service was doing. When inefficient or easily rattled Ministers and Ambassadors have to tackle these sort of problems they tend to panic and even to be downright mischievous. An abhorrence of espionage has led many British Ministers to betray secret agents. One example occurred in Tangier in World War II when a Frenchman employed by the Vichy Government worked for the British Secret Service. One day he had some vital news to pass on to an undercover colleague in the British Consulate-General. The colleague was out so the Frenchman asked to see the Consul-General and handed to him some important stolen documents. The Consul-General not only angrily dismissed the Frenchman, but reported him to the French Consul-General and returned the incriminating documents. It was quite a scandalous case of pomposity amounting to treachery, yet the Consul-General was afterwards promoted to an Ambassadorship. Needless to say the Frenchman never worked for the British again and he was lucky to be able to escape to Algiers before his own Government took action against him.

Compton Mackenzie's efforts on behalf of Venizelos whom both Zaharoff and the Allies were backing at that time were later to be an obstacle to his promotion elsewhere. On one occasion when Mackenzie returned to see Cumming at his offices in Whitehall Court he was asked what he had done to upset Sir Samuel Hoare, who was then head of a British military mission in Rome. Mackenzie was completely bewildered.

"Well," said Cumming, "he writes that 'If there is any suggestion of appointing Captain Compton Mackenzie to be military control officer in Rome, I feel it is my duty to insist that such an appointment would be unfavourably viewed by the Italian Government on account of his conspicuous activities on behalf of M. Venizelos.' "

To which Mackenzie replied that he should have taken with him the card he used to hang round his neck sometimes in Syria.

"What was that?" asked Cumming.

"A card inscribed: 'Talk freely. I do not want your job.' "

Poor Mackenzie was always in trouble. As he describes himself in *Aegean Memories*, on yet another occasion Cumming, who was then under heavy criticism because of Secret Service intrigues in Greece and the Balkans, told Mackenzie that it had been reported that in Paris at Maxim's he had "talked with the greatest indiscretion of diplomatic secrets". The truth about that smear was that Mackenzie had never been in Maxim's on a visit to Paris and that the alleged indiscreet talk could only possibly refer to a dinner party given in the British Embassy.

This is but one of many instances when the Foreign Office have conducted an unscrupulous and mischievous campaign against certain Secret Service agents.

A fairly accurate summary of the official British attitude to Zaharoff at this time was contained in an article in the French review, *La Lumière*, by Alkin E. Johnson, who wrote: "Somebody belonging to Lloyd George's more intimate circle told me, 'we use Basil Zaharoff as a kind of super-spy in high society and influential circles. At the same time we have him watched by two or three of our best agents.' "

During the war Zaharoff was sent on various secret missions by Lloyd George, and these activities certainly substantiate the claim made by Alkin Johnson as also does the fact that he was knighted by the British after the war. It is almost certain that Zaharoff retained complete freedom of action in any spying he did for the British; he was much too powerful to take orders from anyone, even the head of an intelligence service. Sir Guy Gaunt, the naval attaché in Washington, stated afterwards that Zaharoff sometimes had a British destroyer put at his disposal by Lloyd George when he was travelling on incognito missions: "this procedure was adopted by Zaharoff after the passenger steamer in which he had been travelling was stopped by a German submarine".[8]

Unquestionably Zaharoff's intrigues in Greece, disreputable though they often were, helped the Allies, making Constantine so unpopular with his people that he had to leave the country and Venizelos came to power. Completely undocumented, however, is Zaharoff's own story, told to Rosita Forbes on the strict understanding that it was not to be revealed in his life-time, that, disguised as a Bulgarian Army doctor, he went to Germany during the war on a special mission for Lloyd George. "I paid heavily for that uniform," declared Zaharoff, "and the man who sold it died." When he went to London after his mission he was "greeted by Mr. Lloyd George. They say the information I brought ended the war."[9]

As to what this information might have been, the only clue is contained in a Soviet diplomatic dispatch to their diplomatic representative in Turkey in 1921, marked "secret and confidential", which read: "It must be stressed to the Turks that Zaharoff means war, that his every aim is to see the Greeks installed in Constantinople. He is seeking to undermine Turkey by gaining secret control of Turkish banks. It is now clear that was the real purpose behind Zaharoff's secret mission to Germany in 1918. As agent of the British firm of Vickers and the man who financed the Putiloff arms works, he went to Germany to find out how near we were to extending the revolution to the banks of the Rhine. That information be obtained, and it was because of this that he was able to advise the Allies that Germany could be forced to an armistice in the autumn of 1918, when in fact they did not expect to defeat the Germans before 1919. It was Zaharoff who checked the second phase of the revolution."[10]

All that is clear apart from this is that during his secret visit to Germany Zaharoff sent a message to Herr Krupp without revealing his whereabouts. This was a risky thing to do as Krupp had constantly told the German High Command that the capture of Basil Zaharoff was worth the surrender of a whole Army Division. But Zaharoff's appeal to Krupp was really an appeal to the arms magnate's pocket, warning him that unless an armistice could be arranged, Krupp might find his own factories confiscated by the Bolsheviks. This paved the way to a close friendship between Krupp and Zaharoff after the war. There was, of course, a pay-off in Krupp's favour.

Zaharoff was always regarded with the greatest mistrust and dislike by Admiral Hall and he in his turn was irked by the knowledge that the N.I.D. had their own contacts with some of his closest allies, men like Juan March. When war ended Hall had expected to be invited to attend the Peace Conference, but, on Lloyd George's instructions, he was told not to go to Paris. Nor did Hall's name appear on the honours list. Zaharoff had written to Clemenceau, saying: "You must convince Lloyd George that it would be wholly undesirable for Admiral Hall to go to Versailles."

Before the war Zaharoff had been instrumental in obtaining the lease of the fuse patents for the Big Bertha cannon for the Vickers company. A secret agreement was made that compensation should be paid to Krupp at the rate of one shilling and threepence per fuse. In effect this meant that Britain had to pay

Krupp for every German soldier killed by artillery fire. This money was actually collected and used to finance the secret re-armament of Germany and to prepare the way to World War II. According to the Paris paper, *Crapouillot*, Krupp also received "by way of compensation, a share in the steel and lead works from Vickers and Miers in Spain".

19

Defeat in Ireland: Counter-Attack in Russia

WORLD WAR I ended with a Secret Service that had grown out of all recognition from the pre-war set-up, one which had not only scored remarkable triumphs, but had achieved such a formidable reputation that almost every chancellery in Europe imagined it saw the hand of British intelligence behind every political move that was made, not only in London, but throughout the Commonwealth and Empire and in many other capitals as well for many years to come.

The real spy-masters and the principal agents remained in the shadows, sometimes unhonoured, and their identities were carefully guarded secrets from the public at large. Captain Mansfield Cumming, for example, who was knighted in 1923, was still merely referred to as "C" long after his death. It was by this initial that Sir Compton Mackenzie denoted him in his book *Aegean Memories*, published in 1940. Hall, it is true, had never been publicity shy and had acquired a considerable reputation as head of the N.I.D. among the public. It was his seeming fondness for publicity as well as Zaharoff's plea, added to whispers that he had political ambitions, which caused Lloyd George to turn him down when honours lists were prepared. Kell was the least known of the trio and the most self-effacing man in the intelligence world.

But there were others, sometimes men who had been merely on the fringe of intelligence circles, who deliberately stole the limelight and who, by ostentatious behaviour, by creating an air of mystery and by snide innuendoes, created the impression that they were masterminds of the Secret Service. At home this conduct gave them a certain glamour among the uninformed and invoked hero-worship, but abroad much more harm was done. Some of them went so far in building themselves up as Secret Service aces that they caused unnecessary suspicion of British motives among foreign governments.

One such man was T. E. Lawrence, whose legend as a Secret Service ace still lives on. Even as recently as 1967 he was described by two American authors as "both an efficient spy and a self-taught spy-master".[1] Lawrence undoubtedly had talent, but his eccentricities of behaviour and his rather unpleasant characteristic of being such a *fantaisiste* as to be an inveterate and dangerous liar tended to exalt such talents as he possessed into unsubstantiated claims to be the genius of his age. He was never a secret agent in the same sense as Sidney Reilly, nor did he possess the genius of that man. He was essentially an amateur in espionage and a utiliser rather than a begetter of intelligence.

The story is told that Lawrence, after leaving university, had gone to the Middle East to indulge in espionage for the British under the guise of archaeology and that he had been recruited by a university don for this purpose. The truth is really the other way round: archaeological research had brought him in contact with the intelligence services. In the war it had been as an organiser of guerrilla warfare in the Desert that he had really made his name. Naturally such warfare depended a good deal on intelligence reports and it is quite true that on occasions Lawrence, disguising himself as an Arab, pulled off some notable *coups* in obtaining information. But as a spy Lawrence could not be compared with Wolfgang Francks, the German secret agent in the Middle East, who played havoc with the British. Wolfgang, whose exploits are hardly known in Britain, went on long expeditions disguised as a bedouin and on three occasions entered Egypt and even gained entrance to British G.H.Q. in Cairo and frequently crossed from the Turkish to the British lines dressed up as a British staff officer.

It was after the war that Lawrence became such a menace to Anglo-French relations that the French were convinced, quite wrongly, that he was the director of an anti-French drive by the Secret Service. In fact Lawrence had a rôle of no great importance, but Lloyd George used him as a pawn in his schemes for aggrandisement in Arabia. The relations between Lawrence and Lloyd George are of special interest in that they serve as an example of the vanity and deviousness of each man. What Lloyd George did was to exploit the romantic legend which had been built up around Lawrence's name. He was anxious for the Government to draw some benefits from this legend and from Lawrence as the self-appointed crusader for the Arabs. Lawrence knew that Lloyd George was a Francophobe and he played on this by discrediting the French.

Behind these intrigues was also, as M. Poincaré, the French Premier, stated, "the stink of oil". British oil interests and the Secret Service worked in close co-operation in the Middle East, aiming to win oil concessions for Britain and to keep out the French and the Americans. Thus was Lawrence, the minor intelligence agent, built up into a national myth. Lawrence's massacres of sleeping Turks by his gangs of Bedouin killers were built up into the gallant epics of war. As a pro-Arabist and an anti-French agitator Lawrence was exactly the type of man Lloyd George required for his policies in the Middle East. So the Prime Minister gave full support to Lowell Thomas's lectures on Lawrence and the Arab revolt.

Lawrence's character and his whole record were such that he should never have been given scope for intrigues once war was over. A masochistic pervert, a liar who never hesitated to smear relatives and friends by his calumnies, a moral blackmailer, if not one for financial gain, he was a thoroughly unstable character and, by reason of his illegitimacy and his sexual abberations, one who could have been easily blackmailed himself. In short, the last person any Secret Service chief would want to employ in the ordinary course of events. But Lawrence was at least a genius in kidding people. Lloyd George, Churchill and Lord Trenchard were all in their turn taken in by this mountebank and his ridiculous antics. It is fairly certain that Lawrence, by reason of his knowledge of anti-French intrigues and double-dealings in the Middle East, was able to exercise a degree of influence in high circles out of all proportion to his status, even threatening authority with impunity. When he secretly enlisted in first the R.A.F. and then the Army in the ranks under other names, he was protected by all manner of instructions from on high.

The Lawrence legend died hard. In his life-time it was accepted at face value by a number of foreign powers and even after his death in the 'thirties continental newspapers stated that the fatal accident he had on his motor-bicycle was staged by the Secret Service and that he was still alive, aiding the Ethiopians against the Italians in the Abyssinian campaign.

The real director of the Secret Service in the Middle East in World War I was Sir George Aston. Just before war started Aston was called to join the Foreign Intelligence Committee of the Military, Secret and Political Branch of the Admiralty Secretariat. Like many other officers of this era, Aston was an enthusiast for personal observation which he had put into practice in the Boer War and between the wars while on holiday, visiting Continental ports to obtain photographs and details of the fortifications. In his book, *Secret Service*, Aston described how he had liquidated one of Turkey's ace spies. The Turk had been so successful in penetrating the secrets of Allenby's Expeditionary Force that he ensured the Turks had British plans in advance of almost every operation. Aston arranged for thirty pounds in English banknotes to be put inside a letter, addressed to the spy, implying that this was in payment for services rendered to the British. The letter was intercepted by the Turks and simply on this evidence the Turco-German command had their ace spy shot on the grounds that he was a double-agent.

The concocting of fake information has been a favourite ploy of British Secret Service agents throughout history and Aston provided a further example when Allenby wanted to lure the Turks into making a false move so that he could counter-attack. Aston—to use his own words—"baited a haversack" with letters, twenty pounds in notes, entries in a note-book intended to deceive the enemy and a fake letter from home, telling an officer that his wife was expecting a baby. The object was to convey to the enemy that the British would not attack until late in November, and particularly to indicate areas where they would not attack. An officer was sent up to the Turkish lines on horseback. He opened fire and was then chased back to the British lines. While making his escape he dropped the haversack which the Turks promptly secured. Beersheba was attacked on 31 October—the very area where the Turks had been led to believe there would be no attack—and Allenby struck a decisive blow.

Tribute should be paid to others in the intelligence services who, until now, have had little or no mention. On the military side there was General Ewart, Director of Military Operations, who was one of Kell's strongest supporters. There was also the able General Macdonagh, who was such an efficient intelligence officer that he spotted at once when Lloyd George (as he often did) falsified the figures of forces available to suit his own purpose and had the extremely difficult task of preserving secrecy under a Prime Minister who frequently leaked information that should have remained top secret, if it served his own ends. Sir James Edmonds was another of the pioneers of military intelligence in these years of transition and perhaps the best judge of a good agent of any man in the War Office.

Yet of all branches of this now complex and even polyglot Secret Service that of the N.I.D. and the counter-espionage branch, M.I.5, were undoubtedly supreme. Admiral Hall of all the intelligence chiefs was the best known among those of the Allies and was regarded by the enemy as their deadliest and most feared antagonist. Without question he was the great architect of the more spectacular successes in the field of intelligence during the war: Admiral Sims of America described him as "this great Sherlock Holmes". But, as his biographer says, "not a few of his countrymen, both inside and outside the Admiralty, whilst conceding that he was doing wonderful work, regarded him as something of a menace. They were a little frightened of him; they never knew what he was going to do next."[2]

It is true to say that Hall was appreciated more in America than in Whitehall. No other Service chief had done more for Anglo-American co-operation and he might have made a splendid Ambassador in Washington. Certainly he could have helped to check the growing spirit of isolationism that came over America between the wars, for he would have sought to tackle this problem very differently from some of the inept professional diplomats who held that office in the 'twenties and 'thirties. Hall had remarkable qualities of diplomacy for a sailor and because of these, and because of his drive and authority, he acquired a power in wartime which no other Intelligence chief has ever achieved since, or is likely to achieve in the future.

The truth was that Hall too frequently took matters into his own hands. He had no right to deal with intercepted diplomatic messages himself; he should have passed them on immediately, without comment, and without acting on them, to the Foreign Office. If all intelligence chiefs acted in this high-handed manner, disastrous mistakes could be made. On the other hand—and this view was one that Hall sincerely and often in his case rightly held—even more disastrous results could have occurred, if he had followed the rule book on every occasion. Time would have been lost, Civil Service caution would have prevailed and action would have come too late.

But the powers-that-be were quite determined that in future the N.I.D. must be strictly controlled and that the powers that Hall had taken unto himself must be withheld from any future occupant of the office of Director of Naval Intelligence. The result was that the Department never regained its old authority and power during the inter-war years. The legend lived on and even in the 'thirties John Gunter in his book *Inside Europe* was asserting that the Naval Intelligence Department of the Admiralty was one of the most powerful institutions in the British establishment. Alas, the N.I.D. not only declined in its usefulness and failed to live up to its reputation, but it became notorious for leakages of information and indiscretion and when World War II approached there were almost panic moves to build it up again by an infusion of new talent.

One point needs to be made here: it was not Admiral Hall (or Captain Hall as he was when he took office as D.N.I.) who originated Room 40, the brains trust of the N.I.D., but Admiral Sir Henry Oliver, a brilliant intelligence officer in his own right and perhaps one of the best naval brains in the tackling of deciphering problems and the correct interpretation of intercepted signals. The author can recall Admiral Oliver in his eighties when his mind was still lively and his memory for detail astonishing. He could recall almost every U-boat commander of any note, together with the number of his ship, what raids he had made and where he mainly operated, as well as details about his methods of operation.

The most urgent task of the Secret Service, and especially of the counter-espionage services, after World War I was the combatting of Bolshevism at home and of Sinn Fein terrorism in Ireland. There is a tendency today among most historians to suggest that Bolshevism was never a serious menace in 1918–20 and that its threat has been magnified out of all proportion by warmongers and reactionaries. Indeed, if many of these historians are to be believed, world peace would have been achieved years ago if the Western Powers had come to terms with Bolshevism then.

To make this assertion is to ignore completely what was going on in Britain and in Europe in those years and how the sudden collapse of Germany had left a vacuum of instability in the middle of Europe. The aim of the Communists was to spread the revolution as swiftly as possible, first to Holland and Switzerland, then to Germany, Britain, France and Italy.

Sir Basil Thomson had been appointed Security Officer to the British delegation in Paris for the peace talks immediately after the Armistice and in the course of these duties he learned a great deal of communist plots in Europe. Documents which came into his possession revealed that the Communist International expected revolution in Britain within six months. By now Thomson had become an extremely powerful figure behind the scenes and the sphere of his activities extended far beyond the United Kingdom. "February 1919," he wrote, "was the high-water mark of revolutionary danger in Great Britain. Everything was in favour of the revolutionaries. Many of the soldiers were impatient at the delay in demobilisation. The discharged soldiers could not get housing accommodation. Russia had shown how apparently easy it was for a determined minority, with a body of discontented soldiers behind them, to seize the reins of power."[3]

Consequently Sir Basil was forced to concentrate entirely on the political side of his work—that is, with the Special Branch of Scotland Yard, which was then reformed to deal with Bolshevik attempts to spread their doctrines in Britain. Perhaps his zeal for tackling revolutionaries may in the light of their subsequent failure seem somewhat exaggerated and alarmist, and one must admit that this marked a tendency in the British Secret Service to become obsessed with Bolshevism, often to the exclusion of greater menaces and other political developments on the Continent of Europe in the years to come. Nevertheless there was at the time considerable reason for alarm and if there had been less vigilance, the situation might have been much worse.

London, as we have seen, had always been a haven for Russian revolutionaries and the Special Branch knew that many of them were still active, not only in the East End of London, but in Glasgow, Liverpool and other big cities. There had been mutinies at various camps where soldiers were awaiting demobilisation. American soldiers had fought with the police in the Aldwych and outgoing drafts had sung "The Red Flag". By January 1919, the British Army itself was becoming seriously disaffected and many of its units were completely unreliable. Men of the Army Service Corps drove their lorries to London and blockaded the entrances to the War Office, at Folkestone troops refused to embark for France, while in Calais some thousands of them seized control of the town and two divisions had to be recalled from Germany to surround Calais with machine-guns. For some weeks matters grew worse. Workers' Councils were set up to demand "direct action" and to oppose the sending of troops to fight the Bolsheviks. Electrical engineers threatened to plunge London into darkness unless their demands were met and there were attempts to set up Soldiers' and Workers' Councils on the Soviet model in Britain, while the Sailors', Soldiers' and Airmen's Union was established as a revolutionary body in close touch with workers' committees. In February 1919, an attempt was made to seize the town hall in Glasgow.

Three thousand troops in London, detailed to catch trains at Victoria, turned round and marched on Whitehall with their arms. A *coup d'état* seemed a possibility and Churchill, now Secretary of State for War, asked whether the Guards' regiments could be relied on to check the mutineers. Even then he got the very guarded answer that the officers "*thought*" they could depend on the Guards. In the end the Guards rounded up the mutineers and marched them as prisoners to Wellington barracks.

But much worse than this, from Sir Basil Thomson's viewpoint, was the threat of trouble inside the Police Force. Thomson not only had to contend with revolution from without, but from inside the Metropolitan Police as well. The morale of this branch of the force had been affected by a handful of malcontents among the police themselves. The Police Union had been formed with the intention of forcing a strike of policemen linked up with joint action by other trades unions. The sole excuse for this move was that a police constable had been dismissed for circulating strike propaganda material among his comrades.

The situation was thus serious enough to warrant special action and it is to the credit of Thomson that he acted swiftly and ruthlessly and again, like Hall, turned a blind eye to the Cabinet. Lloyd George in particular had given Thomson little encouragement, telling him: "Don't worry, Thomson, the drought will end soon and once it rains and drives people indoors there will be less opportunity for the agitators. Besides the last thing we want to do is to let Churchill know that there are Bolshevists in the Police Force. He's already got Reds on the brain."

Whether Thomson went over Lloyd George's head and raised the problem of disaffection with King George V is a matter of conjecture, but he wrote that he was "summoned to Buckingham Palace to advise the King as to what His Majesty could do to allay trouble when demobilisation began. His Majesty took my advice and by his courage and good sense did much to avert the coming troubles. It was a time when the Russian Bolsheviks were pouring money into the country to incite rebellion. Happily this was averted, but extremist Labour never forgave me and pressed Lloyd George to dismiss me. This he did, but at the cost of a debate in the House of Commons."[4]

It is believed that it was on Thomson's advice that the King intervened and persuaded the Prime Minister to increase the soldiers' pay one hundred per cent—from one shilling to two shillings a day for a private.

Thomson's dismissal came later on, but meanwhile he was busily occupied in snuffing out trouble in the Police Force. He soon found ample evidence that young constables were being bullied and blackmailed into joining the Police and Prison Officers' Union and that there was positive, if not extensive, communist infiltration. But Thomson's own picked men provided him with a complete picture of the rôle of the plotters. Word had been passed round that everyone was to be ready to strike in August 1919. By this time Thomson was able to act promptly: the strike was only partial and the result was the dismissal of the revolutionary constables.

In fact the most dangerous period had been passed, almost without its being generally realised. Zaharoff's warning of the Bolshevik revolution spreading all over Europe if war did not end was accurate enough. It is not now even generally known that revolutions on the Russian plan actually broke out on Armistice Day, 1918, in Holland and Switzerland. If war had not ended then, the authorities in both countries might have had a much more difficult job in checking the revolutionary moves.

The Commissioner of the Metropolitan Police at this time was Brigadier-General Horwood, an ineffective officer who was either unwilling or unable to stamp out corruption and disaffection. Thomson was an outspoken critic of Horwood and barely on speaking terms with the man who was nominally his chief. He therefore insisted on the right to report direct to the Cabinet and not through Horwood and Cabinet Papers of the period show that this plan was approved by the Cabinet.

Horwood, however, got his own back. In his book, *The Scene Changes,* Thomson described how four young Irishmen chalked up in the summer-house at Chequers the words "Up Sinn Fein", while Lloyd George was in residence. They were arrested and brought before Thomson, who, satisfied that this was nothing more than a skylark, let them go. The men had previously been questioned by Superintendent Quinn, one of Thomson's chief aides, and Quinn was satisfied that the four men were not members of the Irish Republican Army. Horwood, who was responsible for the Prime Minister's safety, objected to this leniency and reported the matter to Lloyd George. The latter sent for Thomson and angrily told him that Quinn must be sacked. Thomson replied that he would rather resign than have Quinn sacked. The result was that in November 1921, the Home Secretary, Mr. Shortt, sent for Thomson and told him that if he did not retire voluntarily, he would receive a less generous pension and be summarily dismissed.[5]

Thomson's dismissal was the subject of quite a heated debate during which his old intelligence colleague, Admiral Hall, now a Member of Parliament, stoutly defended the record of the head of the Special Branch. And now, with Hall's departure, only Kell remained of the celebrated counter-espionage trio of war days. Thomson was never in any doubt that he had been hounded from office for purposes of political appeasement, but he also suspected that Lloyd George regarded him as having acquired too many powers. The Prime Minister mistrusted the Secret Service; he felt it had become too vast and autocratic and that in peace-time it needed taming. In matters of intelligence Lloyd George preferred to divide and rule, to have several sources of information, including some that were independent of the Secret Service, and he would frequently play off one section against another.

Thomson's ill luck dogged him into retirement. In December 1925, he and a young woman named Thelma de Lava were arrested in Hyde Park and summoned for committing an act in violation of public decency. Sir Basil pleaded "not guilty" and said that he was carrying out investigations in Hyde Park into reports of soliciting by women with a view to writing articles on this subject. It was perfectly true that since retirement he had written both books and articles for the newspapers on various criminal cases and subjects connected with crime. He completely repudiated the accusations made against him. Nevertheless he was found guilty and fined five pounds. He appealed against the sentence, but lost that, too. Both Admiral Hall and Reginald McKenna, a former Home Secretary, gave evidence on Sir Basil's behalf, testifying to the high regard each had for him and paying tribute to his character.

Was Thomson framed? Two friends, a Major Douglas Straight, and a Mr. H. V. Higgins, testified that Sir Basil had discussed with them the writing of an article on prostitution in Hyde Park before the incident occurred. Even the chairman of the Court of Appeal expressed surprise that in such a case, where a joint offence was alleged, the couple should not have been tried together. Then again Sir Basil's recent book, *The Criminal*, had caused anger and resentment in high places and even vocal disapproval by some Chief Constables, because of his outspoken criticisms of the Police Force. Thomson had many enemies in the police hierarchy and they may well have welcomed a chance to discredit him, especially in the Metropolitan area where Thomson knew a great deal about the corruption and chicanery that was then prevalent in the Metropolitan Force.

It was remarkable that Kell, the least fit of the counter-espionage trio, should have carried on his intelligence work the longest. In 1917 he had been made a Colonel, an appointment that was ridiculously belated when one considers that he had been working for years as a major on equal terms with an Admiral and, in the case of Mansfield Cumming a naval captain. But Kell was one of those rareties in the intelligence world, a self-effacing and utterly selfless man and when at the end of the war he was knighted and made a Major-General this was largely because it was realised that M.I.5 was important enough to be commanded by a senior officer.

Kell was the moulder of M.I.5 policy and principles and from 1910 until 1939—a record of service that has been almost unsurpassed by any modern intelligence chief—he held control of the organisation. But his most outstanding success was not so much in the intelligence service itself as in persuading the Government, when he was only a mere captain, that the Official Secrets Act needed to be amended. For it was through the passing of the revised Act that so many spies were caught during the war: without it the Germans might well have wrought untold havoc in espionage inside Britain.

The troubles in Ireland occupied most of Kell's time in the years immediately after the war and his task was not made any easier by the fact that the Black-and-Tans, (so named because of their black tunics and caps and khaki trousers), the hastily created militia force that was rushed into Ireland by the Coalition Government, often exceeded their duties by indulging in counter-espionage themselves. These thugs—many of them the scum of the Army, including ex-officers with bad reputations, even men awaiting trial who had been freed from jail to join the force—by taking the law into their own hands upset the work not only of Basil Thomson's Special Branch, but of M.I.5 as well.

Thomson certainly did not approve of the Black-and-Tans as constituted. "The whole affair got out of hand," he said. "I was prevented from having any real control over recruitment in the way I wished. It would have saved many lives, if, instead of a force of thugs, a disciplined counter-espionage unit had been organised and moved to Dublin."

In the light of what happened in Ireland it is extremely difficult to define exactly the rôle which the Secret Service played in the campaign of terror, repression, loot, rape, arson and murder which so blackened the British record in Ireland in these critical years. However much I.R.A. terrorism may have justified severe measures, nobody could excuse the excesses of the Black-and-Tans which the authorities permitted. Three distinct bodies were operating on behalf of the British Government in Ireland at that time—the Army, the Black-and-Tans and a Secret Service force which was reputedly independent of Dublin Castle H.Q. and responsible to someone in London. Thomson afterwards denied that he had any control over or say in this organisation; Kell remained silent on the subject, though it was almost certain that he had no hand in it. The probability is that this body was supervised by Sir Hamar Greenwood, the Minister responsible for Irish affairs. Bowen, a former officer with a distinguished war record, was one of these Secret Service agents in the mysterious organisation that reported directly to London. He became so disgusted with the tactics of his colleagues that, according to Brigadier-General Frank Crozier, Commandant of the Auxiliary Royal Irish Constabulary, he "foolishly told his superior she would cross to England and tell David Davies, the influential Welshman, about the irregular way the Service was being run. . . . He was threatened he would be put away."[6]

Sometime later a dead body was pulled out of the Liffey; it was identified as that of Bowen.

Later these same secret agents who had plotted terrorism against the Irish Nationalists and who had completely failed to discover Michael Collins, Director of Intelligence of the Sinn Feiners, were used by Lloyd George to seek out I.R.A. leaders for a basis for negotiations.

The story of the Secret Service in Ireland in the immediate post-war years was one of almost constant failure due to irresponsible political direction, the bungling of amateurs and a complete lack of co-ordination between Dublin Castle and Whitehall. Not only was British intelligence in Ireland inefficient by this time, but it had been infiltrated by the I.R.A. Until 1920 Britain's intelligence system, with its web of agents, informers and spies, had given long warning of any attempted moves against British rule or interests in Ireland. But Dublin in that year saw Michael Collins, the brilliant Irish underground leader, use the British tactics of infiltration against the British, fitting his own agents in the police in almost every village, often in the local post office and even in Dublin Castle.

David Neligan, a Limerick man, has described how at the age of twenty-one, while outwardly a police officer, loyal to the British, he was in fact his own country's most successful spy.[7] Every paper he could copy he copied; every informer who came with news was in turn informed against to the Irish; every plan of which he heard he passed on. Neligan did not always like his work and once he actually resigned from the Force, but was persuaded to carry on by his countrymen. He not only returned to the Force, he joined the Secret Service.

Yet at the same time that the Secret Service was taking a beating in Ireland, it was scoring some brilliant successes inside Russia, based to a large extent on the considerable dossiers that had been built up over the years by those who had been keeping watch on Russian revolutionaries in London. For now the revolutionaries were in power these dossiers had increased in value.

Three men should be mentioned in particular—Sir Robert Bruce Lockhart, Paul Dukes and, inevitably, Sidney Reilly again. In 1918 Robert Bruce Lockhart, then a young man in the Diplomatic Service, was appointed head of a special mission to the Soviet Government, with the rank of acting British Consul-General in Moscow. There was some pressure on the Foreign Office to recall him, but Balfour, then Foreign Secretary, resisted this, for Lockhart's zeal in getting intelligence out of Russia was such that he became much more than a mere diplomat. Not surprisingly the Russians guessed that he was a spy first and a diplomat second and when during the following summer Lenin was shot at, Lockhart with others was arrested for alleged complicity in a plot to assassinate Lenin. As a reprisal the British Government arrested Litvinoff, the Soviet representative in London, and he was held until Lockhart was freed.

Thus Bruce Lockhart remained in Moscow as an agent rather than a diplomat until the collapse of Germany. He was an astute observer of the Russian character and he sent many warning messages that the revolution was not a passing phase and that the clock could never be put back to the days of the Czarists. It was bold advice to give at such a time and it did not help young Lockhart's career. By some in the Foreign Office he was preposterously labelled "pro-Bolshevik", while others turned a cold shoulder on him when the truths he uttered proved unpalatable to them. The Secret Service, alas, completely rejected his interpretations of events. Yet Lockhart spoke Russian fluently, was well acquainted with the leading revolutionaries and was even trusted by them until they became convinced that he was the tool of a Government which favoured intervention against them.

Had the Secret Service listened to Lockhart and had the British Government used its influence to give this young man fuller support at a vital time, all that intervention was intended to do might have been achieved without intervention and bloodshed. Lockhart had made friends with Trotsky and he warned the British that Trotsky might be worth backing now before someone more hostile and suspicious came along, for Trotsky was more fearful of German militarism than of British capitalism and he was willing to co-operate with the British against the Germans and actually asked for a British naval mission to reorganise the Russian fleets and offered to put a Briton in charge of the Russian railways. But the British made no effort to avail themselves of this last opportunity to gain a foothold in Russia and, worse than this, when they actually intervened militarily they had left things too late. They had their chance to land 12,000 men at Archangel when the Czech Army had captured Kazan; then with the pro-interventionist Russians on their side they had a chance of overthrowing the Bolsheviks and at least having a less extreme Government installed. Instead they landed 1,200 men and so transformed Bolshevik apprehensions into joyous ridicule. As Lockhart wrote in his book, *Memoirs of a British Agent*, this blunder was "disastrous both to our prestige and to the fortunes of those Russians who supported us. It raised hopes which could not be fulfilled. It intensified the civil war and sent thousands of Russians to their death. Indirectly it was responsible for the Terror."

It marked the end of Lockhart's career as a diplomat, but as an author and writer he swiftly succeeded.

Paul Dukes was head of the British intelligence service in Russia immediately after the Revolution. He was utterly fearless, he was also a fluent Russian speaker and he undertook the job of sending reports to London. He had many escapes from death and he even quixotically and chivalrously mixed some of his Secret Service work with attempting to rescue White Russians from the prisons of the Cheka. On the other hand this remarkable man also became a pseudo-official in the Cheka, enlisted in the Red Army and became a member of the Communist Party. Originally Dukes had planned a musical career for himself and he had gone to Russia in 1909 to study music in the capital. He had supported himself by giving English lessons and during the early part of the war he was attached to the Marinsky Theatre, studying music under Albert Coates. In 1915 he was made a member of the Anglo-Russian Commission and carried the passport of a King's Messenger, charged with a roving assignment to investigate what was going on in the revolutionary underworld.

In 1919 he obtained a Russian passport which showed him to be an agent of the Cheka and throughout that year he remained in Russia, frequently changing both his name and his residence, sending out reports as often as he could. He was not as percipient as Lockhart, for he did not think the revolution would last, but as a man of action and enterprise, as a veritable free-lance spy he was incomparable. With an ex-Russian officer, Kolya Orlov, he organised raids on the Communists' store of stolen wealth. On one occasion when he was being hunted a Russian woman took him to a cemetery to hide his secret papers in a hole which she dug in the ground: "if anyone sees us," she said, "they will only think we are planting flowers". There must have been weeks when he felt alone and forgotten, even by the authorities at home. As he wrote afterwards: "I was isolated, with a large quantity of information accumulating, part of which I was obliged to destroy. I continued to keep up communication . . . through the medium of an officer who was employed at the Admiralty. As he considered it unsafe to meet in private houses we met in parks or public places, arranging our rendezvous by means of dropping notes into one of a series of little holes—designated originally for flags—in the parapet of the Neva. . . . Towards the end of April I found a note in the parapet hole saying that 'the fruit was ripening' and that a 'postman'—that is a courier—might shortly be available."[8]

Admiral Sir Reginald Hall, Director of Naval Intelligence in World War I

A. E. W. Mason, novelist turned Secret Agent

Sir Paul Dukes and four of the disguises he used in Russia

The Secret Service was at this time, in spring, 1919, using a new type of naval coastal motor-boat, manned by naval personnel, to make contact with British agents in Finland and Russia. Lieutenant W. S. Agar, who was awarded the V.C. for his part in these operations, twice ran the gauntlet of the Kronstadt Forts to bring his courier to contact Dukes. On one occasion Agar took on the might of the Red Navy in his tiny motor-boat and sank the cruiser *Oleg* by torpedo. Later Dukes planned to row out two miles to where Agar was waiting for him, but he was baulked by a leaking craft which sank beneath him. Regaining shore, he was forced to disguise himself as a Red soldier and return to St. Petersburg. The variety of disguises he utilised says much for his versatility—an epileptic, a bearded proletarian, an ailing intellectual and even Comrade Piotrovsky, committee member of the Communist Party. But to Whitehall he was just Agent ST 25 until finally he escaped back to England and received a knighthood.

Sidney Reilly's activities in Russia went far beyond the gathering of information. He was an active instigator of counter-revolution and even a formulator of policy. As a spy Reilly was always a law unto himself and one who not only proffered information, but pressed advice on how it should be used. Prior to 1914, for example, he had done more than any man, not excepting Sir Basil Zaharoff himself, to press Britain to ensure adequate oil supplies from the Middle East. Much of his espionage in Persia and elsewhere had been devoted towards convincing the British Government for the need of this. Very few secret agents indeed have the chance to mould policy as did Reilly: if they attempted to do so, they would probably be sacked for exceeding their duties. Yet Reilly not only did this, but sometimes succeeded in persuading politicians to adopt his policies, for, with the years, he had acquired as much influence with a few politicians as he had in the S.I.S.

Russia in 1918 was to provide him with the chance of actually becoming a policy-maker.

20

Sidney Reilly's Last Gamble

Lloyd George had vacillated so much in his Russian policy that neither the Foreign Office, nor the Secret Service could keep up with his manoeuvres. But as 1918 progressed and as the Germans advanced against the Russians, so it came to be realised that, as the Soviet refused to continue the fighting, they must be overthrown.

Basil Thomson had already made himself unpopular with Lloyd George by his warnings of the threat of revolution at home. Now in desperation he urged Lloyd George to take other opinions. "If you will not listen to what is happening on the home front," said Thomson, "then at least find out what the Reds are doing in Russia. Speak to Cumming."

What, demanded the Prime Minister, could the Secret Service do to get rid of the Bolsheviks? The question was posed more in irony than in any seriousness.

"Cumming will tell you," replied Thomson.

The Prime Minister was also under pressure from some of his Cabinet colleagues so he decided to find out for himself.

Cumming knew only too well that the only man capable of attempting a *coup* against the Bolsheviks inside Russia was Sidney Reilly. His first instinct was not to mention his name to Lloyd George, but the Prime Minister put to him a searching question:

"You are hiding something from me. You have someone in mind. Who is he?"

So it was that, with Lloyd George's knowledge, Reilly set out, armed with a message from the Prime Minister to Litvinoff, to Russia on what was the most formidable and difficult mission he had yet undertaken. This was at the end of April 1918. He arrived in Russia quite openly as Sidney Reilly, but even his confidence, usually unshakeable, was undermined when he saw the rule of terror that had descended on the country. By the usual Reilly methods of charm rather than cunning he managed to secure the goodwill of the Soviet General Brouevitch and through his help was able to secure a pass and move about Moscow freely. Reilly had to pick his way with almost as much care at first through the ranks of British intelligence in Russia as he did through those of the ultra-suspicious Bolsheviks. There had been some misgiving in the hierarchy of the Secret Service when Cumming chose Reilly for the assignment and even more among their agents already in Russia. The fact that Reilly had come with Lloyd George's blessing revived memories among some that he had Leftist tendencies. But then the same kind of people who voiced these suspicions had alleged that Bruce Lockhart was pro-Bolshevik, which was monstrously untrue.

Britain had had two Secret Service chiefs inside Russia within a year. The first was Major Stephen Alley, an old friend of Reilly's, the second was a Commander Boyce. Reilly had some difficulty in convincing Boyce that he should be allowed to use his cipher staff, as Boyce saw his job as being primarily to wage war against the Germans and he viewed Reilly's mission as an ill-defined venture which might interfere with his own activities.

Reilly first played a subtle game of his own. Believing that boldness and directness paid, he went straight to the Kremlin and demanded to see Lenin, but failed. Then he represented to other Bolshevik leaders that the British Government was not satisfied it had received the truth about the Soviet from Bruce Lockhart and wanted an independent report. But these bold tactics failed. The Russians had a dossier on Reilly and they immediately suspected that he was a spy rather than an envoy of Lloyd George. So Reilly had to go underground and change his identity fairly frequently. Sometimes he posed as a Greek from the Levant, at other times a Turkish merchant. He played a considerable rôle in organising a plot to seize power from the Bolsheviks, being aided by some of the most reliable and fearless of the White Russians as well as a few of the moderates among the Revolutionaries. He even began to choose members of an alternative government, and it was in the method of doing this that he raised a remarkable question mark in the minds of discerning people close to him: did Sidney Reilly himself hope to head such a government? For he deliberately left open the post of Premier, choosing a Minister of the Interior (his old friend, Alexander Grammatikoff, a barrister), various other old acquaintances and General Yudenich, a White Russian, as head of the Army.

The full details of Reilly's plotting are even now so confused and conflicting that it is not possible to assess the extent of the conspiracy, but it is certain that at one stage it stood an excellent chance of succeeding. More than two million roubles were contributed to the conspiracy funds by White Russians. Reilly's signal for the *coup* was to be the arrest of Lenin, Trotsky and all the Red leaders at a meeting of the Central Soviet Committee which was to be held in August. But at the last moment the date for this meeting was postponed for a few weeks and then fate upset Reilly's plans completely, for a few days later a woman tried to kill Lenin and this resulted in mass arrests by the Cheka and, in consequence, the capture of documents which gave evidence of the plot against the régime.

The plot was reputed to have been betrayed to the Bolsheviks by a French agent. Reilly had to make tracks for the nearest railway station to get as far from his pursuers as he could. For he was now completely on his own. The British Mission had been forced to leave Moscow, Lockhart was under arrest, and Captain George Hill, his closest fellow agent in Russia, had disappeared. Reilly's fellow conspirators had been caught through the folly of a girl agent who had neglected to obey an elementary rule. As every motor car in Russia had been confiscated by the Bolsheviks it was understood by anti-Bolshevik agents that no house in front of which a motor car stood should ever be visited. She walked right into the trap, had her portfolio opened by the Cheka who found there not only copies of secret Bolshevik documents, but clear evidence that a house in Cheremetoff Pereulok was the secret headquarters of Reilly and his fellow plotters. Meanwhile—proof that Reilly was still finding ample time for his amours—six women among those arrested claimed that Reilly was their husband! They had no idea that he was a counter-revolutionary, or they would assuredly have kept quiet, which shows that he was still remarkably discreet in his love affairs.

Fortunately Reilly had a pass which was signed and stamped by Orloff, the President of the Cheka Criminel, who was in Reilly's pay and one of his contacts. But for all he knew Orloff might already have been arrested; however, the guard at the railway station barrier was sufficiently frightened of the fact that Reilly's pass showed him to be a collaborator of the Cheka that he did not dare to query his movements. It took Reilly nearly two months to make his way out of Russia on that occasion and part of the time he was living in a remote village as a peasant without arousing the suspicions of the local authorities.[1]

"Reckless Reilly" was at heart a romantic and all his life he had a romantic's love of make-believe, of fictionalising his whole existence so that often, in moments of crisis, it was the play-acting, fictitious Reilly who dominated rather than the shrewd, sophisticated business man. A typical example of this trait in his character was the story of his sitting at a special meeting of a Communist body when a messenger brought in a note denouncing him as a spy on the basis of a report from a Russian agent in London. Without hesitating for a moment Reilly turned the tables by not only denouncing the messenger as a spy, but the message as a forgery designed to bring about the downfall of a trusted servant of the Bolshevik cause. The case Reilly put up was so convincing that the messenger was put under arrest and in fact had a narrow escape from being shot without further ado. It was Reilly who persuaded his colleagues to stay their hand until the next day and by then, of course, Reilly himself had fled.

During the next few years Reilly went to and from Russia under various aliases, still seeking to make a further attempt to overthrow the Soviet règime. When in London he switched his attention from Lloyd George to Churchill, believing even then that Churchill was "Britain's man of destiny". It was Reilly who introduced Churchill to Boris Savinkoff, the former revolutionary and now the most violent and indomitable foe of the Bolsheviks.

Meanwhile Reilly obtained a divorce from his second wife, Nadine, and in May 1923, at a London register office married an actress, Pepita Bobadilla, who, like Nadine, knew nothing about his first wife, Margaret. Presumably a bribe, or threats had bought Margaret's silence, for once again Reilly got away with bigamy. Among the witnesses at the wedding was his fellow agent, Captain George Hill, who doubtless knew of "just cause and impediment" to the marriage, but "for ever held his peace". But it is doubtful if Pepita ever knew the real details of Reilly's origins, for in 1931 she stated that "his father was an Irish merchant sea captain and his mother a Russian".[2]

About this time there were changes in the hierarchy of the Secret Service. Sir Mansfield Cumming had retired and by 1923 was dead. Hall and Thomson had gone, so, too, had Cockerill. There had been drastic cuts in the money available for Secret Service operations and to some extent the failure of the plot to seize control from the Bolsheviks had been made the excuse for an economy wave. This is not altogether surprising in view of the fact that awkward Parliamentary questions had been asked about Secret Service spending, one M.P., Joseph King, complaining about gross extravagance in the Secret Service, and claiming that "there are papers on record which show that one officer alone passed £120,000 in one week in Russia with the purpose of starting a counter-revolution".

The next head of the S.I.S. and the controller of M.I.6 was Admiral "Quex" Sinclair, a painstaking man, but one who was never ruthless enough to take authoritative control of the organisation. The organisation of the S.I.S. tended to become departmentalised, with each section going its own away. Economies by successive governments, especially those in Labour's brief periods of office between the wars, made Sinclair's task difficult and he had his work cut out trying to use his limited resources. One of the troubles of the inter-war years was that Secret Service chiefs were indecisive about what the right targets for intelligence should be.

It was to some extent due to this indecision in the hierarchy that intelligence coming out of Germany in the 'twenties and 'thirties was so unco-ordinated and scanty that M.I.6 never had the power to convince the Baldwin and Chamberlain governments how desperate the situation was there.

In 1923 Kell was officially retired and a notice appeared in the *London Gazette* to this effect. His assistant, Captain Eric Holt-Wilson, who had been his deputy since 1913, retired with him. The *News of the World* then announced with banner headlines

"The Spy Destroyer: Famous Secret Service Officer retires," but in fact his retirement notice was just a bluff. The powers-that-be were anxious to conceal the fact that he was still head of M.I.5, for they realised that since the war the counter-espionage service was faced with a new permanent problem—that of communist subversion and saboteurs in factories. As Lady Kell declared years afterwards: "He simply wanted to put people off. That was about the year he really did get down to work. He didn't actually retire until 1940."

Kell's future work was mainly directed to keeping a look-out for communist conspirators and this was totally different counter-espionage than anything attempted before. It called for new techniques and, above all, for a new type of agent who could infiltrate among the workers without arousing suspicion. This meant the employment for the first time of the cloth-cap worker as a counter-espionage agent.

Meanwhile in M.I.6 Sidney Reilly's old friend, George Hill, was rapidly climbing the ladder to promotion. He was more on the operational outside than the organisational inside of the Secret Service, but considerable attention was paid to what he suggested on account of his exploits in Russia. He never completely severed his links with the Service even when in the 'twenties and 'thirties he took civilian jobs, including a year as general manager to C. B. Cochran, the theatrical manager. Later, as Brigadier Hill, he was to become a much more important figure in M.I.6.

The bug of obsession with Bolshevism had bitten deeply into both M.I.5 and M.I.6 in the middle 'twenties and, bearing in mind events at home in 1918–19, this was perhaps understandable. Yet it was an obsession fraught with dangers, as events were to prove, and perhaps the worst of these dangers was that it tended to blind the Secret Service to menaces from other directions. Those who regarded Germany as still one of the primary targets for intelligence were outnumbered by those who were anti-French and pro-German and those who believed that Soviet Russia was the priority target. Then again successive governments—and this included Labour as much as Conservative governments—placed more emphasis on M.I.5 than M.I.6 at this time. It soon became apparent that the authorities, while temporarily saving money on espionage overseas, were not averse to using M.I.5 as a long-term weapon to prepare for the General Strike which they were convinced would come sooner or later. Commonsense may have ended that strike swiftly when it came in 1926, but the counter-espionage organisation played a leading rôle in foiling some of the plots centring around the events leading up to that strike, as well as a somewhat dubious rôle in manufacturing propaganda in the form of various "Red Scares".

In assessing these Machiavellian tactics, one must be fair to the counter-espionage service. Under normal conditions such tactics probably are inexcusable, but when subversion inside a country is actually aided by agents of a foreign government, then the policy of M.I.5 must be equally ruthless. Had a General Strike come at any time between 1918 and 1924 it might well have developed into something far more dangerous.

All the same it is clear that the Secret Service overreached themselves on occasions, especially in the manufacture of "Red Scares". It was in this kind of rôle that Sidney Reilly was next used. Shortly after his marriage he again went out to Russia, posing this time as a British Communist who had come to obtain instructions regarding the cause in Britain. It was Reilly who organised the faking of the notorious Zinoviev Letter which was to bring about the downfall of Britain's first Labour Government.

This letter, allegedly from Gregory Zinoviev, President of the Third Communist International, to Mr. A. McManus, the British representative on the executive of this International, openly incited revolution in Britain, containing such a passage as "Armed warfare must be preceded by a struggle against the inclinations to compromise which are embedded among the majority of British workmen, against the ideas of evolution and peaceful extermination of capitalism. Only then will it be possible to count on complete success of an armed insurrection." A member of M.I.5, Donald im Thurn, who had been employed by a White Russian firm, the Russian Steamship Company, acted as the go-between for the Secret Service in passing the letter on to the Conservative Party Central Office who, for payment of £5,000, exploited it so effectively as an exclusive story in the *Daily Mail* that the scare it produced cost the Labour Government a landslide defeat and returned the Tories to office.

The Labour Party leaders always insisted that the document was a forgery, but, as they could not obtain any proof of this, the damage was done. Nevertheless over the years evidence was unearthed which strongly suggested forgery and in 1929 following German police inquiries in Berlin a confession was obtained that a White Russian named Vladimir Orloff was involved in the disposal of the document. Subsequently in exhaustive research by the *Sunday Times* Insight team in 1966 the whole story of the forgery was revealed, arriving at the conclusion that while Orloff was the culprit the authenticity of the document was probably guaranteed by Sidney Reilly in his own report to the Secret Service.[3]

Now Reilly was no stranger to the job of trading in forged documents. Not only did he purchase them for himself, but he was an expert in detecting them and he was so experienced in these matters that it is highly unlikely that he would ever have been deceived by such a document. It was he who had been chiefly responsible in World War I for the sale by the British Secret Service, for a large sum of money, of the forged "Sissons" documents to the American Secret Service. These documents had originally been purchased by the British Secret Service for an equally large sum—again, as in the case of the Zinoviev Letter—in the alleged, but in any event erroneous belief that they were genuine. The documents purported to show that Lenin and Trotsky were plotting with the Germans against the Allies. This sale to the Americans was a major blunder on the part of the British. To sell such a document to a friendly government was bad enough, but to have sold a forgery was unforgivable. The Americans neither forgave, nor forgot. It was one of the reasons why there was a lasting mistrust of the British Secret Service by the Americans between the wars; the latter were always suspicious that their British counterparts would try and embroil them in some foreign quarrel on the strength of trumped up evidence. Added to this was the Americans' somewhat exaggerated, but not entirely inaccurate belief that Sir Basil Zaharoff manipulated the British Secret Service to keep the Americans away from Middle East oil concessions.

It has been suggested that at the end of his life Reilly was in possession of a considerable fortune. He had certainly acquired a vast amount of money in his pre-war days, but what happened to this wealth, whether it was added to or squandered is far from clear. Certainly during the war he was so completely occupied as a secret agent that he could not possibly have carried on any business activities. It is also unlikely that he was paid any large sums by the British. Mr. Robin Bruce Lockhart, Sir Robert's son, has stated that Reilly was "a big spender and at the time of his 'death' he had exhausted his financial resources on Savinkoff and was heavily in debt".[5] Savinkoff, the former revolutionary, was described by Churchill as that "extraordinary product—a Terrorist for moderate aims."[5] His forthright championship of the White Russians in their crusade against Bolshevism continued after the anti-Bolsheviks had suffered crushing defeats until he organised guerrilla warfare from Prague. It was at this stage of Savinkoff's career that Sidney Reilly came to him in Prague with plans for organising a peasant revolt in Russia. It is not impossible that he provided Savinkoff with funds, but it seems highly unlikely that they were Reilly's funds, though he may have claimed that they were.

Reilly by this time was not only working for the British. He helped the French Intelligence Service, too. There was nothing treacherous about this; France was just as much an ally of the White Russians as was Britain. But no secret service ever really approved of one of its agents, certainly not one of its chief agents, working even for an ally. In December 1924, Reilly brought from Russia documents concerning the imminence of a communist revolution in Paris and Northern France.

This information Reilly passed on to London as well as Paris. As a result Herriot, the French Premier, ordered the arrest of the Communist ringleaders.

Again in 1925 Reilly returned to Russia. It is almost certain that he went on his own volition, but with the full knowledge of the Secret Service and their approval. On the other hand it is equally clear that, though it is normal practice for the British Secret Service to tell their agents that they will be disowned if anything goes wrong, this time they emphasised this very strongly and hinted that there could be no rescue operation. The background to all this is that there had emerged both inside and outside Russia a mysterious organisation calling itself "The Trust". It purported to be anti-Bolshevik with the aim once again of overthrowing the régime. Not unnaturally the Secret Service was sceptical, more so because "The Trust" claimed to have members in high places in the Soviet régime and even in the Secret Police. This could well be another example of the classical tactic of Russians to use *agents-provocateurs* to pose as counter-revolutionaries. It was a tactic which, as we have seen, the Czarists had employed for seventy years and which the Bolsheviks had also indulged in. These suspicions grew when Savinkoff, with Reilly's knowledge, went to Russia to give himself up, with the intention, so he said, of pretending to confess his errors and to pose as a friend of the régime. Savinkoff's theory was that "The Trust" would look after him, ensure his safety and that he himself would be ready to take over the régime at the appropriate moment. Savinkoff went to Russia, was arrested, "confessed" and certainly gave the impression of having betrayed his cause. In May 1925, he was reported to have committed suicide by throwing himself out of a window.

Yet, despite this, Reilly told the Secret Service that he believed in "The Trust" and that, though there was an element of risk, they would still protect him. Eventually news filtered through that he had been caught and shot by frontier guards on the Finnish–Russian border. The Secret Service clamped down on all news of Reilly, declining even to give any information to his friends. They ignored the pleas of Reilly's wife who was convinced that he was still alive. To publicise her dilemma and in the hope of forcing a statement either from the British or the Russians she put the following brief obituary notice in the press:

"REILLY. On the 28th. Sept. killed near the village Allekul, Russia, by G.P.U. troops, CAPTAIN SIDNEY GEORGE REILLY, M.C., late R.A.F., beloved husband of Pepita B. Reilly.

But was Sidney Reilly killed by the G.P.U.? His wife, who did her utmost to clear up the mystery, remained unconvinced and in 1930 declared that the question of her husband's death remained "as open today as it was six years ago".[6] There was some reason for this element of doubt, for M. Brunovski, a Latvian who had been released by the Russians after four years in a Moscow prison, said that he had learned that "an important British spy lay in the hospital at Butyrski Prison". While he was in prison M. Brunovski made secret notes on strips of linen which he brought with him. But the stresses and strains of incarceration caused him to forget the significance of many of these notes. One such series of notes read: "British officer Reilly—Persia—father-in-law" when translated from Russian. But he could not recall the significance of the meaning of "Persia" and "father-in-law." Pepita Reilly, while not throwing any light on the meaning of "Persia", suggested that Brunovski had misread the Russian for father-in-law, *testi* for *l'* S.T.1, which was her husband's code name.[7]

In December 1925, a story in the British press stated that "Sidney George Reilly is the man who brought over the notorious Zinoviev Letter." It was remarkable that somebody either in the Secret Service, or in those political circles who still hoped to gain some credit from this already largely suspect letter, should have been prepared to leak information to the press while Reilly's fate was still in doubt. Two years later Opperut, one of the leaders of "The Trust", arrived in Finland and revealed that not only was he in the G.P.U. counter-espionage movement, but that "The Trust" had been organised by the Soviet as a means of finding enemies of the régime and enticing them into their fold. There was widescale panic among those in various parts of the world who had innocently joined "The Trust", believing it to be a genuine instrument of counter-revolution. Opperut's story was that Reilly had not been shot while crossing into Russia, but that he had gone to Moscow and been put in the Butyrski Prison.

Further reports on Reilly were conflicting. A White Russian who escaped from Russia stated that Reilly was alive in prison, but insane. A British official in the Middle East reported a man, claiming to be Sidney Reilly, saying he had escaped from Russia, calling on him for money, but disappearing immediately afterwards.

The Secret Service were obviously concerned that one of their chief agents might still be alive and might have confessed under torture, or alternatively, have gone over to the Bolsheviks. Perhaps they were anxious that their version of the Zinoviev Letter should be published in the press before news leaked out that Reilly had confessed to his part in it. When the Soviet Government tried to make capital out of the murder of Volkoff in Poland they issued a statement in which they alleged that Reilly was sent to Russia on a "terrorist mission under instructions from Mr. Winston Churchill". The document stated:

"In the summer of 1925 a certain merchant carrying a Soviet passport with the name Steinberg was wounded and arrested by the frontier guard while illegally crossing the Finnish border. During the inquiry a witness declared that this man was actually Sidney George Reilly and that he was an English spy, a captain in the Royal Air Force, one of the chief organisers of Lockhart's plot, who by sentence of the Tribunal of December 3, 1918, had been outlawed.

"Reilly declared that he came to Russia for the special purpose of organising terroristic acts, arson and revolts, and that when coming from America he had seen Mr. Winston Churchill, Chancellor of the Exchequer, who personally instructed him as to the reorganisation of terroristic and other acts calculated to create a diversion. His written testimony is in the possession of the Government. Reilly's evidence was entirely corroborated by material seized during further arrests."[8]

Reilly might have been killed by trigger-happy guards before his true identity was realised, but it is highly unlikely that so vital a spy would have been shot before the Russians had cross-examined him and tried to extort a confession. Mr. Robin Bruce Lockhart as recently as 1967 stated that "the man who admitted to close friends that he was responsible for the Zinoviev Letter was none other than the master-spy, Sidney Reilly. Evidence which has recently reached me from Russia indicated that Reilly later confessed as much to agents of O.G.P.U."[9]

Did Reilly save his life by making a deal with the Russians? He alone of all secret agents had the rare talent of making even his enemies believe him. There are indications that Reilly remained alive for a considerable time and that he became an agent of the Soviet Government, being regarded in Moscow as a defector of the utmost importance. In many ways he was more important to them than Savinkoff, for not only was he in touch with all kinds of Russian enemies of the régime, but he was the ace spy of the British Secret Service and worked with the French and American Secret Services. Also Reilly knew, as few other agents normally do know, most of the ramifications of the British Secret Service, the top personnel, M.I.5 as well as M.I.1.C., for during his visits to London he had also acted as an adviser to M.I.5. If the Russians wanted to infiltrate the British Secret Service for the first time, Reilly was beyond doubt the man to enable them to do it.

One must consider the whole background to Reilly's life to consider whether he would have betrayed the British. On the credit side were his proven ability over thirty years in the British Secret Service, his bravery, which no one doubted, his vehement support of the anti-Bolsheviks and his constant urging on the British Government of the need to stage a counter-revolution, also that his roots were in the Western World, as was his wife. Then, too, he was reputed to have spent money out of his own pocket on the anti-Bolshevik cause.

On the debit side, however, there is much beneath the surface to provide room for doubts. His illegitimacy had removed from him at an early age any feeling of belonging to any one country. No doubt he was grateful to Britain for giving him his first chance in life, but, as he often told friends, "I have spent much more on providing information for Britain than ever the Secret Service has given me." This was not an idle boast; he had frequently used the fringe benefits of espionage—such as the deal with Blohm and Voss—to supplement his meagre Secret Service pay. He was also unscrupulous and ruthless. The probability that he poisoned the Rev. Hugh Thomas has already been mentioned, but there was also the strange case of his long-lost sister whom he once met in Paris and who, a few days later, was found dead on the pavement outside her hotel. It was thought she had jumped from a top floor window. But was she pushed and did Reilly do the pushing? Reilly never hesitated to kill, if he thought the end justified the means. There is also evidence that on more than one occasion he threatened to kill his first wife.

Then again Reilly was certainly not pro-Czarist: he had never forgiven the Czarist's hatred of the Jews, even if he had covered up his Jewish origins. Politically he was to the left of Savinkoff. Indeed there were times when Reilly told friends that he was convinced that he alone knew how an anti-Bolshevik government should be run. He had a Napoleonic complex in a literal sense: Napoleon was not only his hero, but he collected at great expense all kinds of Napoleonic relics. He was not content to be a cog in the wheel of espionage; he delighted in shaping policy himself and in acquiring power. As to his future, if he stayed with the British Secret Service, this appeared to offer him much less scope in 1925 than it had done in 1918. There had been murmurings against him in the hierarchy. Some said that, with awkward questions being asked in Parliament, obviously implicating his activities, Reilly had become an embarrassment to the Service. Others thought the anti-Bolshevik campaign too risky to continue. Cumming, who had never completely trusted him, had none the less loyally supported him. The new head of M.I.1.C. gave the impression of not wanting to have much to do with him. Between 1921 and 1925 he had been forced more and more into the position of a lone agent. The Foreign Office had also voiced some disapproval of Reilly. Even M.I.5 had begun to have doubts about him.

Had the Russians deliberately leaked some information to the British Secret Service, or, more probably to the Foreign Office, to suggest that Reilly was on their side? They certainly knew that Reilly was under a cloud for a period: Shortly before Cumming retired from the S.I.S. Reilly asked his chief to be put on the permanent staff of M.I.1.C. The request was rejected, and Reilly was deeply upset. There are two possibilities here: either Reilly was angered because his request was turned down and there and then decided to work for the Bolsheviks, or he had been asked by the Soviet to apply for permanent membership of the Secret Service so that he could infiltrate their ranks more thoroughly.

Nothing can be proved and there are several people alive today who knew Reilly and who deny absolutely that he ever went over to the Russian side. Indeed, on balance, I do not think that Reilly had any other ploy in mind than a somewhat devious power game of his own inside the Soviet Union. There is some incriminating evidence that, stemming from Reilly's last trip to Russia, the Soviet forged the first link in the chain that led to Philby, Maclean, Burgess and Blake. The parallel between Reilly and Blake is remarkable. Each man was not British-born, thereby in each case the risk was taken of employing as a master-spy a man of foreign origins. Each man had served in one of the British fighting

Services, Reilly in the R.F.C. and Blake in the Royal Navy. Each, to take an even greater risk, had been asked to play the rôle of a double-agent.

With Reilly's disappearance the British Secret Service lost the nucleus of a small, but useful network inside Russia. It took several years before any comparable network could be built up again. On the other hand it was within a few years of Reilly's reported death that the Russians started to build up a new clandestine organisation inside Britain and began to infiltrate the British Secret Service. Moreover Reilly had contacts inside the British Foreign Office and would be able to advise the Russians on which diplomats were pro-Soviet. The first of these was Reginald Orlando Bridgeman, that same Reggie Bridgeman with whom Compton Mackenzie worked in Athens. Bridgeman, a member of a distinguished family, later contested Uxbridge as a Workers' Candidate and was a member of the British-Soviet Friendship Society and Secretary of the League Against Imperialism.

Reggy Bridgeman was perhaps the first fanatically pro-Soviet supporter in the Diplomatic Service, from which he retired on pension in 1923. He once told the author that he had never seriously believed that Sidney Reilly was "so strongly anti-Bolshevik as he made out. To me he always admitted that in the long run it might be better to join them than to fight them, always imagining—for he was an incurable optimist—that his influence could change them. Reilly was, however, realist enough to know that the Foreign Office needed someone who could understand the Soviet viewpoint."

Yet another man paints a picture of Reilly as "romantically eager to re-organise Bolshevism, if he could not defeat it". A Captain van Narvig, a Finnish subject, who had met Sidney Reilly in Finland, had found out that The Trust was a branch of Soviet Intelligence. "There is no question at all that Reilly did not know he was entering a wolves' lair," van Narvig told the author. "He was fully aware that The Trust was a cover for Russian counter-espionage agents. But Reilly was a changed man after 1922. He was disgusted that the British Secret Service had become pro-German. It was that which made him change his attitude towards the Soviet, though it did not unhappily cause the Soviet to change their attitude to him. Ever since Reilly was captured the

Russians have had two of their own agents inside the British Secret Service."

There is no need to doubt the accuracy of most of van Narvig's information, and indeed, later in this book, it will be seen how extremely accurate much of his intelligence was. He served for a time on the staff of General Mannerheim in Finland. Then for several years he disappeared until in June 1939, he turned up in New York after having made a ten thousand mile journey through Siberia, Russia, Czechoslovakia and Germany.

He then brought vital news to New York of the Nazis' war plans and as this far outweighed in importance what he had to tell about the Soviet Union much of it was never committed to paper. Few in America then believed that the Soviet Union was the menace that Western European powers claimed she was.

Van Narvig was partly responsible for the defection from the Soviet Union of General Walter Krivitsky, at one time the head of Soviet Military Intelligence in Western Europe. Thin, tense, perpetually worried looking, Krivitsky ran Stalin's European spy network by posing as an Amsterdam art dealer and he arrived in the United States, uttering dark warnings about the extent to which Russia had penetrated some Western intelligence services. But the British took a keener interest in him than the Americans. By special arrangement between Herbert Morrison (then Home Secretary)—who with Cabinet approval agreed to act as sponsor—and Louis Waldman, a New York lawyer, Krivitsky was sent secretly to Britain by submarine and provided enough incriminating evidence to convict of espionage a code clerk at the Foreign Office named John Herbert King, who was subsequently sentenced to ten years' imprisonment.

He returned to U.S.A. and the State Department gave Krivitsky an American passport. But in London there was a feeling in Intelligence circles that he had not told all he knew, that something was being held back through fear of the consequences. "He told me when he got back to New York," said van Narvig, "that he was certain he had made a great error in going to London. I asked him why and he replied, 'one just cannot trust the British. The Soviet Union have spies there in very high places. One never knows who is a friend or an enemy.' I told him not to be foolish and he added: 'You knew the agent Reilly. It was his information which enabled us to penetrate the British network. He thought by telling us a little he could help Britain and save himself. In the end he did not help Britain and he did not save himself.' "

Early in 1941 it was suggested that Krivitsky should pay a second visit to Britain, but within a few days of receiving that invitation he was found dead in a room in the Bellevue Hotel on Capitol Hill, with the back of his head blown off by a mushroom bullet. At his side was a bloodstained revolver and four ambiguous farewell notes. It was believed then that he had committed suicide. But since then it has been suspected that Krivitsky was killed by Russian agents who had been warned by somebody in London of his activities, silenced to protect the fact that the Russians had penetrated British Intelligence and the Foreign Office.

Van Narvig was convinced that Krivitsky knew how and by whom the British Intelligence had been penetrated by the Russians. The circumstantial evidence for this theory is substantial. Krivitsky spoke of a recruiting agent "in academic circles at Cambridge" who found suitable candidates for Russian espionage and, while not letting it be known that he was in the network, tipped off the British Communist, Douglas Springhall, to do the recruiting. The spy, John Herbert King, was recruited in this manner; so was Philby. Krivitsky knew all about Philby, for Philby met his first wife, Elizabeth Kohlmann, while on assignment for the Soviet Secret Service in Vienna. Krivitsky met his wife, Tonia, in Vienna where she and Elizabeth Kohlmann were in the same underground cell. Isaac Levine, who wrote Krivitsky's memoirs, recalled that Krivitsky had once made a reference to the presence of a "second traitor" in the Foreign Office, whose name was Scottish and whose habits were bohemian, a description which could have fitted Donald Maclean.

Between 1925 and 1933 the Soviet Intelligence Service was already recruiting in Britain. Kim Philby has stated that he was first recruited into the Soviet Intelligence "in Central Europe in June 1933", adding that "all through my career I have been a straight penetration agent working in the Soviet interest. The fact that I joined the British Secret Intelligence is neither here, nor there. I regarded my S.I.S. appointments purely in the light of cover jobs."[10]

Van Narvig's comments on all this were equally shrewd: "There was never any chance that the Soviet Union would make any agreement with Britain when talks began in the early summer of 1939. They knew that in the British Foreign Office and the Secret Service were men of influence who were predominantly anti-Bolshevik and pro-German. They knew because of what their own agents inside both the F.O. and the S.I.S. told them. They knew perfectly well that these forces would like nothing better than to see Germany and Russia engaged in war while Britain and France looked on from behind the Maginot Line."

21

M.I.6 in the 1930s: A Lack of Policy

In the 'thirties, while M.I.5 concentrated mainly on watching communist subversion at home and, to a lesser extent, on keeping an eye on Sir Oswald Mosley's Blackshirt movement, M.I.6 began to build up an organisation in Gibraltar to watch developments in the Western Mediterranean and in Vienna and Prague to keep an eye on Russia and Germany.

Recruitment still came mainly from the ex-officer ranks and, though investigations into the background of recruits were still carried out, it was all rather perfunctory, with family names counting for rather more than they should have done. "It was all very odd," wrote one of the S.I.S. members, recalling his recruitment in that period, "but everything struck me as odd in those early days—including my manner of entry into the Secret Service. I was an Army officer who had had some experience in the Intelligence side of the general Staff. One day in 1929 I phoned an officer in Military Intelligence to try to fix up a job as an interpreter for a man who had left the Army. The sequel was that I met an Intelligence officer who, after several further talks, suggested that I should resign my commission and enter this field. . . . But nobody at this stage gave me tips on how to work as a spy or how to make contact with likely sources, or how to worm information out of them."[1]

Kim Philby's own account of his recruitment to the British Secret Service is interesting. He was working for *The Times* as a war correspondent in the early summer of 1940 and was obviously expecting some kind of an approach from the S.I.S., mentioning that he "watched various irons I had put in the fire, nudging one or other of them as they appeared to hot up". Then came a call by telephone to the Foreign Editor of *The Times* asking whether he was "available for war work". Soon afterwards Philby found himself "in the forecourt of the St. Ermin's Hotel, near St. James's Park station, talking to Miss Marjorie Maxse . . . an intensely likeable elderly lady. . . . She spoke with authority, and was evidently in a position at least to recommend me for 'interesting' employment. . . . I passed the first examination. . . . At our second meeting, she turned up accompanied by Guy Burgess, whom I knew well. I was put through my paces again. Encouraged by Guy's presence, I began to show off, name-dropping shamelessly. . . . Before we parted Miss Maxse informed me that, if I agreed, I should sever my connection with *The Times* and report for duty to Guy Burgess at an address in Caxton Street, in the same block as the St. Ermin's Hotel."[2]

It was all very casual and many other recruits, with similarly superficial investigation of their backgrounds, were brought into the Secret Service in much the same way in the years between 1936 and the end of 1940.

The ex-Army officer recruit mentioned in the first part of this chapter was first sent to Prague to investigate a report on a new explosive with unknown and perhaps unlimited potentialities, which was being developed in Czechoslovakia. But before going to Prague he had to report to a contact man in Vienna. What this contact man told him about his predecessors as British spies in this part of the world must have made depressing intelligence to the new recruit. One of them was in the habit of worrying his superiors by periodically going off on drinking bouts for days at a time. On one occasion this alcoholic who certainly had no business to be a spy, had been picked up by the Austrian police for being offensive and had been put in a cell. In his briefcase, which luckily had not been tampered with, were all kinds of confidential documents which he had collected earlier in the day. This man's successor was a Rugby Blue whose weakness was philandering and he had attracted unwelcome attention from the police as a result of this.

Perhaps the new recruit was being warned for his own good, but, as he declared himself, "I did not find all this encouraging". He was shown files on the subject of the mystery explosive by his mentor, but, not himself possessing any requisite technical knowledge, he found the details singularly unhelpful.

"Could you give me some idea of how to begin?" he asked his superior. "Are there any standard rules?"

"I don't think there are, really," was the reply. "You'll just have to work it out for yourself. I think everyone has their own methods and I can't think of anything I can tell you."

After a year the new recruit made some progress. A technician whom he had contacted asked if he could arrange for an inspection team to come from London to see a demonstration of the explosive. A three-man mission was eventually sent out and the party drove to a wood outside Prague where an experimental explosion was carried out. The noise brought troops to the woods and the technician had some difficulty in explaining away their little experiment.

Four years after the investigation of this explosive had been started the British agent was asked for an advance of one thousand pounds to keep the experiment going. He attended various meetings in London in which the case for and against paying the money was debated. Finally an Inter-Service meeting was held in the War Office to reach a decision. The Navy and the Air Force were in favour of paying the money; the Army were against it. Thus, recalled the agent ruefully, "I am personally convinced that we lost a great opportunity. I suppose we shall never know whether, for the sake of a thousand pounds, we missed the chance of acquiring data which might have had immense importance when the war came."

Agents in the field in the immediate pre-war years found that they were frequently cramped by the rigid system of accounting for every single penny they had to spend in secret work. The system was ruled over by a naval paymaster who not only brought an intensely bureaucratic mind to bear on the subject of agents' expenses, but on occasions travelled overseas to see for himself how the money was being spent. Unfortunately for the agents this paymaster liked to indulge in lavish night life expenditure on his visits abroad and on the mornings after these exploits would rebuke the agents for the wildly extravagant lives they led.

Partly through the S.I.S. and partly through the N.I.D. links were established with important contacts in the ranks of the dissenting generals in Nazi Germany and in Franco's entourage in Spain, but for some reason little attempt seems to have been made to acquire effective liaison with anyone who had the Duce's ear in Italy. Here, in the "soft under-belly of the Axis Powers", was surely a most fruitful ground for infiltration, yet it was sadly neglected and may well have been a contributory factor to Mussolini committing himself so irrevocably to the Nazi cause. For some reason the Secret Service took the view that Spain was the country in which to seek friends. Anyone who had given the impression of being on the Republicans' side in the Spanish Civil War was almost immediately suspect, yet someone like Philby, who had been a war correspondent on the Franco side and had been personally awarded the Red Cross of Military Merit by Franco, was given almost instantaneous approval.

The chief contact on the Spanish side was Juan March, that former head of the smuggling ring who had been won over to the side of British intelligence in World War I. There had been a certain amount of independent lobbying for support in this direction in the early 'thirties and there is no doubt that some of the Secret Service and the N.I.D. had paid more attention to the views of Sir Basil Zaharoff than Admiral Hall would ever have countenanced. Zaharoff had long been a friend of Juan March and he had also struck up an acquaintance with Admiral Canaris, the German intelligence chief. Both men were fond of Spain and Greece and Canaris was much more at home with Latin and Mediterranean peoples than with Teutons. It was Zaharoff who had first interested Canaris through Juan March in the need for underground aid to stamp out Republicanism in Spain. When Juan March escaped from Spain to Gibraltar in 1933 to get away from Republican forces who had sworn he was the enemy of democracy, the N.I.D. tipped him off about his possible arrest and arranged his escape from the Alcara de Henares prison where he had been held on charges of alleged tobacco smuggling. It is also thought that Basil Zaharoff had a hand in this, too.

But by 1934 Zaharoff and Juan March, as a result of talks with Canaris, began to have doubts about the Nazis. Juan March, who was firmly on the side of Franco, nevertheless warned that Hitler would stop at nothing in his aim to dominate Europe. He wrote to a Naval Intelligence friend in Madrid that Canaris had the same forebodings and "does not love, nor trust his new masters. He is our best ally in Europe at the moment." He also added something that was even more significant: "Zaharoff," he said, "is horrified at the idea that Germany may once again perpetrate another world war."[3]

It was Juan March who first put the Secret Service on the track of Canaris as a man to be watched, cultivated and possibly won over as—his own words "a sleeping partner of British espionage." He also advised that contacts should be established with General von Kleist, of the German High Command, the late Baron von Thyssen, the industrialist, and Beigbeder, the Spanish High Commissioner in Morocco. In the light of events all this was very sound advice for any intelligence service. Unfortunately the Secret Service moved far too timidly, always conscious perhaps that the Chamberlain Government was so hell-bent on appeasement of the dictators that they would shrink from any moves to undermine them. Certainly von Kleist and Canaris both seemed anxious in 1937–38 to convince the British that they must call Hitler's bluff. But that chance was lost at Munich after von Kleist had been to London to put forward just such a case. Von Thyssen, first a supporter of the Nazis, later deserted them. Beigbeder was not only strongly anti-Nazi, but he hoped for a German defeat; here the British had a strong, if secret ally, but a blunder was made by the Secret Service when a female British agent was introduced to Beigbeder with disastrous results, he believing there was a deliberate attempt to compromise him. Partly as a result of that incident Beigbeder lost his considerable influence with Franco.

One of the astutest minds in the Gibraltar section of British Naval Intelligence was Don Gomez-Beare, who later became Naval attaché in Madrid during Sir Samuel Hoare's period of ambassadorship. Gomez-Beare was always close to Juan March and through him had a good deal of indirect information about what Canaris was thinking. Most of it was cautiously encouraging; in fact it almost seemed as though Canaris was inviting the British to open up communications with him.

Not surprisingly the hierarchy of the Secret Service was deeply split on the question of whether an understanding with Canaris was desirable. At best it seemed to be a wildly optimistic gamble that might come off; at worst it could be an invitation to walk into a well-laid trap with disastrous consequences. Those who saw Bolshevism as the main enemy naturally tended to take more notice of the optimistic reports on Canaris. They pointed out that if the British Secret Service could come to an understanding with Canaris, it might be possible to pool information on the machinations of international communism. But those who regarded Germany as Britain's potential enemy were highly suspicious. Canaris' whole career was one which did not suggest he was any better than a good German patriot and in some respects he was a downright scoundrel. He had fought against the British when he served in German cruisers in the South Atlantic in World War I; he was reputed to have paid Mata Hari to spy on the French and the Secret Service knew that in World War I he had worked against the Allies in Madrid and organised the sabotage of French installations in Morocco by giving subsidies to Moorish tribes. In 1916 he had landed in New York from a neutral ship under the name of Moses Meyerbeer; in fact he was a saboteur who carried bombs in his violin case to plant in American arms factories. He escaped back across the Atlantic in a British ship with a forced Chilean passport under the name of Mr. Reed-Rosas. After the war he was suspected of having been behind the murders of German Communists and Social Democrats, but nothing could be proved. He had also negotiated for U-boats of German design to be secretly built in Holland, Spain and Japan during those years when the Versailles Treaty had forbidden these craft to Germany.

As a man he possessed immense charm, but the coldness of his piercing eyes struck terror into the heart of anyone unfortunate enough to be cross-examined by him. He could be gentle, softly spoken and disarming, but with the slightest change of inflection in his voice his whole personality changed. He had a passion for Spain and visited the country as often as he could; to intimates he would also profess a love of Britain and a great admiration for her Navy, but to most, even of those who worked closely with him, he remained an enigma, a man who seemed to want people to believe he trusted them, but who in fact trusted nobody, a man who would pit his own judgement against that of all others.

This was Admiral Wilhelm Canaris, head of the *Abwehr*, the German intelligence organisation which he had built up as efficiently as had Colonel Nicolai many years before.

The Secret Service also knew that it was largely-through Canaris' influence that Hitler had promised to intervene in the Spanish Civil War at a time when the Fuhrer's more conservative generals opposed such a plan. They had discovered that Canaris had organised the sale to the Spanish Republican Government of defective arms, carefully sabotaged, through intermediaries in Poland, Holland and Finland. All this suggested that any overtures from such a man should be treated with the greatest misgivings.

One interesting and significant item of news which the N.I.D. learned from Juan March was that Canaris had in fact discussed with a few such intimates as Fabian von Schlabrendorff a young Conservative Prussian, the possibility of working clandestinely with the British Secret Service against Hitler. Canaris was prepared to listen to such talk, but equally he was astute enough to point out the dangers of such a plan. "The N.I.D. of today," he told Juan March, "is not so circumspect as that of Admiral Hall's day. It is run by amateurs, brilliant men no doubt, but often irresponsible and apt to talk too much. I have penetrated them and M.I.6, and I know. So if any German, however important and discreet, felt tempted to work with the British Secret Service, be sure I should find out about it. Now in that Secret Service there are conflicting minds and it could well happen that one section of the Secret Service would keep faith, but that the other would not hesitate to betray any such Germans either to me, or someone else in the *Abwehr*. And that might force me to take action I should not wish to take."

This was somewhat obscure advice and open to various interpretations. It could be that Canaris was simply warning the fellow plotters against premature moves. But it was more likely that Canaris, always very much of a lone plotter, preferred to keep matters entirely in his own hands and wished to dissuade other even friendly Germans from opening up their own lines of communications with the British, possibly allowing them to think he was hostile to the project while secretly going ahead with it. On the other hand Canaris had good reason, according to Juan

March, for suspecting that there were people in the Secret Service who would deliberately sabotage any secret communications between him and the British. In Canaris' opinion this risk was great because the "two extremes of opinion in the Secret Service" were hostile to such a plan. By this he meant those who took the Chamberlain line and feared that war would be inevitable if an attempt was made to link up with Hitler's enemies in Germany and the Nazis discovered this, and those who preferred to risk war and chaos rather than make a deal with the kind of forces in Germany Canaris represented.

Whatever his doubts Canaris did all he could to warn Britain of the folly of not standing up to Hitler, never directly, of course, but sometimes by leakages from Spain to the N.I.D., and also by mysterious envoys who came to London. The N.I.D. was singularly unimaginative in not paying more attention to these reports, but it would seem that while news from Spain encouraged them to strengthen their links with the Admiral, reports from their agents in Central Europe were quite the reverse. In Germany the N.I.D. at that time was very badly served. Yet Canaris persevered. He was especially active at the time of the Munich crisis, even hinting that the German General Staff were prepared to arrest Hitler if he went to war. In 1938 he sent a close friend, General Edwald von Kleist, to London to urge the Chamberlain Government to state openly that if Hitler attacked Czechoslovakia, Britain would declare war. But Chamberlain did not want to listen. Obstinately, in spite of all warnings, he insisted on continuing a policy of appeasement.

While Chamberlain and his government must take most of the blame for missing these opportunities, the Secret Service, too, can be faulted for not taking fuller advantages of the situation. There was a total lack of co-ordination of the reports of their own agents in many cases, a lack of co-operation between M.I.6 and the N.I.D. and a failure on the part of the hierarchy of the Secret Service to give coherent guidance to the Government. A stronger government would have asked more questions; this particular government just did not wish to know.

In the middle and late 'thirties M.I.5 considerably increased its personnel. By 1939 Major-General Kell had approaching six thousand persons working for him in some capacity or other, part-time or full-time. He had not only infiltrated the Communist and Fascist ranks in Britain, but had most efficiently penetrated the organisation which was handling recruitment for the Spanish Republican Army. The result was that when World War II came some six thousand people were rounded up and interned as suspects, though only thirty-five of these were Britons. Before this there had been an intensive search for would-be saboteurs in the dockyards which had culminated in 1937 in the dismissal of five dockyard workers from Chatham and Devonport. M.I.5 had not wanted any publicity and the men had been dismissed without any charges being brought against them. Immediately an outcry arose of "secret police methods" and questions were asked in the House of Commons. In fact M.I.5 had abundant evidence of sabotage—one case of sand and brass filings being put in the machinery of a Fleet oil-tanker and another case of an attempt to damage the motors of a submarine. The First Lord of the Admiralty, Sir Samuel Hoare, was not able to reveal much in reply to these criticisms, but he was at least able to give an assurance that as a double check on the allegations the whole case had been referred to a tribunal of three Senior Civil Servants.

As it became apparent that Germany was once again building up a network of spies and saboteurs inside Britain so the problem became one of patiently tracking the network to its source rather than making premature arrests. Risks had to be taken, but Kell did not hesitate to repeat his tactics of World War I. A labourer named Joseph Kelly, working at a Royal Ordnance factory in Lancashire, had been seen visiting the German Consul in Liverpool. Immediately orders were given for Kelly's mail to be opened and one letter revealed the name of a German agent in Holland, offering Kelly work as a spy. M.I.5 had enough evidence to arrest Kelly when he was seen to break into the works office of his factory and steal site plans. But no action was then taken. It was a gamble, but it paid dividends. Shortly afterwards Kelly received money for his fare to Germany and M.I.5 watched him all the way to his port of departure and then handed the matter over to M.I.6. This enabled them to track down the agent in Holland and to several other German agents whose cover names and addresses were now discovered. Later Kelly was arrested, tried and sentenced to ten years' imprisonment.

By 1938 M.I.5 had to take in the work of screening all the refugees from Nazi-occupied Europe who flocked into Britain. Not until it was too late did the authorities realise that this sudden rise in the number of foreigners in Britain imposed a severe strain on the police and M.I.5. By that time many German spies had entered the country in the guise of refugees. This created a chaotic situation for the security forces and when war came there was something akin to panic in their ranks. A great many genuine anti-Nazis were interned in the summer of 1940, while a few, but a very dangerous few escaped altogether and wrought much mischief. While not wishing to make an irrelevant digression into the controversial question of coloured immigrants into Britain during the post-war years, it seems apposite enough from a security point of view to state that in the event of another conventional war (as distinct from a nuclear war) the problem of screening something like three million immigrants, thousands of whom have got into the country illegally, would be well nigh impossible.

Security in the immediate pre-war years was not merely lax, it was often non-existent. There is also no evidence that the Secret Service—and here the emphasis is on M.I.6 more than M.I.5—gave any adequate warnings about it. No wonder that Canaris was so critical about this aspect of British intelligence and diplomacy. German intelligence had in part at least penetrated British diplomatic ciphers, but in their interpretation of what they learned the Germans made several mistakes and miscalculations. The British Embassy staff in Berlin were appallingly careless and indiscreet in their use of the telephone, despite the fact that it was known the Germans were tapping their wires. The biggest offender was the Ambassador himself, Sir Nevile Henderson, who on 31 August 1939, committed three gross breaches of security by telephoning the Polish Embassy in Berlin, the French Embassy in Berlin and the British Foreign Office, passing on a warning he had just had from the Italian Ambassador and Ulrich Von Hassel, a confirmed anti-Nazi, that Poland was to be invaded.[4]

One reason undoubtedly for Italian apprehensions about considering even as a remote possibility some rapprochement with Britain was that they had discovered that there was already a traitor in the British Foreign Office even if the Secret Service was unaware of this. Italian intelligence had been shocked by the appalling lack of security in the British Embassy in Rome, where the safe was burgled regularly every week and confidential papers copied out and passed on to the Italian authorities. The agent who performed this task was a professional thief who, emboldened by his success, also stole the Ambassador's wife's (Lady Perth) tiara. Despite this Lord Perth declined absolutely to improve the Embassy security services. Thus the Italians not only secured the British diplomatic ciphers, but gained a close insight into British policy and the ineptitude of the British Foreign Office in that period.

But another factor must have made the Italians shake their heads even more about Britain. Their agent also worked for the Russians (unknown to the Italians, of course) and there is no doubt that the Russians fed him with a certain amount of information to pass on to the Italians. One such tit-bit he did pass on was that the Russians had one of their agents actually working in the archives section of the British Foreign Office. At first the Italians refused to believe this. Later they found it to be correct.

At this time Donald Maclean was in the British Embassy in Paris, so it was not Maclean who was involved, which poses the question of who was the fifth man in the British diplomatic and Secret Services who was a traitor, the man who preceded Philby, Maclean, Burgess and Blake.

However the British had their successes even in these doldrum days. They penetrated the Japanese ciphers, they gained some limited insight into Italian ciphers and in 1939 they obtained keys to German military ciphers from the Polish military intelligence.

In 1939 Sir Paul Dukes had yet another of his spectacular adventures in the sphere of espionage. He was sent to Germany, ostensibly on behalf of a group of London industrialists, to ascertain the truth about the disappearance of a wealthy Czech business man on his way from Prague to Switzerland.

The Czech, Alfred Obry, had fallen foul of the Nazis at the time of the German occupation of Czechoslovakia. The Nazis coveted the huge enterprises he controlled and wanted to force him to sign them away. His relatives, who had escaped to England a few days previously, knew that he had bought a false passport and was planning to escape there as well, disguised as an artisan. But Obry failed to turn up.

Paul Dukes was always a meticulous agent in paying attention to detail. He combed all the local papers of Czechoslovakia and in one he found this paragraph:

"A thirteen-year-old boy found on the railway line near Tuschkau the completely unrecognisable corpse of a man. The body was mutilated beyond recognition and the right hand was missing. The police pronounced a verdict of suicide. From papers found on the body it appeared that the individual was Friedrich Schweiger, a tailor of Prague."

Dukes immediately suspected that Schweiger was in fact Alfred Obry, especially as this was the route Obry was to have taken on his escape. He built up a strong case against the Gestapo of murdering Obry and not only demanded the exhumation of the body, but succeeded in persuading the Germans to do this. The corpse was undoubtedly that of Obry.

During 1939 the re-organisation of the Secret Service was begun in earnest. M.I.1.C. had now disappeared and the espionage and counter-espionage branches were now respectively M.I.6 and M.I.5, the former being usually designated the Secret Intelligence Service and the latter the Security Service. It should perhaps be pointed out that "M.I." stands for military intelligence, but that this is an anachronism, since neither agency is concerned directly with military intelligence, and the military intelligence sections of the Defence Ministry are quite separate from either.

Both M.I.5 and M.I.6 are known as such to every other Secret Service in the world, yet while the Russians, the French, the Americans and the Germans acknowledge the existence of their own intelligence services by name, secrecy is still carried to absurd lengths in Whitehall. A perfect example of this fatuity was provided in Lord Denning's official report on the Profumo Scandal, published in 1963. He stated that "the Security Service in this country is not established by Statute nor is it recognised by Common Law. Even the Official Secrets Acts do not acknowledge its existence."[5]

Responsibility for the Secret Service falls directly on the Prime Minister of the day. He alone (in theory at least) has access to the

Joint Intelligence Committee, which is comprised of the heads of four intelligence services—M.I.5, M.I.6 and Military Intelligence and the N.I.D. At the outbreak of war in 1939 Military Intelligence was in the process of being reorganised, but this work was not completed until the following year when it became imperative to speed it up owing to the S.I.S. having lost some of their networks when the Germans overran Europe. Then, under the direction of Winston Churchill, the S.O.E., or Special Operations Executive was formed by Dr. Hugh Dalton, Minister of Economic Warfare, combining under its command D section of the S.I.S., which, incidentally, was the section in which Kim Philby worked.

To grasp fully the implications of the intelligence set-up in 1939, it must be realised that there was no overlord of intelligence, a fact which in war-time inevitably forced the Prime Minister to be sole arbiter in this sphere. But to prevent this from putting too much power in one man's hands, or giving him the burden of too much responsibility, there was the theoretical safeguard that the head of M.I.5 had direct access to the Home Secretary, the head of M.I.6 to the Foreign Office, and those of Military Intelligence and the N.I.D. to the Ministry of Defence and the Admiralty respectively.

M.I.6 had a new chief at the outset of World War II, Colonel Stewart Menzies. This section of the Secret Service had suffered severely between the wars through undermanning and lack of funds and while Sinclair, a more forceful character than Menzies, was unable in peacetime to persuade the powers-that-be to do anything about this, Menzies in war-time, despite his mild manner, managed after some preliminary tussles in obtaining a much freer hand. Where Sinclair had failed had been in his personal uncertainty as to what the priority targets for espionage should be, a failing which unfortunately was shared by the various governments under which he served. Certainly Germany had not been a priority target for M.I.6 and the fluctuations in policy towards Russia had also caused a great deal of confusion. Menzies made one of his first tasks to lay down clearly what the various targets were. The tragedy was that he had to start from the disadvantage of an organisation singularly ill-equipped to assess intelligence coming out of Germany.

Right, Sir Vernon Kell, founder of M.I.5; *below, left,* Sir Basil Thomson; *right,* Sir Robert Bruce Lockhart

Above, Prae Wood, near St. Albans, H.Q. of Section V of the S.I.S.; *below,* one of the Vichy cipher books captured by 'Cynthia'

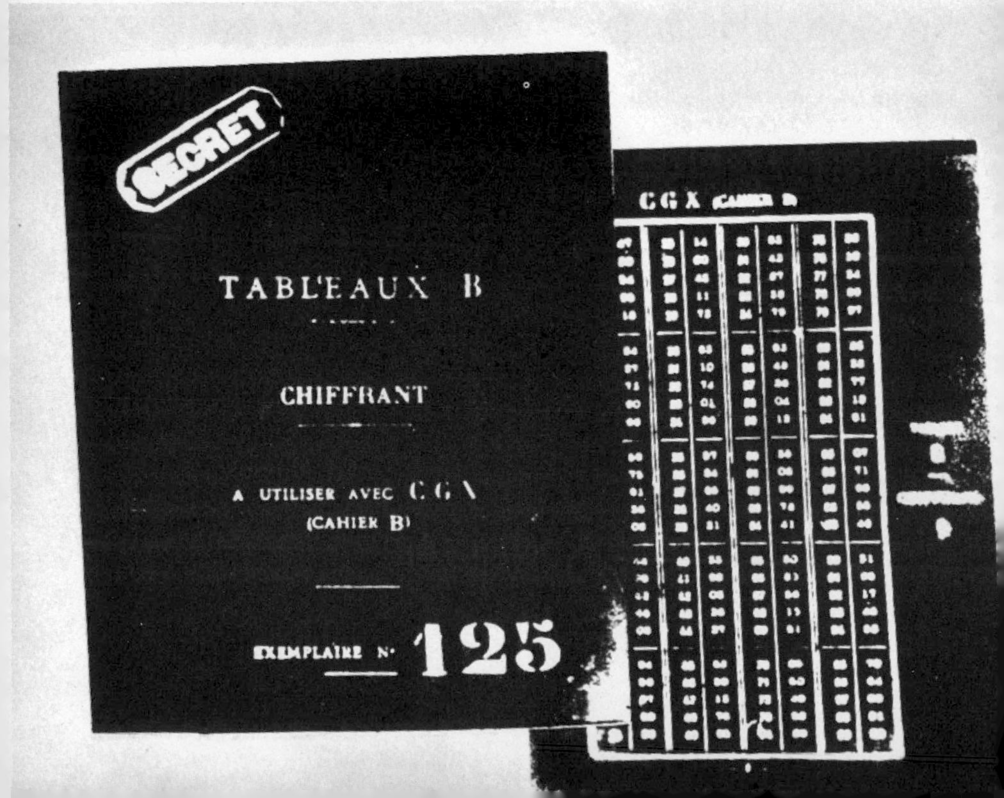

The legend of a supremely efficient, diabolically clever and utterly ruthless British Secret Service had lived on during the inter-war years. If the Germans had contempt for the British armed forces, at least they still had a great respect for the Secret Service. This respect was to prove an unexpected bonus for the Secret Service in 1940. Yet the truth was that the legend masked a run-down, unimaginative and badly staffed Service. Under Admiral Sinclair recruiting for personnel had been mainly from ex-Naval officers, especially from those who had been axed in the stringent economy cuts of 1931. As in all such cuts the least promising material is always axed first, this meant that the S.I.S. received many recruits who did not measure up to their jobs.

Menzies' most exacting task was in his dealings with a Prime Minister who was more probing, more critical and demanding than any of his predecessors. Churchill was not the man to be in awe of an intelligence chief, nor did he wish to listen to excuses for past failures and lengthy catalogues of the reasons why this or that task could not accomplished. He also made it quite clear to Menzies that he must change his methods of recruitment and not follow Admiral Sinclair's policy of recruiting bowler-hatted ex-officers.

The background of the new M.I.6 chief was conventional enough—Eton, service in the Grenadier Guards in World War I, in which he won the D.S.O. and M.C., and, more recently, Army Intelligence. It is easy to see that anyone with this background, unless he had had Churchill's warning, might well have chosen ex-Army officers if only because it would be easier to enforce Service discipline. All his life Menzies had kept to a rigidly conventional military pattern in his career and was quite unlike some of the more bohemian characters who had previously filled this post. While lacking any great intellectual powers, he possessed a remarkable gift of intuition and this enabled him to weave his far from easy path through the maze of problems in the political arena. He was generally respected both among his own staff and other intelligence chiefs with whom he came in contact, but he was always conscious that the S.I.S. was the most criticised branch of the Secret Service and that his job was coveted by others.

Menzies' gift for intuition was remarkable in that while it never seemed to range over the rank and file of his staff, or even over his junior executives, it frequently showed almost clairvoyant qualities in assessing men he had never even met. He was peculiarly sensitive to making unfair snap judgements on his own staff and this inhibited him. On the other hand when judging the enemy he showed sound powers of assessment. One of his staff once said that " 'C' understood Admiral Canaris better than he did me." That may have been an overstatement, but if Menzies had allowed himself to follow his hunches on Canaris, he might have brought off the biggest *coup* of the war. From the very beginning he had a great respect for and curiosity about Canaris, and believed that the S.I.S. had made a great mistake in not establishing better contacts in that quarter years before. He set out to make these contacts himself through various intermediaries, despite the fact that he had no encouragement from on high and no co-operation from other intelligence departments in doing so. By the end of 1942, when the Allies had invaded North Africa, he was in a position to open direct negotiations with him. Menzies had no illusions about Canaris: he realised that the Admiral's chief concern was to preserve German power intact as a price for helping to end the war. But he was sufficiently realistic to know that with Canaris' co-operation some means might be found of removing Hitler from power, shortening the war and bringing about a negotiated peace. Menzies thought this solution was in Britain's long-term interests, but the "unconditional surrender" theme of the Casablanca Conference sounded the death knell of any such plan. He stated afterwards that he was thwarted in certain Foreign Office quarters "for fear of offending Russia".

As the Secret Service had then already been penetrated by Russia and the Soviet had at least two spies in the British Foreign Office, it is not unlikely that Menzies' ideas were leaked to Russia who duly put pressure on the Foreign Office.

22

Sir David Petrie's Task

When World War II broke out M.I.5 believed it could repeat its success of 1914 of rounding up all enemy agents in Britain. But to some extent this pious hope was thwarted partly by the stream of refugees from Nazi Germany who had come to Britain in the two previous years and partly by improved German methods of espionage.

Some spies managed to slip in with the refugees. But the body blow to M.I.5 came in October 1939, when a German U-boat glided into the hitherto impregnable anchorage of Scapa Flow and sank the battleship, *Royal Oak*. This feat owed everything to the careful planning of a German spy named Alfred Wahring, a former naval officer, who had established a cover for himself as a Swiss watch-maker under the name of Albert Oertel. In 1927, using a Swiss passport, he had come to Britain, eventually becoming a naturalised Englishman, settling in a jeweller's and watchmaker's shop at Kirkwall in the Orkneys, close to Scapa Flow. He had provided German intelligence with reports over many years and in October 1939, had informed his masters that there were no anti-submarine nets at the eastern approach to the naval anchorage.

Of course, the failure to detect Oertel was a black mark for M.I.5: it was criminal negligence not to have checked more carefully on a naturalised watch-maker who had had a Swiss passport. But worse was to come. In the early months of 1940 time-bombs wrecked an arms factory at Waltham Abbey in Essex. Again M.I.5 failed to find the saboteurs.

Not unnaturally criticism was directed against M.I.5 who until then had been remarkably free from the kind of prolonged nagging fault-finding to which M.I.6 had been subjected. It was unfortunate that this criticism came when Kell's health was rapidly deteriorating. Inevitably, when he resigned in 1940 it was suggested that he had been made a scapegoat for M.I.5's failures. In fact he had carried on at his post despite his chronic asthma, standing up to suffering which would have defeated a lesser character years before. But by 1940 he realised that he could not do his job properly under war-time conditions and ill health alone was the reason for his departure. It was an unhappy end to a career which in length of service is still unparalleled in the history of M.I.5.

Then came the panic measure introduced as Regulation 18 B, a clumsy, hastily contrived and thoroughly unsatisfactory piece of legislation. Even worse was the vicious and cynical manner in which it was interpreted by the new Home Secretary, Herbert Morrison. The latter, though he was a member of a Coalition Government, sought every possible means of gaining kudos for the Labour party by showing how guilty were those of the Right Wing. At the same time he pursued a vendetta against the Blackshirt Movement of Sir Oswald Mosley which was out of all proportion to its importance in terms of national security. A large number of innocent Britons were rounded up and imprisoned without being charged, many of them having only been guilty of ventilating indiscreet opinions in war-time. To the extent that the general public believed that by making these arrests the Government was at last alive to the dangers of the much-vaunted Fifth Column, 18 B can be said to have succeeded. In its long-term effects it was of little use to the war effort and gave M.I.5 a great deal of unnecessary work.

There was no Fifth Column in Britain as there had been on the Continent. Not even the I.R.A. gave much trouble once war was declared, though they had been active right up to that time, convinced that after Chamberlain's flight to Munich they had only to cause a few bomb explosions to bring that same Prime Minister post-haste to Dublin with a guarantee that he would hand over Ulster to Eire. One or two I.R.A. men played along with the Germans, but more to take their money and mislead them than to be active spies. For example when the Germans persuaded a group of I.R.A. men to establish a radio link in Liverpool and encouraged them to carry out acts of sabotage, they were superbly hoodwinked. Over the secret radio came reports of the sabotage they had carried out. Then came the report that they had wrecked the Manchester Ship Canal. On checking this information the Germans learned that the report had been made the moment the bomb was placed in position and that in fact it had failed to explode. Even those Irish who actively collaborated with the Germans (and there were relatively few of them), such as Sean Russell, detested the Nazis and only co-operated in the larger cause of a "Free Ireland". Colonel Lahousen, officer in charge of the sabotage section of the *Abwehr* (German Intelligence), declared that his associations with the Irish had been "disastrously unlucky" and that Irish agents were "devilishly independent and undisciplined".

On the whole M.I.5 roundly defeated German espionage inside Britain during World War II, though not so easily as they had in the previous war. As has been stated, German methods of espionage had vastly improved and the few who succeeded were highly successful. For some months after Kell's departure M.I.5 underwent a constant change in personnel and so much reorganisation that, instead of being able to concentrate on their own tasks, they frequently found themselves involved in those of M.I.6. This, however, was not the fault of the new war-time chief of the service, Sir David Petrie, who had an immensely difficult task to perform, for M.I.5 not only had to keep a watch on German spies, but on Russian, Italian and even Spanish agents as well. To make this task more manageable Sir David brought in various experts to form sections to deal with the various types of agent.

David Petrie, a Scot, educated at Aberdeen University, had served in the Indian Police from 1900–36 and had at one time been Assistant Director of Criminal Intelligence to the Government of India, finally rising to the post of Director of the Intelligence Bureau to that Government. Perhaps his most notable achievement was to bring the various sections of his department into closer and tighter liaison with their counter-part sections in M.I.6. For example when Petrie brought in Roger Hollis, a former representative of the British-American Tobacco Company in China, to head the department of M.I.5 handling communist affairs, a direct link was established with the section of M.I.6 which assessed Soviet and communist espionage.

One serious omission by M.I.5 at this time was its failure to appreciate that though no worthwhile Fifth Column of German spies existed in Britain, there was a tiny, but compact and potentially highly dangerous network of German agents among the Welsh nationalists, some of them actually members of the Welsh Nationalist Party. It should be made clear that the Welsh Nationalist Party itself had nothing whatsoever to do with the net-work and perhaps because of this organisation's respectability and religious undertones (its members were mainly Welsh Nonconformist teetotallers) M.I.5 had ignored the possibility of trouble from this quarter in the years immediately preceding the war.

Faulty liaison with M.I.6 was partly to blame for this, as well as inadequate intelligence from Germany in the immediate prewar period. It should have been noted that not only had the Germans paid special attention to Welsh nationalism, but they had used key members of their intelligence service to make contacts among them.

What made the Germans place so much importance on what would appear to have been very infertile ground for recruiting spies? It dated back to the visit paid to Hitler in 1936 by Lloyd George who had returned home enthusiastically to praise the Fuhrer and the German experiment. Then Lloyd George had defiantly backed Edward VIII against the Baldwin Government at the time of the Abdication and had lamented the fact that he was far away in Jamaica and could not oppose the King's departure in Parliament. The Germans thought that an alliance between Lloyd George, the most famous living Welshman, and the ex-King, who had been Prince of Wales, could be exploited to bring about a negotiated peace.

Alleging that Germany had active sympathisers among "a group of Welsh nationalists", Dr. L. De Jong, a Dutch historian, in his book *The German Fifth Column* stated: "In the spring of 1940 a group of Welsh nationalists lent themselves for this purpose. Six months later it was noted in Berlin that they had developed along the lines of the task set by the *Abwehr*."[1]

De Jong's book was compiled with the aid of captured German documents, including diaries of the *Abwehr*. There is abundant evidence that in 1940 this group was extremely active.

Hauptmann Nikolaus Ritter, former head of the *Abwehr* branch, *Ast-Hamburg*, has recorded that two German agents were dropped by parachute near Salisbury in the summer of 1940 to "contact Welsh nationalist circles who had already expressed themselves as willing to help in the event of a Nazi invasion of Wales". Referring to a fire started in an aircraft factory at Denham in April 1940, the *Abwehr*'s official diaries state that this was "the first major sabotage task set for the Welsh agents' group, while a note dated 15 August 1940, signed by Colonel (later Major-General) Lahousen, says: "The dispatch of agents to take up direct contact with the Welsh group has been approved by me."[2]

The Nazis must have been encouraged by these developments for they worked out a plan to capture Wales by a combination of paratroops and seaborne divisions which were to be based on Ireland. This was "Operation Green", linking up the invasion of Wales with that of Ireland, and it was to have been launched at the end of August 1941. A subordinate part of this project, code-named "Whale", concerned the Welsh part of this operation, and the *Abwehr* diaries again reveal that "an attempt is to be made to set down the agent Lehrer with a wireless operator on the coast of South Wales in order to establish better communications with the Welsh nationalists".[3]

However, in this case German hopes far exceeded realities. The number of Welshmen who were prepared to betray their country and work with the Germans was mercifully few. The ablest of these spies was one Arthur Owens who had volunteered to serve the Germans as early as 1937 and, because he travelled as a salesman in electrical equipment, was able before the war to visit the Continent without arousing suspicion. Owens quickly proved his worth by passing on information about arms factories, munitions dumps, air fields and port installations. It was largely through a detailed map of the port area of Swansea that he enabled the *Luftwaffe* to deliver a deadly blow against vital strategic targets there.

Owens was well paid by the Germans who regarded him in many respects as their prize agent. But when war came communications with Germany proved to be difficult, if not impossible. So Owens was ordered to travel to Lisbon. As Lisbon was then one of the most notorious spy centres in the world the British authorities should have been alerted, but they seem to have failed to make any check on his movements. Owens arrived safely, contacted a German agent and handed over more information. This time he had amassed an amazing amount of material from plans of new airfields, details of new radar equipment and sketches of the latest developments in bomb-sights. Owens was pressed to give details of how he obtained the material: his story was that he had been given it by an officer who had recently been dismissed from the R.A.F.

The Germans were anxious to meet this ex-officer. They suspected a possible "plant", but agreed to put the matter to the test by asking Owens to arrange for the man to come to Lisbon. Much to their surprise Owens agreed to fix this and, to their even greater amazement, the ex-officer eventually arrived at the Portguese capital.

Now although M.I.5 would appear to have been singularly lax in not catching up with Owens, somebody elsewhere in the Secret Service had been working for some time to track down the Welsh nationalist spy net-work. The most curious feature of this story, which has never been told before, is that the member of the Secret Service responsible for this initiative was almost certainly a double-agent, undoubtedly working with the Americans as well as the British, and possibly also for the Russians.

Early in 1940 a free-lance American agent who had managed to get himself on the staff of Admiral Canaris' intelligence service reported back to Washington news of a conversation between Hitler and Dr. Robert Ley, founder of the *Arbeitsfront*, about working for a secret understanding with Lloyd George in the hope that he might yet be called to form a British Government which would make peace with Germany. He added that Hitler had personally urged that steps must be taken to speed up contacts with Welsh nationalists.

There seems no doubt that Canaris allowed this message to be leaked for reasons best known to himself, but for a long time Washington refused to take the information seriously. When Churchill became Premier the State Department was even less inclined to pay any attention to the report. However, somebody, either the American agent working in the *Abwehr*, or an agent in the U.S. Government, decided to act on his own accord. For this information was next repeated to a free-lance informer in Tangier who was known to be anti-German and pro-Soviet, while actually working for both the British and American intelligence services. The informant insisted on keeping his anonymity and said he was making this roundabout approach because he suspected the Americans would not believe him and that the British were not to be trusted because there were "too many secret German sympathisers and appeasers in the British Secret Service". But, he added, if proper use was made of this information the German intelligence could be effectively penetrated in one section that Canaris did not control—the sabotage section. What was more, such penetration could be used to delay indefinitely German plans to invade Britain.

The Tangier free-lance informer was impressed by the details given of the Welsh nationalist spy net-work, but was curious to know exactly how he was supposed to use this intelligence if he could not pass it on officially to the British or Americans. He was then given the name of a pro-Soviet sympathiser inside M.I.6 who would "shortly be coming to Tangier".

In due course the information was passed on as requested and there was then a surprising chain of reactions. First the ex-R.A.F. officer turned up in Lisbon and met the German agent. So important seemingly was the information which he brought along that the German agent took him to Germany. There the ex-officer met several key men in different intelligence sections and inevitably learned a great deal about the German spy network. However, the Germans, while delighted with the material he had brought with him, decided that a check on his past career was essential, being puzzled as to why he had been dismissed on the grounds of "political unreliability". Exactly how they made their check is not absolutely clear, but it would seem that they examined a tiny snapshot which the ex-officer carried around with him without his realising that it had been "borrowed". An enlargement of the snapshot revealed code numbers and these were identified as an address used by Soviet agents. The ex-officer was apparently a communist spy.

Admiral Canaris refused to allow the spy to be detained, insisting that he must be taken back to Lisbon as though nothing had happened and then watched. But when he had to change planes in Madrid the man disappeared.

From then on little more was heard of the Welsh spies. By a simple tip from Tangier their net-work had been infiltrated and exploited in the heart of Germany. From that moment attempts were made systematically to feed the Germans with information calculated to make them believe that Britain was much more strongly defended than previous reports had suggested. The S.I.S. aimed to use its own net-works to delay any attempt to invade Britain. In case reports of a Britain growing stronger every day failed to convince them, the alternative plan was to lure them into believing that there was no need to invade Britain because sooner or later a Fifth Column inside the country would overthrow the Churchill Government and come to terms with the Nazis.

The frustrating of invasion plans was in many respects the British Secret Services's biggest *coup* of the war. The full story still cannot be told because it is extremely confused and complicated and involved many individual efforts by people who were on the fringes of the Service, or, in some cases, were acting as double agents.

There is no doubt at all that some people in high places, even in the Secret Service, were disposed to look for and to examine any feelers that were being put out by the Germans for peace negotiations. Some even considered it their duty to give these sympathetic consideration and to let the Germans know this. But any such moves were kept secret from the Prime Minister, for Churchill would have clamped down on them ruthlessly.

Others in the Secret Service went to the other extreme and took the view that none of their agents should have any truck with people peddling peace feelers and that these should be vehemently discouraged and blocked. A third and more imaginative viewpoint was that the Secret Service should establish links with anyone proposing peace talks and track these down to their source both in enemy territory and at home. In this way they felt that the peddlers of peace could be infiltrated and exploited to mislead the Germans. This was the sanest viewpoint and, fortunately, the one which eventually won the day, but not without the aid and encouragement of Soviet agents. Even if

Stalin remained unconvinced that Germany would attack Russia, the Soviet Secret Service was convinced that sooner or later an attack would come. They were desperately anxious to keep Britain in the war and to go to any lengths to snuff out peace plots.

Unless there had been some unofficial action by Russian agents and the very few pro-Soviet sympathisers in the Secret Service, Hitler's invasion of Britain might not have been prevented. Russia feared having to fight Germany alone even more than Germany feared a war on two fronts at once. To that extent infiltration of the Secret Service and the Foreign Office by pro-Soviet sympathisers may well have had more beneficial results in 1940–42 than the harm created in the post-war years. To make this assertion is not to approve the action of traitors in peacetime, but to make a realistic assessment of their services to their country in war-time.

To complicate this picture of intrigue with its deceptive patterns of behaviour was the recurring enigma of Admiral Canaris's interventions. Canaris was surely the most flexible of all intelligence chiefs, always soft-pedalling and by doing so allowing himself scope for switching his policy at the appropriate moment. In 1938–39 one finds him bent on preventing war between Britain and Germany and aiming to oust Hitler and give power to a junta of generals. From late 1939 until at least the late summer of 1940 he appears to have encouraged peace feelers; from the end of 1940 he even gave the impression of wanting to exploit these same peace feelers for the purpose of stopping a German invasion of Britain.

Volume X of the *Documents on German Foreign Policy* shows that Von Ribbentrop and the German Foreign Office were convinced after the fall of France that they could induce the Duke of Windsor —then spending his time in Madrid and Lisbon—to stay on in Europe instead of leaving to become Governor of the Bahamas. They were certain that he would lend himself to their peace campaign and that he and Lloyd George could be brought into a secret accord. Their efforts in this direction range from the sinister to the fatuous and, as the book rightly states, "the German records are necessarily a much tainted source. The only firm evidence they provide is of what the Germans were trying to do in this matter and how completely they failed to do it."

An elaborate plot to kidnap the Duke and Duchess was ordered by Hitler and Ribbentrop, and the man chosen to organise it was Walter Schellenberg, who was then developing his own spy organisation. The kidnap attempt was to have taken place while the Duke was hunting near the Spanish frontier. He was to have been "inadvertently" lured over the frontier by a ruse and taken to the German Embassy in Madrid. But at the last moment the British Secret Service had warning of the plot, the Duke cancelled his shooting trip and guards were posted around the villa where he was staying just outside Lisbon. Schellenberg, who went to Madrid to organise this ambitious *coup*, wrote in his journal: "I had accomplices in the house where the Duke was staying. Servants at table were in my pay and reported to me all that was said."[4]

The two most surprising features of this story are, first, that the British authorities allowed the Duke to stay in such a dangerous, spy-infested city as Lisbon, and, secondly, the extraordinary credulity and wishful thinking of the Nazis. Von Stohrer, the German Ambassador in Madrid, reported that "Churchill had threatened W. with arraignment before a court-martial in case he did not accept the post [i.e. Governorship of the Bahamas]. . . . The Duke was considering making a public statement and thereby disavowing present English policy and breaking with his brother. . . . The Duke's agreement [for the Germans' future plans] can be assumed as in the highest degree probable."[5]

The Duke of Windsor has since refuted these allegations, but the truth is that the Germans were even then being deceived by the information which was being leaked to them by the British Secret Service. Just after the fall of France it was frequently touch and go whether Hitler gave the go-ahead for the invasion of Britain. Any suggestion that important Britons were in a position to encourage peace talks, or that the Duke of Windsor might be secured as an ally enabled the British to play for time, to regroup their shattered armies and to delay matters by causing the Germans to examine possibilities of achieving an armistice with Britain without actually invading the country. Even some former sympathisers with Germany among the ranks of ex-Fascists and right-wingers who had now come to see the menace of Hitlerism allowed their names to be lent to this kind of false encouragement to the Nazis.

From the Tangier informer already mentioned came a further piece of intelligence. The Germans, working with the Spanish Falangists, planned to send a representative of the Spanish Youth Movement to Britain ostensibly to study the Boy Scout Movement, but actually to give a detailed report of British defences and preparedness against invasion. In October 1940, France's Government sought permission for the Falangist to make the trip. S.I.S. knew perfectly well that everything he saw and heard would be reported back to Berlin, but they persuaded the Foreign Office to agree to the request and then, in co-operation with M.I.5, took charge of the plans for his arrival.

The Falangist was given V.I.P. treatment. He was given a suite in the Athenaeum Court Hotel in which concealed microphones and tapped telephone wires were laid on. At the time there were only three anti-aircraft batteries in the whole London area. One of these was moved into Hyde Park close to the hotel and given orders to fire continuously throughout every air raid whether enemy planes were directly overhead or not. M.I.5 even allowed the spy to be shown the A-A batteries and he must have been convinced that London was bristling with such guns. He was then taken to Windsor Castle outside of which the only fully equipped tank regiment in the whole of the British Isles suddenly appeared in full view. When the Falangist expressed surprise at so impressive an array of strength he was told that this was merely a ceremonial bodyguard for the Royal Family. Again, when he was flown to Scotland, the S.I.S. arranged for squadron after squadron of Spitfires to be seen in the air: in fact there was only one squadron which had been detailed to appear and re-appear, but it suggested that Britain was covered from north to south by a constant air patrol, despite the serious lack of fighter planes at that time.

When he was taken to a sea-port the S.I.S. saw to it that that port was packed with warships of every shape and size. Immense pains were taken to give the impression of an impregnable, armed to the teeth Britain, with defence in depth. Later the authorities learned details of the spy's report to Berlin. It warned against any invasion attempt and declared that stories of Britain's unpreparedness were merely wiles of the British Secret Service to lure the Germans into making what would be a disastrous onslaught on the British Isles.

This alone did not prevent the invasion, but, coupled with all the other efforts to mislead, it played an important part. What finally clinched the calling off of an invasion was the supreme effort made to encourage those Nazis who wanted to make war on Russia by providing further evidence that peace could be made with Britain.

A report came from Helga Stultz, an agent working for the British and the Americans in Munich that "Hitler has been in a terrible mood. I am sure he will repudiate the German-Soviet Pact. Ribbentrop is most anxious not to upset the Russians, but I do not think his view will prevail. Rudolf Hess sides with Hitler; he believes that Germany must settle her account with Russia and that by doing this some agreement can be reached with England. *Hess is so confident of this that I am sure he has had important news from England.*"

The S.I.S. then knew that their attempts to infiltrate the *Verbindungsstab*, the intelligence agency set up by Hess, who was contemptuous of the *Abwehr*, had succeeded. Hess' aim was to set up listening posts in Britain with a view to establishing contacts with sufficiently powerful sympathisers inside the country to pave the way to a negotiated peace. This move to infiltrate the *Verbindungsstab* was equally linked with the communist agent who had been sent out to Lisbon to pose as a German agent, quite unknown, of course, to the Welshman Owens who had sponsored him originally.

To make the case of their undercover agents stronger those in the S.I.S. who were playing this dangerous game—and the ploy was a secret between less than half a dozen of them—deliberately recreated The Link, that suspect Anglo-German friendship organisation which had been a source of some concern to the Secret Service immediately before war broke out.

The declaration of war, then the invasion of France and the Low Countries, the German-Soviet Pact and the imprisonment of pro-German extremists under Regulation 18 B had struck a mortal blow to The Link. The impression had to be given that it was being secretly revived, a risky game to play because it could equally have been exploited by the Germans for propaganda purposes, had they wished. But there were good reasons to believe that as long as Hess was bent on playing his own secret political game with the *Verbindungsstab*, the intrigue would not be publicised and that there were few risks of its boomeranging against Britain.

Suddenly tiny cells of The Link were established in Tangier and Lisbon. The former was an exceptionally useful site for such intrigues because, being an international zone, it offered great scope for the ploy of the double-agent. The Link cell in Tangier soon proved to be an excellent source of information. A report from here stated: "Hess is contemptuous of the *Abwehr* and is pursuing his own ideas of espionage through the *Verbindungsstab*. For some time he put his faith in the Welsh section of this organisation and believed that contacts made in that way would prove fruitful. Now he is inclined to think that the prime target for further conversations lies in Scotland. The Cafe Chiado in the Rua Gambetta in Lisbon is one meeting place for intermediaries between The Link and the *Verbindungsstab*, the Hotel Riff in Tangier is another."

At last it was clear that the bait had been taken. Hess at least was clearly interested in the re-creation of The Link. But another and even more important factor had been revealed to the Secret Service: Admiral Canaris' much-vaunted *Abwehr* was being bypassed and two new German intelligence services were being forged, one master-minded by Walter Schellenberg, the other by Rudolf Hess.

If Germany could be convinced that if she attacked Russia, Britain would sue for peace, the course of the war could be changed overnight.

23

The Formation of S.O.E.

Such purely defensive espionage as that described in the previous chapter was about all that could be seriously expected from the British Secret Service in the grim days of 1939–41. Even in the first year of the war, when some bold spirits envisaged enterprising and imaginative espionage onslaughts, the Service was held back by lack of funds.

A section of the S.I.S.—Section D (for Destruction) had been set up in 1938 under Colonel Lawrence Grand. It was intended, as its name implies, to be an aggressive unit aiming at inflicting damage on the enemy by sabotage. Its original purpose was not to operate outside the country, but in the event of a German invasion to organise subversive operations and sabotage in enemy-occupied territory in Britain. Grand had plenty of good ideas, but some of them went beyond his brief. For example he put forward a scheme to stop the supply of Rumanian oil to Germany by acts of sabotage. But when it came to finding funds to implement these ideas, even if they had been possible to implement, the Treasury proved a stumbling block. Soon the grandiose schemes had to be abandoned, or at best pigeon-holed.

Bickham Sweet-Escott in his *Baker Street Irregulars*, a first-hand account of some Secret Service work in World War II, has summed up the position of the S.I.S. by the mid-summer of 1940: "Our record of positive achievement was unimpressive. There were a few successful operations to our credit, but certainly not many; and we had something which could be called an organisation on the ground in the Balkans. But even there we had failed to do anything spectacular . . . our essays in Balkan subversion had succeeded only in making the Foreign Office jumpy. As for Western Europe, though there was much to excuse it, the record was lamentable, for we did not possess one single agent between the Balkans and the English Channel."[1]

This state of affairs requires some explanation. The S.I.S. was weak enough in Europe when war was declared. When Hitler made his swift *blitzkrieg* across the Continent our spy net-work was destroyed overnight. But an unexpected disaster in the early months of the war had made matters worse than they need have been. Prior to the war Holland was one of the chief bases from which spying on the Germans was organised by the British Secret Service. The headquarters of this organisation in Holland was the Passport Control Centre of the British Consulate at 15 Nieuwe Uitweg, The Hague, curiously enough next door to the house in which Mata Hari had lived in 1915: an ill omen that was overlooked. For years the Secret Service has used its various Passport Control offices and often its Passport Control Officers as the local control centre for S.I.S. activities. There was one very good reason for this: it enabled the local spy-master to be in a position to examine passports presented for visas and gave him an excuse for detaining suspects on the grounds that inquiries needed to be made about their passports and records. There was also the advantage that records and files were easily available for inspection.

The great disadvantage of the system was that it gave away to any potential enemy the address of the spy centre and the name of its controller. Sometimes such centres were used as a decoy and the real local spy chief would be elsewhere, but far too often this system played into the hands of rival intelligence services.

The principal of this spy centre at The Hague was Major H. R. Stevens and his deputy was Captain S. Payne Best. The Germans had little difficulty in finding out what was going on and in making effective plans to counter the British effort. Thus in the late autumn of 1939 agents of the *Abwehr* successfully laid a trap for Major Stevens and Captain Best. By posing as anti-Nazis who could supply the British with vital military intelligence, they persuaded the two officers to meet them at Venlo on the German frontier and on 8 November 1939, they kidnapped the pair and drove them by car across the border. At one and the same time the Germans captured two of the most senior intelligence men the British possessed on the entire Continent and effectively broke up their network. Later the Nazis captured a number of other British agents and obtained secret files from the British outpost at The Hague.

The blow which the Germans had struck at this section of British intelligence not only wiped out the espionage net-work in Holland, but forced the S.I.S. to withdraw agents from other parts of the Continent. By the time the Germans had invaded the Low Countries and France in the spring on 1940 Britain was left with practically no effective intelligence service in Europe.

Thus Stewart Menzies had the task of re-building from scratch, while at the same time he had to learn the hard way that information won by technical means—especially by the study of wireless traffic—was now of prime importance. Unless some drastic measures had been taken the task of re-building a net-work of spies in Europe would have taken years. Fortunately Churchill decided that Menzies should be relieved of the full burden of this enormous task and the result was the creation in July 1940, of the organisation called Special Operations Executive, or S.O.E. This was easily the biggest reform of the Secret Service carried out during the war and it fell to Dr. Hugh Dalton, as Minister of Economic Warfare, to undertake the formation of the S.O.E. The original idea was sound enough: its purpose was simply and solely the economic sabotage in enemy countries and enemy sources of supply in neutral territories. But the phrase "economic sabotage" is itself open to a variety of interpretations and a great deal went wrong in the actual organisation and planning. It is doubtful whether by the end of the war S.O.E. had justified the vast sums of money spent on it. The adjective "economic" was swiftly dropped in practice and often of necessity S.O.E. was acting independently of anything the S.I.S. was planning; sometimes it was running contrary to S.I.S. and quite frequently it was concentrating on the wrong targets. Also, as a new organisation in the hands of men with no professional experience of intelligence work it was wide open to infiltration by the enemy, and infiltrate it the enemy did, not once, but consistently throughout the war.

Dalton was assisted in the founding of S.O.E. by Gladwyn Jebb and Philip Broad from the Foreign Office, Brigadier Willie van Cutsem from the War Office, and the banker, Leonard

Ingrams. Dalton himself was not an ideal choice for the creator of such an organisation. Voluble, extrovert, often indiscreet, given to fraternising with the rank and file, and with an academic mind, he tended to view S.O.E. as primarily a weapon for propaganda against the enemy and for obtaining economic intelligence. It would have been better if a separate department had tackled the first of these jobs and for S.O.E. to have been a smaller organisation, with much more rigid screening of recruits, solely concentrating on building up a specialised spy network in Europe to advise on economic sabotage and to specify targets and where feasible linking up with Resistance groups.

Perhaps it was too much to expect that an organisation so hastily formed in war-time, with little time to spare for effective screening of recruits, could fail to commit serious errors in its early stages. But few could have envisaged how costly these errors would prove to be.

In the early days of S.O.E. some risks had to be taken. Among the influx of French, Belgians, Dutch, Norwegians and Poles who fled to Britain from Nazi-occupied territory were many whose aim was to infiltrate British intelligence, and relay information back to the Germans. The influx was so great that even M.I.5 could not spare the time for thorough screening in all cases. Those who offered their services for work in the British intelligence and whose bona fides seemed all right were passed on to S.O.E. But S.O.E. was an infant service whose executives were totally inexperienced in the selection of recruits. On the one hand there were at best enthusiastic and often blundering amateurs, on the other unsophisticated personnel officers in S.O.E. itself who had to try to sort out potentially sound agents from rogues and incompetents. It was a situation in which treachery could easily flourish.

The most dangerous of these refugees were the Dutch and, as has been mentioned before in these pages, the Dutch are notorious for producing double-agents and treacherous agents. It may seem unkind and even unjust to make so sweeping an allegation against a whole nation, but, though the Dutch are often perfectly delightful, peaceful, honest citizens, when it comes to espionage they are thoroughly unreliable, with few exceptions. It should have been obvious to the S.O.E. executives that there were many secret Nazi sympathisers among these Dutch refugees, just as in the ranks of the Dutch Resistance movement in Holland were many Nazi agents. But for some reason the policy-makers decided to speed up their attempts to develop an operationally effective Dutch section of S.O.E. before all others.

Two senior *Abwehr* officers exploited this situation by blackmailing three members of the Dutch Resistance and acquiring from them intact three S.O.E. radio posts in Holland. As a result of this S.O.E. Dutch recruits who were parachuted into Holland were captured and from two of these the Germans obtained the secret code signals of the S.O.E. Dutch section in London. The Germans then sent faked messages to London, receiving messages in return and by this means slowly built up a picture of the whole S.O.E. net-work in Holland.

In this way the Germans conducted a radio dialogue with the Dutch section of S.O.E. in London for nearly three years before it was discovered. Germany was all this time effectively controlling British espionage in Holland and the supplies of arms, explosives and cash parachuted into Holland, as well as the agents, went straight into German hands.

Yet, despite this set-back, S.O.E. in London had ample warning that something was wrong. One of the captured Dutch operators, tapping out faked messages under Nazi orders, though he was closely supervised and monitored by the *Abwehr*, managed to slip a warning into his messages. He did this by omitting the identity check which was that each genuine message must carry a deliberate mistake in every sixteenth letter of the text. Failure to do this should have alerted London to the fact that something was wrong. Either London had careless operators, or else, as was eventually suspected, there was treachery at the London end.

For not only was the operator's warning ignored, but even warnings from other sections of British intelligence. Commander D. W. Child, a British intelligence operator who, after being hunted by the Gestapo, had escaped to England late in 1942, warned the British Secret Service that the Germans had infiltrated a number of S.O.E. radio posts in Holland. Regardless of all this London continued to carry on communications with the S.O.E. in Holland at enormous cost, permitting the Germans to capture

28,000 pounds of explosives, 3,000 Sten guns, 5,000 revolvers and considerable currency, all dropped by parachute.

After the war the Dutch Parliament conducted its own inquiry into these disasters and the Commission appointed to investigate the matter described it as "a catastrophe which assumed proportions far in excess of any failure in any of the other German-occupied countries in Western Europe . . . grave mistakes made at Baker Street [the Dutch section of S.O.E.] were caused by lack of experience, utter inefficiency and the disregard of elementary security rules."[2]

The site of the S.O.E. headquarters in Baker Street was certainly badly chosen from a security point of view. The building was so ill-suited for accommodation that an army of workmen were continually being called in and out to put up partitions, or pull them down, to change a door here and take one away there. All that was not conducive to security, nor was the presence of a departmental store below where there was ample scope for infiltration. The training of would-be saboteurs and agents was ludicrously amateurish and would have made excellent material for a farcical novel by Evelyn Waugh. The D for Destruction Department was removed from the S.I.S. and placed under the command of Frank Nelson, who had taken over from Dr. Dalton as the head of S.O.E. shortly after it was formed. Nelson, who was knighted in 1942, had arrived at the S.O.E. by a somewhat more versatile path than Stewart Menzies had reached the summit of the S.O.S. Educated at Bedford Grammar School and Heidelberg, he had served in the Bombay Light Horse in the 1914–18 war, then graduated upwards via the chairmanship of the Bombay Chamber of Commerce, membership of Parliament for Stroud in the Conservative cause, Consul at Basle and then, having joined the R.A.F.V.R., became Acting Air Commodore during his stay at S.O.E.

George Hill, Sidney Reilly's old friend, was put in charge of one section of training of S.O.E. agents who were destined for parachuting into Occupied Europe. Before the Germans invaded France Hill had been in Paris liaising with the *Deuxième Bureau.* It was while Hill was in charge of this training course that Kim Philby and Guy Burgess were transferred to S.O.E.—"wished on us by the Foreign Office", declared Hill. Hill, like many others in S.O.E. and the S.I.S., found Philby quick and perceptive and full of ideas and sound advice. Burgess, however, appears to have got himself into trouble within a few weeks of joining S.O.E., a corporal complaining that this notoriously irresponsible character had been "trying to muck about with him". This, of course, did not prevent Burgess from continuing in secret work, only involving his transfer to another unit.

There was almost criminal negligence in the selection of personnel at this time, in both S.O.E. and the S.I.S. Burgess, a homosexual whose indiscreet talk was even then common knowledge, was the last person who should have been introduced to the S.O.E. Nobody had bothered to make any check on Philby's career with any thoroughness and the fact that he had married an Austrian communist was either unknown or ignored. Nerve-shocked Army and Navy officers were put in charge of S.O.E. recruits for training purposes; at least one of them was almost permanently on the verge of a nervous breakdown. It was not until Colonel Colin Gubbins arrived from the War Office to supervise and organise a new training programme that some order was restored amidst the initial chaos, and a new school for recruits to learn the arts of sabotage and wireless communication was set up at Beaulieu.

George Hill, now a brigadier, fully lived up to his previous reputation as a first class intelligence man and an exceptional agent. He was fully aware of the ineptitude of many of the S.O.E. executives for their work and longed for a return to field work. Eventually he had his chance. When Russia entered the war on the side of the Allies Hill was sent to Moscow to liaise with the N.K.V.D., who asked for and obtained reciprocal facilities to send three N.K.V.D. men to London. Hill exchanged training experience with the N.K.V.D. and was able to make comparisons between them and S.O.E. Despite the follies of S.O.E. and the limitations of some of their training programmes, he nevertheless formed the opinion that the latter was better than that of the N.K.V.D. Hill went into action with Soviet Partisans two hundred miles behind the German lines near Minsk in 1943 to learn Soviet techniques at first hand.

The Naval Intelligence Department eventually developed into

an extremely efficient machine, not perhaps as spectacular as that of Admiral Hall's rêgime, for the simple reason that it did not indulge in anything like the same amount of private buccaneering espionage that Hall delighted in. But to appreciate what the N.I.D. achieved from 1939–45 one must understand the political neglect of the branch after 1918, the extremely bad staffing of its higher posts between the wars and a general carelessness in signal security which existed throughout the Navy prior to World War II.

Laxity in signal security extended to an appalling slackness in almost everything appertaining to security matters. From 1927–30 the Director of Naval Intelligence was none other than Admiral Sir Barry Domville who was a member of the sinisterly pro-German organisation, The Link, and who in 1940 was arrested under Regulation 18 B largely on account of his having been chairman and founder of this society. In fairness to Domville it must be said that he was more a fool bitten by the bug of racial purity than a knave and that there is no question of his having betrayed any secrets. In fact he did not come under the Nazi influence until 1936. He attended the Nuremberg Reichsparteitag in 1937 together with such pro-German sympathisers as Lord Stamp, Lord Lymington, Lord Brocket, Colonel Yeats-Brown, author of *Bengal Lancer*, and Sir Jocelyn Lucas, M.P. But the fact that such an unstable character should be chosen as the D.N.I. is no credit to the Admiralty.

As early as 1936 German cryptanalysts penetrated the wireless security of British ships in the Red Sea and this failure in naval security was not completely overcome until the middle of 1943. Perhaps its worst effects were felt in the disastrous Norwegian campaign in 1940.

One of the prime blunders of Admiralty in peace-time—and they have repeated the blunder in two World Wars and again in recent years—is their failure to select an intelligence-trained specialist for the job of D.N.I. and then to allow their nominee to hold the job only for a few years. This makes it almost impossible for any D.N.I. to get to know his Department and to formulate long-term policy. Even Rear-Admiral John Godfrey, who became D.N.I. in 1939 only held the post for three years, but in that period he achieved a remarkable success, bringing in civilians of distinction and talent, men such as Ian Fleming, who became Assistant to the D.N.I., Sir Norman Denning, Ewen Montagu, Patrick Beesly and Frederick Wells.

Godfrey seems to have followed closely the methods of Admiral Hall in his original selection of candidates from the civilian ranks for the N.I.D., again going to the Stock Exchange for men such as Fleming just as Hall had chosen a stockbroker in Claud Serocold. Just as in World War I Room 40 in the Old Admiralty Building was the nerve centre of the N.I.D. So in World War II it was Room 39 in the same building. The process of gathering information was much more scientific than in World War I and the N.I.D., having failed so lamentably in signal and cipher security before war started, at least learned the lesson by concentrating on this branch of intelligence both as regards espionage and counter-espionage from the very outset. Its first spectacular success in this respect was in 1941 when the British captured two German weather ships, the *Muenchen* and the *Lauenburg* in a calculated sweep in mid-Atlantic and so acquired enemy ciphers.

A great weakness in these early years of the war was the disregard by the N.I.D. and even more by the Operations Division of the Admiralty of the possibilities of Combined Operations as a source of intelligence. The Royal Navy was half-hearted in its attitude towards Combined Operations in its early stages and this was not entirely due to the antagonism of some of the Navy's top brass towards Admiral of the Fleet Sir Roger Keyes, the first Chief of C.O., which was an admirable attempt to combine units of the Army, Navy and R.A.F. under a single command firstly to harry the enemy with lone raids on occupied territory, and, secondly, to prepare for the eventual invasion of Europe. The Admiralty showed its contempt for Combined Operations by foolishly relegating it to a Cinderella of the Services, giving it as personnel officers those it wished to be rid of and ratings who were either Active Service men so undisciplined that they could not be controlled in a battleship, or the poorest material among the Hostilities Only entries. Had Combined Operations been used more intelligently and more actively from 1940 to the end of 1942, a much greater wealth of intelligence could have been obtained much earlier in the war and might conceivably have shortened it.

The man who was mainly responsible for rectifying this omission was Ian Fleming who combined a sense of humour which was both sardonic and bizarre with an imagination which, had it been given full rein, might have produced the kind of Secret Service *coups* which Sidney Reilly pulled off. It is not without significance that Sidney Reilly was one of Fleming's greatest heroes: he always lamented that James Bond, his own fictitious hero, was "not in the Sidney Reilly class".

Fleming's most effective quality in the N.I.D. was a gift for jollying along senior officers. He could take a somewhat prosaic idea, mould it into something more imaginative and proceed jocularly to nudge a senior officer into letting him develop it. This was the case with No. 30 Assault Unit which he supervised so closely that it became known as Fleming's Private Navy. It was one of his relatively few releases from purely desk work. The idea of No. 30 Assault Unit came from the lessons learned from the German activities in Crete in 1941. In that campaign the Germans achieved great success with a special assault unit that penetrated British G.H.Q. to make a swift appraisal of our ciphers and technical equipment. Thus was 30 A.U. born and it began to operate in somewhat tentative fashion in the Middle East under the dual command of Dunstan Curtis, a Coastal Forces officer, and Quentin Riley, a pre-war Polar explorer. The Admiralty continued to regard the project with distaste if not actual disapproval and it required all Fleming's champagne-talk and gay bantering to keep it jogging along and to maintain the morale of its members. Then in North Africa, Sicily and Italy Fleming's Private Navy eventually proved its worth. In beach reconnaissance, in probing enemy territory secretly and bringing back information Fleming's Private Navy was ultimately a great success. By this time Admiral Godfrey had left the N.I.D. and had been succeeded by a very different type of officer, the tall, reserved and serious-minded Rear-Admiral Rushbrooke.

As an assault intelligence unit 30 A.U. surpassed anything the Germans could contrive of this kind and when it came to operations sustained its difficult task with a camaraderie, insouciance and piratical spirit such as one can only get from civilians turned into naval uniform. One R.N.V.R. officer, for example, captured three hundred Germans and their radar station with the aid of only half a dozen ratings. The briefing, cajoling, cursing and direction of the unit was carried out almost single-handed by Fleming himself by means of a stream of terse, but often highly amusing signals from the Admiralty and sometimes he would himself make trips across the Channel to meet the courageous desperadoes who formed his Private Navy.

Somewhat ruefully Fleming once described one of his less fortunate war-time escapades which he utilised later for the gambling scene in his first novel, *Casino Royale*. "I and my chief, Admiral J. H. Godfrey," wrote Fleming, "were flying to Washington in 1941 for secret talks with the American Office of Naval Intelligence before America came into the war. We were taking the Southern Atlantic route and our Sunderland touched down at Lisbon for an overnight stop. We had talks there with our Intelligence people and they described how Lisbon and the neighbouring Estoril were crawling with German secret agents.

"The chief of these and his two assistants, we were told, gambled every night in the casino at Estoril. I immediately suggested to the D.N.I. that he and I should have a look at these people. We went there and there were the three men playing at the high *Chemin de Fer* table.

"The D.N.I. didn't know the game. I explained it to him and then the feverish idea came to me that I would sit down and gamble against these men and defeat them, reducing the funds of the German Secret Service. It was a foolhardy plan which would have needed a golden streak of luck. I had some fifty pounds in travel money. The chief German agent had run a bank three times. I 'bancoed' it and lost. I 'suivied' and lost again and 'suivied' a third time and was cleaned out. A humiliating experience which added to the sinews of war of the German Secret Service and reduced me sharply in my chief's estimation."[3]

This was a typical Fleming story against himself. Partly because of his flippancy and tendency to tell stories against himself there has been a tendency among those who have attempted to write about this complex character to dismiss him as an amiable, but lazy amateur bluffing his way through life. Fleming himself cultivated the legend of his indolence, but the portrait often drawn of him is unfair. In fact as an administrator he was first-class and thoroughly professional and he could efficiently get through more positive work in an hour than most men could achieve in three and many intelligence *coups* which he personally initiated were credited to other people.

The first-class intelligence agent—and this applies even more to an intelligence executive—must possess a sense of the bizarre and even some conception of translating the impossible into the possible. That, very often, is just what espionage is about. Philby has said that every good agent should have an element of irresponsibility in his make-up: this is both a safety-valve and a cover. Fleming had these qualities in finely balanced proportions leavened with a slight streak of puritanism which provided the necessary sprinkling of caution. He knew when to meddle outside his own field of operations and in extra-mural activities of his own department. Prior to the establishment of 30 A.U. he had to do this quite a lot. Also he possessed another rare virtue in the intelligence man: he lacked ambition, partly because he detested pomposity and preferred the rôle of the dilettante.

One of the stories about Fleming that has never been told is of his hunch that it should be possible to lure one of the Nazi leaders to Britain. Fleming had studied the dossier on Admiral Sir Barry Domville, the pro-German D.N.I. of 1927–30, and this had led him to examine, first out of idle curiosity, the history of The Link. He also had a keen insight into the psychological make-up of the German character and of the preoccupation of top-ranking Nazis with astrology and the occult. As a result of this he thought up the idea of re-creating The Link and building up a fictitious picture of how it had gone underground and acquired new and even more influential members which could pave the way to a negotiated peace with Germany and the overthrow of the Churchill Government. If this kind of information could be leaked to some gullible Nazi leader, then he believed that not only might Germany's invasion plans be shelved, but the Nazis could be misled into secretly sending some important figure in their hierarchy to Britain.

Nobody knew better than Fleming that such an extravaganza of Secret Service technique would be unlikely to commend itself to the N.I.D. and that the project posed all kinds of political objections. To leak the fiction of a powerful movement inside Britain prepared to make a deal with the Nazis could easily backfire on its planners and produce alarm and despondency at home rather than among the enemy. Therefore he decided it was far too hazardous a project for him to handle on his own. But, reluctant to let go of a scheme which appealed to his imaginative mind, he passed the idea to two trusted friends, one who was in another branch of British intelligence, the other a contact in Switzerland who was an authority on astrology.

It is not possible to reveal the names of these two friends, both of whom ran grave risks in acting on Fleming's hunch. The first risk was of acting independently of higher officers in the Secret Service and without their knowledge, the second was of falling into enemy hands. Fleming had himself decided that Rudolf Hess was their likeliest candidate for the rôle of a gullible Nazi leader. He was delighted when his friends confirmed that Hess was indeed the best man on whom to concentrate. Not only was Hess the keennest of the Nazi leaders to make peace with Britain to free Germany for the task of attacking Russia, but he was also a mystic, a student of astrology and a consorter with occultists and fortune-tellers, even credited with being Hitler's secret astrologer.

Fleming's contact in Switzerland succeeded in planting on Hess an astrologer who was also a British agent. As Fleming himself kept firmly in the background and avoided direct association with the development of the plot, it is impossible to say just how much he may have urged on the plotters. One can easily imagine Fleming, tongue-in-cheek, briefing the astrologer for the task in hand, allowing his imagination full play and painting a picture of aristocratic plotters in British country houses waiting for the signal from a Nazi leader to bring about the downfall of the Churchill Government. But to make this assertion would be guess-work and, as the author of this book is aware from personal experience, Fleming's methods of work were frequently peculiarly circumlocutory. He had an uncanny skill when briefing people to give less than the information required, thus completely disguising the purpose of an operation, yet cajoling the mystified subordinate into doing the right thing without his knowing why he was doing it.

To ensure that the theme of the plot was worked into a conventional horoscope the Swiss contact arranged for two horoscopes of Hess to be obtained from astrologers known to Hess personally so that the faked horoscope would not be suspiciously different from those of the others. Where skill would be required would be in working the necessary faked details into a conventional horoscope of Hess in a manner that would not conflict too drastically from anything Hess might be told by other astrologers whom he had consulted.

The Swiss contact probably did not know that another member of the Secret Service, playing a lone hand, was working on much the same theme, but in a different manner. Yet the recreation of The Link was skilfully being developed to fit in with the horoscope forecast and towards the end of 1940 agents in the Cafe Chiada in Lisbon and another in Berne were slowly but surely shaping events which led to one of the most dramatic incidents of the war.

24

Occultism and Espionage: a sidelight on the Hess Mission

IT HAS already been shown how in Elizabethan times occultism had been employed as a weapon of espionage by the British. What is not so well known is that this trend in the British Secret Service has also been maintained in modern times. The use of occult practice by the British Secret Service has been often noted by Britain's enemies, so much so that in World War I it was believed that there was something supernatural about the British Secret Service and that much of their information could only have been obtained by occult means, or by some telepathic genius.

Himmler was so convinced of this that he seriously stated that the Rosicrucians were a branch of the British Secret Service. In the First World War Aleister Crowley, the most picturesque and notorious occultist of modern times, indulged in pro-German propaganda writing for Vierveck in *The Fatherland* and *The International*, which he edited for about a year. However, Crowley always claimed that he did this merely to ingratiate himself with the Germans so that he could spy on them. The American Intelligence Service in World War I seemed to have believed Crowley's story, though the N.I.D. rejected him and his occult temple in London was closed down by the police.

After the war Crowley was very nearly prosecuted for his alleged activities in helping the enemy, but it was eventually proved that he was genuinely intending to help the Allies. What clinched the decision to exonerate him was his revelation that the international head of the Hermetic sect which he joined was in fact a highly dangerous German agent and Crowley had revealed this to the Americans. In the inter-war years Crowley spent a great deal of time in Berlin and supplied the S.I.S. with information on Continental communism. The German Intelligence Service certainly knew all about Crowley's ventures in espionage for Crowley lived in Berlin with another notorious spy, Gerald Hamilton. Crowley was spying on Hamilton for M.I.5 and Hamilton was almost certainly spying on Crowley for the Germans. Living together as friends, they concocted reports on each other.

There has been from time immemorial a strange union between occultism and espionage, probably because occultists tend to go underground and therefore make good agents. Himmler was right about Rosicrucian links with espionage, though he went too far in believing the Rosicrucians to be a branch of the British Secret Service. Himmler may have got this idea through knowledge of Crowley's activities, or because Saint Germain, one of the best known eighteenth century Rosicrucians, was an intelligence agent.

Ian Fleming's acquaintance with Crowley was certainly not a close one, but he did know that Crowley had put forward some madcap ideas to the intelligence authorities at the beginning of World War II, one of them being a plan for dropping occult information by leaflet on the enemy, which was rejected. Crowley claimed afterwards that he persuaded the authorities to adopt the famous V sign, which Winston Churchill took up. But to Crowley the sign was not intended to be V for victory, but the ancient satanic sign of destruction known as the sign of Aphis and Tiphon. In fact credit for the V sign must go to David Ritchie of the B.B.C.

It was known in some sections of the British Secret Service that many leading Nazis were secretly interested in the occult and especially in astrology. Hitler's own interest in the subject had also been noted. For this reason the Secret Service gave serious consideration to the part that astrology could play both in the way of psychological warfare and counter-espionage. One of the keenest minds employed on this kind of work was a friend of Fleming's, Sefton Delmer, formerly Berlin correspondent of the *Daily Express*.

Delmer was in the Political Warfare Executive indulging in

both "white" and "black" Propaganda. "White", in the jargon of the Service, referred to straightforward propaganda put out by the British by radio or leaflet dropping, or similar means. "Black" propaganda referred to material that was put out in such a manner as to disguise its British origins. One of his agents was an Hungarian-born astrologer, Louis de Wohl, who before the war escaped from the Nazis to England. De Wohl, largely on account of his claims to an intimate knowledge of the workings of one of Hitler's own astrologers, was made a captain in the British Army and attached to the Department of Psychological Warfare. He had to fight one of the strangest battles of the war, forecasting Hitler's intuitions and what he was likely to do next. To do this he had to study Hitler's horoscope and send reports on it to the War Office. "I had learned the technique of Karl Klafft, Hitler's favourite astrologer," said de Wohl afterwards, "and I knew what his advice to Hitler would be long before he was even summoned by the Fuhrer."[1] In this manner he was able to some extent to forecast what Hitler's moves would be.

If it seems somewhat bizarre that the War Office should employ an astrologer and the other branches of the Secret Service should make use of them, one must understand that the Germans themselves had in recent years become increasingly astrologically-minded. In 1932 one Martin Pfefferkorn founded a Nazi Astrologers' Study Group and by the time the Nazis came to power quite a number of them had begun to pay attention to astrology. Goebbels fully appreciated the value of astrology in propaganda and in his Ministry was a special department of occultism from which Nazi astrologers used to send articles to newspapers all over the world to pave the way to forthcoming events on which Hitler wanted attention focused. This was the department A.M.O. (Astrology, Metapsychology and Occultism).

The British had to counter this astrological propaganda and the Secret Service subsidised a number of astrologers in foreign countries to put out their own horoscopes and forecasts that would be rather more favourable to the British prospects and rather less so to Hitler's. Many American magazines had been unwittingly used to print the forecasts of Goebbels' own astrologers that there would be peace on 15 February 1941. It is interesting to note that both the British and German agent-astrologers used the prophecies of Nostradamus for propaganda purposes. Louis de Wohl even went so far as to compose a letter to which he attached a forged signature of Ernst Krafft, Hitler's astrologer, in which it was suggested that Krafft had forecast that Germany would lose the war and Hitler die a violent death. Even faked copies of such German astrological magazines as *Der Zenit*, which were infiltrated into Germany, were edited by de Wohl and used to convey predictions unfavourable to Germany.

De Wohl had not found it easy to press his services on the British authorities which he had begun to do some few years before the war. "It was not easy to find a niche for me," he wrote in his book *The Stars of War and Peace*. "Neither the War Office nor the Admiralty could employ an astrologer." But eventually the S.O.E. employed him and, even if the War Office and the Admiralty would not employ him, they were glad to have his reports from S.O.E. passed on to Military and Naval Intelligence respectively. Sir Charles Hambro, the second-in-command in S.O.E., commissioned him to do his astrological propaganda and ultimately he was sent to the U.S.A. for this purpose. De Wohl himself, however, believed that his talents could be more usefully and effectively used in direct counter-espionage—i.e. using astrology to mislead the Nazi leaders and for developing a series of red herrings.

It was essential in any astrological predictions put out to mislead the enemy that they were presented in such a manner as to accord with orthodox astrological principles. The German intelligence not only paid great attention to all astrological predictions, but had them analysed by experts to see if, in their working out, they conformed to the known rules and data. Thus anyone wanting to put through misleading information in a horoscope had to be exceptionally skilled and knowledgeable of all the precepts of German astrology.

While most naval and military intelligence men were paying scant regard to the evidence of the tremendous interest in astrology by the Nazi leaders, Fleming's friend in Switzerland followed up every scrap of information he could glean on the subject. Not only did he obtain a detailed dossier on every astrologer Hess had been known to consult, but, through his Swiss contact (a fellow-countryman of Krafft, Hitler's astrologer), he learned of the kind of information Hess was being given. By the end of 1940 it was clear that Hess was stepping up his interest in astrology and that in some way this was linked up with his geo-political research.

It was, of course, essential that the secret plan which Fleming originally envisaged should not be shared with anyone else other than the trusted astrological expert in Switzerland. For the plan went far beyond the feeding of vague general information about the feasibility of peace moves in Britain, but to direct Hess's attention to specific people, to a re-created Link, and to a specific date for action by Hess. Once the information had been passed on there would be little hope of knowing what Hess's immediate reactions were. Only by contriving some independent evidence (faked, of course) to support the faked astrological forecasts could they be sure that there was rather better than a fifty-fifty chance of Hess falling for the bait.

Thus all kinds of false information, much of it substantiated by the cleverest faked evidence, was disseminated by British agents. In *Documents on German Foreign Policy, 1918–45* it is stated that one message came to Germany "from the secret agent of military intelligence in London, who boldly signalled from Madrid: British Under-Secretary Butler is at heart a great admirer of the Führer. In an intimate circle he refers to the English situation as desperate."

It was dangerous to name too important a personage as the man with whom Hess might be able to deal. For the Nazis could very easily check on the reliability of such a source. Ambassadors of neutral countries in Britain could still be relied upon to give accurate checks on such rumours. It was then that the plotters decided to play the risky, but infinitely subtler game of using the Duke of Hamilton's name to mislead Hess. There were good reasons for this choice: first, both Hess and his principal adviser, Professor Karl Haushofer, were inverted romantics with a snobbish awe of titles and royalty. The Duke of Hamilton, apart from coming from one of the most ancient titled families in England, was Lord Steward of the King's Household, and therefore would be, in the eyes of Hess and Haushofer, close to royal circles. In this way, if the Duke's name was put forward as a would-be peace negotiator, it could be hinted that he had the full support of the King himself, and, to a certain type of German mind, the King, quite erroneously, was still supposed to have more influence than the politicans. All that was necessary was to build up a picture of the former chief pilot of the Everest Flight Expedition and an ex-amateur boxing champion as the "hero-figure" around whom a small, but influential group of pro-Germans was being developed in London.

There was another excellent reason for using the Duke's name. The latter was at that time serving in the R.A.F. and was in command of a fighter squadron stationed in a relatively remote part of Scotland. This provided the possibility of suggesting an actual landing place for Hess in Scotland with a promise that instructions would be given that his plane would not be interfered with. By a lucky coincidence Dungavel House, the Duke's Scottish home, was in the same area as that where his squadron was stationed.

If one searches for the evidence of this plot, both the counter-espionage angle of it and of the game of astrological bluff, there is conclusive proof of how well it worked. German reports now make it indisputably plain that Hess "conceived the insane notion of working through Fascist circles in Great Britain to induce the English to yield" and that he sought out the Duke of Hamilton because "he considered the latter, quite erroneously, to be a friend of Germany". That was Ribbentrop's assessment after Hess's flight.

Ernst Schulte-Strathaus, an intimate of Professor Haushofer, had served on Hess's staff since 1935 and, on the testimony of Dr. Gerda Walther, was Hess's adviser on "occult and astrological matters". In January 1941, Schulte-Strathaus told Hess that an unusual conjunction of the planets would take place on 10 May 1941, which was the date of Hess's flight to Britain. On that date six planets in the sign of Taurus coincided with the full moon, though Schulte-Strathaus afterwards denied emphatically that Hess chose this date on any advice from him. Nevertheless he was imprisoned by the Nazis because he was suspected of being Hess's astrological adviser.

In Dr. Ranier Hilderbrandt's biography of Haushofer, there is some clue to this astrological prediction. He states: "Hess's astrological foible strengthened his own conviction that everything possible must be done and hazarded in order to end hostilities without delay, because at the end of April and the beginning of May 1941, Hitler's astrological aspects were unusually malefic. Hess interpreted these aspects to mean that he personally must take the dangers that threatened the Fuhrer upon his own shoulders in order to save Hitler and restore peace to Germany. Time and again Hess's astrological adviser had told him that Anglo-German relations were threatened by a deep-seated crisis of confidence. . . . Indeed, at this time there were very dangerous [planetary] oppositions in Hitler's horoscope. Haushofer, who dabbled a great deal with astrology, seldom left his friend [Hess] without a hint that something unexpected could 'happen' in the near future."[2]

Thus it would seem that Hess sought astrological advice from more than one person, probably from several, but that Haushofer had rather more influence and certainly was more acquainted with his plans than the others. The organisation of the plot on the British side in its careful attention to astrological detail was extremely thorough. The Swiss astrologer-agent had full advanced knowledge of what Hess's own astrological advice would be: the conjunction of the planets and the deductions to be drawn from that in general terms could easily be foretold. All that was needed was to signify in the horoscope to be "planted" on Hess that the date of 10 May was particularly promising for "a journey in quest of peace" and that the indications were that the place in which to "seek peace" was in Scotland and some hints, deliberately vague, incomprehensible to the average person, but sufficient to enable a man like Haushofer to identify as the Duke of Hamilton. For it was clear that Hess would check with other astrologers, who would certainly confirm that conjunction of the planets and the significance of the date in question, and that Haushofer, who was bound to be brought into the discussions would himself insist that the intermediary so vaguely named must be the Duke of Hamilton.

Albrecht Haushofer was the son of Karl Haushofer, who had been responsible for the theories of *lebensraum*. The younger Haushofer was not only a keen student of political affairs, but took a scientific interest in astrology and because he was himself not an astrologer, but an objective appraiser of astrologists' work, Hess paid a good deal of heed to what he advised. Both the Haushofers had begun to have doubts about Hitler's sanity and Albrecht Haushofer was already suspected to being highly critical of the Fuhrer. As the younger Haushofer was murdered by the Nazis in 1945 it is possible that even in 1941 he may have been concerned in underground opposition to Hitler. If the British Secret Service, or Fleming knew this, there was an even sounder reason for bringing Haushofer into the plot.

It would seem that the plot succeeded admirably. For it was a report by Haushofer which provided the basis for the Hess plan. This report was discovered immediately after Hess's flight and sent to Hitler. It was headed "English Connections and the Possibility of Using Them." The "connections" were tenuous and the means of using them were vague. But the Duke of Hamilton was named as "a young Conservative with close links at Court", who frequently dined with the King and "Sir Samuel Hoare". In Haushofer's mind there was a "Round Table group of younger Imperialists" anxious for peace with Germany and a small number of senior men at the Foreign Office, including "Strang" and "O'Malley", who seemed approachable.

Here then was the basis for the Hess flight to Britain. But the plan almost went wrong. For the Haushofers had become so enthusiastic about the idea that they had themselves made cautious attempts to contact the Duke of Hamilton. Fortunately the Secret Service got wind of these and were able to take precautions against the plot being prematurely exploited.

There is a curious sidelight on all this in the astrologers' Convention that was held at Harrogate in the month preceding Hess's flight to Britain. Then a British astrologer, T. Mayby Cole, predicted that a momentous historical event would occur on 10 May 1941, and that "some great spiritual force is going to be released on this planet". This could have been a coincidence, or it could have been a "plant", but the fact remains that Mayby Cole was killed in an air raid on London *on 10 May 1941*.

Saturday night, 10 May, was the occasion of the last major air raid on Britain from Germany, and on that night Rudolf Hess, Deputy Fuhrer, Reichminister without Portfolio, piloted his own plane to Britain and parachuted on to Scottish soil, asking the

Scottish police and Home Guards who arrested him to "take me to the Duke of Hamilton".

The full story of the Hess affair will probably not be revealed for many years to come. For one thing, though the actual story of a group of Britons prepared to negotiate for a peace with Germany was manufactured by the Secret Service, there were still enough wishful thinking pro-Germans in high places in Britain prepared to envisage such a state of affairs. A few of these were inside the Government, some are still alive today. The would-be traitors had to be exploited in order to be destroyed. But, as so often happens, the authorities covered up the would-be traitors and only publicised the imaginary ones. Indeed, one reason why the name of the Duke of Hamilton was released to the Press was that too much silence on the subject might have led to conjecture about even more important and embarrassing names from the viewpoint of the British Government.

Hess himself has gone on record since the war with his statement of what happened. "I solemnly declare that neither Hitler, nor anybody else knew in advance of my intention to fly to England, except my Adjutant whom I took into my confidence. Herr Messerschmidt was not informed of my intentions".[3] (It had been stated that Messerschmidt arranged for a plane to be put at Hess's disposal.)

Hess went on: "As to Professor Haushofer, I merely asked him for a few lines of recommendation to the Duke of Hamilton under the pretext that with Hitler's knowledge I wanted to meet the Duke on neutral soil."[4]

There seems little doubt that the plans to lure Hess to Britain originally aimed at a date far earlier than May 1941. Hess himself declared that he had "decided to fly shortly after a conversation with the Fuhrer in June 1940. The delay of nearly a year was caused by difficulties in obtaining a machine and long-range equipment as well as unfavourable weather conditions. . . . I also postponed my flight for a certain time because our military setbacks in North Africa carried the danger that my sudden arrival in England might give rise to false interpretations as to my motives."

What remains obscured in mystery is the arrangement made for Hess to fly to Britain. He admits himself that it was difficult to find a plane. Did the Americans help unofficially? An American who was a close friend of Fleming and who was then working for the American Secret Service told the author that "you can take it that there was American co-operation at an unofficial level in this wildly optimistic plan. Perhaps you could say that American help alone made it feasible."

A clue may be found here from looking at newspaper reports of the period. When Hess came to Britain, the National Savings Committee announced that his aeroplane would be shown in London to help raise funds for War Weapons Week. That plan was swiftly revoked on the official grounds that "circumstances have made this impracticable". The reason for official coyness may perhaps be found in the statement a few months later by an American aircraft engineer, Donald Dunning, that he had examined Hess's plane and found American products in it. The tyres bore the imprint of an American firm, a well-known brand of American aviation fuel was specified above the intake-valve, and the fuel tank was marked "100 Octane", an American designation.

The luring of Hess to Britain was a brilliant Secret Service *coup*, but as far as propaganda was concerned it was sadly muffed. The Americans regarded the event as one of the most important of the war to date and believed it to be a tremendous potential victory for Britain in her darkest hour, provided the British Government exploited it. The truth was that the Government handled the Hess affair with singular ineptitude and left many neutral nations wondering whether what they had first regarded as a crack in the Nazi régime might not be a crack in the British hierarchy.

The truth was that the Cabinet was unsure of how the Hess flight should be handled in a propaganda sense and a majority of them were afraid to exploit the subject too vigorously. Not even Churchill could be sure of all the Secret Service manoeuvres regarding the Hess affair—he certainly did not know about the unofficial scheme which Fleming had hatched—and, contrary to general belief, Secret Services do not always tell their governments all they do. But the inhibitions which prevented the Government from fully exploiting Hess's arrival were due to the fear that the pro-German influence in high places was still strong and that the enemy might counter-attack with their propaganda about the existence of a pro-German movement in Britain if the British exploited the Hess affair to any great extent.

Churchill must have suspected that there were still prominent people in Britain, even on the fringes of his own nominal supporters, who believed that the best prospect of an armistice with Germany was in return for giving her a free hand against Russia. For this reason he probably did not show his hand immediately for he desperately needed to know what had been going on behind the scenes. Thus the official British line on Hess coincided exactly with the German line—that Hess was insane. No doubt the Germans were greatly relieved about this. It was a major blunder by the British Government and it played right into the hands of the Germans.

This blunder was bad enough: it spoiled the effects of a great intelligence *coup*. But the statements made by prominent people created an even worse impression. Sir Nevile Henderson, the former British Ambassador in Berlin, referred to Hess publicly as "honest and sincere", while Mr. Harold Nicolson of the Ministry of Information, declining to have photographs taken of Hess, said that "such ignominy should not be put on this fundamentally decent man". All of which only caused neutrals to wonder what the British were really up to and whether they might not yet capitulate to German peace feelers.

Fleming undoubtedly felt that a great chance of a propaganda victory had been lost. One of his more whimsical ideas as Assistant to the D.N.I. was to suggest that Aleister Crowley should be sent to interview Hess in captivity. No doubt he wished to pursue the astrological inquiries much further and, zany as this idea might seem, it is just possible that it might have led to some interesting revelations about the influence of astrologers in the Nazi hierarchy. But the interview which might well have made a fascinating interlude in the history of intelligence work never took place. Authority had had enough of Hess. Sir Ivone Kirkpatrick was convinced that Hess was quite mad, though those few people who have spoken to him in recent years have found him lucid enough.

The story of this master-plot of a few individualists working on their own has been carefully guarded over the years, probably because it was an unofficial effort. Quite probably it will still be denied by some, but German astrologers were convinced of its authenticity and Kapitän zur See Alfred Wolff, who had been flag officer to Admiral Doenitz, was insistent that Hess's defection had been schemed by the British.

25

Examples of Imaginative Planning

THE HESS Affair was one of the biggest shocks dealt out to the German espionage organisations during the war and one from which they never recovered. It marked the beginning of the end for Admiral Canaris; the new intelligence organisation that Hess left behind him disintegrated; all the German Secret Service hopes of winning over the Duke of Windsor and other prominent Britons broke down completely that May of 1941.

Evidence of the panic which Hess's flight created in Berlin was soon available, though it took some time for news of it to filter through to the West. Heinrich Muller, head of Section IV (Gestapo) of the R.S.H.A. helped to organise the *Aktion Hess*, a widescale operation which entailed the arrest of hundreds of people, including many astrologers who were closely interrogated by the Gestapo. In June 1941, Martin Bormann signed a decree which led to the banning of "public performances", if they involved demonstrations of the occult, astrology, fortune-telling and telepathy. On 9 June 1941, astrologers were rounded up and questioned as to whether they had had any associations with Hess. One of the chief astrologers cross-examined was Ernst Schulte-Strathaus and it is clear from German records that the Gestapo suspected him of having advised Hess to make his flight to Scotland on 10 May, whereas all he had done was to lend a certain amount of support to the Swiss astrologer who had contacted Hess. Then it was discovered that in March 1941, Hess had asked a Frau Maria Nagengast, a Munich astrologer, what would be a propitious day for a trip overseas in the near future. She recommended the tenth of May and was duly paid for her advice.

Louis de Wohl, the Hungarian astrologer who had done so much to make the British Secret Service take astrology seriously, had quite a success in the summer of 1941 when he went over to the United States. His mission was quite straightforward: without in any way showing he was interested in Britain's well-being, he had to demonstrate astrologically to the American public that Hitler was not an infallible master of the arts of war. At the same time the object of the exercise was to build up the reputation of de Wohl as something of an infallible prophet. So it was arranged for de Wohl to give a press conference in New York at which he would make various dire predictions of Hitler's fate and that in other parts of the world shortly afterwards other astrological predictions should appear in magazines and newspapers more or less confirming de Wohl.

The tame astrologer of the S.I.S. stated in New York that Hitler's horoscope showed the planet Neptune in the house of death and that this clearly showed his decline was imminent. Shortly afterwards a Cairo paper published in Arabic had a statement from an Egyptian astrologer that "a red planet will appear on the eastern horizon four months hence . . . this means that an uncrowned emperor will die, and that man is Hitler". De Wohl's activities were remarkably successful in making a singularly gullible people believe that Hitler was on the way out, and the efforts of Nazi astrologers were thwarted.

It was at this stage of the war that the British Secret Service at last drew level with the German Secret Service and began in the matter of solid achievement to forge ahead of the enemy. As has been seen, much of the credit for this must go to those painstaking back-room planners in British Intelligence who decided that until they had rebuilt their organisation in Europe the only way to success lay through counter-espionage planning at home and, to a very limited degree, in undercover counter-espionage in the United States where the enemy was still extremely powerful. From mid-1941 onwards the British Secret Service took the initiative and swiftly established a reputation for being by far the most efficient of all the powers' intelligence services for the next three and a half years.

Many of their exploits are now well known and have been described in some detail in recent years. It is probable that in another decade some of these exploits can be told in even greater detail. In the interim no useful purpose can be served here by simply recording what is already well known. The aim will be to list some of these achievements, to correct some misapprehensions about them and to try to interpret them in the light of the development of the various British intelligence services. At the same time, in the interests of accuracy, it will be necessary to put the record right on some legends of World War II Secret Service work which have hitherto been accepted as the correct versions.

One such case is that of Lieut.-Colonel Alexander Paterson Scotland, who suddenly came into the public eye as a result of a chance remark he made when he was testifying during the trial of Field-Marshal Kesselring after the war. When the German defence counsel objected to a question put by the prosecutor, he said: "Only someone who has served in the German Army can answer that." Whereupon Lieut.-Colonel Scotland was asked: "Have you ever served in the German Army?"

Lieut.-Colonel Scotland's unexpected answer was "Yes".

This immediately gave rise to the legend that Lieut.-Colonel Scotland had, as a British Secret Service agent, served on the German General Staff in two world wars. Without in any way detracting from his services to his country—and these were considerable by any standards—this legend is incorrect. Born in Perth, Alexander Scotland spent the early part of his career cattle-farming in South Africa. In the early part of the twentieth century there was a native uprising in the area of South-West Africa, which was under German control, where Scotland was farming. Together with other non-Germans, including other Britons and Scots, he joined the German forces to assist in keeping order. That period of service gave him a valuable insight into the German mentality, a grasp of their military organisation and tactics which later proved of much use to British intelligence. He served quite openly as a Briton and there was never any question then of his being a British agent. In 1914 he was interned by the Germans, but within three months he had engineered the surrender of a fort to General Botha, after which he returned to England.

In World War I he became G.H.Q. interrogator as an Intelligence Officer and in World War II he fulfilled much the same rôle. It was Lieut.-Colonel Scotland's silence which allowed the legend to develop around his name. The explanation of his statement at the Kesselring trial was that he had served in the German Army in South-West Africa in 1903–7. He was again after World War II head of the team interrogating German prisoners-of-war in the "London Cage", the intelligence unit set up for this purpose.

The legend of Scotland's activities—it was even said he held the rank of a German General in two World Wars—was gilded even further by a film based on the story in which Jack Hawkins played as a Briton who masqueraded as a senior German staff officer. Similarly the story of "The Man Who Never Was" became public indirectly as a result of a novel written by Sir Alfred Duff Cooper, a former British Minister of State, and published in 1950, entitled *Operation Heartbreak*. The publication of this book led to certain strong criticisms that the Official Secrets Act had been breached and some muted and half-hearted objections by the Secret Service, not upheld by the Government of the day. Yet, though the unfortunate Lieut.-Colonel Scotland had his flat raided by Special Branch police and was threatened with prosecution when he proposed to publish a book about the "London Cage", Duff Cooper seems to have got away with what was undoubtedly a breach of the Official Secrets Act without any trouble, the point being that he could only have known of the "Man Who Never Was" through his official position.

There seems to be no uniformity in the application of the Official Secrets Act and the failure to prosecute, or at least to restrain, in some cases suggests there is one interpretation of the law for the minor executive and altogether different and preferential treatment for those higher up and especially for the politicians. The Duff Cooper novel caused Ian Colvin to do some research on his own account. When he discovered that Rommel had admitted he was "sent in the wrong direction" as a result of a British courier's body being washed up off the coast of Spain and that there was the grave of a mysterious "Major Martin" in Spain, Colvin wrote a series of articles which paved the way to the next revelation, that of Ewen Montagu's book, *The Man Who Never Was*.

The general outline of this story is now well known and it is given in a wealth of detail that makes a fascinating narrative in this book by the man who, as a Lieut.-Commander, R.N.V.R. was in charge of the planning of the operation in the Naval Intelligence Department. When planning "Operation Torch", the invasion of French North Africa, the Intelligence services were anxious not merely to mask their intentions, but deliberately to mislead the enemy as to their target. It was realised that the gradual build-up of Allied shipping at Gibraltar prior to the invasion could not fail to alert enemy agents in Spain to the fact that an operation was being planned. Therefore the best that could be hoped for was that the Germans should be persuaded that the convoys of shipping were destined for somewhere else. So the aim was to mislead the German High Command by planting on the Spanish coast a corpse, supposedly that of a major of Royal Marines, with fake plans for an Allied invasion of Greece in his pouch. The object of this operation was to cover up the impending invasion of North Africa by the Allies and to make the Germans prepare instead for landings in Crete, Rhodes, Greece and Salonika.

What Ewen Montagu, himself an officer serving in the N.I.D., did not reveal in his otherwise detailed book was the surprising problem of obtaining a body in complete secrecy in war-time. Ewen Montagu approached his friend, Sir William Bentley Purchase, the Coroner for St. Pancras, saying that he needed a body and that his plan had the full support of the Prime Minister.

"You can't get bodies just for the asking," Sir William told him. "Even with bodies all over the place, each one has to be accounted for."

Finally Sir William found the right corpse. It was of a man roughly the right age, height and weight, who had been ill for some time before his death. When the mythical "Major Martin" was being dressed, difficulty arose in fitting on his boots. "I've got it," said Sir William, as the officers stood around the frozen corpse, "we'll get an electric fire and thaw out the feet only. As soon as the boots are on, we'll pop him back in the refrigerator again and re-freeze him."

In Robert Jackson's biography of Bentley Purchase, *Coroner*, the author states: "Purchase's action in providing the body had the sanction not only of the Government, but the man's own relatives, but he was still worried about the effect on public opinion of the unorthodox disposal of a body which had been in his keeping."

The surprising thing about "The Man Who Never Was" *coup* is that while the most thorough precautions had been taken in the planning of the operation to ensure success, there seems to have been an extraordinary laxity when it came to finding a body. Not only had a detailed picture been built up of the mythical "Major Martin", but he had been given a girl friend whose photograph and letters were found on his person and even a bank account showing an overdraft of £79 19s. 2d. Yet the one vital part of the operation—the selection of the corpse—seems to have filled the planners with inhibitions about propriety. Ewen Montagu admits: "At one time we feared we might have to do a body-snatch . . . but we did not like that idea, if we could possibly avoid it. We managed to make some very guarded inquiries from a few Service Medical officers whom we could trust; but when we heard of a possibility, either the relatives were unlikely to agree or we could not trust those whose permission we would need not to mention to other close relatives what had happened."

Many people, therefore, must have heard of the quest for a body, even if they did not know the purpose of the quest. One cannot help feeling it would have been safer to have "acquired" a body by unorthodox means without asking questions or getting permission.

The most remarkable feature of "The Man Who Never Was" operation was the extent of the imaginative planning that went into it and the fact that there was no leakage despite the fact that so many people were in the secret. On the lower levels of the operation, for example, the obtaining of a body, this seems to have been a weakness, but at the higher levels it was imperative to make the plan known because of the problems posed by strategy and the risk of a leak back from the enemy. What Lieut.-Commander Ewen Montagu did not reveal was that this operation had to cleared personally with President Roosevelt. This task fell upon William Stephenson, who was the Secret Service's chief link between the British and the Americans in World War II.

Stephenson was in many respects the outstanding executive on the British side of the Secret Service in World War II and in his relations with the Americans he was as adept and successful as had been Admiral Hall in World War I. Certainly he deserves to have a prominent place in the Secret Service's history, for his services were exceptional in that he possessed the gifts of diplomacy as well as those of Intelligence.

For a Canadian William Stephenson was singularly unobtrusive and indeed, but for the First World War, he might have lived the life of a quiet business man in his native Winnipeg. In that war he joined the R.F.C. in which he served with distinction and from that time began to take a keen interest in Britain and world affairs, an interest that was stimulated by his entering the field of the then adolescent world of wireless and broadcasting. He was a pioneer in this field both on the technical side and in broadcasting experiments and especially in the transmission of photographs by wireless. One activity led to another and by the 'thirties Stephenson had become unostentatiously a figure of importance in several spheres, in broadcasting developments in Canada, in a film company in London, in the manufacture of plastics and in the steel industry. As a sideline he also won the King's Cup air race in 1934 with a machine which had been built in one of his factories.

As a business man with world-wide interests Stephenson travelled extensively and made contacts with many important figures in all countries. He was quick to absorb and to interpret information that would have been overlooked by most men and as a result of the trips he made on behalf of the Pressed Steel Company he was alarmed to discover that practically the whole of the German steel production had been turned over to armament manufacture. This not only made him aware of the German threat at a time when the British government was ignoring it, but made him carry out a lone campaign to inform responsible people of the need to combat it. Only one man was willing to give him a ready ear and to encourage him to find out more—Winston Churchill. From then until the outbreak of war William Stephenson became one of a small, unofficial team of men who supplied Churchill with intelligence on Germany.[1]

It was a simple step from this rôle to that which Churchill

offered him after the outbreak of war, the job of co-ordinating an unofficial relationship between the British and American intelligence services. It was but a short step from some temporary work on behalf of his friend, Lord Beaverbrook at the Ministry of Aircraft Production, to his appointment in New York in the inevitable cover of British Passport Control Officer. There, with a Secret Service officer from London and recruits of his own choosing, Stephenson set about the difficult task of combining propaganda for the British cause with intelligence work and counter-espionage and, by far the most hazardous, carving out a working arrangement with American Intelligence.

It must be remembered that at the beginning of the war America was still neutral, there was not only a great deal of isolationist feeling still prevalent, but in some places lack of faith in the power of Britain to "go it alone" and some downright, old-fashioned American prejudice of Britain as a colonial power. Any co-operation with American Intelligence was therefore fraught with danger and needed to be kept secret even from the State Department. At one stage the frigidity of the State Department was so marked that it was suspected on the British side that there were over-eager plotters inside the State Department working for peace terms with Germany which would have placed Britain in an extremely difficult position. It was thought that Roosevelt was not fully informed of these moves, with the result that a well-meaning, but somewhat rash ex-Army officer working as a British agent took it on himself to burgle the safe of the Under-Secretary of State, Mr. Sumner Welles. It was a successful operation that revealed certain German manoeuvres which the State Department had been hushing up and led to the forestalling of the sabotage of British ships. The agent was forced to flee to Canada for some months and did not return until America entered the war. Even then he was conspicuously shadowed by Edgar Hoover's G-men from bar to bar.

Edgar Hoover and his F.B.I. were practically all that America had to offer in the form of an intelligence service at that time. Hoover, traditionally a somewhat heavy-handed police chief, who had rescued the Federal Bureau of Investigation from the corruption into which it had fallen during Harding's presidency, was not an easy man to handle. It is extremely doubtful whether any Briton other than William Stephenson could have handled him so skilfully at that time. Many have tried since and failed lamentably, especially since Hoover's obsession with communism and his crude methods of combatting this menace. Stephenson knew that Hoover, a man who brooked no interference and who was of a much tougher calibre than any similar figure in World War I American Intelligence, had to be handled carefully. Without his tacit co-operation British espionage and counter-espionage in U.S.A. would have been out on a limb.

But the two men quickly settled down to a working arrangement, though it was perhaps not always so smooth as has sometimes been represented. Hoover himself thought up a typically American bureaucratic title for Stephenson, which the latter adopted. It was Head of British Security Co-ordination. So B.S.C. became the vital link between London and New York and Washington. Whether the alliance would have been achieved without Stephenson's diplomacy—no doubt the fact he was a Canadian helped—or Roosevelt's strong backing is a matter of some doubt.

The lone wolf operator in British intelligence in World War II was hardly seen at all. The brilliant eccentric disappeared almost completely after World War I. The aces of World War II—on paper, if not in fact—were more often business men who had a cover for their work and who, used to soft living and the deadening influences of bureaucracy, rarely emerged from their shells to indulge in any feats of the calibre of Sidney Reilly, or Baden-Powell. Yet this history would fail completely if it did not reiterate the importance of the lone wolf in the entire history of the Secret Service even in modern times. The crucial moment in all Secret Service work is when one agent sees the path ahead clearly, appreciates the objectives and, ignoring the rules, drives ahead on his own against opposition, if necessary, and with absolute conviction that his own methods are right. In espionage there should be precautionary rules, but no others: whether a government likes it or not, if the end justifies the means, all should be forgiven. Morality does not, indeed should not, enter into this subject. The burgling of Sumner Welles' safe was one example of the success of the unorthodox lone agent who goes beyond his brief, even though he is left unprotected.

Another man who had something of this spirit and one in whom patriotism and eccentricity lived on into this more prosaic era of espionage was Lieut.-Colonel Alfred Daniel Wintle. He is worthy of far more space than can be spared in this history, for he exemplified the value of supreme optimism at a time when the British Government, even the Churchill Government, was riddled with inhibitions, doubts and pessimism at the time of the fall of France. Having denied France fighter cover in her hour of greatest need, Britain had a tremendous task to convince her ally that she still meant to carry on the war. Alfred Wintle believed he could do just that.

Born in South Russia, of English diplomatic stock, and having been educated in France, Germany and Rumania, Wintle spoke several languages and, while remaining almost defiantly English, had the unusual knack for a soldier of his type of understanding foreigners. A Dragoons officer at the age of nineteen, he was wounded in Flanders and lost four fingers of his left hand and the sight of one eye, at the same time winning the Military Cross. After the war he learned his training as an intelligence officer in Secunderabad and later he worked in Egypt in Intelligence with Prince Aly Khan, who described him as "the bravest man I ever met". Shortly before World War II Wintle became a lecturer at the French Army Staff College in Paris and he struck up close friendship with a number of high-ranking French officers. At least two of these became prominent in the Vichy Government and his influence over them was such that it could well have been vital in persuading them to change allegiance at this time. When France fell and the authorities in Britain were panic-stricken as to whether the French Navy would go over to the enemy, or what would happen to the French Air Force, Wintle believed he could persuade most of the French Air Force and some of the French Navy to come over to the British side. Nobody would listen to him. He was in fact thwarted by a still influential minority in the Intelligence Services who believed that France must be written off and that capitualation to Germany was a matter of weeks, if not days. Such was the divided state of British Intelligence at the time.

Wintle, however, decided that, single-handed, on his own initiative entirely, he could achieve his aim. He telephoned the commander of the airfield at Heston and, using all the password and code-signs he knew, gave an order, purporting to come from a staff officer at the Air Ministry. He said that a certain Colonel Wintle would shortly be arriving and was to be flown to Bordeaux and left there. Bordeaux was then the seat of the French Government who had been driven from Paris by the Germans.

The ruse worked only too well. Unfortunately Wintle was delayed in getting to Heston and the plane was ready beforehand, with the result that the airfield authorities rang the Air Ministry to say the plane was waiting. Some moments of panic ensued when it was realised that someone was trying to obtain a plane in the Air Ministry's name without first obtaining their authority. Wintle was not allowed to go to Bordeaux when he reached Heston. Instead he had to go to the Air Ministry to explain to the official he had impersonated what he had intended to do. "I told him there was a chance of getting something back," said Wintle afterwards, "most probably a considerable portion of the French Air Force and also some of the French Navy. I was known to all of them. I got on well with them, I not only spoke their language fluently, but I spoke their own form of Service jargon. There were some among even the senior French officers who expected me to come. At that precise moment what they wanted was somebody they trusted to give them a lead."

The officer said "no". Wintle demanded to be allowed to speak to the Air Minister, but the mere suggestion was waved aside as being "preposterous". Wintle then played his last card. He offered to blow off his own right hand to show he was in earnest. The officer, according to Wintle, "turned a billious green and implored me to put my revolver away."

Subsequently Wintle was arrested and placed in the Tower to await court martial. There is little doubt that however foolhardy his plan was, Wintle would have stood just as good a chance of success with the French as some of the inept envoys sent out by the British Government at that time, men who only succeeded in arousing profound suspicion of British motives by their clumsy diplomacy. In his defence Wintle called Generals Ironside and Wavell and, after a severe reprimand, was eventually set free.

Undaunted by this set-back, Wintle next served on Wavell's staff in the Middle East. Wavell, shrewd, taciturn and unostentatious himself, often showed a marked appreciation for the very opposite characteristics in others. The panache which he himself lacked was what Wavell admired in others and he had a high regard for the swashbuckling Wintle. The dashing major grew a beard, with official permission, disappeared, and, posing as a pro-Vichy French officer, got himself repatriated to France. Once inside French territory Wintle indulged in a one-man espionage and sabotage mission of his own. He planted bombs, gleaned French military secrets and even had the audacity to try to contact the French War Minister in an effort to win him over to the Allies. When this plan was thwarted, Wintle landed himself in a French prison, eventually escaping by sawing through the bar of his window and, leaping into a hay-cart, hiding himself under the hay.

His escapades in the war were the subject of much ribaldry in Cairo where, after months of absence, he would suddenly reappear in Shepherd's Hotel, having completed some mission or act of sabotage in France. When he was drinking with those he could trust, he had the most amusing line of patter such as: "Lovely weather along the Riviera coast last week. Had a bathe at Monte Carlo."

Alfred Daniel Wintle was an engaging and attractive character and an amusing companion, but he was also somewhat of a clown and exhibitionist, dangerous combinations in wartime. He was far too much of an individualist to fit easily or safely into an intelligence unit, or a team in the field, for Wintle was the type to take risks and by taking them he could have compromised the lives of others. Nevertheless as a lone wolf secret agent he had valuable qualities and was a great Englishman in the best tradition of Edwardian eccentricity.

There was at least one lone female agent who played a tremendously important rôle in the British Secret Service in World War II. She was American-born Amy Thorpe Pack and shortly after marrying a member of the British Diplomatic Service, she joined the ranks of British Intelligence in Poland in 1937.

The combination of blonde hair and green eyes is supposed to be irresistible and Amy, apart from the initial advantage of possessing these attributes, was extremely smart, sophisticated and highly intelligent. She conquered men's hearts as much by her alert mental qualities as by her looks. She was also fanatically devoted to the British cause.

Using the cover-name of "Cynthia", she turned up in New York in the early years of the war and became William Stephenson's prize agent. The mission he gave her was to penetrate the secrets of the Vichy Government's diplomatic team in the U.S.A. and to find out what pro-German activities they might be indulging in. In his biography of Sir William Stephenson, H. Montgomery Hyde had this to say about her: "As a product of British intelligence her achievement was to prove of incalculable value to the allied war effort. For sheer bravado it probably has no equal in the records of espionage during the last war. Not only did she secure the texts en clair of nearly all the telegrams despatched from and received by the Vichy Embassy, but she was also instrumental in obtaining the key to both the French and the Italian naval ciphers, which enabled the British Admiralty to read for the remainder of the war all relevant cablegrams, radiograms and fleet-signals which were intercepted in code or cipher."[2]

Amy Thorpe Pack's method was to cultivate the acquaintance of the French diplomats by her physical charms. She bewitched an Italian admiral and persuaded him to talk, as a result of which she learned of Italian sabotage plans in the U.S.A. Finally in the Vichy Embassy in Washington she won the confidence and the active support of one of the French attachés. She persuaded him to help her obtain the Embassy codes and ciphers from the strong-room, which was guarded throughout each night by a full-time watchman.

Working on the assumption that any Frenchman will be sympathetic to *l'amour*, Amy and her attaché pleaded with the watchman to be allowed to spend the night on a divan in the Embassy. The assumption, aided by a generous tip, proved to be correct and the ploy was repeated on other nights. Then one night the pair arrived with bottles of champagne and offered the watchman a drink. The champagne had been slightly drugged and soon the watch-man was sound asleep. During his snoring slumbers, Amy and her new-found friend opened the Embassy door to let in a locksmith who found the combination of the code-room safe for them. Two nights later the pair returned to the

Embassy and found the night watch-man in somewhat wary mood. Realising that it was just possible that the man may have suspected he had been drugged a few nights earlier, Amy had a hunch that he would keep a close watch on them. So, stripping herself of her clothes, she arranged herself in a provocative pose on the divan. When the watchman stealthily opened the door and peeped inside to see what was happening, he was covered in embarrassment and hastily retired never to show himself again that night. The locksmith was let in through a window, the safe was opened, the books removed and photographed and then put back in the safe.

It was one of the coolest espionage tricks of the war and the codes and ciphers were valid for many months afterwards as the French never suspected what had happened. The story also had a happy ending for Amy married her French attaché after the war.

Incidentally, with the outbreak of war quite a few professionally-skilled safe-breakers in Britain were freed from prison to work for the Allies. The majority were given the chance of joining the Commandos, while a select few were accepted for Secret Service work purely as locksmiths, safebreakers and dynamiters.

An altogether different category of lone-wolf in the Intelligence field in World War II was the author, Dennis Wheatley. He was a lone wolf in the sphere of ideas.

"Wheatley's War", as his friends jokingly called it, began with a lunch at the Dorchester Hotel in London three days after the surrender of France. Sir Louis Greig, a Wing-Commander Lawrence Darvall and a Czech armaments manufacturer were in the party with Wheatley, the purpose being to discuss a paper which Wheatley had written giving his own, unofficial and highly original ideas for repelling a German invasion. Wheatley was asked to develop his theme. The result was that he spent the greater part of the rest of World War II in Churchill's secret underground fortress just off Whitehall, the only civilian member of the Joint Planning Staff. True, this was work that was only on the fringes of Intelligence, but in essence it was the job of feeding ideas into the Intelligence machine, for Wheatley not only worked out his own projects, but was also involved in providing some of the background details for two such successful Secret

Service *coups* as "The Man Who Never Was" and the creating of General Montgomery's "double."

Making himself think like a Nazi, Wheatley initially wrote a 12,000 words paper on a plan for the conquest of Britain as it might have been prepared by a member of the German General Staff. The object of this exercise was to imagine every possible horror, or diabolical trick which the Germans might think up and try out if they attempted invasion. Then, having contrived an invasion plan with Teutonic thoroughness, to think up moves to counter every plan they had in mind. Wheatley planned various hazards for the Germans such as the blacking-out of the names of railway stations on the platforms and the uprooting of sign-posts as well as a 230-mile barrier of fishing-nets to foul the propellors of Nazi landing-craft.

Not all of Wheatley's ideas were accepted, of course: many were rejected on the spot. But a great many of them formed the basis for further discussions and quite often for action. One of his pet ideas was a plan to invade Sardinia, which he had worked out like a thriller story. He was convinced that the war could have been won at least a year earlier if Sardinia had been invaded instead of Sicily, but "Operation Brimstone", as the project was labelled, remained in the pigeon-holes. General Eisenhower was said to have favoured the plan which was finally vetoed by Sir Alan Brook, the Chief of General Staff who had been in the habit of pouring a douche of pessimism on every invasion plan that was put forward from Admiral Keyes' plan to capture Pantellaria to Wheatley's scheme for Sardinia.

So successful had been the deception of the Germans by the "Man Who Never Was" *coup* that shortly before the invasion of Normandy by the Allies the Intelligence chiefs asked for ideas for tricking the enemy on this occasion. The idea that was finally accepted was to find a man who could impersonate General Montgomery and for him to be sent on a mission to Gibraltar and North Africa just before the landings in Normandy were to take place. An ex-actor, M. E. Clifton-James, was selected to play the role of "Monty" and he carried it out so convincingly that, as he wrote afterwards, "I *was* General Montgomery. Even when alone I found myself playing the part."[3]

26

Aid to French Resistance Movements

THE TASK of M.I.5 became relatively a light one as the war progressed. It is true that in the beginning Germany showed signs of improved methods of espionage inside Britain itself and the few really first-class agents who escaped detection were highly successful. But by far the greater number of agents sent over were of poor material, badly trained and easily caught. The Germans had devoted a vast amount of expenditure to espionage, but their trouble was that they had too many intelligence units, too many warring intelligence leaders and far too many agents in the field. Quantity was there, quality was lacking. One of the incredibly stupid blunders made again and again by German agents was their tendency to have a farewell drinking party before being sent on a mission. A small party of them would drink themselves into a state of near intoxication before setting off either by plane, or by rubber dinghy to reach the coasts of Britain. The result was their wits were dulled when they landed and they quickly gave themselves away. Lord Jowitt, who was Solicitor-General during the war and conducted a number of espionage trials, stated afterwards that in the German espionage machine there were "all the marks of hasty and very imperfect improvisation . . . if they were a fair sample of German espionage, then that espionage must have been remarkably inefficient".

It would, however, be a great mistake to write off the espionage of any nation as entirely inefficient merely on the evidence of the inexperience or poor quality of several of its agents. The few, or even the one, can do as much damage as a whole battalion of spies. One such man achieved spectacular successes in Britain throughout the war. Defying all efforts of M.I.5 to catch him, he worked for the Germans in Britain for seven years from his arrival from Canada in 1937 to 1944 when all trace of him was lost. Even Lieut.-Colonel Edward Hinchley-Cooke, who was M.I.5's chief interrogator of spies during the war, paid tribute to him. Hinchley-Cooke, a barrister and an excellent linguist, had served in M.I.5 before the war as controller of postal and cable censorship and he remained in the organisation until 1954, acquiring a reputation as one of the most feared interrogators in the Department.

The mystery spy who spent seven years in Britain was responsible for passing on information from the Kirkwall watch-maker about the Scapa Flow defences, providing charts of the docks of Liverpool, Hull, Southampton and Newcastle, plans of the system of airfields in South-East England and preparing an outline of how the Luftwaffe raids should be directed during the battle of Britain. There were many other *coups* which were sometimes attributed to this man, but they may well have been the work of other German spies.

The identity of this undetected spy is still somewhat obscure. It is known that he was operating in March, 1944, and that when General Eisenhower moved his headquarters from London to Bushy Park as a security precaution, the fact was reported to Berlin within a few days. M.I.5 was convinced that he was a man with great knowledge of and many contacts in the Midlands and suspected that he had provided the target information for the massive raid on Coventry in 1941. If this was the case then he could have been a German-Canadian calling himself Karl Dickhenhoff, who lived in Edgbaston, whose real name was Hans Caesar, and who is reputed to be still alive, but in an asylum. The authorities have been singularly coy about this phantom spy and the reason for this may well have been that he was a double-agent whose cover was almost unshakeable.[1]

Another dangerous German spy who entered Britain was Dr. Jan Willem Ter Braak, a Dutch refugee who arrived in Cambridge and, claiming that he was writing a book on the medicinal properties of plants grown in Dutch territories overseas, requested permission to do research in the University libraries. Somehow Ter Braak had been allowed in without proper screening: his story was that he had come with a crowd of refugees and had been passed by the authorities. Certainly he had a Dutch passport and had registered with the police. His arrival would probably have gone unremarked, but for two facts. First, M.I.5, while accepting that he might have slipped into the country with a crowd of refugees, thought that the police or someone should have a positive record of his arrival: there was none. Secondly, one member of M.I.5 made a habit of checking on records of arrivals of strangers from abroad immediately after they had received news of parachutes being found anywhere in the country, as the Germans dropped a number of spies by this means. A few days before Ter Braak had appeared a parachute had been found in a field in Buckinghamshire. They decided to watch Ter Braak. It was quickly discovered that though he spent most of his time in Cambridge libraries, he also paid occasional visits to London and that during these he went to Downing Street and the vicinity of Storey's Gate, where the Prime Minister's underground offices were situated. So on one occasion when he was in London Ter Braak's lodgings in Cambridge were searched. Here were found note-books containing codes, pistols and a radio-transmitter, enough evidence to warrant an arrest. But Ter Braak never returned to his lodgings: whether he suspected he was being followed and decided to commit suicide, or whether he was killed by a counter-espionage agent, cannot be stated for certain. It has been asserted that he had been sent over by the Nazis with the express intention of organising Churchill's assassination.

Such assertions are, however, only too frequent when spy stories are told. Both the British and the Germans sometimes tended to make some of their exploits sound more exciting than they were. At one time it was suspected that Ter Braak was the mystery spy who had been providing so much top secret information to the enemy, but this is almost certainly not the case, though there is evidence that he was an associate of the elusive Karl Dickenhoff, and of another German spy, a Dutchman named Johannes Marius Dronkers who had come to Britain in a small boat flying the Dutch flag and claiming to be a Dutch Resistance worker.

According to German records a more successful spy was one

Hans Schmidt, a Danish Nazi, who was dropped by parachute near Salisbury in 1940. His story has been told by Charles Wighton and Gunter Peis in their book *They Spied In England*, based on the diary of former General Erwin von Lahousen, chief of the Sabotage Division of the German Secret Service. It is claimed that he owed his success to a link-up he achieved with Welsh Nationalists. Not only did Schmidt radio messages to Germany throughout the war, but he even married and had a son during this period. He sabotaged railways and factories and later warned Berlin of the preparations for the Dieppe landing of 1942 and the Normandy invasion of 1944. But even the Germans admit that little use was made of his information. The authors of the book claim that Schmidt is still living in the London area with his wife and family.

In retrospect, however, one must suspect the story of the German version of Schmidt just as much as of the British version of Ter Braak. The latter was certainly a very careless and amateurish spy to allow himself to be compromised in such a manner and surely extremely faint-hearted to have committed suicide merely because he suspected he was being watched. It is hard to believe that the Germans can seriously have used a man of this calibre to try to assassinate Churchill. Similarly the story of Hans Schmidt does not altogether have the authentic ring of truth. Mr. Harry Agerbaak, a Danish Embassy official, stated that he had read the account of Schmidt's alleged espionage activities and that he was not satisfied: "I was in London during the war. I know the steps that M.I.5 took to vet every refugee. I do not believe that any slipped through their fingers for long."

The accuracy of General von Lahousen's diary may be questioned. It is more than likely that Schmidt was unmasked by M.I.5 and that in the latter part of the war he was being fed information by the British to be passed back to the Germans. If he is still living in Britain, this is even more probable: a genuine German agent would have gone to Ireland or somewhere else further afield. Again, any German agent who had worked so long and so successfully in Britain, as is suggested, would have been regarded with more respect than Schmidt. Why were his later reports ignored? The answer may be that they suspected that false information was being planted on him. It is even probable that Schmidt eventually became a British agent, though continuing to accept German money.

A German who actually worked for British Intelligence was Baron Ridiger von Etzdorf, a Prussian landowner and former German Navy officer. He was born to vast wealth, moved in the highest circles and, spied for Britain from 1935 to 1945, eventually being given British nationality for his services.

The Baron had become convinced as early as the early thirties that the Nazis were a threat to European peace and that Hitler was planning a second World War, and, when he joined the British Secret Service his aristocratic connections enabled him to pick up a good deal of worthwhile information. Immediately after the fall of France he was posted to Casablanca, where as "Mr. Ellerman", he created an escape organisation to enable British soldiers and airmen to get back to Britain. Many of these had been trapped in France at the time of the French collapse and the Baron provided them with false papers which identified them as neutrals and got these stamped with Moroccan exit visas and Portuguese transit visas. Then his activities were discovered by the Vichy police, but, being warned in time, he made good his own escape.

His next mission for the British was to spy out the coast and off-shore islands north and south of Dakar in search of submarine hideouts and refuelling depots. His wife described how he had "a hair-raising journey to Africa in a flat-bottomed Rhine river barge .... His cover story was that he was a coastal trader in coconuts. So at Freetown he filled up the barge with nuts, then sailed for several weeks around the islands and inlets, selling the nuts to native traders."[2]

Von Etzdorf spied for the British later in Chile and the Argentine, being mainly engaged on economic espionage. After the war he undertook a number of jobs ranging from salesman to chef and language teacher. He did not have the luck he deserved and life was somewhat of a struggle in his later years when he became the proprietor of a working men's snack and coffee-bar known as Jack's Café in Boundary Road, London, N.W. Little did the men in dungarees who greeted him as "Jack" know that he was a German baron who had spied for the British. That was a secret he guarded carefully along with his true identity, especially as at one time his brother was a post-war German Ambassador in London. Even though the Ambassador had also been hostile to Hitler, it would have been embarrassing for him if it had become generally known that his brother was a former British agent. Von Etzdorf died in 1967.

Further changes in the leadership of the Secret Service occurred in the early 'forties. "It was much harder to keep up with the Germans in World War II than in World War I," declared Sir William Wiseman, who had been in charge of counter-espionage for the British in U.S.A. in the previous war. "True, the German espionage machine made mistakes and we always kept ahead of them, but they were full of ideas and far better organised than in the First World War."[3]

Wiseman himself had not lost his touch and not only gave his successor, Sir William Stephenson, a great deal of help and advice, but even indulged in a little espionage himself. The latter included talks with the Princess Stephanie Hohenlohe-Waldenberg-Schillingsfurst and Captain Fritz Weidemann, then Consul-General in San Francisco, on the possibility of a *coup* of Monarchists and Army officers against the Hitler régime, and Weidemann revealed a great deal of what Hitler was thinking and of current German strategy. Even more important Weidemann told Wiseman that Hitler was seriously planning to drive through Bulgaria and to invade Yugoslavia and Greece.

Wiseman also gave much sound advice on the handling of co-ordination matters with the Americans in the field of intelligence. For the next step from the setting up of the British Security Co-ordination Service was to help the Americans to create a new intelligence organisation of their own, a scheme which came to fruition with General William Donovan's American Office of Strategic Services. That the co-operation was effective can be judged from Donovan's own assessment that "Bill Stephenson taught us all we ever knew about foreign intelligence".[4]

This was one of Stephenson's great triumphs. He had felt the need for a thoroughly professional American espionage set-up and he had hoped that Donovan would become the head of it and, to quote David Bruce, U.S. Ambassador to Britain, Stephenson had "to achieve this end, brought through subtle influences the merits of such a proposal to the attention of President Roosevelt".

Back in London changes were also made in the S.O.E. Sir Frank Nelson was succeeded as head of this organisation by Sir Charles Hambro who was in his turn succeeded by Major-General Sir Colin Gubbins who had been in charge of operations and training in S.O.E. The propaganda division of S.O.E. was situated at Woburn Abbey, the country house of the Duke of Bedford, while the operations staff remained in Baker Street. As has been previously indicated, there was much to criticise about the organisation of S.O.E. in its early stages and though it undoubtedly improved, it is becoming increasingly evident that it was never at any time during the war as powerful a body as has sometimes been suggested. In achievements, in professionalism and in organisation it never matched up to the S.I.S.; in many respects it was downright inefficient, wasteful and even damaging to the war effort. This may seem a harsh judgement, but it is one that is shared by many on the Continent of Europe who saw and sometimes suffered from S.O.E. blunders.

S.O.E. was least effective in its relations with the Secret Services and the Resistance groups of Britain's Allies. Writing in *Le Nouvel Observateur* on 1 June 1966, Jean Daniel declared that the official history of the S.O.E. in France confirmed that "Secret Services fight on several fronts—against the enemy, against rival services of their own country and sometimes against their Allies." He pointed out that in 1940 the French section of S.O.E. was under orders to make no distinction between De Gaulle and Pétain and thus to have no special ties with the Free French.

Admittedly this was the view of a left-wing journal, but to a large extent it was justified by the facts. There is ample evidence that relations between the French Resistance and the S.O.E. French section were never very satisfactory and allegations have been made both from the French and the British sides that not all the blunders were due to inefficiency and that some were positively criminal, accusing the authorities in London of hiding guilty secrets behind the cloak of the Official Secrets Act. Even Ian Fleming used to tell his colleagues in the N.I.D. that "those boys in S.O.E. make as much trouble for us as they do for the enemy".[5] Fleming's sardonic witticisms were frequently made at the expense of the S.O.E.

Many have tried to probe the full story of the muddle, suspected treacheries and chaotic relationships which typified much of the S.O.E., but few have succeeded in solving what one critic has called "a skein so tangled, a story so convoluted, attitudes of mind so Byzantine as so far to have defied rational analysis".

Colonel Maurice Buckmaster, the head of F Section of the S.O.E. published two accounts of work done by the Section, the first, *Specially Employed*, in 1953, and the second, *They Fought Alone*, published in 1958. The second book in particular was singled out for considerable criticism on the grounds that parts of it flatly contradicted his first book about S.O.E. One critic contended that it was "as riddled as a pistol target—with wrong names, wrong dates, wrong details". The author in reply said that "any pretension that the book constitutes a detailed and meticulously accurate day-to-day record of happenings which, by their very nature, were shrouded in secrecy, would be absurd".

Then Dame Irene Ward, M.P. agitated for a probe into what she regarded as the misdemeanours of Baker Street and in December 1958, in the House of Commons, called for a "full and frank investigation" of certain phases of the S.O.E.'s work. It was alleged that forty-seven British agents had deliberately been dropped to the Germans to distract their attention from other under-cover operations. Colonel Buckmaster replied to such criticisms in an article in the *Daily Mail*, of 1 December, 1959, stating: "I can now say categorically that nothing is further from the truth than that we deliberately dropped the agents to the Germans." But he admitted that the Germans did penetrate one "important *reseau*, but this was only one of fifty".

"The penetration by the Germans in the summer of 1943," he added, referring to the breaking of the Prosper Circuit, "was a serious set-back to our operations. I have never tried to conceal the importance of this German success, admittedly with grave repercussions."

The truth about S.O.E. will not easily be established even when the files are fully available to all researchers. Even Mr. M. R. D. Foote, when writing the official history of *The S.O.E. in*

Above, left, Alexander Foote, a member of the 'Lucy Ring'; *right,* 21 Queen Anne's Gate, H.Q. of M.I.6; *below,* Sir Stewart Menzies, head of M.I.6 in World War I

Left, Lt.-Cdr. Ian Fleming; *belo*
Sir William Stephenson receive
the Medal of Merit from Gener
William J. Donovan

France, found the files in "a state of authentic confusion". There had been no central registry and many papers had been destroyed by fire, or deliberately removed or censored.

In reading between the lines of the official history and in comparing this with independent narratives it is abundantly clear that many of the activities of the S.O.E. have escaped the searchlight of truth because they have been so well hidden. It becomes increasingly apparent that many of the agents were sent into the field with imprecise instructions and inadequate briefings as to the dangers they would meet. Often they saved their skins only by masterly improvisation and presence of mind. As Jean Overton Fuller has pointed out in her three books about the work of British secret agents in France, it has never been explained why S.O.E. in London accepted as genuine communications from France which did not comply with the pre-arranged security codes. For a long time some of these messages were being sent by the Gestapo, who had penetrated the network and arranged to "receive" and so capture the agents as they parachuted into France.

It is still not possible to make an accurate assessment of many of these criticisms of the S.O.E. in France. Relations between the S.O.E. and the S.I.S., M.I.5 and the P.W.E. (Political Warfare Executive) were never cordial and at times marked by an almost venomous mutual distrust.

The hasty recruitment of agents, the uninhibited behaviour of some of them when they landed in Occupied France and the brevity of the training periods tended to produce indisciplined and careless conduct. For example the Security Training Course at Beaulieu in the New Forest often lasted only a week. Blunders were perhaps inevitable, but they were also too numerous. There was the case of an agent named Labit who was parachuted into France and was soon asked for his identity card in a routine check-up. He produced two identity cards at once from the same pocket, each bearing his photograph and yet made out for two different people. This stupidity cost the agent his life.

Agents who were supposed to send messages back to London often forgot to give their true identity checks. There was the Prosper Circuit Disaster, already referred to, which resulted in the break-up of an entire operational circuit in a single blow and the arrests of hundreds. The French alleged that this circuit had been betrayed by the British to the Germans, but it was carelessness—criminal carelessness, perhaps—which was really responsible. The circuit was too large, its security inadequately controlled from London, and it now seems almost certain that it was infiltrated at an early stage by a double-agent. By far the biggest mistake was that one address was used as "post office" and rendezvous point for as many as ten agents. Such failure to spread the risk was courting disaster.

Yet by far the worst disaster and one which robbed the French of the greatest of all their Resistance leaders, a man who undoubtedly would have been a political leader of eminence after the war, was the capture of the inimitable Jean Moulin. Here again lack of security precautions led to his arrest and barbaric torture and murder by the Germans. He was one of the bravest, most efficient and imaginative of the Resistance leaders and his comments on links with the S.O.E. are of special interest. The Resistance, he wrote in a report, dated October 1941, had done their best to communicate with the British, but "the results obtained have been disappointing, a few communications conveyed out of the Occupied Zone by British planes, or a few information pamphlets received from London by the same means, constituted the only fruits of their labours until recently. They have several times had the opportunity to complain and set out in detail their wishes to British agents in France, with whom they had worked very successfully. These agents had promised to put their case before high authorities, but none of these pleas have had any effect. . . .

"One recent attempt could, however, have had useful results if it had been made under different conditions. I mean the mission in France of the Aspirant Z., who was to have entered into contact with movements of resistance in France, as a result of an interallied conference. Was it the youthful age of the agent, or his insufficient knowledge of the problems at stake that made the attempt a failure, resulting only in a series of misunderstandings?"

Moulin may have been an impatient man, but he was neither stupid, nor hostile to the idea of S.O.E. But towards the end of his life he warned close friends that he suspected that not all the blunders of British agents could have been accidental and that it sometimes seemed as though someone in London had links with the enemy, or was deliberately sabotaging the Resistance Movement, or those parts of it who wished for swifter action.

The official history of the S.O.E. angered one Frenchman in particlar, M. Dewavrin, better known as Colonel Passy, General de Gaulle's war-time intelligence chief. His verdict on the *History* was that it had "accumulated the errors of others and added others to them". One of the things which harassed the Gaullists in war-time London was a sniping force of French politicians who sowed mistrust of the Gaullists and whose war aim was to restore the discredited Third Republic in its entirety. They passed on anti-Gaullist rumours to the British intelligence machine—to any department of it which would listen to them—and misled both M.I.5 and the S.O.E. Fortunately the S.I.S. was somewhat more discriminating. Passy, who, with other Gaullists, had been a victim of these rumours, was particularly angry about a reference in *S.O.E. in France* to the French codes which, the author recorded, were broken by the British practically on sight and that it was generally believed that every message the French sent out in their own code could be read by the Germans as late as March, 1944. "If this were true," commented M. Dewavrin, "then it was surely criminal of the British to allow us to go on using them."

S.O.E. in France also makes reference to persistent rumours that the Germans had an agent on de Gaulle's staff, but the author admitted that he had not found proof for or against this. In which case why record the rumours? The truth is that the official history still reflects a good deal of the antagonism of the heads of S.O.E. towards de Gaulle and his followers. Its publication drew such widespread evidence of inaccuracies in the official version of events that the author found it necessary to reply to his critics in an article in which he admitted that "S.O.E's. own archives are of course in many respects sadly incomplete. . . . There have been heavy losses by accident and by ill-advised intent. . . . *All* the files of A.M.F., the section that worked into southern France from Algiers, were burned at—or even before—the end of the war; and almost all the messages exchanged between Colonel Maurice Buckmaster's F section and France by wireless have disappeared."

Yet these were vital documents which could have completely changed the whole picture of S.O.E. It is significant that the A.M.F. files were burned, because the French have repeatedly claimed that Resistance leaders who visited Algiers and returned to France during the war after having contacts with S.O.E. agents were betrayed and, in some cases, like that of Jacques Médèric, were ambushed. But what is even more disturbing is the fact that agents named in the official history again and again refute the versions of their activities given in that book. For example, here is the official version of an operation in October 1941:

"The Corsican mission—J. B. Hayes, Jumeau, Le Harivel and Turberville—arrived by parachute on 10/11 October to a reception near Bergerac arranged by Pierre Bloch (Gabriel), a former Socialist deputy recruited by de Guélis. They were all four trained sabotage instructors (Le Harivel was also a wireless operator); and they were all in prison before ten days were out. Turberville dropped wide of the others, but with all their containers; he was arrested by the gendarmerie next morning, and the others fell successively into a Vichy police trap when trying to make contact with Turck at the Villa de Bois, because his address had been found on Turberville. The same trap, manned by someone who resembled Turck closely enough in voice and figure to deceive several agents, also caught Robert Lyon, Roche, Pierre Bloch, and—last and worst of all, on 24 October—Georges Bégué. On one of these captured agents Fleuret's name was found, and Fleuret was arrested, too. . . . The result in fact of giving that one Villa des Bois address to fourteen incoming agents had been that five of them had been arrested at it; these arrests had led the police to a sixth newcomer, to several of S.O.E's. new French friends and to the almost indispensable Bégué. Turberville escaped some weeks later, by jumping off a train while being transferred from one prison to another; lay low in Auvergnat village; and finally got back to England in 1943."

Daniel Turberville refutes this version indignantly. First he states that the address of the Villa des Bois could not have been found on him as he did not even know of its existence. In any event his mission was to go to the French Riviera. "For security reasons we never took down in writing any names or addresses,"

Mr. Turberville wrote after reading the official version, "and when questioned by the French police I always pretended I was parachuted alone. In prison at Pengueuse I was put with the *Prisonniers de Droit Communs* (thieves, murderers, etc.), the others were put in the *Section Militaire*. The War Office received the full details of my interrogation and they should know that never did the French police suspect I was not alone. Turck, who had been working for the *Deuxième Bureau* is, according to the other boys, responsible for their arrest. He turned over to us later, but he was the guilty man."

There is absolutely no reason to doubt Mr. Turberville's version of events, which is supported by independent evidence. Why, if he was as careless as has been alleged, was he given other important missions later, no mention of which appears in the official history? Was the official record of the Corsican Mission "doctored" and, if so, how many other records were also treated in this manner? Were guilty men being protected by the S.O.E. executive? These are questions to which answers are needed not only in the interests of the agents concerned, but for getting a better perspective of S.O.E's. work overseas.

There were of course some successes which can be credited to S.O.E. After all there were 10,000 men and 3,200 women agents and operatives who took part in their activities. Again, as was the case with the Germans, the emphasis was often on numbers rather than quality. It can be shown that for less expenditure of both men and money, however, S.O.E. was more effective than R.A.F. Bomber Command, which is perhaps the answer to "Bomber" Harris's damning description of the Ministry of Economic Warfare which controlled S.O.E. as "amateurish, ignorant, irresponsible and mendacious".

Without the organisation and arms of S.O.E. the French Resistance movements would not have received the supplies of arms and cash they needed. In adversity the S.O.E. kept alive the spirit of hope when the Resistance groups were suffering set-backs. During the Normandy landings S.O.E. agents were particularly successful in delaying vital German Panzer divisions bound for the coast. In the area of the Normandy beach-head, it is true, little, if anything was accomplished by S.O.E. (as has been stressed before, its link-up with Combined Operations H.Q. was never really adequate), but in the premature rising that occurred in France following the B.B.C's. announcement of *Des Violins d'Automne*, there were positive achievements: 950 planned interruptions of the French railway system were carried out of the 1,050 planned on the first night. Traffic between Toulouse and Montauban was blocked for three months and traffic between Marseilles and Lyons after D-Day was incessantly interrupted.

There were also many instances of individual bravery and initiative by agents. More than once a sense of humour saved lives. A flamboyant radio-operator agent said in French to the German who stopped him: "I am a British officer and here is my radio set." The German laughed at the mad-man: "All right, run along then," he replied. Trained agents used to carry messages on thin, tight rolls of paper, inserted into a cigarette with a needle. If captured, they could smoke their secrets away. So much perfume was brought back to Britain by returning agents that much of it was used as lighter fuel.

To dwell too long on the work of individual agents whose enterprise and initiative lend some light to the largely sombre picture of S.O.E. would be to confuse the overall assessment of this organisation. Many of these agents have already had their stories told in great detail and the controversies about whether these stories have been told accurately, or whether they have been highly coloured and fictionalised are hardly relevant to the subject as a whole. Mr. Foot makes the somewhat uncharitable allegation that some of the "stories of torture come from the prurient imaginations of authors anxious to make their books sell". This is a thesis which I do not propose to examine.

One cannot, however, whatever reservations one may have about some of the S.O.E. agents' activities, neglect to pay tribute to Wing-Commander Forest Frederick Yeo-Thomas, whose field-name as an agent for S.O.E. was "Shelley". A Welshman, who had lived in Paris, latterly as a director of the fashion house of Molyneux, Yeo-Thomas was one of the most indomitable and resourceful agents S.O.E. put in the field. On one occasion he was driven out of danger hidden under a pile of flowers in a hearse, with vital information stowed away beside him in a coffin. During this macabre journey through the ranks of the enemy he gripped a Sten gun as did his companion the other side of the coffin. Yeo-Thomas had been told to return to London, but was dismayed about the orders because a German division was camped over almost the whole area between Arras and the pick-up field. It was Berthe Fraser, a middle-aged Frenchwoman with a British husband, who remembered the graveyard near the pick-up spot and organised the "funeral".

Yeo-Thomas was parachuted to France on a number of occasions until eventually he was betrayed by an arrested subordinate and captured on the steps of the Passy Metro station just below his father's flat. He was thereafter subjected to appalling tortures which were to precipitate his death in Paris in 1964. He escaped first from Buchenwald, then after recapture and posing as a French Air Force prisoner from a P.O.W. camp. For his "exceptional gallantry" he was awarded the Military Cross and the George Medal.

Yet, despite the heroism of individual agents, it is still a moot point as to whether it would have been better to have left occupied Europe alone until liberation from without became possible. When Churchill told Dalton that the purpose of S.O.E. was "to set Europe ablaze", the idea was romantic and grandiose, but it went off at half cock. It was not until the spring of 1941 that any agents reached France and not until the beginning of 1944 did they seriously worry the Germans. There is an attempt now to blame the amateurism of the agents, but the real culprits, in the beginning at least, were the conservative-minded and timorous chiefs of the S.O.E., whose internal wranglings were notorious for their wasting of time and opportunity. The naval and military authorities showed marked hostility to S.O.E. and the Air Force Chief of Staff, Lord Portal, was reluctant to release aircraft from the bombing of Germany for dropping agents, which he considered a "gamble". There was also a great deal of insane jealousy of S.O.E. among the Service chiefs and emotional anti-French prejudice which hampered operations. On one occasion when the R.A.F. begged for S.O.E. to ambush the pilots of a particularly troublesome Luftwaffe squadron, Portal scotched the operation by refusing to associate himself with "assassins". Here was the mid-Victorian attitude to espionage and sabotage rearing its head again. Thus, in mitigation of some of S.O.E's. shortcomings, the hostility of the conventional forces can be blamed.

F Section of the S.O.E. took its orders entirely from London and was completely run by the British, without liaison with De Gaulle's Free French organisation. Not only was this a source of grievance to the Gaullists, but it meant that, in effect, F Section was a "private army", a law unto itself and thereby wholly responsible for the appalling lack of security in most of its operations. Of four hundred agents sent out by F section twenty-five per cent did not return.

On the other hand there is a good deal of evidence that some of the earliest agents to be sent out, while acquiring a good deal of favourable publicity for themselves after the war, took the line of least resistance and, realising they had been despatched too soon, settled down to a life of relative comfort on the Riviera and elsewhere. It is easy perhaps to criticize the agents concerned: in war one takes what bonuses come one's way unquestioningly, if one is wise. But disciplined control of some of these agents from London was sadly lacking.

The most effective part of S.O.E's. work was its moral influence on Resisters and Europeans generally. Its agents were in effect waging an ideological war, the creating of the idea that liberty was something worth fighting for. Had these ambassadors of liberty had the intellectual capacity of a Jean Moulin, the discipline of the Maquis, or the single-mindedness of the Communist Resistance, much more might have been achieved more quickly. As it was in the end the real triumph lay with the undoubtedly heroic and disciplined men of the Maquis.

27

The "Lucy" Ring

By the time the United States entered the war at the end of 1941 the structure of the British Secret Service and its various appendages had become unwieldy and perhaps unavoidably complicated. On the other hand its unwieldiness and complicated interlocking departments provided to a very great extent a system of checks and balances against the risks of one-sided, or distorted intelligence, the gravest threat to the effectiveness of any intelligence organisation in wartime.

At this stage it is interesting to denote certain subtle changes in the evolution of the British Secret Service during its history. In Tudor times it was the statesman in charge of intelligence gathering who was all powerful: Cecil and Walsingham held the reigns of power and passed on, even to the sovereign, only those items of information which they deemed advisable to be disseminated. Later the power passed more to the Foreign Secretary of the day and it was not until World War I that the Prime Minister himself had to take steps to control the dissemination of intelligence and to ensure that he was kept fully in the picture. Even then much information that was acquired by some departments was not always passed on to the Prime Minister even when it was a matter of grave importance.

However, the development of espionage and counter-espionage both before and during World War II made it inevitable that the Prime Minister should in fact as well as in theory be the supreme arbiter of intelligence. This was a rôle for which Chamberlain, like Baldwin before him, had little taste, or indeed talent. With Churchill, with his experience in Cabinet office in World War I and his desire to influence events personally, the control of the Secret Service was a job for which he was fitted both by temperament and inclination. Of all the war leaders, including Roosevelt and Hitler, Churchill was easily the most powerful as regards access to intelligence and control over it, with the possible exception of Stalin. Even Stalin was invariably suspicious of intelligence reports given to him. As to Hitler he was confronted by a number of warring intelligence services and with an intelligence chief in Canaris who increasingly worked against him and even misled him. Roosevelt suffered because in the United States there was no centralised agency that could co-ordinate the scattered information which came in from the Office of Naval Intelligence, the Army, the O.S.S. and other organisations, while the State Department, which should have been the clearing-house of diplomatic intelligence, was often strangely lacking in information, especially on Japan and the Far East. Indeed, most of the information that came from the State Department was prejudiced, unobjective and wrong. It relied far too much in the early stages of the war on intelligence from Vichy-ites in France, which was one reason for both its and Roosevelt's antagonism to de Gaulle.

Churchill relied on the machinery of the Joint Intelligence Committee, which not only brought him in touch with all his intelligence chiefs, but with the S.O.E., the Foreign Office and M.I.5, and on the intelligence summaries which were prepared for the War Cabinet by Professor Arnold Toynbee. The intelligence summaries were on Churchill's instructions kept terse and factual and for this reason the work was much more suitable for an international historian such as Toynbee, who had a long record of association with British Governments. He had undertaken confidential work for the Government from 1915–19, had been in the Political Intelligence Department of the Foreign Office in 1918 and a member of the Middle East section of the British Delegation to the Peace Conference in Paris in 1919. His post as Director of Studies in the Royal Institution of International Affairs, dating from 1925, had provided the right kind of background for his new task and for that of Director of the Research Department of the Foreign Office, which he held from 1943–46.

Churchill, more than any other modern British Premier except Lloyd George, was always determined to find things out for himself, especially in intelligence matters. While relying on a machinery in most respects admirably designed to keep the war leader fully informed, he also turned to personal specialist advisers, to men like General Ismay, his military adviser, and William Stephenson, to whom he paid a great deal of attention. At the same time he managed to keep himself reasonably well informed even on such remote sections of the Secret Service as the Iberian Section (devoted to Spain, Portugal and North Africa), Section Nine (Russian affairs) and Section Five, which was responsible for counter-intelligence from foreign countries. The result was that the British Prime Minister was easily the best informed of all the Allied war leaders.

With the United States having entered the war, liaison between the respective intelligence services of the U.S. and Britain became of paramount importance. Although J. Edgar Hoover, the chief of the Federal Bureau of Investigation, had agreed to co-operate with Sir William Stevenson in the early stages of the war before America entered the fray, he had remained somewhat resentful of British intelligence activities in U.S.A. This resentment became more marked when America joined the Allies. The creation of the Office of Strategic Services embittered him, for he felt that power was slipping away from him and that Government funds which might have gone to the F.B.I. would now be devoted to the O.S.S.

On the surface relations between Stephenson and Hoover had been amicable enough. From now on Hoover decided to by-pass Stephenson and to establish his own relations with London, sending over one of his subordinates, Kimball by name, as a liaison officer to co-operate with the S.I.S. and M.I.5. It was a clumsy move and it did not take London long to realise that this was an attempt to undermine Stephenson's influence. Meanwhile the O.S.S. countered this move by sending over to London a liaison officer of their own.

In fairness to Hoover it must be admitted that M.I.5 was the British counter-part of his own organisation and that there was a strong case for working with them. Tactically, of course, Hoover greatly strengthened his own position by aiming to transfer co-operation with the British away from the United States to Britain and by obtaining a working relationship with M.I.5 to lessen his dependence on Stephenson. It was also suspected, not without justification, that Stephenson's close personal relationship with Churchill not only gave him too much political influence, but enabled him to push this influence with Roosevelt himself, as Stephenson's friend, Ernest Cuneo, was one of the men to whom the President paid a great deal of attention. These machinations in the hierarchy of Anglo-American intelligence left their scars and as the war developed there was a tendency on the American side to keep back a good deal of information from the British and to seize on any defect in the British intelligence organisations and use this as an excuse for regarding co-operation with them as a security risk for the U.S.A. Unfortunately there were two schools of thought in American intelligence, both of which clashed with the British on policy; on the one hand the left-wingers of the O.S.S. were always suspecting Britain of imperialist Machiavellianism and of anti-Soviet motives, while on the other hand the right-wingers, some in the O.S.S., but mainly in the F.B.I., became increasingly concerned about a tendency for the British Secret Service to be "soft on communism". There was far less vocal right-wing criticism and even Hoover, who seems to have been one of the first to become uneasy about some personnel in British intelligence, held his counsel on this until the war was over. Hoover had himself made a long and detailed study of communist tactics ever since in 1919 he was assigned to prepare a legal brief on the newly formed Communist Party in the U.S.A. as a special assistant to the Attorney General. He may have had a life-long obsession about communism, but he never lost sight of the fact that in a young nation like America, lacking traditions and drawing its citizens from the immigrants of many countries, communism could be less easy to contain than elsewhere. He was also concerned that the party's membership in U.S.A. had risen from 7,500 members in 1930 to a peak of 80,000 in 1944. Hoover more than once pointed out to members of the B.S.C. that the "Communist Party in the United States was stronger in numbers than the Soviet Party was at the time it seized power in Russia". When in the immediate post-war years serious leakages of information occurred on the British side and one traitor after another was unmasked, sometimes as a result of American investigations, Hoover claimed that his suspicions about British Intelligence had been proved fully justified. As a result relationships between the two countries in this field rapidly deteriorated.

The British Secret Service outlook was naturally quite different from that of the U.S.A. Britain was the nation which would suffer most if Hitler's drive into Russia succeeded. While caution needed to be exercised in dealing with the Russians, it was also necessary to try to work with them. Above all, however great the risks involved, the British could not afford to ignore the occasional employment of double-agents. This was something which many American intelligence chiefs could not and would not comprehend.

Meanwhile in Europe the S.I.S., finding the task of co-operation with Russian Intelligence a frustrating and one-sided arrangement, sought to make their own plans for handling relations with Russia. Fortunately there were some Soviet agents who, not being themselves Russian and therefore not narrowly suspicious of British motives, were prepared to co-operate. One or two of these had assisted in the Hess Affair and again in providing intelligence on the state of affairs in Vichy-controlled Algeria. But the real problem was often something totally different: it was how to help the Russians without the Russians knowing who was helping them.

Under the Stalin régime Russia was not merely a dictatorship, but a tyranny where everyone, even a loyal Communist Party member, could never be sure that he was not being secretly singled out for liquidation. If Russia was so riddled with manic suspicion internally, how much more was its attitude to the outside world, even to its allies, consumed by mistrust and disbelief. Stalin had consistently ignored British warnings of German intentions to invade Russia. Once the Nazi hordes were let loose upon Russia and that country was slowly being devoured by the German war machine, it became imperative to try to stem the tide by providing the Russians with intelligence.

But how to make them accept that intelligence and to act on it? If it was once suspected that it came from British sources, that intelligence would cease to be of any value: it would be contemptuously ignored. Yet this was the only way, other than sending convoys, in which Britain could help Russia at that stage.

In their book *La Guerre a été gagnée en Suisse*[1] Pierre Accoce and Pierre Quet have described how the "Lucy Ring" in Geneva made all the difference between a Russian victory and defeat. Through this unique clandestine Secret Service set-up plans and orders of the German High Command on the Eastern Front right down to brigade level were transmitted to Moscow daily. It was an incredible feat and it may well have been the most effective intelligence operation in history. Certainly its long-term effect was to save countless Russian lives and eventually to help stabilise the front.

"Lucy's" own identity was revealed after the war. He was Rudolf Roessler, a German publisher who moved to Switzerland after the Nazis came to power and started up a firm called Vita Nova Verlag in Geneva. He was eventually employed by Brigadier Masson, of the Swiss security organisation, in the Bureau Ha, and after the fall of France when the Swiss were temporarily concerned about the possibility of a German invasion, his job was to assess military intelligence relating to Germany. Roessler proved not only to be a most competent analyser of such information, but to provide extremely accurate forecasts of what the Nazis would do next. At the same time Roessler began to send out information to the Russians, intelligence so valuable that the Soviet eventually gave him a retainer equivalent at that time to £350 a month plus various commodity emoluments.

The mystery of Roessler, who is now dead, has always been how he obtained his detailed information of German military plans and troop movements. The authors of *La Guerre a été gagnée en Suisse* suggest that ten Bavarian officers who served with Roessler in World War I became anti-Nazis, but joined the German Army and, having reached high rank, were jointly able to send to Roessler in Geneva by German Army radio channels intelligence of all operations on the Eastern Front. It only requires a cursory examination of this theory to realise that it defies belief. The ten Bavarians are never named, nor is it explained how they could continue to use official channels for sending such information until the end of the war and it must surely be obvious that if ten high-ranking German officers in the German High Command were traitors in 1940–41, that Army would never have lasted as a military force as long as it did.

The truth is that the "Lucy Ring" was really only an instrument used by the British Secret Service in one of the most effective long-term intelligence operations of the whole war. For, in order to pass intelligence to the Russians without its being suspected that they were doing this, the British used a Soviet spy as their link-agent. It was perhaps the best use made of a double-agent in any war and undertaken in such a way that it helped both the Russians and the British, for, without question, a Soviet defeat would have been disastrous for the Allied cause.

To understand the full ramifications of the "Lucy Ring" it is necessary to turn back to the time of the Spanish Civil War. Among the officers of the International Brigade on the Republican side at that time was an Englishman named Alexander Foote, a left-winger who had strong communist sympathies but more in the connotation of the establishment of a Popular Front than in any ideological sense. He was recommended as a likely agent to the Russians and late in 1938 was recruited into the Soviet Secret Service. In his book, *Handbook for Spies*, Alexander Foote records that he was "for three vital years of the war a member of, and to a large extent controller of, the Russian spy net in Switzerland, which was working against Germany. The information passed to Moscow over my secret transmitter affected the course of the war at one of its crucial stages. I was a key link in a network whose lines stretched into the heart of the German High Command itself; and it was I who sent back much of the information which enabled the Russians to make their successful stand before Moscow."[2]

It was this recollected passage in Alexander Foote's book which provided me with the clue to some of the unexplained mysteries of the "Lucy Ring". While it was always possible that the Russians, like any other power, might get duplicated intelligence from one area, it seemed highly unlikely that they would obtain such detailed information of German High Command plans for so long a period from two sources in Switzerland.

Just as in Walsingham's day Italy was used as the country from which to mount espionage operations against Spain, so in modern times it has been the tradition of most of the powers to use a neighbouring country as the base for espionage activities directed towards the nation which is their target. In this way the

Soviet Union used Canada as a base for espionage against both the U.S.A. and Britain and Switzerland for activities directed against Germany. In Switzerland between 1934 and 1940 the Russian intelligence organisation was carefully built up, developed and wisely and widely dispersed in the disposition of its agents. The Resident Director of Soviet espionage in Switzerland at this time was Alexander Rado, who had been in charge of operations since 1937. His cover was that of partner in a firm of Swiss map-makers.

Alexander Foote worked under Rado's directions and set himself up in an apartment in Lausanne. In his book he mentions the code names of various contacts he had and in particular he refers to '"Lucy", our link with the German High Command' whose identity was known only to another link, the recruiter of "Lucy", named "Taylor".

Foote is coy about the identity of "Lucy", insisting that he was the "most important actor in this peculiar drama, but adding that "where he got his information and how it came to him were his own secrets". But it is quite clear that this "Lucy" was, in fact, Rudolf Roessler who was still alive at the time Foote wrote his book and for that reason Foote would not reveal his identity. Not only did "Lucy" provide information, but he frequently gave the answers to queries which the Russians put to him. Even when he was asked for information about a German force on the Eastern Front, he would come back with details of its composition, strength and location. Foote states that "in effect, as far as the Kremlin were concerned, the possession of 'Lucy' as a source meant that they had the equivalent of well-placed agents in the three Service Intelligence Staffs, plus the Imperial General Staff, plus the War Cabinet offices".[3]

"Lucy" insisted on keeping his identity a secret as a condition of his working for the Russians. Only the link-man Taylor was to be allowed to know who he was. Naturally the Russians were extremely suspicious and at first regarded "Lucy" as a plant who might well "blow" their network. For a long time they declined to take any notice of his information, but, says Foote, "despite the Centre's [the Russian espionage network] attitude, we continued to 'plug' 'Lucy's' information over to Moscow".

In the end of course Moscow were only too eager to lap up

everything "Lucy" could send them and indeed based their war plans on what he told them. Foote, as the radio-operator for the Russian network in Switzerland, was in an excellent position to judge "Lucy's" performance and to assess its value. Though Foote, like Roessler (or "Lucy") is now dead, his subsequent history enables the mystery of this super-spy with contacts inside Germany to be unravelled to some extent. Amazingly, he carried on rapping out messages to Moscow despite the fact that the Swiss security service has always had a reputation for efficiency. It is almost certain that Brigadier Masson, who was both pro-French and pro-British, knew what was going on and that he connived at it. Only in November 1943, when the tide of war had turned in the Allies' favour did the Swiss start making arrests of the Soviet spy network and even then they were extremely lenient towards Foote who had a relatively comfortable time in prison and was released in September the following year. It was clear to Foote that the Swiss knew all about Roessler's activities and that the same man who had been giving them information about the German High Command had also passed it on to Russia. But Roessler was not arrested until some time later and then released after three months with a certificate from (and probably the blessing of) the Swiss General Staff.

Foote went to Paris after leaving prison and from there on to Moscow. The Russians wanted him to go to Mexico and operate from there as a spy against the U.S.A. But Foote had other ideas. When he reached East Berlin he crossed over to the West and contacted British Intelligence. Returning to Britain he eventually settled down as a civil servant in the quiet bureaucratic back-water of the Ministry of Agriculture and Fisheries.

Officially nothing has ever been admitted about Foote's true rôle in the war. That he worked for Russia faithfully and competently is not in doubt; equally it is certain that he had all along been an agent of the British Secret Service and he was thus able to salve a left-wing and anti-fascist conscience at the same time as he performed a patriotic service to his own country. Alexander Foote made the most effective penetration of the Soviet Secret Service Britain has yet effected and yet the Russians will never be able to deny that he rendered them service of incalculable value.

What must remain a matter of conjecture is whether "Lucy" also was a British agent. There is no doubt that he was protected by the Swiss and must be regarded as one of their own most valued agents. Though neutral during the war, Switzerland was divided in opinion between pro-Germans in the predominantly German-speaking part of that country and pro-French in the French-speaking part, but on balance the pro-French outnumbered the pro-German and as long as there was a man of Brigadier Masson's calibre in charge of Swiss security, there was no risk of the pro-German element acquiring any power. It was in Switzerland's interests that Germany should not win the war, as Germany was the only nation which was a threat to her integrity. If passing on information to the Russians helped to defeat Germany, then Swiss security forces were prepared to turn a blind eye to this move.

The Swiss are above all things realists and ultra-cautious. Neutrality is something they regard as something almost written into their constitution: probably the greatest crime a Swiss can commit is to compromise his country's neutrality. Therefore it is equally certain that the Swiss would never have connived for so long at the activities of the Russian network unless they knew that the information they were receiving from Roessler would only come to them, if they permitted it to be passed on to the Russians. Roessler might have fooled the Swiss that his information came straight from Germany, but it is extremely unlikely. Indeed, if the Swiss knew that such information was coming regularly from Germany, they would probably have been even more suspicious and unlikely to have allowed themselves to be mixed up with Roessler. If the Germans had discovered that the Swiss security had been obtaining intelligence out of Germany, it would have given them an excuse to intervene in Swiss affairs. Such a risk the Swiss would not knowingly dared to have taken. It is much more likely that the Swiss, if they did not actually know, at least guessed that the information came not from Germany, but from Britain. The fact is that the information came with such clockwork regularity, in such a steady daily flow of up-to-date, professionally presented intelligence that it could not have come straight from Germany. No agent could have risked sending material in such bulk and so frequently by radio from inside Germany. Even the most efficient agent is forced by circumstances to go "off the air" on occasions.

It is possible that a small amount of information was obtained from Germany direct, but it is certain that the bulk of it was passed direct to Roessler through British Secret Service channels and that Foote, as a British agent, saw to it that, despite Russian initial suspicions of the material, he transmitted it to Moscow whereas another Soviet agent might have rejected it completely as a plant. The success of the ploy depended equally on both men—Roessler and Foote. As to the Swiss, they must have been hugely delighted to be getting Roessler's own assessment of the material as it affected Switzerland, for he was providing them with his own admittedly skilful analysis at a low cost. They were getting the kind of intelligence which would normally have cost a fortune and several agents to obtain. One can also be sure that they would know that this analysis intended to suit their own requirements was not being passed to the Russians even if the "raw" material was.

Anyone unacquainted with the methods of modern espionage might argue that if it was well nigh impossible to obtain such a wealth of information directly from Germany, it would be absolutely impossible for it to be obtained from London. Superficially that might seem so; in fact, it would have been much easier. British Intelligence succeeded quite early on in cracking German military codes and ciphers. Even as early as the spring of 1940 British Intelligence was occasionally getting from a roundabout freelance source interception of some signals of German troop movements, but, with no means of checking the accuracy of these, was disposed not to place too high a value on the information. Menzies had insisted that every priority must be given to the job of cracking German military ciphers, mainly because he was under constant pressure from Churchill to get intelligence from the Continent and to set right the clamp-down on such news which had resulted from the Venlo disaster. Consequently a team of cipher experts was closeted away at a country house near Bletchley under Captain Edward Hastings, R.N. The Germans in their thorough manner had learned two lessons from World War I, first the skill with which the N.I.D. had broken their codes, secondly, that the job of de-ciphering had been greatly speeded up. To counteract this they had developed a machine cipher which they believed was extremely difficult to break, as to crack it involved not merely deciphering by analysis, but obtaining a machine similar to the one used for transmission. By a lucky chance on 27 August 1941, the Royal Navy captured a German submarine which was equipped with one of these machines. Having gained possession of this machine the task of breaking the German ciphers was made much easier. The capture of the submarine, the U-570, was kept secret from the Germans while the deciphering team furiously got to work. Even more important, however, had been the capture intact of U-110 on 9 May 1941. The intelligence coup was one for which the Navy must take credit, but as the Cipher Organisation run by Captain Hastings came under Menzies' sphere of operations the Secret Service gained the glory. Soon it was possible to speed up the process of deciphering German messages so as to prepare a day-to-day analysis of German intelligence and it was this that was fed through "Lucy" to the Russians. It was because a whole team of decipherers were working on this material and that so many men were processing the information at high speed that the Russians were able to get such up-to-date material so swiftly. Because much of this comprised intercepted signals from the *Oberkommando der Wehrmacht* it appeared as though it must have come straight out of Germany. Neutral Switzerland, where diplomatic communications by radio and bag were securely available, was the ideal place for disseminating it and hiding its British origins. No doubt the story of the ten Bavarian officers was Roessler's somewhat extravagant "cover story" if ever he had been closely questioned by the Russians. He must have relied heavily on immunity from Russian probes by reason of his membership of the Bureau Ha.

A good deal of additional information was, however, obtained through a mysterious character known for code purposes as "Walter". He also had the *nom de guerre* of Captain Van Narvig. A former officer of the Russian Imperial Army, he was not really a Russian, but one of that cosmopolitan band from whom secret agents are so readily recruited, having been born in St. Petersburg of an English mother and a German father, while he himself was actually a citizen of Finland. He was in fact the same Van Narvig who had known Sidney Reilly, mentioned in chapter twenty. The link between Reilly and Van Narvig is an interesting one; it is almost certain that Reilly provided Van Narvig with introductions both to the British Secret Service and to that of the Czechs. Van Narvig himself insisted that he "owed a lot to Sidney Reilly, who taught me that the best spy was a free lance agent, a precept I have always followed up".

Van Narvig, apart from indulging in espionage, for reasons best known to himself passed on a great deal of information to his friend, Wythe Williams, the editor of a small, almost insignificant suburban newspaper, the *Greenwich Time*, of Greenwich, Connecticut. Readers were puzzled that so modest a newspaper could produce so many scoops of what was going on in Europe. Lowell Thomas wrote of the owner and editor: "Wythe Williams had been one of the ace reporters of the European scene. When he earned that reputation he got his stuff with the formidable machinery of the foreign service of the *New York Times*, of the Northcliffe Press and the United Press at his back. After he returned from Europe, he had apparently nothing but the resources of *Greenwich Time* . . . from his desk . . . Wythe proceeded to pull one news rabbit after another out of his hat. He had us not only guessing, but more than slightly sceptical. How could one man, we asked, dig up information not available to the great American wire services, to say nothing of the great newspapers who had their own news-gathering machinery? So some of us looked upon the beats that Wythe was scoring with raised eyebrows. But, by jingo, history began to vindicate and corroborate him."[4]

Wythe Williams had many sources for his news, all of them tucked away in European capitals, but his ace reporter was Van Narvig himself. He warned Williams that war would come in September 1939, that Russia would stay aloof for as long as possible and even make a pact with the Nazis. He continued when war started to ply Williams with regular dispatches smuggled out of Europe, and eventually rigged up a special wireless receiving set by which he enabled Williams to intercept coded messages from the German High Command. By this means on 8 May 1940, Williams was able to reveal in a broadcast that two German armies were deploying towards the Dutch frontier, one from the direction of Bremen towards Groningen, the other from the direction of Cologne towards Limburg, clearly indicating the invasion of the Low Countries. Thirty-two hours later the world received confirmation in the official news that the invasion of Holland, Belgium and Luxembourg had begun.

Van Narvig's policy in using Williams was to alert the American public to the dangers that lay ahead: it was first rate propaganda and all the more effective because it was also the truth. Van Narvig had also known Roessler in Czechoslovakia before the war and it is suspected that at one time Roessler was a spy for the Czechs: he certainly worked for the Czechs for a short time after World War II. Working indirectly with the British Van Narvig also provided a great deal of the German intelligence culled by his wireless receiving set.

28

Exploiting the Mafia and the Enigma of Admiral Canaris

One of the most commendable axioms of waging World War II on the British side was a determination to avoid the senseless waste of life which characterised World War I. When an offensive operation was being planned, the vital question put to the planners was always—how can we minimise casualties.

For this reason the Secret Service had to be brought into planning operations at a very early stage and without question this strategy saved a great deal of bloodshed and shortened many operations. To those who condemn espionage as a dirty game it would be salutary to ponder on the benefits it bestowed on combattants at least in World War II.

One of the best examples of this was the campaign to invade Sicily. A great deal of hard grafting and information gathering had been undertaken by agents in the field prior to "Operation Husky," as the Sicilian campaign was code-named. Under Mussolini every effort had been made to stamp out the dreaded Mafia secret society because it was feared that it might become a rival to his own Fascist Party. The task of defeating the Mafia had been given to the Duce's own chief of police, Prefect Mori, who arrested suspects by the thousand and shipped them off to penal islands so that by 1927 Mussolini was able to announce to the Fascist Parliament the end of the war against the Mafia.

But, as Norman Lewis remarks in his book, *The Honoured Society*,[1] "the effect of the Mori repression could be only temporary, as at best it scythed the heads off a crop of weeds when what was needed was a change in soil and climate. All the more astute members of the Mafia—professional men such as lawyers or doctors—were clever enough to put themselves beyond Mori's reach by joining the Fascist Party. It was the unimportant rank and file of the 'Honoured Society' who went to prison."

This was fully realised by the British Secret Service, though with perhaps the cautious proviso that while disgruntled Mafia members might be employed usefully as agents, it would be extremely dangerous to revive the Mafia and allow it unbridled authority. The Americans, however, had other, more uninhibited ideas. In 1943 "Lucky" Luciano, born Salcatore Lucania in Sicily, and head of the American Mafia, was in prison in the U.S.A., serving a 35-year prison sentence for compelling women into prostitution. The U.S. intelligence, aided and enthusiastically abetted by the U.S. Navy, decided to make use of Luciano's services and through him to make contact with the underground head of the Mafia in Sicily. In return for these services Luciano was given his freedom, officially in 1945, but, according to some Italian sources unofficially in 1943 when, some claim, he was taken secretly to Sicily by the U.S. Navy and was seen in the vicinity of the U.S. Seventh Army's headquarters shortly after the invasion.

A somewhat unfair portrait has been painted of the Sicilian campaign, comparing the fact that the Americans, who had the allegedly stiff task of conquering the mountainous centre and western half of the island, reached the north coast of Sicily in seven days, while the British and Canadians fighting up the east coast in much easier terrain took five weeks to reach Messina. This is a most misleading portrayal of events. The route to Messina was vital and required the very best troops to tackle it, for the capture of Messina was in effect the establishment of a bridgehead to Italy. Thus the British and Canadian troops faced the bulk of the German armoured strength and it was here that the backbone of the resistance to the invasion was offered. Also in this area the Mafia was not nearly so strong as in the terrain in which the American troops were operating, confronted only by half-hearted Italian forces and aided by a Mafia rising. The American troops may have been given the most difficult terrain geographically speaking to tackle, but this was more than compensated by the lack of opposition and the extensive Mafia aid in an area partly dominated by Don Calo, the Mafia leader. Something like fifteen per cent of the American troops were of Sicilian origin, deliberately selected for the operation on orders from the U.S. Intelligence.

While it would be churlish to detract from the imaginative way in which the United States exploited the Mafia in Sicily and so paved the way to a more or less bloodless invasion of the western area of the island, it cannot be denied that in retrospect the policy of co-operation with the Mafia was carried too far and with detrimental effects which have been felt ever since the war. Don Calo, the Mafia leader, was appointed Mayor of Villalba by the American Officer of Civil Affairs and the cheering crowds hailed the announcement by shouting "Long live the Allies! Long live the Mafia!" Those Mafia who were in prison were speedily released and within weeks most of the Sicilian towns had mayors who were members of the Mafia. One of them, Serafino Di Peri, Mayor of Bolognetta, immediately formed a gang which terrorised Palermo for the next five years.

The British took an altogether more sober view of the policy of exploiting the Mafia. British Secret Service agents who had been operating in Sicily were not influenced in the same way by Sicilian propaganda as the Americans had been. They had, with a few exceptions, taken a long-term and more objective view of the advisability of using the Mafia as allies. This was that what really mattered was the future of post-Mussolini Italy and that to give the Mafia a new lease of life in Sicily before Italy was completely liberated was to pave the way for a revival of Mafia power in Rome itself. Indeed, within a few months of the Sicilian landings Scotland Yard was asked to send men to track down and round up the worst of the Mafia gangsters in Sicily. These 'Yard officers were made members of a special Intelligence Section of the Army and their brief was to concentrate on known terrorists. They quickly arrested and imprisoned two of the ringleaders as well as seventeen district chiefs. Unhappily the American officials in their sectors of Sicily failed to take similar action.

In preliminary soundings with Mafiosa before the invasion the British detected a note of blackmail: Mafia terms not only included assurances of office and the "right" to govern Sicily, but of a guarantee of independence for Sicily and complete separation from Italy.

"There is no problem about winning support from the Mafia," reported one British agent in January 1943. "It is the price for such co-operation which presents the problem. If we concede the terms the Mafia want, Allied Military Government in Sicily will become a farce and a black market entirely dominated by the Mafia will result. I believe that two months ago we might have got very much better terms, but the Americans have obviously been intriguing with some of the American Mafiosa and the message has reached Sicily. In Syracuse it is reported that some Americans have actually hinted at independence for Sicily after the war and that they take the view that as the Mafia is violently anti-communist, this might be a good thing. There are some Mafia who would actually be prepared to consider becoming an American colony."

The British Secret Service plan was to utilise independent anti-Fascist bandits in preparing the way for invasion rather than the Mafia themselves. One of Sir William Stephenson's agents who was trained at Stephenson's Sabotage Training School outside Toronto was an Italian with close contacts with Sicilians who had been carefully selected well in advance of the operation. This man became a lieutenant-colonel in the British Army and was second in command of the Special Operations mission which went into Sicily with the advance party of assault troops. He immediately organised Sicilians for sabotage and other work behind the enemy lines.[2] Some of these were Mafia, but the aim was not to become too heavily involved with the Mafia as an organisation. Indeed, part of the policy was to win peasant support above all else.

The independently-minded anti-Fascist bandit who was friendly to the peasants was the type the British sought to recruit. Such types not only knew the terrain, but were used to operating independently and to living dangerously. One of those who had been singled out for special recommendation was Salvatore Giuliano, a twenty-year-old desperado who then had no affiliations with Mafia, but whose charm and gifts of leadership and organisation suggested he might well play a useful rôle in planning a rising to coincide with the invasion. Plans were made to give Giuliano authority to organise such a rising and he himself went ahead to raise a raiding party and equip it with arms. But for some reason permission for this plan to be put into operation was delayed. Giuliano felt he had been badly let down, but, fired by enthusiasm for freeing his country, turned to the Americans and secured their backing at the last moment. The result was that Giuliano held two German divisions in check with a force of only one hundred men in the area of Mount Cammarata. British dilatoriness drove Giuliano into making a bid for Mafia support. He was never actually a member of that organisation, but afterwards he flourished as a legendary Robin Hood-type bandit with Mafia support until eventually they betrayed him.

Giuliano was so strongly pro-British at one time that he actually talked of helping to create a British naval base in Sicily and establishing a government which would recognize the British Crown in return for aid. Whether, if handled differently, he would have behaved as a good citizen remains open to doubt, but some believe that the British erred is not making full use of him. After the war he fought an impudently brave campaign from his mountain stronghold outside Palermo, repudiating all links with the Mafia and claiming that he was the only man in Sicily who had fought against communism effectively. He even made a request to U.S.A. for Marshal Aid, in return for which he said he would be prepared to raise an army to make Sicily American territory. He backed his aims with some subtle propaganda, claiming he only robbed the rich to pay the poor. He dumped ration gifts on the doorsteps of Sicilian peasants at night and sent money by post to people facing starvation. A remarkable young man, full of ideas, but by his challenge both to the Mafia and to Italian authority, doomed to a violent death, being shot dead by a police force after defying capture for more than seven years.

But it was the Americans who, with reckless indulgence, brought the Trojan horse of American-Sicilian gangsterism back to Sicily to revive the Mafia. The methods of the *mafiosi* had taken well in the U.S.A. In Chicago Sicilian gangsters extorted money for protection and they were also strong in New Orleans. Many of these gangsters were among the troops landing in Sicily and they swiftly co-operated in the drive to make Mafia the only power that counted on the island.

Whether the British blundered in their failure to use Giuliano is an academic point in comparison to a real blunder which they made in the British Legation at Berne in 1943. A German called there and asked to see the British military attaché, saying that he was employed by the German Foreign Ministry and that he had with him a case full of important documents which he had brought from Berlin.

The military attaché told him to go away, so the German then tried to contact the Head of Chancery and, finally, the Minister. He was still rebuffed and apparently no effort was made to check up on his admittedly somewhat astonishing story. What was worse nobody at the Legation had the sense to suggest he should see one of the Secret Service intermediaries in Switzerland of whom there were a number, for Colonel Claude Dansey, Assistant Director of the Secret Service, had taken great pains to ensure that the Secret Service network in Switzerland was efficient. Dansey had been stationed in Switzerland before the war and took a personal interest in intelligence from this territory. Therefore he was highly displeased when eventually copies of the documents the German had brought with him reached the S.I.S. via the O.S.S. in Washington. For the German, having failed to interest the British, had gone to see Allen Dulles, then in charge of the O.S.S. office in Berne. Rather foolishly, Dansey, who was jealous of Dulles, after giving them only a cursory examination, insisted that the documents were fakes and had been planted on the Americans.

This incident was to precipitate the beginning of the end of Dansey's Secret Service career. For the documents were genuine all right; the mysterious German caller had been able to prove that he was an assistant to the *Auswaertige Amt* liaison officer for for all the German armed forces in Berlin and also anti-Nazi. He had come to Berne as a courier, with the documents strapped to his leg. What was more he was prepared to go back to Berlin and bring out further information later. Wisely, the Americans gave him the cover name of "George Wood" and arranged for him to make future contacts with U.S. Intelligence at Stockholm and elsewhere. The material which he supplied to the O.S.S. proved of immense value: it contained details of new German radio stations, of how tungsten was smuggled into Germany from

Spain in orange crates, troop movements and changes in command in Central Europe.[3]

Meanwhile the enigma of Admiral Canaris continued to fascinate those in the Secret Service hierarchy who followed his career with interest. Some of them were so afraid of being hoodwinked by reports of his antagonism to Hitler that they frowned on any attempts to discuss the matter. At least one Intelligence chief threatened to discipline anyone who dared to suggest Canaris might be a secret ally of the British. But a few were more discerning and began to see that it was important to study Canaris' likely reactions to various events. It was known for example that Canaris had been asked by the Nazis to have General Giraud murdered in captivity. Nothing happened and then Giraud escaped from Saxony and made his way into Vichy France. Canaris' excuse for having failed to see that Giraud was liquidated was that he had given this assignment to Heydrich, the Commissioner General for Security in Occupied Territories, and that presumably Heydrich had been assassinated before he could do anything about it. But did Canaris himself have a hand in Giraud's escape? The odds against the General, who spoke hardly any German, escaping from prison unaided must have been high indeed: in addition to which he was conspicuous because of the loss of an arm.

Certainly Canaris was playing a very strange game throughout 1941–2. According to the testimony of General Erwin Lahousen, of the *Abwehr*, Canaris was also in touch with Admiral Darlan as well during 1942. Lahousen, who was an *aide* of Canaris, should know, and he stated afterwards that the intermediary between Darlan and Canaris was one Deloncle, a former *Cagoulard* terrorist and head of a brigade of French anti-Soviet volunteers in the *Reichswehr*. Deloncle seems, however, to have been privy to Canaris' intrigues to save Germany by thwarting Hitler.

The information was given to the British Secret Service as early as May 1942, that Canaris had had communications with both Giraud and Darlan, but this information seems to have been treated with distrust. However, more attention was paid to the fact that Canaris tended to give Hitler information which showed that Britain was stronger than she was and that a good deal of intelligence was withheld altogether. It was noticeable that either with intent, or unwittingly, Canaris was passing on only information which tended to help the Allies. Indeed one reason why the body of the "Man Who Never Was" was dumped off the southern coast of Spain was that the British knew the Iberian Peninsula was Canaris' special sphere of operations and that any intelligence from this area would be sure to reach him. It might, of course, have been argued that if Canaris was secretly on the side of the Allies, he might not have passed on the information to the German High Command, if he thought the dispatches on "Major Martin's" body were authentic. On the other hand if Canaris suspected they were not authentic, then he would be the first to profess his belief in them.

It must be a matter of conjecture as to whether Canaris himself suspected that "Major Martin" was a British plant, or whether by devious means this idea was conveyed to him by the British. From what one knows of the extreme caution shown by the Secret Service towards the theme of collaboration with Canaris, it is extremely unlikely that they would have risked making any overtures in this direction in connection with so vital a ruse. None the less the deviousness of Canaris's mind and the ambiguity of his actions must have worried the planners of the "Man Who Never Was" operation, not least because they would know that Canaris must suspect that the presence of so large a convoy of ships at Gibraltar meant an invasion of North Africa.

Therefore it is interesting to ponder on the case of "Major Martin" and that of a similar incident which occurred a few days before the invasion fleet sailed into Gibraltar. "Major Martin's" papers had been found by the Spanish authorities, shown to German Intelligence and the information passed on to Canaris and Berlin. Yet when, within days of D-Day for the invasion of North Africa a plane carrying a British messenger with actual plans of the invasion was shot down off the coast of Spain, the papers were swiftly returned to the British apparently untouched. It is hard to believe that on this occasion the papers were not first shown to the Germans. If they were, then Canaris did not pass on the information.

Even up to the last moment Canaris gave no cautionary warning when more than five hundred Allied ships were either in or approaching Gibraltar and merely suggested they were bound for

Malta. It must have been obvious to the Admiral with his considerable naval experience that such large convoys would not simply be going to Malta where they courted certain disaster by being wiped out by German bombers in the Grand Harbour. After Darlan's murder Canaris provided Deloncle with a false passport to go to Spain to sound out Sir Samuel Hoare, then British Ambassador in Madrid, and British agents on the possibility of a compromise peace. Later, when he went to Paris, Deloncle was murdered in his flat by the Gestapo. As for Canaris himself, his calmness after his failure to give the German High Command the correct assessment of Allied intentions towards North Africa was matched only by his astonishingly light-hearted spirit on New Year's Eve, 1941. His biographer, Abshagen, records that Canaris went to Algeciras and celebrated the New Year by giving a party for his *Abwehr* officers in Spain at the Hotel Reina Christina and, donning a chef's cap and apron, cooking their dinner for them. One would have expected him to be roundly abusing them for dereliction of duty, not indulging in such frivolity.[4]

Why did Canaris make this trip at that time? If it was intended to cover up his own failure and to suggest to Hitler that he had gone to rebuke his staff, such festivities hardly seem in keeping with such a pretence. It seems much more likely that Canaris was waiting hopefully for some news from Deloncle. But the Casablanca Conference shortly afterwards which demanded "unconditional surrender" by Germany must temporarily have sounded the death knell to Canaris' hopes.

It is even possible that on New Year's Eve in Algeciras Canaris was half hoping he might be contacted by the Governor of Gibraltar, General Mason MacFarlane. There had been a plan at one time for a British Secret Service kidnapping of Canaris on one of his visits to Algeciras. It was so close to Gibraltar that the Admiral could have been smuggled out by a fast speed boat within minutes. But the operation was cancelled on instructions from London, the view being that Canaris was much more useful to the Allies if he remained in his post.

In his book, *The Murder of Admiral Darlan*, Peter Tompkins states that when he was waiting aboard ship in Gibraltar prior to the invasion of North Africa, "we were puzzled that the Axis had not already spotted and attacked our convoys—visible to agents on either side of the Strait in Algeciras and Tangier—and could not decide whether to attribute this lack of Axis action to the brilliance of Allied cover operations, to stupidity on the part of the Axis, or to sabotage within their own intelligence. It was, as we later learned, a mixture of the three."[5]

General N. K. Mason MacFarlane took a special interest in intelligence while Governor of Gibraltar and sought to keep a close watch not only on operations at Gibraltar, controlled by Colonel Brian Clarke, but in Tangier, too, where the nominal controller of intelligence was Lieut.-Colonel "Toby" Ellis. MacFarlane had had plenty of experience himself as an Intelligence officer in Russia and possessed a flair for this kind of work. He was an imaginative Governor, extremely popular with the Gibraltarians for whom he did a great deal, sometimes unorthodox and not above indulging in espionage on his own account. MacFarlane in fact had a finger in many intrigues which somewhat unfairly gave him the reputation of playing politics and being a Machiavellian and these attributes brought him into disfavour with some politicians who would have preferred a less independently minded Governor.

Mason MacFarlane's popularity with the Gibraltarians brought him into contact with many persons who were prepared to give him information which they would have withheld from the official Military Intelligence circles: there lay much of his strength and influence. Consequently he learned of some of the skirmishes indulged in by the rival Intelligence service of Gibraltar and Tangier. The latter city, being an international zone, though in wartime under Spanish administration, was a focal point for spies of all nationalities, even the Japanese having a spy network there. For this reason it was a key centre for British Intelligence and a most important listening post, as well as being a rendezvous point for itinerant spies drawing their pay.

Mason MacFarlane is credited with having personally suggested the kidnapping of Admiral Canaris from Algeciras, this being one of the first incidents to bring recrimination down on him. He always maintained that the North African campaign was badly planned, that it should have meant an invasion much further to the east, envisaging the capture of the ports of Bone and

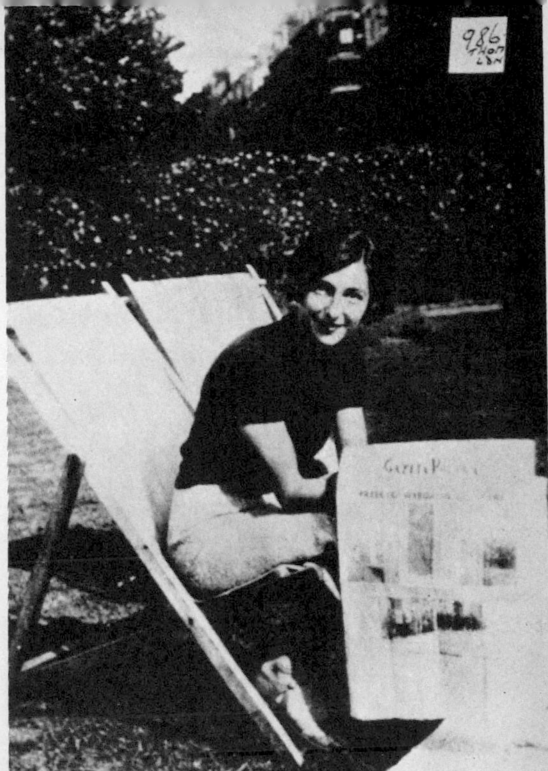

S.O.E. agent Christine Granville survived World War II but was murdered shortly after

Sir Percy Sillitoe, head of M.I.5 in the immediate post-war years

Two of the most successful espionage agents to operate in the West: Kim Philby and . . .

. . . George Blake

Bougie and that the whole affair was unnecessarily snarled up by the British Secret Service losing control of their side of the planning to the Americans.

Much more serious, however, was the trouble which Mason MacFarlane brought on himself by his rôle in the mysterious Sikorski affair. In July 1943, General Sikorski, the Commander-in-Chief of the Free Polish Forces, was killed when the plane in which he was to travel failed to take off the ground at the Gibraltar airstrip and crashed into the sea. Within a few days Goebbels' Propaganda Department was putting out the story that Sikorski had been murdered by the British Secret Service. The story at the time was that Sikorski was a stumbling block to the Allies' relations with Stalin and that strategy required his sacrifice for the sake of future relations with Russia.

Far too much has been written about this affair without any further evidence having been produced. However, as any allegation against the British Secret Service must be examined in what purports to be a history of that organisation, certain evidence needs to be considered here. The chief factor in the case which gave cause for suspicion was the blanket of silence on the British side, continued during and after the inquiry into the incident and persisting until the present time. This could be explained as bureaucracy in its occasional moments of stubborn stupidity, especially as so many people have been threatened with prosecution under the Official Secrets Act that disbelief in the German allegations were turned into gnawing doubts about the British version of the crash.

Controversy about the case has recently been aroused by the production of Rolf Hochhuth's play, *The Soldiers*, which implies that Winston Churchill himself connived at a plot to murder Sikorski, and by the writing of David Irving, the historian, who is equally convinced that there was sabotage. The issue has been unnecessarily complicated by dragging in Churchill's name without an iota of evidence to link Churchill personally with the incident and by mysterious references to a box containing vital proof of sabotage which lies in a Swiss bank.

More important than the box containing the alleged evidence which cannot be seen is Hochhuth's other allegation that General MacFarlane knew in advance of British plans to kill the Polish

C.-in-C. and that he warned Sikorski and his daughter against flying in the Liberator bomber in which they crashed to death. There is no doubt that, whether MacFarlane knew of any plot, British or otherwise, he certainly went out of his way to warn Sikorski not to take the plane, but declined to give any specific reason for his warning. The Governor of Gibraltar even went so far as to suggest that Sikorski should travel in another plane in which M. Maisky, the Soviet Ambassador in London, was going to Cairo. To suggest that the Polish general should travel with a Russian Ambassador at a time when the Free Poles had no diplomatic relations with the Soviet certainly sounds like counsel in desperation. Apart from this Sikorski was virulently anti-Russian.

General Kukiel, who was the Minister of Defence in the Polish Government-in-exile, confirmed this story, both of MacFarlane's warning to Sikorski not to travel in the Liberator and the suggestion that he should go in Maisky's plane. Not only did MacFarlane give such a warning, he repeated it three times. Mrs. Olga Lisiewicz, who acted as interpreter at MacFarlane's conversation with Sikorski's widow after her husband's death, also confirmed the story and claimed that MacFarlane was in "an exceptionally distressed state" about his failure to impress the seriousness of his warning on the General.

MacFarlane's warnings to the General and his subsequent conversation with Madame Sikorska certainly caused grave displeasure in the Secret Service hierarchy and angered Churchill so much that he refused to speak to MacFarlane, cutting him dead on the steps of a London club when the two men met face to face after the war and when MacFarlane was Labour M.P. for Paddington.

The British Foreign Office and Service Ministries have consistently refused information to writers on the subject, particularly on the identity of the two Secret Servicemen who were supposed to be on the plane, but whose bodies were never recovered and who were said to have left the plane before the crash occurred. It must have been too dark for the Airfield Control Officer to have seen whether the men left the plane shortly before take-off, but it is curious that the page in this officer's log-book containing the entries about passengers and details about Sikorsky's aircraft was later found to have been torn out. The subsequent inquiry produced a good deal of contradictory evidence and left many questions unanswered.

Yet, having conceded this much to those who profess to see sabotage in the incident, it must be stressed that there was probably a simpler, yet none the less culpable reason for the crash. When V.I.P's. flew during the war it was normal practice to ensure that they were given two experienced and first class pilots. The pilot who is still alive, Captain Edward Prchal, a Czech, was in this category, but his co-pilot on this occasion was a man who had never before flown in a Liberator. Evidence which was not produced at the court of inquiry suggests that when ordered to take up the undercarriage, this second and inexperienced pilot pulled the flap lever in mistake for the undercarriage lever and that this caused the plane to crash into the sea.

This seems a much more plausible explanation of what happened than the suggestions of an act of sabotage which wiped out so many people. Unfortunately the second pilot was killed, so there is no confirmation of this report.

Sikorski had been demanding that an independent Red Cross inquiry should be made into the discovery of the bodies of the murdered Poles found in Katya Forest, alleging that these crimes had been perpetrated by the Russians. Certainly the Russians stood to gain most by Sikorski's death, for the problem of the future of Anglo-Soviet relations. The Russian need to silence Sikorski was certainly politically important to the Soviet at this juncture. But why did not the Germans suggest the Russians rather than the British as the culprits for the deed? It would have been better propaganda for them at this stage of the war.

Some historians, notably A. J. P. Taylor, take the view that Sikorski was not the principal obstacle in the way of a Soviet–Polish agreement. "On the contrary," writes A. J. P. Taylor in a review of David Irving's book *Accident: The Death of General Sikorski*, "he was the best hope for agreement and his death, which strengthened the Polish right-wing in exile, was a disaster for the British policy of conciliation. This statement is, however, an oversimplification of the situation. Sikorski was slightly more open-minded on the subject of a reconciliation with the Russians than those of his right-wing allies, but any terms he might have agreed to would almost certainly have been inadequate to the Soviet from a long-term viewpoint.

The British Secret Service had, it is true, discovered that Sikorski knew that some of his fellow Poles were secretly in league with the Germans and maintaining contacts with them. As a Polish patriot Sikorski cannot be faulted; as one of the Allies his knowledge of and connivance in this intrigue was tantamount to treason. From this moment all Sikorski's movements had been constantly shadowed by British intelligence. There had been links between the Poles and Admiral Canaris' *Abwehr*, but these were forged by the right-wingers and not by Sikorski personally. It is possible that right-wing Poles wanted Sikorski out of the way. Closely guarded though he was, there were two attempts on his life during the war. Doubtless a further attempt on Sikorski by enemy agents was suspected prior to the Gibraltar tragedy and the knowledge of this may well have given rise to stories of sabotage. MacFarlane had served in Intelligence in Russia and probably understood full well Sikorski's appalling dilemma—his need to fend off Soviet demands on Polish territory and loyalty to his Allies. Quite obviously MacFarlane, regardless of his position as Governor, considered it a moral duty to save a fellow officer and friend, if he could.

What remains a mystery is why MacFarlane was so convinced that danger to Sikorski lay in his going by the Liberator. Admiral Sir Guy Guant, who made his home in Tangier and who, despite his retirement from the world of intelligence, kept a close watch on these matters, was convinced that MacFarlane suspected an attempt at sabotage. He told the author that General MacFarlane, who was his personal friend, had been tipped off from Tangier of a plot to sabotage the Liberator. "This was the reason for his warnings. I don't think MacFarlane had any details whatsoever of the plot, but he was particularly disturbed because he could not be sure who was behind it. He suspected that it had been planned from Tangier and that British intelligence in Tangier had failed to warn Gibraltar. He was extremely angry that the Intelligence Department in Gibraltar pooh-poohed the idea."

If MacFarlane had alerted British Intelligence, this may have explained the presence of Secret Servicemen at the time of the crash. In this way coincidences were built up into myths. Stalin tended to encourage the rumour that the British "arranged" Sikorski's murder, not publicly, but occasionally in private conversation. He delighted in letting it be thought that he not only knew what the British Secret Service was doing, but that he had ways and means of using the organisation. In this way he terrorised his opponents. According to Milovan Djilas, who was Yugoslav military attaché in Russia during the war, Stalin gave him a warning to pass on to Marshal Tito shortly before Yugoslavia's break with Russia. The warning was enigmatic, but the meaning was clear: the British Secret Service might arrange for Tito to be killed in the same manner that they had removed Sikorski.

29

Feminine Exploits in World War II

THE RÔLE of women in the field of intelligence acquired far more importance in World War II than ever before and this applied to the British Secret Service. No longer were women employed in routine, part-time espionage, but in many instances were given key parts to play in actual operations on enemy territory as well as executive posts in Intelligence departments. Both M.I.5 and the S.I.S. used female executives and a number of spy chiefs abroad were women operating as Passport Control Officers. Indeed, when the war ended, a number of women were promoted to such rank.

It was a highly resourceful young W.R.A.F. officer who, at secret R.A.F. Intelligence headquarters at Medmenham, brought off one of the best scoops of the latter period of the war. Constance Babington-Smith was one of a group of officers whose job it was to examine reconnaissance photographs brought back by the R.A.F. from missions over Germany. This branch of intelligence became of supreme importance in searching out new targets and in building up a picture of what the enemy was doing. In May 1943, she came across a picture taken the day before during a flight over Peenemünde. Using a stereoscope and a measuring magnifier, she noticed a small, curved black shadow with a T-shaped white blob above it. From this she deduced that the black shadow was a new kind of launching ramp and that the white T must be a remarkably small aircraft of some kind. As a result of this discovery enlargements of the photograph were made and these confirmed her deduction: it was quite obviously a ramp and also a tiny aircraft. That single piece of intelligence work, the result of painstakingly sorting through hundreds of similar photographs of aerial reconnaissance, was to save tens of thousands of British lives.

For Peenemünde was on the German island in the Baltic where Hitler had ordered the carrying out of experiments with rocket bombs and guided missiles with which he hoped to swing the war back in Germany's favour. Work here had begun as early as 1933, but the Secret Service had not only been uninformed about the project in its early days, but had failed lamentably to follow up various scraps of information which should have alerted them to the possibilities of top-secret German experiments in this area. News of the Nazis' development of a secret weapon of devastating power filtered through in 1939 on the eve of war, but it had been dismissed as alarmist propaganda by Goebbels in his war of nerves on the West. Further warnings came during the war, one in an unsigned letter posted from Norway, which, not unnaturally, was suspect, but another report from an agent in Denmark should have been taken more seriously.

Constance Babington-Smith's discovery resulted in an immediate drive for more reports on Peenemünde and all the previous reports which had been carefully filed away were re-examined. More positive details about the production of the deadly V-1 and V-2 flying bombs resulted in the bombing of Peenemünde by the R.A.F., which meant that the first flying bomb attacks on Britain were postponed by at least six months. Even then the Intelligence organisations had great difficulty in getting the politicians to agree to make the flying bomb bases priority targets.

One of the most accomplished secret agents of the war was Christine Granville. The daughter of a distinguished Polish family, born Countess Krystina Skarbek, this tall, attractive, slim, vivacious girl was outwardly everything that a fiction writer could desire as a model for a glamorous female spy. She was half Jewish which explained to a large extent her detestation of the Nazis, while her family background explained the extraordinary courage and determination which she displayed. In her late teens she had lived somewhat of a playgirl existence, even entering for and winning a "Miss Poland" beauty contest. Stanley Moss, another British agent who knew her and worked with her, said of Christine: "The almost mesmeric attraction she had for men was a blend of vivacity, flirtatiousness, charm and sheer personality.

She could switch that personality on and off like a searchlight that could blind anyone in its beam."

Her first marriage to the son of a wealthy family lasted only a few weeks. Her second husband was George Gizycki, twenty years her senior, who was a poet, explorer and foreign correspondent, and she was with him in Addis Ababa when war broke out. Immediately Christine travelled to England, offered her services to British Intelligence and was accepted. She was first assigned to Budapest, where, living as a journalist, she repeatedly crossed into Poland to smuggle out Poles and other Allied officers. She linked up with a Polish Cavalry officer named Andrew Kowerski, who later under the name of Andrew Kennedy became a British agent. He was organising the escapes of Polish soldiers from internment camps all over Hungary and he placed his resources at Christine's disposal. On one journey into Poland Christine was arrested, but managed to escape. On a third mission she found that the Gestapo were offering a reward of 100,000 zlotys (£2,500) for her capture. Again she was arrested, this time on the Yugoslav frontier just after she had smuggled four pilots across, but she talked the guards into believing she was on a picnic, at the same time persuading them to start up her car which had stalled.

There were many other narrow escapes such as the occasion on which she skied away from the enemy with machine-gun bullets spattering all around her, driving into the shelter of rocks with such speed that she seriously injured herself. On another occasion when she was arrested she bit her tongue, causing it to bleed, and, spitting up blood, feigned tuberculosis. She was taken to hospital and later released. Later she went to Cairo and became the first woman parachutist in the Middle East, working quietly for thirty months learning the arts of sabotage and preparing herself for parachute missions in France. Under the auspices of the S.O.E. she was parachuted on the Vercors Plateau in Southern France. There she maintained contact with the French Resistance and the Italian Partisans across the frontier, operating as a courier for the Hockey network under the command of François Cammaerts.

Christine Granville was then serving in the W.A.A.F. and using the code-name "Pauline". She insisted on doing far more than the work of a courier, participating in raids and sabotage missions and much of what she achieved has not even been mentioned in the official history of the S.O.E. in France. Even in that book, however, the author, in describing how the agents Cammaerts and Xan Fielding were captured by the Gestapo, tells how the "new courier the Polish Christine Granville by a combination of steady nerve, feminine cunning and sheer brass persuaded his [Cammaerts'] captors that the Americans' arrival was imminent and secured the party's release three hours before they were to have been shot".

By this time Christine was a hardened campaigner. Once when threatened with arrest by the Germans she had opened her right hand to reveal a hand grenade which she threatened to throw unless she and others with her were freed. In fact on the occasion referred to in the official history she had gone to the jail where Cammaerts and Fielding were incarcerated, not only warned that the Allied Forces were not far away and that they would be shot as war criminals if anything happened to their prisoners, but even pretended that Field Marshal Montgomery was her uncle and would personally see that the Germans were executed. Lieut.-Colonel Cammaerts, who later became the headmaster of Alleyn's School, stated afterwards that Christine Granville "was perhaps the greatest person I have ever known".

Her immediate superior said of her activities in France that "Christine Granville accomplished her task in a manner that no other person, man or woman, could have done." Yet though she was awarded both the George Medal and an O.B.E., she was churlishly treated by the British Government, being paid off at the end of the war with two months' salary— £100. She was forced to find what work she could and, surprisingly, no worthwhile job was found for one of her remarkable attainments. She became a stewardess on a liner, became acquainted with a steward who fell madly in love with her and who, finding his love unreturned, stabbed her to death.

It remains a mystery why Christine Granville was treated in so miserly a fashion and why she ended her days in comparative poverty. She was as brave in criticising her superiors as she was in tackling the enemy and some of her strictures on the S.O.E. hierarchy caused her to have powerful antagonists. Because she was Polish and had close contacts with the Poles in exile she was also regarded with some suspicion. What is more Christine Granville claimed she had evidence to show that Sikorski's death was due to sabotage. This she did not hesitate to proclaim: it spelt her death knell as far as the British Secret Service was concerned.

In France alone the S.O.E. employed no fewer than fifty-three women agents and some of these, such as Odette Sansom and Violette Szabo, are already legends of the war, whose stirring deeds have been immortalised in book and film, but whose actual achievements have been dealt with in rather curmudgeonly fashion in the history of the *S.O.E. in France*. The hierarchy of the various intelligence services seems to have been oddly jealous of its women agents in World War II and even to have resented descriptions of their heroism. True, books and films can exaggerate heroic deeds, but this does not excuse the extraordinarily churlish attitude of the authorities towards many of these women. We have seen how Christine Granville was cast aside; others suffered similarly. Yet many of these women agents were exposed to far greater dangers than their male colleagues. Some were caught and executed in circumstances which suggest they were never too well protected. As one of them told the author: "There was a feeling in the London control centre of S.O.E. that we were expendables, that, being females, there was no special reason to protect us. This may seem hard to believe, but we were often unduly exploited and exposed to unnecessary dangers. The case of Noor Inayat Khan was a perfect example of this."

Noor Inayat Khan, code-name *Madeleine*, was an Indian princess, born in Russia, but who had spent a great deal of her life in France and England. She had escaped from France in 1940, joined the W.A.A.F. and been transferred to S.O.E. An emotional, artistic and in many ways an unworldly character, Noor Inayat Khan should almost certainly not have been recruited for such work. She was the antithesis of Christine Granville and her imaginative powers would have been better employed in her talent for writing children's stories than in the work of an agent in the field. There is evidence that efforts were made to prevent her being used as an agent overseas. A fellow agent described her as being "a splendid vague, dreamy creature, far too conspicuous,—twice seen, never forgotten—and she had no sense of security. She should never have been sent to France."[1]

But sent she was, by Colonel Buckmaster, in charge of F Section, backing his judgement to employ her as a radio operator against that of the training department. Yet the incredible thing is that this sensitive dreamer, though almost inevitably doomed to death in the harsh world of espionage, revealed an amazing courage in adversity. On one occasion she left her code-book on the kitchen table of her rooms in Paris. Fortunately the landlady gave it back to her. She was supposed to stay in the Bois de Boulogne area, yet she could not resist paying visits to old friends in Suresnes where she had spent her girlhood. Eventually she was betrayed by somebody who sold her address to the Germans for 100,000 francs, and there is some reason to believe that she was deliberately liquidated for her indiscretions and lack of a sense of security. There was certainly a singular lack of concern in London for this agent and no serious effort was ever made to protect her, or to relieve her. She was arrested by the Gestapo, taken to Dachau and executed. She refused to reveal anything to the enemy and, despite threats and torture, maintained silence until the end.

It is doubtful whether any young recruit in the Armed Forces would have been treated so shamefully as was Noor Inayat Khan, or left to fend for herself in such circumstances. In many respects it was unforgiveable, in all respects it was bad judgement. But one must salute this inexperienced lone agent as one of the many heroines of the war. She was merited the George Cross and M.B.E. which were awarded her in a belated attempt to make amends to a very brave young woman.[2]

In conclusion it is worth noting that of the fifty-three women agents S.O.E. put in the field, twelve were executed by the Germans and twenty-nine were either arrested or died in captivity.

30

Treachery in High Places

It would be rash indeed to attempt any detailed history of the Secret Service since the end of World War II. Not only does the Official Secrets Act to a large extent preclude any such attempt, but in very many instances judgement must necessarily be reserved. It is not always possible in assessing espionage and counter-espionage within the past twenty years to say for certain that this was treachery and that that was a brilliant *coup*. Subsequent evidence may easily show that what seemed like treachery was an act of service of which our own Secret Service was cognisant, but remained silent. Similarly some incidents which have been hailed as brilliant achievements may have been either propaganda, or, at best, considerably short of the truth.

The truth is that the whole business of secret service has undergone a tremendous metamorphosis, as it always will after any major war. The feats of such wars, when publicised, reveal new techniques of intelligence that cannot be repeated: consequently a new approach is essential. Then again, the targets of espionage are always changing. From 1945 onwards the prime targets for all major powers were atomic secrets and the development of nuclear techniques. Then the emphasis was on aircraft and secret missiles and later on naval and underwater developments in both craft and nuclear missiles. The nuclear stalemate brought about a change of attitude: the emphasis now is much more on the obtaining of diplomatic secrets and information on conventional ground forces, and it has shifted from naval bases to laboratories like that of Porton experimenting in germ warfare and methods of counteracting it.

Espionage has in fact been speeded up. There are many reasons for this. First and foremost is the fact that with the coming of nuclear warfare techniques the margin of warning is considerably less. This makes it much more important for spies to be placed high up in the hierarchy of a rival power. Secondly, sky-spying has speeded up the work of intelligence. The spy jet-plane, flying at a great height can photograph enemy installations with impunity until it is shot down and spy ships with infra-red long-distance cameras and electronic telescopes can perform the work of a score of agents. The replacement of even these weapons by satellites in the sky, circling the earth and providing a steady stream of information from cameras which can photograph from 150 or 200 miles what can be seen by the human eye at only fifty yards is but another example of changing techniques of intelligence.

All this has not eliminated the need for the individual agent, but it has meant that the type of backroom rôle such as was played by Constance Babington-Smith at Medmenham in World War I has assumed far greater importance. Even in the last war the part played by the Medmenham establishment was so vital that the Air Ministry's history of air operations recorded that "a very high proportion of successful landing operations in Western Europe can be directly attributed to the work done at Medmenham, the air force photographic interpretation station".

There was no sudden folding up of the various Intelligence branches in Britain in 1946 as there had been after World War I. Indeed, the organisations were so large that it would have been impossible to disband all personnel speedily and as the Cold War began to develop at the end of 1945 any ideas of a sudden dispersal of agents became unthinkable. But the Secret Service as a whole in 1945 was not nearly so well geared to fighting a Cold War as were its American counterparts. The O.S.S. and the F.B.I. had learned a great deal in a very short time and in many respects had overtaken the British. With the creation of the Central Intelligence Agency, U.S.A. had a machine designed to combat communism in peace-time, not merely in counter-espionage, but in more aggressive forms as well.

The first shock in what proved to be a series of devastating shocks in the world of espionage came in Ottawa in September, 1945, when Igor Gouzenko, a young cipher clerk in the Russian Embassy there, defected. It was fortunate that the British Secret

Service, who had been tipped off, took an immediate interest in Gouzenko, otherwise he might not have been alive today and a whole network of Soviet agents might not have been broken up. For the Canadians behaved with a stupidity and lack of understanding equalled only by the British in the Legation at Berne when the German arrived with confidential papers. The Canadian newspaper on whom Gouzenko first somewhat surprisingly called showed little interest, turned him away and casually suggested he might try the Royal Canadian Mounted Police. Government officials told him to go back to the Russian Embassy and the Canadian Premier showed no desire to be mixed up in the affair, saying it was "too hot a potato to handle". But, not by any means by chance, William Stevenson was in Ottawa at the time and when officially told about Gouzenko immediately went into action, making sure that the Russian was given instant protection for his wife and himself and personally supervising the whole operation.

Gouzenko's information quickly revealed the existence of a powerful Russian spy network in Canada and more ominously pointed to Soviet penetration of British and American atomic secrets. One of their agents was code-named "Alek". It was not long before M.I.5 established that he was Dr. Alan Nunn May, a British physicist working on research into nuclear fission at the Montreal laboratories of the Canadian National Research Council.

Thus what had been a feather in the cap of British Intelligence proved in the long run to be the means of revealing grave weaknesses in national security. The United States' doubts about British security dated from the arrest of Dr. Nunn May. From that date U.S. Intelligence was almost as much concerned about looking for suspects in the ranks of British Intelligence as for Russian agents. J. Edgar Hoover started the feverish witch-hunt long before Senator Joe McCarthy appeared on the scene. Screening of people working on top secret or semi-secret work in Britain had been inadequate for a long time. Even up to 1950 it remained woefully inadequate, amounting to little more than a cursory examination of backgrounds to show that there was no actual membership of the Communist or Fascist Parties at any time. The toll in terms of treachery of varying degrees was appalling: Nunn May, Klaus Fuchs and Pontecorvo were all examples of this laxity.

It is almost certain that other scientists employed by the British also passed information on to the Russians, though nothing was ever proved. The revolt among scientists against what they regarded as irresponsible political gamesmanship with nuclear science was far-reaching. It did not mean that all, or even a majority of these scientists were traitors in the ordinary sense of the word, or that they were Communists. They simply felt that science was being misused and exploited against a former ally: rightly or wrongly they felt that to spread the information would in the long run prevent a nuclear war rather than to allow one or two powers to keep the secret and be able to use the deadly weapon with impunity. From a patriotic point of view they may have been wrong, from a rational long-term assessment events which have led to the present nuclear stalemate may have proved them to be right. It was the use of the bomb at Hiroshima which stirred many scientific consciences.

Attlee, who was Prime Minister at the time, seems to have realised this moral dilemma which would present itself to some scientists and that this meant a tightening up of security. Indeed Attlee showed more commonsense in tackling this knotty problem than many in the Secret Service. He decided to make all nuclear research and experiments top secret and to keep the question of nuclear development not only out of politics, but out of the Cabinet as well. He ordered the strictest security; his orders were ineffectively carried out.

M.I.5 underwent various changes after the war in an effort to cope with the problems posed by the new style espionage—the realisation that traitors were often to be found in high and unexpected places and that among the Iron Curtain countries at least the swollen personnel of their Embassies masked a large-scale network of spies. For from 1946 onwards it was not a case of Russia carrying out espionage single-handed, but often in close collaboration with the Czechs, Poles, Rumanians, Hungarians and others who had diplomatic representation in London.

Yet for the best part of twenty years M.I.5 has frequently been obstructed in its work by lack of co-operation by the Foreign Office and the S.I.S. On too many occasions when M.I.5 has pointed out a potential suspect in either the Foreign Office or the S.I.S., a blunt refusal to co-operate has been met with. The Foreign Office has obstinately persisted in the fiction that it has its own methods of security screening and these have been proved highly deficient.

The liaison between the Foreign Office and the S.I.S. was after the war somewhat ill-defined as far as security was concerned. For example there was a purge of the S.I.S. with a view to weeding out any undesirables who had been brought into the Service in wartime. Many wartime recruits were asked to leave the Service, but Burgess, Maclean and Philby, all of whom should have been detected by such a purge either escaped notice, or were passed as satisfactory. It is hard to believe that anyone as flamboyant as Burgess, or as brilliantly erratic as Maclean could have escaped notice, yet both apparently were cleared in a similar probe carried out by the present Lord Caccia which covered both the S.I.S. and the Foreign Office.

That there was an acute need for such a purge and that it should have been very much more drastic, probably involving revised vetting at six monthly intervals for the next three years is now beyond doubt. Some of the people who had been brought into the S.I.S. during the war, not only in posts in London, but overseas, too, were utterly unfitted for further service. Many of them were security risks and even outrageously ostentatious homosexuals.

Nor did M.I.5 escape unscathed from this type of recruit. During the war even this organisation began to hand out jobs to some doubtful characters such as Brian Howard, old Etonian and homosexual poet who, presumably, was employed because of rather than in spite of his perverted tastes. Howard was an absolute disaster, recruited at the end of Sir Vernon Kell's era. He behaved in a childish and amateurish way in carrying out his duties, frequently getting drunk and then revealing his membership of M.I.5 in bars and at the same time accusing his fellow drinkers of being German spies on the flimsiest of pretexts. Howard was finally axed in a purge carried out during the war by Lord Swinton who was then the Minister responsible for this branch of security.

It was through the prolongation of such an unhealthy climate in the world of intelligence and the Foreign Service that such exotic plants as Burgess, Maclean and Philby flourished and survived. Burgess was an Old Etonian who, despite frequent indiscretions, drunken bouts and homosexual orgies, survived a brief spell in Intelligence to join the Foreign Service. Donald Maclean, the son of a highly respected and respectable former Liberal Minister, had by the charm of his personality and undoubted talents endeared himself to the hierarchy of the Foreign Office. Others might make mistakes and pay for them, but Maclean's rapid progress up the ladder of the Foreign Service matched the retrogressive steps he took in his private life. Not even his violent behaviour at parties in Cairo where he smashed up furniture and attacked people interrupted his career more than a posting for leave. Yet Guy Burgess had been an active Communist while at Cambridge and as Maclean said afterwards: "We abandoned our political activities not because we in any way disagreed with the Marxist analysis of the situation in which we still both find ourselves, but because we thought . . . that in the public service we could do more to put these ideas into practical effect than elsewhere."

It was little wonder that all three became careless and convinced that a lucky star protected them. Neither Burgess nor Maclean tried to mask indiscretions and Philby, the most discreet of the three, finally compromised himself fatally by association in Washington with the now notorious Burgess. Gradually the counter-espionage service built up their case against Maclean, yet even when convinced reluctantly that Maclean must be interrogated on the subject of leakages of information to the Russians, a dilatory Foreign Office decided he need not be questioned until the weekend was over. Thus was Philby able to warn Burgess and Burgess to persuade Maclean to escape with him via Southampton and Le Havre on a secret route which took both behind the Iron Curtain.

The tradition that M.I.5 must have a Service chief ended with the war. Sir David Petrie had gathered under him a highly professional team of counter-espionage agents and the organisation was in much better shape at the end of the war than it had been at the beginning. Sir Percy Sillitoe become head of M.I.5 on 1 May 1946, the day that Allan Nunn May was charged at the Old

Bailey with communicating information contrary to the Official Secrets Act. Since then all directors of M.I.5 have been civilians. Sir Percy, though a policeman, was in a very different tradition from that of Sir Basil Thomson. Joining the British South African Police Force in 1908, he was gazetted in the Northern Rhodesian Police in 1911, served in the German East African campaign in World War I and then returned home to embark on a spectacularly successful police career in Britain. As Chief Constable of Sheffield he set up Britain's first forensic science laboratory in 1929 and later as Chief Constable of Glasgow became famous as the most effective gang-buster which that crime-torn city has ever known.

From 1943–46 he was Chief Constable of Kent and, being situated in an area where security was much more of a predominant issue than in other parts of the country, he learned in wartime to work closely with the Intelligence. When he became Director General of M.I.5 he found, however, that the ramifications of the Service were somewhat baffling even to a man of his experience. "I cannot deny," he wrote, "that during my first few weeks as head of M.I.5 I found it so extremely difficult to find out precisely what everyone was doing that I felt its popular reputation for excessive secrecy was in no way exaggerated. The men whom I was attempting to direct were highly intelligent, but somewhat introspective, each working, it seemed to me, in a rather withdrawn isolation, each concentrating on his own especial problems."[1]

Sir Percy held the post from 1946–53 and was a shrewd, competent administrator, often still underrated. He had no pomposity and did not believe in trying to hide what could not be hidden. Of all heads of M.I.5 he was the one who never made any nonsensical pretence of not having anything to do with the organisation. He even disclosed the exact position of his office in *Who's Who*—"War Office, Room 055." When he travelled it was under his own name: he never used disguises or *incognitoes*, a fact which caused him occasional embarrassment. Once, for example, in 1951, shortly after the disappearance of Maclean and Burgess, he went on holiday to La Baule in the south of France and, by an odd coincidence, Mrs. Maclean was there, too. The press was persistently but misguidedly convinced that the head of M.I.5

had gone to La Baule for a secret interview with the missing diplomat's wife. So intense was the press coverage of his visit that the Sillitoe family had to return home. There has been criticism of what was somewhat unfairly alleged as Sillitoe's complacency about the defection of Burgess and Maclean. The truth is, however, that neither the Foreign Office, nor the S.I.S. would listen to M.I.5. Sillitoe believed that as the public could play a useful rôle in helping the security organisation, it was equally important that the existence of this body should be well known to the public. In this he was undoubtedly right for if M.I.5 ceased to have tips from the public, their work would be much more difficult.

Sillitoe took the view that the British counter-espionage service should not be given powers which would put it into the same category as the Secret Police of a totalitarian state. "I myself would rather see two or three traitors slip through the net of the Security Service than be a party to the taking of measures which could result in such a régime," was his comment. "M.I.5 has no executive powers. And the head of the Security Service—fortunately in my opinion—is not empowered to take the law into his own hands and put people under arrest because he suspects them of being spies, or for any other reason."[2]

This is undoubtedly as true today as it was in Sillitoe's time. Where criticism can be directed is to the failure of the authorities to root out suspects inside the Intelligence Services when growing evidence, not only from M.I.5 and other sources in this country, but from U.S.A., pointed to treachery in the S.I.S. and the Foreign office.

While M.I.6 (S.I.S.) has always diversified itself by having various offices with improbable names (often in even more improbable Ministries) scattered all over London, it was for years known that M.I.5's hierarchy, apart from a liaison office in the Defence Ministry, maintained premises at Leconfield House in Curzon Street. Indeed that office has sometimes been called "The Pink Elephant" in a joking comparison with the White Elephant Club in the same street.

Secret Service estimates remain secret despite official figures which are released annually. Though Parliament votes an annual figure for a Secret Service grant, the details are naturally not divulged. Nothing like a true picture of all Secret Service expenditure can be gauged from these official figures. Some of this expenditure is spread over other departments like the Admiralty and the Air Ministry and other departments, too. Probably a truer picture would emerge if one multiplied the official figures by four or five. Until recently even the salaries of officers in the Intelligence services were unknown even to Inland Revenue and were tax free so that no clue should be provided as to the nature of their activities. That, at least, is the official view: it might also be argued that the very fact that their salaries are tax free could provide a clue as to the nature of their work. In 1951 Secret Service men won a record pay award, back-dated for nearly six years. A tribunal, headed by Sir David Ross, heard officers' claims for increases in their salaries ranging from £12 to £18 a week. It was then disclosed that salaries paid to men (including ex-officers of the rank of major who had been specially chosen for Intelligence work) had been getting less than £12 a week. Top men were getting only £18 a week. This was a relic of the pre-war Secret Service when rich young men who did not need large salaries joined up happily because they had these tax-free benefits.

Shortly after the war Secret Service spending was running in the region of £3 millions a year, but this, it should be stressed, merely refers to the declared estimates. By 1959 an extra allocation of two millions in that year brought the total up to £7 millions, which shows that relaxation from the Cold War had by no means reduced spending. By 1963 the figure was £8 millions and in February 1967, despite the fact that it was reported that the Secret Service had underspent during the previous year by £17,236 14s. 7d., the allowance for the future was increased to £10 millions. Any "surplus" had to be "surrendered" to the Treasury: it could not be earmarked for future use. The current estimates are in excess of £11 millions a year.

In 1936 a young schoolmaster, who had been educated at the universities of Oxford, Michigan and California, joined M.I.5 with a view to making a permanent career in intelligence. He was Dick Goldsmith White, who swiftly proved his capacity for hard, incisive work and by the middle of the war was regarded by many as the ablest man in the organisation. Some even thought he should have been made head of M.I.5 when Sir David Petrie retired, but it was Attlee, then Prime Minister, who decided to appoint Sillitoe, a well known figure outside the Service, in the belief that this would inspire more confidence with the Americans and that Sillitoe's police experience would be invaluable in coping with nuclear development security, always a subject uppermost in Attlee's mind. However, White, who was later knighted for his services, succeeded Sillitoe.

There had been a growing contempt among the impatient young professional counter-espionage executives of M.I.5 for the methods of recruitment, vetting and the whole structure of the S.I.S. This contempt had, during the war, been based on a realisation that the S.I.S. in the 'thirties had been in many respects recruited and directed in an amateurish manner. M.I.5 had always been made to feel very much the junior branch of Intelligence and was regarded by the S.I.S. rather as the Army proper looks upon the Military Police. This caused resentment and the resentment was increased when it was noted that the S.I.S. more or less vetted itself: the immediate pre-war inspection of the S.I.S. had been carried out by Lord Hankey, an aged and autocratic civil servant, and Gladwyn Jebb, then an up and coming Foreign Office man. Apart from this the agents of the S.I.S. continued to be a very assorted collection of unimaginative ex-Indian Army officers, young men who had failed at stockbroking and a fair sprinkling of playboys in the idle rich category. Even in the middle of the war many of these S.I.S. types used to congregate at White's Club, which became almost an annexe of the Secret Service, even Stewart Menzies and his personal assistant, Peter Koch de Gooreynd, spending much of their time in the bar there.

Contempt and resentment, however, gave way to dismay and frustration when towards the end of 1949 and in early 1950 M.I.5 began to realise that something was amiss in the S.I.S. set-up. It was then known that there were leakages of information which could only have come from somebody in the S.I.S. or the Foreign Office. M.I.5 blamed lack of co-operation with the Foreign Office and the S.I.S. on the failure of the authorities to dismiss Burgess as a drunken incompetent and to catch Maclean before he fled the country. Even Philby's belated tip-off to these two men would not have prevented the escape of Maclean if the authorities had acted promptly. There was enough evidence to call Maclean's bluff several days, if not weeks, before he fled the country. M.I.5 were also certain that Philby, then the liaison officer of the S.I.S. with the American C.I.A. in Washington, was the "third man" in the Burgess—Maclean case by the end of 1951. But the S.I.S. continued obstinately to insist that Philby was beyond suspicion.

One M.I.5 executive was energetic enough to make inquiries with his American opposite number after the abject failure of the C.I.A.-S.I.S. operation in Albania in the spring of 1950. On that occasion well-armed bands of agents were infiltrated into Albania which was considered then to be ready to stage a revolt away from the Soviet regimé. Obviously somebody had betrayed the news of the operation in advance to the Russians for more than half of the infiltrators were killed. We know now that Philby was responsible for the leakage. The C.I.A. were certain even at the time that Philby was responsible and this information was passed on to M.I.5. But the S.I.S. remained as obdurate as were the top men of the Foreign Office in protecting Burgess and Maclean after constant M.I.5 reports that each man was a security risk on account of his drunkenness, homosexuality and outrageous behaviour, quite apart from suspicions of treachery.[3]

This crass stupidity on the part of the S.I.S. caused the C.I.A. and the F.B.I. to become highly critical of the whole British Intelligence set-up. It was the era of Senator Macarthy's witch-hunts and denunciation of communism in high places, and they can perhaps be forgiven if they took the view that the British Foreign Office and the Secret Service contained men at the top who were knowingly protecting traitors. If this seems to be an hysterical and exaggerated view of things, it is worth noting the comment of Geoffrey McDermott, who spent twenty-seven years in the British Diplomatic Service and was at one time Foreign Office adviser to the S.I.S. Mr. McDermott states: "Parts of his [Philby's] confession could well have been bogus too. He might have been protecting the real 'third man' so that he could continue his activities among us."[4]

One must, however, remember three aspects of the Philby affair. First, his undoubted ability, judgement and intellectual capacity had won him the respect and confidence of the hierarchy of the S.I.S. Quite a few of these who worked with him admit that he inspired loyalty. Secondly, as a double agent, he must have supplied the S.I.S. with plenty of good intelligence about Russia, under Russian guidance of course, otherwise he would not have got away with his double game for so long. Thirdly, Philby was an astute psychologist, not in a theoretical way, but intuitively and he knew personally the characters and foibles of the leading men not only in S.I.S., but in M.I.5 as well. This would enable him to anticipate their reactions. Yet against all this, and the most damning indictment of British Intelligence, is the fact that the Americans suspected him all along. They just could not obtain enough proof, though one imagines that had British co-operation been forthcoming, that proof should not have been impossible.

Philby was the man who, after more than a decade in the service of Soviet Intelligence, found himself at the end of the war in the vital post he had wanted for so long—head of the department of the S.I.S. known as Section IX in charge of anti-Communist and anti-Soviet counter-intelligence. Philby himself throws some interesting light on the way in which he set about getting this appointment: "I did not want to be dependent solely on the loyalty of my colleages in S.I.S. The particular danger facing secret servants is the charge of insecurity, or of related offences, which are the province of M.I.5. In case anything should happen to me in my new job, it would be well, I reflected, if M.I.5 could be officially embroiled in my appointment. What I wanted was a statement from M.I.5 on paper to the effect that they approved my appointment."

There was one other sound reason for this wish. In tackling counter-intelligence work the S.I.S. were to some extent treading on the preserves of M.I.5 and in any event had to co-operate with this body. But Philby got his approval from M.I.5 from Sir David Petrie himself.

Oddly enough Philby's counterpart in M.I.5 was Roger Hollis, the head of its section investigating Soviet and Communist affairs. To complete a somewhat complicated picture of comings and goings in the Intelligence Services it was Roger Hollis who became head of M.I.5 some years later when Sir Dick

Goldsmith White was transferred to the S.I.S. as head of the Secret Service.

Hollis was the son of a Bishop of Taunton and a brother of Christopher Hollis, a former Member of Parliament. Apart from having worked as the representative of the British-American Tobacco Company in China before he entered intelligence, he had remained entirely in the background since his Oxford days. While at Oxford he had been a member of a club called the New Reform which, curiously enough, was partly subsidised by cash from the mysterious Lloyd George Political Fund. Other members at that time were Evelyn Waugh, Roger Fulford and Maurice Richardson. The last-named recorded that "Roger Hollis and I had a romantic plan to abandon Oxford and seek our fortunes in Mexico. We got as far as applying for Mexican visas. I never saw him after Oxford, but used to inquire about him during the early 'sixties from his brother, Chris, who either didn't know what he was doing, or else was diplomatically evasive."[5]

Changes in the S.I.S. after the war were inevitably gradual. It took time to adapt for peacetime purposes an organisation which had included at one time or another during the war such diverse personalities as Malcolm Muggeridge (who functioned in Lourenco Marques) and Graham Greene (who watched the Vichy French in Freetown). The S.I.S. had always suffered much more from the presence of amateurs and eccentrics in its ranks than had M.I.5. At one time the S.I.S., who called themselves "The Friends", considered themselves socially superior to the "The Snoopers", as they called M.I.5. To spy, they averred, was a cut above spy-catching. But such snobbism swiftly disappeared during the war when the recruitment to M.I.5 brought in men who, taken all round, were probably stabler, more professional and better at administration than those of the Secret Intelligence Service. There were more dons and barristers in the ranks of M.I.5 and few playboys or stockbrokers.

Stewart Menzies remained at the head of affairs for a few more years, surviving one of those prolonged bouts of internecine warfare to which all secret services seem strangely prone. There is little doubt that Philby himself played some part in the internal disputes, never directly, but cleverly using them to secure advancement for himself. It is, however, doubtful if his influence in the imbroglios which at one time threatened to split the S.I.S. into rival camps was as marked as some have suggested. Colonel Vivian, who had been Deputy Chief of the S.I.S., was made Adviser on Security Policy, a sinecure of a job created for him, while Colonel Claud Dansey became Vice-Chief, an unfortunate designation, but one specially chosen rather than Deputy Chief out of deference to Vivian. It was a shuffle in top jobs which did not amount to much change in general policy until shortly afterwards Dansey retired, his place being taken Major-General Sir John Sinclair, who had been Director of Military Intelligence at the War Office. "Sinbad" Sinclair, so called because he had served as a Midshipman in the Royal Navy before being commissioned in the Army in 1919, had only been active in intelligence work during the last two years of the war.

Menzies' retirement in 1951 must have come at the unhappiest moment of his career. It went completely unnoticed in the press because the newspapers were observing the Whitehall request that the head of the S.I.S. should not be embarrassed by identification and publicity. Yet some few years later when the storm burst about Philby's defection to the Russians and the revelation came that he had been a Russian agent since the 'thirties, Menzies had to remain silent while criticism raged about the inefficiency of the S.I.S. in employing such a man in vital posts over so long a period.

Menzies cannot escape a high degree of personal responsibility for the harbouring of such a man all these years in the S.I.S. There is ample evidence that some at least of the S.I.S. knew that Philby had been a communist while at Cambridge and the fact that later he posed as a pro-German should have made the authorities if not doubly suspicious, at least sufficiently cautious to keep him away from any post in which he could wreak damage. After all Philby was not even in the S.I.S. when he joined the Anglo-German Fellowship or became a war correspondent on Franco's side. After the disappearance of Burgess and Maclean in 1951 an investigatory team, headed by G. A. Carey-Foster, the head of Q-Branch at the Foreign Office, went out to Washington to question Philby and after this Philby was removed from his post of liaison with the C.I.A., though this was due more to American pressure than British suspicions. Yet even then the S.I.S. showed their loyalty to Philby and Menzies tried to seek a compromise by which he personally would have a talk with Philby on his return to London to find out whether his agent's indiscretions could not be interpreted more charitably. This interview never took place. Had it done so and had Menzies personally "cleared" Philby, the head of the S.I.S. would have irreparably damaged his reputation. The best one can say for Menzies was that he had a high estimation of Philby's qualities and was reluctant to lose a good man because of what might be even minor indiscretions. However, the Philby affair, damaging as it was, should not be allowed to detract from Menzies' war-time services and the manner in which at the outbreak of war he retrieved the Secret Service from its peace-time sloth and restored it to something like its former prestige. In any event, even if Menzies had wished to get rid of Philby, all the evidence suggests that the powerful pro-Philby body of opinion in the Foreign Office would still probably have overruled him and insisted on hushing the matter up and allowing Philby to continue in a minor rôle. Very few Secret Service chiefs in modern times have been able to go against the Foreign Office, as Menzies knew from personal experience.

There was another body of opinion, albeit not large, that thought that to leave Philby free might eventually lead British agents on the track of the Soviet spy network. Dr. Otto John, former head of the West German counter-espionage, asserts that in 1954 Soviet agents kidnapped him solely to determine whether Philby was not, after all, a double agent, betraying the Russians to the British.

31

Changes in S.I.S. and M.I.5

MAJOR-GENERAL SINCLAIR succeeded Menzies as head of the S.I.S.; again, it will be noted, promotion in the Civil Service manner of seniority, to which the S.I.S. then seemed increasingly dedicated. Sinclair, however, neither had Menzies' experience, nor his knowledge of agents, nor his anticipatory sense of diplomacy and political nous. On top of this he had the misfortune to be head of the S.I.S. at the time of the Crabb incident of 1956. Subsequent inquiries into this affair showed that it was not held to be his personal responsibility.

Commander Crabb, one of the Royal Navy's best underwater sabotage experts and divers, dived into Portsmouth Harbour in April 1956, on a secret mission near the Russian cruiser *Ordzhonikidze*, which had brought Khrushchev and Bulganin, the Russian leaders, to Britain. He never reported back to duty and his disappearance caused a Parliamentary storm. There were, of course, the usual denials that Crabb was operating on behalf of British intelligence, with some rather snide hints that he might have been a free lance agent for the Americans which were ventilated in the press. Fourteen months later a headless body was washed ashore near Chichester and at an inquest, on the flimsiest evidence, a verdict was recorded that it was that of Crabb.

Since then there have been sporadic reports that Commander Crabb has been seen in the Soviet Union living under a Russian name. Mrs. Patricia Rose, the Commander's fiancé, is convinced that the body was not Crabb's and that he is still alive. She claims to have had a message from Crabb delivered by a man who had actually spoken to him in Russia. "He said he met Crabbie at Sebastopol and that he was training frogmen for the Russians. He sent me his love. The man even described the characteristic way Crabbie smokes and coughs."

Bernard Hutton, whose book *Commander Crabb is Alive*, was published in 1968, declares that he was told that Captain R. Melkov, a Leningrad seaman, who often sailed to Britain, had spoken to Crabb. Crabb gave Captain Melkov a personal message for Mrs. Rose and mentioned his pet name for her as proof that he was Crabb.

"For further proof," declared Bernard Hutton, "Crabb also described a conversation with his old friend Sidney Knowles, which had taken place just before his disappearance in 1956. Before I received this communication—by a roundabout route—Melkov himself died."

On 8 May 1968, Captain Roman Melkov, master of the Russian ship *Kolpino*, then in London docks, was found shot dead in his cabin. On the following day a verdict that Melkov "killed himself" was recorded at Southwark Coroner's Court.

Sidney Knowles, a diver who worked with Crabb for thirteen years, confirmed that the conversation with Crabb stated to have been mentioned by Melkov had in fact taken place.

The Admiralty officially announced that Commander Crabb was "presumed to be dead as a result of trials with certain underwater apparatus" at a spot three miles from where the cruiser had been anchored.

It can be argued that the Russians might find it useful propaganda to put out the story that Crabb had been caught, taken back to Russia and turned over to the Soviet. But this is not typical Russian procedure. They waited years before revealing that Burgess and Maclean were actually in Moscow. For a long time they remained silent on Philby. They never claimed that Sidney Reilly went over to them. Whatever the full truth about the Crabb affair it was once again that old failing of British Intelligence that the left hand did not know what the right was doing. In private Randolph Churchill maintained that Ian Fleming had had something to do with the Portsmouth "prank", even referring to "Frogman Ian Fleming" and his exploits in connection with the Crabb affair in an amusing skit in an American magazine. True, the article was fictitious satire, but Randolph had an unerring nose for embarrassing gossip of this kind. The only light the author of this book can throw on this suggestion is that at the time of the Portsmouth incident Fleming was supposed to be taking a cure at a health farm, yet in fact he was not at the address he named. Whether he had another alibi I cannot say. The Crabb episode would have been the type of intelligence prank that might have appealed to Fleming, who, though no frogman and even then in none too good a state of health, was a keen skin-diver and underwater explorer.

The Crabb affair, however, did neither the S.I.S., nor the N.I.D. any good. It suggested sheer mischievousness, or a prank on the level of a schoolboy lark. On the other hand to many Members of Parliament, especially those of left-wing persuasion, it looked as though the S.I.S., possibly abetted by the C.I.A., were trying to sabotage the Russians' goodwill visit to Britain. Sir Anthony Eden, then Prime Minister, took umbrage to the extent of regarding the frogman incident as a personal slight to his statesmanship. In any event, if this was a serious attempt to carry out probes for an underwater examination of the Russian ship's hull in a search for special electronic equipment, or nuclear devices, it was incredible that Crabb should be selected for the job. He was then a diver not fully fit, already beyond the age when he should have attempted a serious or difficult diving operation of this nature, and a notorious gossip incapable of keeping quiet about anything of a secret nature. To make matters worse some security officer visited the hotel at which Crabb had last stayed in the Portsmouth area and clumsily tore a page containing a list of guests from the visitors' book. There was a wild panic in Intelligence circles and at least two health farms not far from London were visited by counter-espionage agents who instructed them to maintain absolute silence on any inquiries about visitors.

There was an immediate call from the highest level for a shake-up in the Intelligence Services and the Foreign Office Adviser to the Secret Service was among the first casualties. It was generally conceded that advice to the S.I.S. on the occasion of the Russian leaders' visit should have been categorically against any indiscreet operations at such a time. Shortly after this Sir Dick Goldsmith White was appointed chief of the S.I.S. It was a great pity that he had not been switched to this post from M.I.5 much earlier, for his gifts as a counter-espionage executive were vitally needed for an organisation which since 1945 had shown such laxity in security, such incredible obstinacy to face facts and such clumsiness in conducting operations. Sir Dick was at last able to put into effect some of the reforms of the S.I.S. which were long overdue.

It has been under Sir Dick's regimé that much useful work has been done in obtaining information from Russian defectors and, more important, in making on the whole the right deductions from that information. Apologists for the Secret Service point to the fact that American defectors and spies in the post-war period far outnumber those of Britain. It is perfectly true that the American list of such names includes Alger Hiss, Soble, Soblen, Gold, the Rosenbergs, Slack, Greenglass, Brothman, Moskowitz, Abel, Coplon, Haynahen, Scarbeck, Bucar, Cascio, Verber, Dorey, Sobell and Boeckenhaupt. But America's population is not only far greater than that of the United Kingdom, but also much more diversified and containing a vast number of barely assimilated Poles, Czechs, Chinese, Germans and people of other races. One would expect their security problems to be far greater and the number of defectors and spies to be proportionate to these factors. Mr. Donald McLachlan has written that "those who harp on the Philby story as if it were the beginning and end of British Intelligence run the risk of undermining that loyalty by advertising a bogus set of values." This is, of course, begging the question: it is not conceded that the Secret Service needed reforming and that appalling mistakes, if not indeed criminal negligence, occurred. Would these reforms have been carried out if there had not been open and healthy criticism at last of what the S.I.S. was doing? Even today there has been no adequate answer to many of the criticisms. Both Labour and Tory Governments must take their share of the blame. Hector McNeil, when Minister of State at the Foreign Office, was sufficiently cognisant of the facts to warn Burgess that he must not indulge in left-wing politics and open homosexual misdemeanours. Burgess was sufficiently contemptuous of the warning as to ignore it almost completely. As for the Tories, either they turned a blind eye to what was going on, or they uncritically accepted the briefing they were given by the Foreign Office.

The main criticism to be levelled against British Intelligence over the past quarter of a century is that far too many of the spies and agents eventually unmasked proved to be either British agents, diplomats or diplomatic employees, or even worse, members of the Armed Forces.

The notorious "Cicero" in Ankara was a valet of the British Ambassador: he revealed to the Germans details of the forthcoming Teheran Conference which led to a plot to assassinate the Allied war leaders. Maclean and Burgess were both employed by the Foreign Office, Philby and George Blake were in the S.I.S., Vassall was in the Admiralty, Harry Houghton was in the Royal Navy. In every case the authorities had ample evidence to throw suspicion on each of these men. Maclean and Burgess should have been dismissed years before on the grounds of misconduct, let alone suspicion of being agents; Philby had revealed communist leanings in his university days before he posed as a pro-Fascist in the time of the Spanish Civil war; in giving S.I.S. employment to Blake the authorities were overlooking the fact that he had an Egyptian father and a Dutch mother; Vassall's unsuitability for work involving handling confidential papers should have been known from the time he worked in the British Embassy in Moscow, while Houghton's fraternisation with the Poles when he was stationed in the British Embassy at Warsaw (he was sacked from this post because he had been mixed up in the black market) should have precluded his being employed later at the secret Underwater Weapons Research Establishment at Portland. Further blame can be laid on the authorities because of their failure to acquaint M.I.5 with many of these facts.

In eventually trapping the Krogers, Houghton, Gee and Gordon Lonsdale M.I.5, assisted by the Special Branch at Scotland Yard did an excellent job. It was a splendid example of teamwork in counter-espionage. The selection and screening of M.I.5 personnel is today most carefully carried out and the rules for selection are much more rigidly enforced than in the S.I.S. A man such as George Blake, however impeccable his qualifications, would not find work in M.I.5: Kell's maxim about employing British-born nationals still holds. Since the Vassall case several surprise checks have been carried out on security precautions in several Government departments.

Electronic aids to espionage, the technique of "bugging" and microphones have all added to the work of security agents. One of the greatest of menaces is the "sensitised ear". This device is the size of a match-box. It needs no connection to wires or cables. All that is needed is for, say, an office cleaner to hide it in a room, office or laboratory. From a hide-out a mile away, a transmitter operated by an agent sends out electronic waves which sensitises a small disc in the device. The disc then picks up and reflects the waves of conversation on the frequency of a receiver by the spy's hideout and this is recorded. Since the discovery of this device every vital security office in Britain is searched periodically. But the main counter to such activities is the laborious screening of personnel who have access to security-vital places.

In May 1961, George Blake, nominally a member of the Foreign Office staff, but actually an agent of the S.I.S., was sentenced to forty-two years' imprisonment for spying for the Russians. Blake was the son of Albert William Behar, an Egyptian Jew, married to a Dutchwoman, and was born in Rotterdam in 1922. The father had a British passport and considered himself British. During World War II, when still a boy, George Behar joined the Dutch Resistance against the Nazis, escaped to Britain and was enrolled into the Dutch and British secret organisations in London. Eventually he took the name of Blake, joined the R.N.V.R. as an Intelligence officer and, after the war, was transferred to the Foreign Office. He was sent to Korea with the rank of vice-consul, fell into the hands of the Communists and suffered hardships in Korean prison camps. Whether he succumbed to brainwashing while in these camps is a subject of some controversy. When it was suggested by the authorities that this must have been the case, various Britons who had been in prison camps with him vehemently denied this, saying that nobody stood up more vigorously to the Communist jailer.

When Blake was released he was given even more important work to do as a secret agent. He had in fact been a secret agent ever since he went to Korea. This time he was posted to Berlin not only to spy on the Russians, but to play the rôle of a double-agent, infiltrating the Soviet espionage set-up with the full knowledge of his employers. For almost eight years he worked for the

British without arousing any suspicions. In the end he was only caught because a German informer and a Polish defector gave him away. The latter disclosed the cells which the Soviet Secret Service had established inside British and American Intelligence in Berlin which proved that Blake had been not only a double, but a triple agent. It was alleged that Blake had not only betrayed secrets to the Russians, but had given away the names of a whole network of British agents, causing some of them to be caught and killed by the Russians. Despite the allegations and Blake's subsequent conviction, however, much of what Blake is supposed to have done has not yet been proved. Indeed, it is salutary to ponder on the question posed by Blake's biographer, E. H. Cookridge. Mr. Cookridge asks "why George Blake, on becoming a double agent in Berlin, was allowed access to so much information which was not designed for Russian consumption. If, with the connivance of his British employers, Blake had to throw out baits to the Russians in order to gain their confidence, then he had of course to deliver to them some secrets. . . . But however trusted a double agent may be, the danger of his being unmasked by the enemy, of blackmail, torture and submission, makes it an elementary rule of Secret Service work not to allow him near secrets which much be kept inviolate. In Blake's case his superiors in Berlin and at the Foreign Office should have been aware of his ambition to excel and of the danger that in his zeal to bring back from the Russians secrets wanted by his British employers, he might overstep the limits of discretion afforded to him. The responsibility for such acts must, therefore, be shared by at least some of his superiors."[1]

Who were these superiors? Leaving aside the question of the executives of the S.I.S. and the Foreign Office, the head of the Russian section of the S.I.S. on the Continent up to about 1958 was Colonel Charles Gilson, who was stationed at Minden in West Germany. This section was later moved to Rome and Gilson, who retired shortly afterwards, blew out his brains in Rome because, it was stated at the time, of money difficulties and that he found he could not live on his pension in the style to which he was accustomed. This sidelight on the Blake affair is one of the little known and unexplained mysteries of the case.

The Blake affair was followed in quick succession by the

Vassall, Profumo and Philby bombshells, all of which considerably weakened the authority of the Macmillan Government in its last years of office. When Vassall was sent to prison for eighteen years for passing secrets to the Russians, it was learned that not only had he previously worked in the office of the Deput[illegible]ector of Naval Intelligence at one time, but that he had [illegible]d passed after positive vetting tests. On each occasion [illegible] by a two-man team and, though his homosexual tende[illegible]had been noted by some of his colleagues in Moscow, this fact was either not revealed, or completely missed by the vetting team.

Nor did the vetting team notice that Vassall was spending far in excess of his salary. The subsequent inquiry revealed that the people principally to blame were members of the Admiralty staff in London and of the British Embassy staff in Moscow.

The Profumo case was in no sense as serious as the other cases, for no betrayal of secrets was involved, but it was alarming in its revelations not only of laxity in security, but of the failure of M.I.5 to bring home to the Prime Minister and the War Minister the risks involved. In July 1961, the War Minister, Mr. John Profumo, met Miss Christine Keeler who was a guest of Dr. Stephen Ward who was tenant of a cottage of the Cliveden estate of Lord Astor. Through Stephen Ward Miss Keeler had met Eugene Ivanov, who was assistant naval attaché at the Russian Embassy in London, a gregarious lover of the good things of life who mixed freely in the social life of London's official and fashionable circles. That the Minister of State for War had been sharing the favours of a girl with a Russian naval attaché was bad enough, that the same Minister had lied to Parliament in denying the allegations against him was worse, but that the security services had failed to draw proper attention to the serious risks involved and that the Prime Minister had not bothered to find out the truth was almost unbelievable. This deplorably mishandled case, which culminated in Mr. Profumo admitting that he lied to the House and resigning from office sounded the death knell of the Macmillan Government and reduced its credibility to zero.

Security authorities made a routine check on Ivanov and thought he might be operating as a spy. They kept a watch on him and in this way discovered that both Ivanoff and the War

Minister were visiting Miss Keeler at her flat in Wimpole Mews. Then M.I.5 learned from Stephen Ward that Ivanov had asked him when the Americans were going to arm Western Germany with atomic weapons. The security officer's report on this was tha[illegible]uld not think Ward was "a security risk in that he would [illegible]ally disloyal, but his peculiar political beliefs, coupled w[illegible]vious admiration of Ivanov might well cause him to be [illegible]reet unintentionally".[2] This sounds like an attempt to damn with faint praise and an effort on the part of the security services to suggest that Ward was more of a security risk than the War Minister: in short, the classic technique of security services in telling the authorities what they wanted to know rather than what they ought to know. The real risk was not that the Minister of War would be a security risk, but that the Russians, armed with the knowledge of his association with Miss Keeler, the mistress of Ivanov, would use this for blackmail or for political exploitation.[2]

The Denning report on the Profumo case states: "A thought occurred to the Security Service that, perhaps, with Mr. Profumo's help, it might be possible to get Ivanov to defect. Mr. Profumo might be a 'lead-in' to Ivanov. The Director-General carefully considered what to do. He felt that he could hardly approach Mr. Profumo direct on the matter. So on 31st July 1961, he spoke to Sir Norman Brook [Secretary to the Cabinet] about it."

The Denning Report's comment on all this was that "if the Security Service had had such knowledge, I should have thought it was one of those matters of extreme delicacy where they might approach the Prime Minister direct; or, if they had reported it to Sir Norman, I would have thought that Sir Norman would have reported it to the Prime Minister. In failing to do so, he would have made a mistake."

Incidentally during a debate in the House of Commons on 17 June 1963, Harold Wilson, then Leader of the Opposition, suggested to the Prime Minister, Harold Macmillan, that the security services had first heard of the affair from the executive of a Sunday newspaper. "If this is true," Wilson added, "and the Prime Minister must be frank about this, this would imply that the sixty million pounds spent on these services under the right honourable gentleman's premiership have been less productive in this vitally important case than the security services of *The News of the World*."

Despite the omissions of the security services to carry their deductions to a logical conclusion in the early stages of this case Lord Denning gave them at least a qualified approval of action: "I find that they covered the security interest fully throughout and reported to those concerned. . . . They took all reasonable steps to see that the interests of the country were defended." Nevertheless the impression remained that the security services could not be expected to do their job properly while vital information was withheld from them by such departments as the Admiralty and, for that matter, by the Ministry of Defence. Only a year before Colin MacInnes had written in *New Society* on 15 November 1962, that "one of the first lessons President Kennedy learned, or which disaster taught him, was that elected authority must control the institutional (Pentagon, C.I.A.) and prevent these becoming policy-making states within the State. In our country this can scarcely be assured by the Prime Minister's office alone; so that to control the Security Services, both operationally and politically, it might seem the time has come for stricter, broader supervision. . . . A supervising body of this kind should operate continually."

Macmillan would have done well to heed this advice. But the then Prime Minister had a somewhat cynically indifferent attitude towards intelligence work, not, let it be explained, in any matters which he considered vital to the safety of the nation. Macmillan was a man who believed in getting to the root of a question, who refused to allow himself or others to be bogged down by irrelevant details, or sidetracked by "a little local difficulty". This is an admirable trait in many respects, indeed a virtue in a Prime Minister, but a highly dangerous one in modern intelligence matters where it is not always possible to separate the trivial from the important. Macmillan believed, not without some reason, that sixty per cent of intelligence was a waste of time and unimportant. This is certainly true as a generality, especially in modern times when executives often create unnecessary work merely to extend their own private empires and when so much duplicatory intelligence work is carried out. But the point the Prime Minister missed is that it is not always possible at the time such work is carried out to know what is useful and what is wasteful, to assess what is trivial and what later might become of national importance. Only time can prove that. It was this indolence, this desire not to be told, or to become too involved, which led to the Profumo Scandal. Macmillan's predecessor had fussed and interfered too much on matters of detail; Macmillan himself went to the other extreme. Another explanation is that there was so much relief in Ministerial circles that the Profumo case was merely a heterosexual scandal after a series of homosexual scandals affecting the Government, or the ruling party, that they failed to appreciate the inherent dangers of the affair.

Sir Roger Hollis remained at his post as head of M.I.5 until he retired at the normal age of sixty in 1965. He assisted in the shake-up of the security services which followed the Profumo case and the subsequent Denning Report. There was a feeling in M.I.5, at least on the lower levels, that a more vigorous assertion of their requirements was needed at the top and that perhaps in future younger men could more easily implement awkward or unpopular decisions, even when it meant ensuring that the Prime Minister should be made aware of them. One result of such thinking was the decision to reduce the retiring age from sixty to fifty-five in future. Sir Roger Hollis was succeeded as head of M.I.5 by Sir Martin Furnivall-Jones.

In 1955 Macmillan, then Foreign Secretary, had declared that "no evidence has been found to show that [Philby] was responsible for warning Burgess or Maclean. . . . I have no reason to conclude that Mr. Philby has at any time betrayed the interests of his country, or to identify him with the so-called 'Third Man', if indeed there was one."

Nevertheless even at this time it was officially known that Burgess had warned Philby, even though it might have been possible for the credulous to interpret this as a mere indiscretion. Yet no one, it would seem, had taken the pains, or had the courage, to make the then Foreign Secretary aware of the seriousness of the situation. Philby had been interrogated by security officers and he said then that he had blurted out to Burgess: "Can you imagine the bloody nonsense the F.B.I. is peddling now? They're claiming you're a Soviet spy." Philby said that

Burgess took the remark calmly and then burst into seemingly incredulous laughter.[3]

The only charitable explanation one can put on subsequent events after Philby's questioning is that somebody in the S.I.S. had the crazy idea of using him as a double agent without Philby knowing this, the idea being to feed stuff to Philby which he would be certain to pass on to the Russians and to keep tabs on Philby and see whether he led them to the Soviet spy network. It was a thoroughly unworkable idea, first because Philby would have been far too shrewd not to have guessed what was happening, and, secondly, because the Russians would soon have realised that Philby was suspected by the British. One doesn't let a top man in the S.I.S. go to the Middle East in the guise of a newspaper reporter and anyone who thought the Russians would fall for this must have wanted his head examining. In fact this plan led to a major row between M.I.5 and the S.I.S.

In the end Philby walked out on the British and on his job as a correspondent for the *Observer* and followed Burgess and Maclean behind the Iron Curtain. And on 1 July 1963, the Prime Minister admitted that Philby had worked for the U.S.S.R. before 1946, and that he was that same "third man" whose existence he had doubted in 1955 when he was Foreign Secretary.

A Labour Government is perhaps always more vulnerable to espionage scandals or Intelligence blunders than a Conservative one, as the Zinoviev Letter showed. Perhaps for this reason when Labour returned to power in 1964 the new Prime Minister, Harold Wilson, made a special effort to learn some of the lessons in this respect which his predecessor had failed to profit from. At the latter end of Macmillan's period of office the Prime Minister had given his Home Secretary, the unfortunate Henry Brooke, part of the responsibility for Intelligence which normally fell on the Prime Minister's shoulders. The new Prime Minister decided to keep a close grip on Intelligence by appointing George Wigg as Paymaster General and making him his *eminence grise* on security service matters. This was in part a reward to George Wigg for his persistence and skill in breaking the Profumo Scandal. Significantly in 1967 it was disclosed that the cost of the department of Paymaster General went up by £56,000 to £806,000.

To what extent the relative lack of major espionage scandals during the Wilson Government's era has been due to luck, to improvements in the security services, or to the new policy of having a watch-dog Minister for security, only time can show. There is some suspicion that the new policy only serves to clamp down on security with occasional threats to newspaper editors about "D" (security) notices, but there has been more watchfulness at Ministerial level.

The escape of George Blake from Wormwood Scrubs Prison in October 1966, and his subsequent getaway to Russia was perhaps the one vital security lapse during the Labour Government's term of office. Curiously it aroused less criticism and far less effective Parliamentary questioning than any of the security lapses in the Macmillan era. This may have been due in part to the Opposition feeling inhibited because of failures during the life of the previous Government. Yet the escape again revealed many minor details of bad organisation at a security level: to mention only one, Scotland Yard officers desperately searched for a photograph of Blake so that they could circulate it to airports and docks, having discovered that there was no photograph of him in the Criminal Records Office.

Events such as described in this chapter have tended to put the S.I.S. and M.I.5 on the defensive since the war. It may be argued that a Secret Service should be purely on the defensive in peacetime. In the sense that espionage should never be allowed to worsen political relations as has happened in America with the C.I.A., this corrolary is true. But in the long run it is the offensive spirit which, even in peacetime, pays off. It should be made abundantly clear that there are two types of "offensive", or "aggressive" espionage. There is the *agent provocateur* form of aggression such as the C.I.A's. activities which led to the Bay of Pigs' disaster, or aggressive infiltration of the type which the Russians employ when fomenting strikes in other countries, or disrupting industry. These tactics are not only apt to boomerang against their instigators, but can in some cases lead to war, or at best disastrous incidents. They are escalatory and therefore damaging. The saner type of "aggressive" espionage is that which aims to keep abreast of all developments in territories of potential enemies, i.e. spying on nuclear and armament developments and diplomatic secrets, and at the same time sees to it that the potential enemy knows that this information has been obtained. One cannot make hard and fast rules of the question of when or when not to tell a potential enemy that one has his secrets. But failure to let him know that, at least occasionally, can mean that the effectiveness of the espionage is lost.

No potential enemy will declare war on a nation because that nation has stolen its secrets, but it may be deterred from going to war if it is realised that those secrets have been discovered. This is one of the chief lessons of the era of the nuclear stalemate. The other lesson is that the nation who through "aggressive" espionage wins the most defectors to its own ranks must in the long run have the most effective Secret Service. While British traitors and defectors can be disturbingly numerous, the most obvious weakness of the Soviet system is that Russian defectors are inevitably more numerous and, for this reason, there is considerably more scope in this direction for the British Secret Service than there is for the Russian.

The Soviet Secret Service has had to win its defectors from British ranks on a very narrow front. Realising that the purely ideological defector in Britain is a relatively rare animal, it has often had to fall back on blackmailing, or compromising the homosexual, a technique which has in the past succeeded in Britain because of the legislative bias against homosexuals. Concurrently the Soviet security services have realised that Whitehall has neglected to screen homosexuals adequately and that the S.I.S. had had a tradition of regarding homosexuals as useful agents. The theory is that the homosexual can be used to seduce male enemy agents, while he is unlikely to be vulnerable to the attractions of female enemy agents.

One important development in Secret Service work as far as Britain is concerned is that of literary espionage. This can in the future be almost as important as scientific espionage. Indeed, the creation of a Director of Literary Intelligence might pay useful dividends, for in the post-war period the writings of Djilas, of Pasternak and Danielski have all had as much value in their way as military secrets. The battle of ideas is a field in which espionage in future can be usefully aggressive and win substantial victories.

Supplementary Notes to Chapters

CHAPTER 1

1 *Calendar of State Papers, Venetian,* 1202–1509. See also *Four Years at the Court of Henry VIII. Selection and Despatches written by the Venetian Ambassador, Sebastian Giustiniani,* edited by R. Brown, London, 1854.
2 *Thomas Cromwell and The English Reformation,* by Professor Dickens.

CHAPTER 2

1 Correspondence of Sir Nicholas Throgmorton with Cecil, published by Forbes (vol. i, 137, 148), chiefly from MSS. in the P.R.O. and British Museum.
2 Cited by Conyers Read in *Mr. Secretary Walsingham,* vol. i.
3 State Papers Domestic, Eliz. xlv. 2.
4 Letter to Burleigh, 20 August 1573, Brit. Mus. Harleian MSS. 6991, no. 39.
5 See Camden *Annals* (1635), p. 394. Walsingham's will is published in full in *History of Chislehurst,* Webb, p. 383.
6 State Papers Domestic, Eliz., ccii, no. 41 in Walsingham's own handwriting.
7 P. Pellegrini to Walsingham: Harleian MSS. 286, f. 122 (partly in cipher).
8 See *Mr. Secretary Walsingham,* Conyers Read. This refers to "The Copy of the General and Particular Relation which the Marquis of Santa Cruz and the Secretary Barnaby de Pedrosa sent to the King of Spain on 22 March 1587, containing a list of ships in various ports, of sailors, soldiers, stores, details of wages and other expenses.
9 Harleian MSS. 6994m f. 76.

CHAPTER 3

1 The Public Record Office in London has three volumes of approximately 200 cipher codes dating from the reign of Elizabeth I.

Lord Burghley frequently used signs of the Zodiac for codes, *Aries* for the Duke of Parma, *Cancer* for Estates-General, etc. Latin words were also used: *visus* for Burghley, *oculus* for Lord High Admiral, *olfactus* for Walsingham.

2 This correspondence with Cecil is contained in State Papers, Eliz., vol. xxvii, no. 63.

3 See *The Posthumous Works of Robert Hooke,* Richard Waller, London, 1705, and *John Dee: Scientist, Geographer, Astrologer and Secret Agent to Elizabeth I,* by Richard Deacon.

4 *John Dee,* Deacon.

5 *History of the Jesuits in England,* E. L. Taunton.

6 Cotton MSS., Caligula C ix, f. 566.

7 Berden to Phelippes, undated, State Papers, Domestic, cxcv, no. 75.

8 See *John Dee,* Richard Deacon.

9 *Ibid.*

Chapter 4

1 Cal. Spanish, 1587–1603, p. 578.

2 See *Life and Letters of Sir Henry Wotton,* by L. P. Smith, Oxford, 1907.

3 *Ibid.*

4 Cited by J. W. Thompson and S. K. Padover in *Secret Diplomacy: A Record of Espionage and Double-Dealing: 1500–1815,* p. 66.

5 See *A Project for the Acquisition of Russia by James I,* by Lubimenko, *English Historical Review,* XXIX (1914), pp. 246–56.

6 See *Dictionary of National Biography.*

7 Cited in *Secret and Urgent: The Story of Codes and Ciphers,* by Fletcher Pratt, pp. 140–1.

6 See *John Dee,* by Richard Deacon.

Chapter 5

1 This quotation from Pepys is taken from his diary as transcribed from the tachygraphical manuscript in the Pepysian Library in Magdalene College, Cambridge, by the Rev. Mynors Bright.

2 Giovanni Sagredo was Venetian Ambassador to London and his comments on English intelligence are cited in D. J. Hill's *A History of Diplomacy in the International Development of Europe.*

3 See *Secret and Urgent,* Pratt.

4 From letters sent to Thurloe by agents in November and December 1856.

5 Cited in *Secret Diplomacy,* by Thompson and Padover.

6 See History of the *Commonwealth and Protectorate,* by S. R. Gardiner, vol. III.

7 Cited in *Secret Diplomacy,* Thompson and Padover.

8 This letter is now in the Lambeth Library (vol. 645, No. 33), forming part of the Tenison Collection.

9 See *Thomas Scott's Account of his Actions as Intelligence Officer during the Commonwealth,* by C. H. Firth, *English Historical Review,* VII, 1892, 72 f.

CHAPTER 6

1 Transcribed from the Pepys Diary manuscript in Magdalene College, Cambridge, by the Rev. Mynors Bright.

2 *Ibid.*

3 See *The Secret Service under Charles II and James II,* by J. Walker, *Transactions of the Royal Historical Society,* 4th. Ser., XV (1932), pp. 211–35.

4 See *Secret and Urgent*, Fletcher Pratt, p. 148.

5 See *The Letter Book of Sir George Etherege,* edited by S. Rosenfeld, 1929.

6 Mr. Shelton's tachygraphy bore some resemblance to modern shorthand in that consonants were represented by lines and curves and dots were used for the vowel sounds. But the system differed in that Shelton employed many arbitrary signs, such as the figure 4 for "heart", 5 for "because" and 6 for "us". Pepys adapted the system by inventing arbitrary signs of his own.

7 The official historical account of how the secret of the Argyle revolt was learned by the authorities is that it was obtained following the capture of the Duke's secretary, Spencer, and his surgeon, Blackadder, when the Duke made a brief stop at Cariston in Orkney. This is, however, erroneous. These men were captured on 6 May 1685, only a day before Argyle made his landing, long before news obtained from Spencer and Blackadder could have reached Edinburgh, let alone London. In fact the proclamation calling out the militia and the arrests of the hostages in Argyle occurred on 28 April, as a result of the capture of Argyle's courier and his coded despatches.

8 See *The Diplomatic Service under William III, Transactions of the Royal Historical Society,* 4th. Ser., X (1927), pp. 87–109, by M. Lane; also *Matthew Prior, A Study of his Public Career and Correspondence,* by L. G. W. Legge, Cambridge, 1921.

CHAPTER 7

1 See *The Life of Daniel Defoe,* by Thomas Wright.

2 See *Defoe,* by James Sutherland.

3 See *Thirty-Three Centuries of Espionage,* by R. W. Rowan and R. G. Deindorfer.

4 See *A Dialogue between Louis the Petite and Harlequin le Grand*: cited by Sutherland in *Defoe.*

5 Portland MSS., vol. iv, p. 148.
6 His Majesty's Commissioners Ninth Report, Pt. II, p. 469.
7 Portland MSS., p. 396.
8 Portland MSS., pp. 444–5. In another letter to Harley Defoe added plaintively: "... his Lordship's goodness to me seems like messages coming from an army to a town besieged that relief is coming, which heartens and encourages the famished garrison, but does not feed them; and at last they are obliged to surrender for want, when perhaps one week would have delivered them . . . 'tis like a man hanged upon appeal, with the Queen's pardon in his pocket." Some of the delay in funds reaching Defoe may have been due to the fact that Harley often paid him out of his own pocket and not from official funds. The Lord Treasurer had told Harley that he ought not to be making secret service payments out of his own pocket.
9 Public Record Office: State Papers 35/11/24 (letter dated 26 April 1718).
10 *Ibid.*

CHAPTER 8

1 *Memoirs and Correspondence of Sir Robert Murray Keith,* edited by G. Smith, London, 1849.
2 See *English Historical Review,* XLII (1928), pp. 606–11.
3 There are no records extant of the early days of this society, but it is believed to have started at the George and Vulture Inn in Cornhill, London, which may have been one reason why it was erroneously dubbed the Hell-Fire Club as one of the original "Hell-Fire clubs" had its headquarters at this tavern earlier in the century. There was, however, no connection between the two and the Knights of St. Francis of Wycombe probably began their existence about 1746. After that the society established itself at Round Tar Island in the River Thames until they settled at Medmenham Abbey and later in the caves under West Wycombe Hill. See *The Hell-Fire Club: The Story of the Amorous Knights of Wycombe,* by Donald McCormick.
4 Cited in *The Hell-Fire Club.*
5 See *Correspondence of Catherine the Great when Grand Duchess with Sir Charles Hanbury-Williams*, edited by the Earl of Ilchester and Mrs. Langford-Brooke, London, 1928, and *The Life of Sir Charles Hanbury-Williams*, by Lord Ilchester and Mrs. Langford-Brooke, London, 1929.
6 *Ibid.*
7 See *The Hell-Fire Club*, McCormick.
8 While philandering at the *Parc aux Cerfs*, his royal bordello, Louis XV went incognito as a Polish count and took extreme precautions to disguise his true identity.

CHAPTER 9

1 The reports of the French spies and surveyors of the English coast are now in the Public Record Office in London.
2 See *Secret and Urgent*, Fletcher Pratt.
3 See *A Memoir of the Right Hon. Hugh Elliot*, by the Countess of Minto, Edinburgh, 1868.
4 King George III had some barbed comments to make on Bancroft: "The man is a double-spy," said the King, "if he ever came over to sell Franklin's American secrets in London, why wouldn't such a fellow return to France with a British cargo for sale?" *The Published Letters of King George III,* revised edition, 1932, provide much evidence on Bancroft's intrigues.
5 See *The Correspondence of the Right Honourable William Wickham from the Year 1794*, 2 vols., London, 1870; also see *La Trahison de Pichegru*, by Caudrillier.
6 *Ibid.* See also *General Pichegru's Treason*, 1761–1804, by J. Hall, London, 1915.
7 For the story of British espionage and the detecting of the Treaty of Tilsit see *A British Agent at Tilsit,* by J. H. Rose, English Historical Review, vol. XVI (1901), pp. 712–18; also Temperley's *Life of Canning: A British Agent at Tilsit*, by O. Browning, *English Historical Review*, vol. XVII (1902), p. 110; *The Mystery of Tilsit*, by J. Hall in *Four Famous Mysteries*, (1922), pp. 9–33.
8 See *Life of General Sir Robert Wilson*, edited by H. Randolph, 2 vols., London, 1862.

CHAPTER 10

1 See *Les Grands Espions*, by Paul and Suzanne Lanoir.
2 The Duke of Wellington had a superior espionage service to that of the French at this date, notwithstanding the efficiency of the formidable Fouché, Europe's chief spy-master, as he was so often dubbed. But he was never able to unravel the cipher of Joseph Bonaparte, the temporary French-imposed King of Spain. It was not until Napier came to write the history of the Peninsular War that the key to Joseph Bonaparte's cipher was discovered and Wellington's comment on that occasion was: "I would have given £20,000 for this secret during the war."
3 See *Behind the Scenes in Espionage*, by Winfried Ludecke.
4 See *Narrative of a Secret Mission in 1908*, by James Robertson, edited by A. C. Fraser, London, 1863. Also D.N.B., XLVIII, p. 410.

CHAPTER 11

1 See *Thirty-Three Centuries of Espionage*, by Rowan and Diendorfer.
2 See *Dear Robert Emmett*, by Raymond Postgate.

3 See *Secret Service under Pitt*, by Dr. W. J. Fitzpatrick.
4 *Twenty-five Years in the Secret Service: The Recollections of a Spy*, by Henri Le Caron, Heinemann, London, 1892. Born as Thomas Beach in Colchester in 1841, Le Caron ran away to France as a youth, then went to America and enlisted in the Northern Army, playing the part of a Frenchman and calling himself Le Caron.
5 *Ibid.*
6 *Ibid.*
7 *Ibid.*
8 Details of the accounts of the "Skirmishing Fund" of the Irish rebels list the following items under the heading of expenses in 1881: "Old submarine vessel 4,042.97 dollars; new submarine vessel 23,345.70 dollars; subsidising foreign newspapers 2,000 dollars.
9 *Great Contemporaries*, Winston S. Churchill.
10 *Twenty-five Years in the Secret Service.*
11 *Great Contemporaries*, Churchill.
12 *Twenty-five Years in the Secret Service,*

Chapter 12

1 *Twenty-five Years in the Secret Service.*
2 See *Rapports militaires écrits de Berlin: 1866–1870*, Stoffel, Garnier Frères, Paris, 1871.
3 See *Die Communisten-verschworungen des neunzehnten Jahrhunderts*, Wermuth und Stieber. Also *Les Grands Espions*, Paul and Suzanne Lanoir.
4 *Ibid.*
5 See *London Labour and The London Poor*, 4 vols., Henry Mayhew, 1851–62.
6 See *Things I Know*, William Le Queux, 1923.
7 *Ibid.*
8 *Ibid.*
9 See *History of the C.I.D. at Scotland Yard,* by Margaret Prothero, Herbert Jenkins, London, 1931.
10 *The Story of Scotland Yard*, Sir Basil Thomson.
11 The earliest evidence that the French and Germans believed that British espionage was linked with the occult and supernatural influences was to be found in sixteenth century writings, undoubtedly due to the strange activities of John Dee. Niçeron was convinced that Dee employed astrology to obtain secret information and Dee's "angelic conversations" in Bohemia and Poland undoubtedly led the Germans and Central Europeans to draw the same conclusion. But even in the present century, according to Professor H. R. Trevor-Roper, Himmler was convinced that the Rosicrucians were a branch of the British Secret Service (*Last Days of Hitler*), while Aleister Crowley's claims to having indulged

in espionage were sometimes given credence on the Continent and again strengthened the belief that British Secret Service and the occult were synonymous.

12 See *Burton: A Biography of Sir Richard Francis Burton*, by Byron Farwell.

13 *Ibid.*

14 For this and the preceding information on McMorrough Kavanagh see *The Incredible Mr. Kavanagh,* by Donald McCormick.

15 See *My Thoughts Past and Present: The Memoirs of Alexander Herzen*, Chatto & Windus, 4 vols., 1968.

16 See *Ace of Spies*, by Robin Bruce Lockhart.

CHAPTER 13

1 Letter from Admiral Sir Francis Beaufort to Capt. R. P. Cator, 1868.

2 *Urgent and Secret*, Fletcher Pratt.

3 See *Secret Service in South Africa*, by Douglas Blackburn and W. W. Caddell.

4 *Great Contemporaries*, Winston S. Churchill.

5 See *Baden-Powell*, by William Hillcourt with Olave, Lady Baden-Powell.

6 *Ibid.*

7 See *The Mystery of Lord Kitchener's Death*, by Donald McCormick, Putnam, London, 1959.

8 See *The German Secret Service,* by Colonel Walther Nicolai, translated by George Renwick.

9 See *Steinhauer: The Kaiser's Master Spy*, by Gustav Steinhauer and S. T. Felstead.

10 *Hansard*, 1908.

CHAPTER 14

1 See *The Eyes of the Navy*, by Admiral Sir William James.

2 *Ibid.*

3 See *M.I.5*, by John Bulloch.

4 *The Scene Changes*, by Sir Basil Thomson.

5 See *Azeff the Spy*, by Boris Nikolajewsky, and *The History of Azeff's Treachery*, by Ratayeff. While it is abundantly clear that Azeff worked for the Ochrana as a double spy, there also seems to be evidence that he loved his play-acting as a revolutionary and that possibly at heart he was more of a rebel than a police spy. Mercenary considerations made Azeff a police spy. There is a curious comment on him by Col. Victor Kaledin, of the Russian military intelligence in World War I (himself a double spy), who declared that an *agent provocateur* was "held in the greatest contempt in Service circles, and is generally chosen from the lowest types".

But, he added, "Azeff was a noticeable exception . . . a genuine revolutionary and his work fulfilled more the rôle of a double spy."

6 *Lost London*, by B. Leeson, Stanley Paul, London, 1924.
7 *Statement*, by Gerald Bullett.
8 See *The Ochrana*, by A. T. Vasil'ev, 1930.
9 *Lost London*, B. Leeson.

Chapter 15

1 See biography of Dr. Walter Page by B. J. Hendrick.
2 See *The Life of Sir Alfred Ewing*, by his son.
3 See *Secret and Urgent*, by Fletcher Pratt. Pratt states: "This was to have the most important effects on the German naval effort, and through it on the whole course of the war. Twice in the early days the Germans tried slipping flotillas of destroyers down along the coast of Holland in an effort to raid the British troop convoys across the Channel. Each time Room 40 read their radio signals and knew of the project. The first time fog and a storm forced the raiders back to harbour; the second time a fast and powerful British light cruiser waited across their path and sank four of the German ships before they could get away."
4 *The World Crisis: 1911–1918*, by Winston S. Churchill, Thornton Butterworth, London, 1923–31.
5 See biography of Walter Page, Hendrick.
6 Farewell message to the staff of the Directorate of Special Intelligence by Brigadier-General Cockerill, 1 January 1919, published in *The Times*, 2 January 1919.

Chapter 16

1 See article entitled *Battle of Wits with Enemy Spies*, published in *Sunday News*, by Sir Basil Thomson, 15 March 1925.
2 The German General Staff proved extremely gullible in accepting the fantastic story about the arrival of Russian troops in Britain. On 5 September 1914, the representative of German O.H.L., Col. Hentsch, told General von Kluck: "The news is bad. . . . There are reports of a Russian expeditionary force in the same parts [referring to disembarkations on the Belgian coast]. A withdrawal is becoming inevitable."
3 See article in source shown in footnote 1: *Battle of Wits with Enemy Spies*.
4 *Ibid.*
5 See *Eyes of the Navy*, Admiral Sir William James.
6 *The Star*, 30 March 1948.
7 See *The Autobiography of an Adventurer*, by Ignatius Timothy Trebich Lincoln, Leonard Stein, London, 1931.

8 See *The Mask of Merlin*, by Donald McCormick, Macdonald, London, 1963.
9 *Ibid.*
10 *Ibid.*
11 See *Eyes of the Navy*, James.

CHAPTER 17

1 *Eyes of the Navy*, James.
2 See *The Mystery of Lord Kitchener's Death*, by Donald McCormick. See also *Die Weltkriegsspionage*, by W. Bley, 1931.
3 See *Admiralty White Paper* Cmd. 2710, 1926.
4 See *With the Battle Cruisers*, by Filson Young, London.
5 *Secret and Urgent*, Fletcher Pratt.
6 See *The Intimate Papers of Colonel House*, Arranged by Charles Seymour, Ernest Benn, London, 1926.

CHAPTER 18

1 See *Ace of Spies*, Lockhart.
2 See *The Romance of the Last Crusade*, by Vivian Gilbert, New York, 1923, pp. 183–5.
3 *Eyes of the Navy*, James.
4 *A. E. W. Mason*, by Roger Lancelyn Green, Max Parrish, London, 1952.
5 *Ibid.*
6 See *Vickers: A History*, by J. D. Scott, Weidenfeld & Nicolson, 1962. A detailed and factual account of Zaharoff's rôle with the firm of Vickers and Vickers-Armstrong is given in this book.
7 See *Athenian Memories*, by Compton Mackenzie, Chatto & Windus, 1940.
8 Zaharoff to Rosita Forbes (Mrs. A. T. McGrath): see *Sunday Chronicle*, 29 November 1936.
9 *Ibid.*
10 See *Documents Politiques de la Guerre*, Barthe, Menevée & Tarpin.

CHAPTER 19

1 *Thirty-three Centuries of Espionage*, Rowan & Deindorfer.
2 *Eyes of the Navy*, James.
3 From an article entitled *Scotland Yard from Within*, by Sir Basil Thomson, in *The Times*, 2 December 1921.
4 Autobiographical note in unpublished papers of Sir Basil Thomson, by permission of Mr. Nigel Seymer.
5 See *The Scene Changes*, by Sir Basil Thomson, Victor Gollancz, London, 1939.

6 See *Ireland for Ever*, by Brig.-Gen. F. P. Crozier, Jonathan Cape, London, 1932.
7 See *The Spy in the Castle*, by David Neligan, McGibbon & Kee, London, 1968.
8 From a series of articles entitled *The Scarlet Pimpernel*, by Sir Paul Dukes, in the *Daily Sketch*, January 1938.

CHAPTER 20

1 See *Ace of Spies*, Lockhart, and *The Secret Documents of Sidney Reilly*, series of articles in the *Evening Standard*, May 1931.
2 *Evening Standard*, 11 May 1931.
3 See *The Zinoviev Letter*, by Lewis Chester, Stephen Fay and Hugo Young, Heinemann, London, 1967.
4 Letter by Robin Bruce Lockhart in *Sunday Times*, 20 March 1966.
5 *Great Contemporaries*, Churchill.
6 *Daily Express*, 23 July 1930.
7 *Ibid.*
8 Extracts from the Soviet report quoted by Reuter.
9 Letter by Robin Bruce Lockhart in the *Sunday Times*, 8 January 1967.
10 See *My Silent War*, by Kim Philby, Grove Press, New York, 1968.

CHAPTER 21

1 See *Secret Agent*, by John Whitwell, *Sunday Express*, April 1966.
2 *My Silent War*, Philby.
3 For further background see *Pedlar of Death*, by Donald McCormick, Macdonald, London, 1965.
4 See *Breach of Security*, edited by David Irving.
5 Lord Denning's Report (on the Profumo case), H.M.S.O., Cmnd. 2152, September 1963.

CHAPTER 22

1 See *De Duites Vijtde Colonne in de Tweede wereldoorlog*, by Louis De Jong, Arnhem, Amsterdam, 1953.
2 See *They Spied in England*, by Charles Wighton and Gunter Peis, based on the diaries of General Erwin von Lahousen.
3 *Ibid.*
4 For background to German wishful thinking on the subject of the Duke of Windsor see *Schellenberg Memoirs*, edited and translated by Louis Hagen, Andre Deutsch, London, 1956, and the War Diaries of Abwehr II (Sabotage and Subversion), at present in the Munich Institute of Contemporary History. The latter is incomplete and contains only extracts from the Diaries.
5 *Documents on German Foreign Policy*, vol. x.

CHAPTER 23

1 See *Baker Street Irregulars*, by Bickham Sweet-Escott, Methuen, 1965.
2 There is a detailed account of the S.O.E. debacle in Holland in E. H. Cookridge's *Shadow of A Spy*, Leslie Frewen, London, 1967.
3 See article by Ian Fleming entitled *How to Write a Best-Seller* in *Evening Standard*, 18 August 1964.

CHAPTER 24

1 The spelling of "Klafft" is wrong: this refers to Karl Ernst Krafft, the Swiss astrologer who was Hitler's personal adviser. The statement quoted was made by Louis de Wohl in an article entitled *Strangest Battle of the War*, in the *Sunday Graphic*, 9 November 1947.
2 See *Wir sind die letzen*, by Ranier Hildebrandt, 1949.
3 Statement made by Hess in reply to a questionnaire submitted to him by Pierre J. Huss, published 9 December 1945.
4 *Ibid.*

CHAPTER 25

1 For a full account of Sir William Stephenson's life and further details of his wartime activities see *The Quiet Canadian*, by Montgomery Hyde.
2 *Ibid.*
3 See *I Was Monty's Double*, by M. E. Clifton-James.

CHAPTER 26

1 See *Entlarvter Geheimdienst*, by T. Bush, (pseudonym of Arthur Schutz), Zurich, 1946.
2 See article entitled *The Life and Death of A Master Spy*, by Rhona Churchill, *Daily Mail*, 29 July 1968.
3 See *The Quiet Canadian*, by Montgomery Hyde.
4 *Ibid.*
5 Cited by Donald MacLachlan, a colleague of Fleming in the N.I.D., in a review he wrote of M. R. D. Foote's *The S.O.E. in France*.

CHAPTER 27

1 *La Guerre a été gagnée en Suisse*, by Pierre Accoce and Pierre Quet, tells the story of the "Lucy Ring" in considerable detail. Also worth reading on the same subject is *La Chasse aux Espions en Suisse*, by Col. R. Jaquillard, Librairie Payot, Lausanne, 1947.

2 *Handbook for Spies*, by Alexander Foote, Museum Press, London, 1949.

3 *Ibid.*

4 Quoted from a preface by Lowell Thomas to Wythe Williams' book, *Secret Sources*, Ziff-Davis Publishing Co., New York, 1943. Wythe Williams wrote in 1942: "Because of the transmission expenses connected with our exclusive reports from overseas I had always been faced with a considerable overhead. This in turn could be met only by a commercial sponsor, as the radio stations themselves carry no provision for such expenses. Without a sponsor willing to carry the cost, I had to abandon broadcasting over a nation-wide network. . . . After Hitler's declaration of war against the U.S., we did not hear from our German friends for a long time. . . . By the very nature of things all such information was turned over to the U.S. authorities and only the data made available for such a purpose were presented in my broadcasts."

CHAPTER 28

1 *The Honoured Society*, by Norman Lewis, Collins, London, 1964.

2 *The Quiet Canadian*, Montgomery Hyde.

3 For details about this agent, "George Wood", see Allen Dulles' *The Secret Surrender*, Harper & Row, New York, 1966. Dulles described Wood as "one of the best secret agents any intelligence service has ever had".

4 See *Canaris*, by Karl Heinz Abshagen, Union Verlag, Stuttgart.

5 *The Murder of Admiral Darlan*, by Peter Tompkins, Weidenfeld & Nicholson, 1965.

CHAPTER 29

1 See *S.O.E. in France*, Foote.

2 For the full story of Noor Inayat Khan see *Madeleine*, by Jean Overton Fuller, Gollancz, 1952.

CHAPTER 30

1 Article entitled *My Answer to Critics of M.I.5*, by Sir Percy Sillitoe, in the *Sunday Times*, 22 November 1953.

2 *Ibid.*

3 For further information on the Burgess and Maclean affair see: *The Missing Diplomats*, by Cyril Connolly, The Queen Anne Press, London, 1952; *The Missing Macleans*, by Geoffrey Hoare, Cassell, London; *Guy Burgess*, by Tom Driberg, Weidenfeld & Nicholson, London, 1956.

4 Article entitled *James Bond Could Have Learned from Philby*, by

Geoffrey McDermott in the *New York Times Magazine*, 12 November 1967.

5 In *Views* by Maurice Richardson in *The Listener*, 26 October 1967.

Chapter 31

1 See *Shadow of A Spy*, by E. H. Cookridge, Leslie Frewen.
2 The *Denning Report*.
3 *My Silent War*, Philby.

Bibliography

ABSHAGEN, K. H.: *Canaris,* Hutchinson, London, 1956.

ASTON, Sir George: *Secret Service*, Faber & Faber, London, 1939.

BABINGTON SMITH, Constance: *Evidence in Camera,* Chatto & Windus, London, 1957.

BLACKBURN, Douglas and CADDELL, W. W.: *Secret Service in South Africa.*

BUCKMASTER, Colonel Maurice J.: *Specially Employed,* Batchworth, London, 1952; *They Fought Alone,* Odhams, London, 1958.

BULLOCH, John: *M.I.5: The Origin and History of the British Counter-Espionage Service,* Arthur Barker, London, 1963.

COCKERILL, Brig.-Gen. Sir George: *What Fools We Were,* Hutchinson, London.

CHURCHILL, Peter: *Of Their Own Choice,* Hodder & Stoughton, London, 1952; *Duel of Wits,* Hodder & Stoughton, London, 1957.

COLVIN, Ian: *Chief of Intelligence,* Gollancz, London, 1951.

COOKRIDGE, E. H.: *Shadow of A Spy,* Leslie Frewin, London, 1967.

DALTON, Hugh: *The Fateful Years,* Frederick Muller, London, 1957.

DEACON, Richard: *John Dee, Scientist, Geographer, Astrologer and Secret Agent to Elizabeth I,* Frederick Muller, London, 1968.

DULLES, Allen: *The Craft of Intelligence,* Harper & Row, New York, 1963.

FARAGO, Ladislas: *War of Wits: Secrets of Espionage and Intelligence,* Hutchinson, London, 1956.

FARWELL, Byron: *Burton: A Biography of Sir Richard Burton,* Longmans, London, 1963.

FITZGERALD, Brian: *Daniel Defoe: A Study in Conflict,* Secker & Warburg, London, 1954.

FITZPATRICK, Dr. W. T.: *Secret Service Under Pitt.*

FOOT, M. R. D.: *SOE in France,* H.M.S.O., London, 1964.

FOOTE, Alexander: *Handbook for Spies,* Museum Press, London, 1949.

FREEMAN, W.: *The Incredible Defoe,* Herbert Jenkins, London, 1950.

GARDINER, Samuel Rawson: *The History of the Commonwealth and Protectorate: 1649–1656,* 4 vols., Longmans, Green, London, 1903.

GRAY, Austin K.: *Some Observations on Christopher Marlowe, Government*

Agent, from *Modern Language Association of America,* 1928, vol. XLIII.

GREEN, Roger Lancelyn: *A. E. W. Mason,* Max Parrish, London, 1952.

HILLCOURT, William: *Baden-Powell: The Two Lives of a Hero,* with Olave, Lady Baden-Powell, Heinemann, London, 1964.

HYDE, H. Montgomery: *The Quiet Canadian: The Secret Service Story of Sir William Stephenson,* Hamish Hamilton, London, 1964.

JAMES, Admiral Sir William: *Eyes of the Navy,* Methuen, London, 1955.

JOWITT, The Earl: *Some Were Spies,* Hodder & Stoughton, London, 1964.

LE CARON, Major Henri: *Twenty-five Years in the Secret Service: The Recollections of a Spy,* Heinemann, London, 1892.

LEWIS, Norman: *The Honoured Society,* Collins, London, 1964.

LINCOLN, Ignatius Timothy Trebich: *The Autobiography of an Adventurer,* Leonard Stein, London, 1931.

LOCKHART, Sir Robert Bruce: *Memories of a British Agent,* Putnam, London, 1932.

LOCKHART, Robin: *The Ace of Spies,* Hodder & Stoughton, London, 1967.

MACKENZIE, Sir Compton: *Aegean Memories,* Chatto & Windus, London, 1940. (See also: *Greek Memories,* 1932.)

MALMESBURY, Susan, Countess of: *The Life of Major-General Sir John Ardagh,* John Murray, London, 1909.

MCCORMICK, Donald: *The Incredible Mr. Kavanagh,* Putnam, London, 1960.

MONTAGU, Ewen: *The Man Who Never Was,* Evans Bros., London, 1953.

NICHOLAS, Elizabeth: *Death Be Not Proud,* Cresset Press, London, 1958.

OVERTON FULLER, Jean: *Madeleine,* Gollancz, London, 1952; *The Starr Affair,* Gollancz, 1954; *Double Webs,* Putnam, London, 1958.

PHILBY, Kim: *My Silent War,* Grove Press, New York, 1968.

PRATT, Fletcher: *Secret and Urgent: The Story of Codes and Ciphers,* Robert Hale, London, 1939.

READ, Conyers: *Mr. Secretary Walsingham and The Policy of Queen Elizabeth,* 3 vols., Oxford University Press, London, 1925.

ROWAN, Richard Wilmer and DEINDORFER, R. G.: *Thirty-Three Centuries of Espionage,* Hawthorn Books, New York, 1967.

SUTHERLAND, James: *Defoe,* Methuen, London, 1937.

THOMSON, Sir Basil: *The Story of Scotland Yard,* Grayson & Grayson, London, 1935.

THOMSON, Sir Basil: *The Scene Changes,* Gollancz, London, 1939.

THOMSON, H. W. and PADOVER, S. E.: *Secret Diplomacy: A Record of Espionage and Double-Dealing, 1500–1815,* Jarrolds, London, 1937.

WHEATLEY, Dennis: *Stranger Than Fiction,* Hutchinson, London, 1959.

WRIGHT, Thos.: *The Life of Daniel Defoe,* Cassell, London, 1894.

Index